# AMERICAN PRAGMATISM AND DEMOCRATIC FAITH

# AMERICAN PRAGMATISM AND DEMOCRATIC FAITH

Robert J. Lacey

NORTHERN ILLINOIS UNIVERSITY PRESS DEKALB

© 2008 by Northern Illinois University Press

Published by the Northern Illinois University Press, DeKalb, Illinois 60115

Manufactured in the United States using recycled, acid-free paper

All Rights Reserved

Library of Congress Cataloging-in-Publication Data

Lacey, Robert J.

American pragmatism and democratic faith / Robert J. Lacey.

p. cm.

Includes bibliographical references and index.

ISBN-13: 978-0-87580-379-1 (clothbound : alk. paper)

ISBN-10: 0-87580-379-2 (clothbound : alk. paper)

1. Democracy—Philosophy. 2. Pragmatism. 3. Political participation—Philosophy. I. Title.

JC423.L26 2008

320.01'1—dc22

2007016726

For Rebecca

# Contents

Acknowledgments    ix

Introduction    3

1 Charles Peirce
*The Joyful Nirvana of the Unlimited Community*    25

2 The Lonely Courage of William James    45

3 The John Dewey School of Democracy    82

4 C. Wright Mills
*The Oracle of the New Left*    127

5 Sheldon Wolin and Melancholic Democracy    170

6 Benjamin Barber and Quixotic Democracy    198

7 Participatory Democracy
*An Impoverished Theory and Its Legacy*    228

Epilogue    252

Notes    257
Bibliography    275
Index    282

# Acknowledgments

I would not have finished this project without the support of a large number of people. I would first like to thank Jerry Mileur, who encouraged me throughout my graduate school career and lent me his time and expertise to help me turn what was at best a vague idea into a viable dissertation topic—and finally a book. Further, I must credit Jerry for teaching me much of what I know about American politics and political thought. His influence has left an indelible mark on my thinking and general approach to the discipline.

I would also like to express my gratitude to Mike Hannahan and Ralph Whitehead, who were both willing to sacrifice precious time and energy for me during the dissertation phase of this project. For a while I worked in an office adjacent to Mike's, which meant he endured my constant intrusions to bounce ideas off him and borrow his books. He was always willing to humor me in these impromptu discussions, and he often provided useful insights that compelled me to view my project from different perspectives. I have had the good fortune of working with Ralph on a number of projects over the years, which often involved marathon discussions that would invariably meander from the task at hand but would, more often than not, turn out to be indispensable brainstorming sessions. Ralph is the master of productive digression, and his willingness to devote hours at a time talking about my project helped me make useful connections that would not have occurred to me otherwise.

I also thank the Department of Political Science at the University of Massachusetts for its many years of academic and financial support. I am especially grateful to George Sulzner, who shared both humor and encouraging words throughout my graduate school career and guided my research on the initiative and voter turnout. I am also indebted to Nicholas Xenos, an inspiring teacher and scholar, whose seminar on Sheldon Wolin was invaluable, and whose seminars on a number of other topics rounded out my education in political theory.

Since I left the nest of graduate school, I have received support from a number of other people without whom I could never have finished this book. Patrick Deneen, whose work on democratic theory is unparalleled, has given me indispensable advice and encouragement. I must also thank my new colleagues at Iona College—especially Mary Hagerty, Tricia Mulligan, and Jeanne Zaino—who offered advice on how to balance my teaching responsibilities with research and writing. I cannot sufficiently thank my editor, Melody Herr, who believed in this project from the start and helped me improve the manuscript considerably.

I would like to express my gratitude to those friends and colleagues who have been willing either to read portions of my manuscript or listen to my long-winded accounts of it. Larry Becker, David Claborn, Jon Keller, Dan Lorge, Sean Molloy, Jason Schrieber, Noelle Shough, Carlos Suarez-Carrasquillo, and George Thomas stand out for providing useful feedback over the years on this and other projects. Perhaps more important, they have challenged me to view American politics in a different light and to reconsider my political convictions.

I could never have completed this manuscript without the support of my family. I would like to thank my parents, Joseph and Susan, who always showed an interest in my education and encouraged me to pursue an academic career. I am particularly indebted to my brother, David, his wife, Lisa, and his children, Ryan and Mariah, for encouraging me to finish and for providing me refuge from academia. Dave also played a vital role in my education as a child, encouraging me to read a wide range of fiction, history, and biography, and it is highly doubtful that I would have pursued a Ph.D. without his early influence.

Finally, I must show my appreciation for Rebecca Root, who is not only my best friend but also a colleague. Busy with her own research and teaching commitments, she still found time to read every word of every draft of my manuscript and to give me indispensable advice and guidance along the way. And with good cheer she took on the arduous task of copyediting the final manuscript and helping me assemble and format the bibliography and hundreds of citations. I cannot thank her enough here, but I hope to express my gratitude further through reciprocation, assisting in any way I can when she completes her book in the near future.

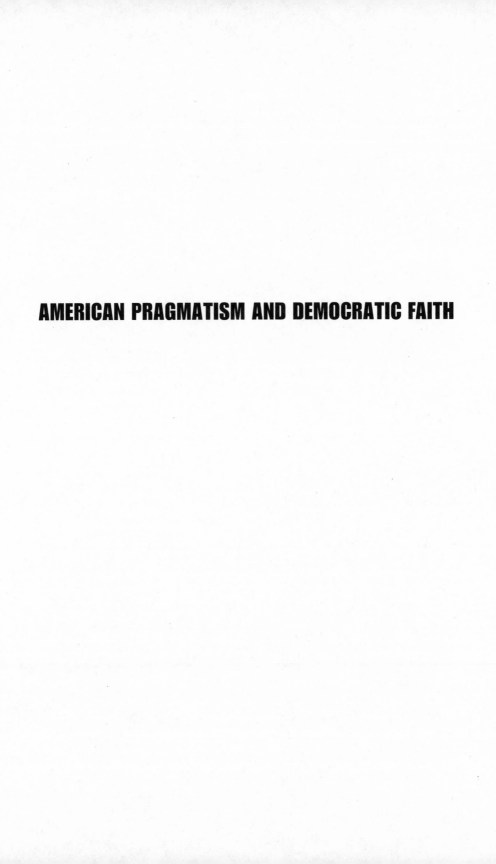

# AMERICAN PRAGMATISM AND DEMOCRATIC FAITH

# Introduction

In June 1962 the Students for a Democratic Society (SDS) met together at a United Auto Workers retreat in Port Huron, Michigan, and released their founding manifesto, the *Port Huron Statement,* expressing the authors' growing disenchantment with the world in which they lived. Racial bigotry in the South and the paranoid logic of the Cold War, in particular, led the SDS activists to question the status quo—the political and social institutions that most Americans accepted, even embraced, without question. Those in the SDS found that American principles of democracy, liberty, and equality—regularly invoked by politicians—rang increasingly hollow. Despite the growing popularity of the civil rights movement, blacks were still disenfranchised and oppressed in the South. The nation seemed to be dangling over the precipice of annihilation, and its citizens had little, if any, control over the direction of American foreign policy. The moneyed elites of the country had a firm grip on the pillars of power, and they alone controlled the nation's destiny—a destiny portending disaster: stark inequality, poverty, racial discrimination, greed, alienation, war, famine, even world annihilation. Most Americans were politically complacent because they enjoyed unprecedented prosperity, but beneath the veneer of satisfaction, the SDS believed, lurked a widespread anxiety.

The authors of the *Port Huron Statement* were in part reacting against the 1950s, a decade often associated with repressive conformity and an almost military-like regimentation, but in particular, they were concerned with the lack of popular control over political institutions. While most of the country's citizens remained either apathetic about or unaware of their own political impotence, the Students for a Democratic Society posited that only "participatory democracy" could restore sanity to politics. Conventional democratic institutions, which at best represented the will of the people only obliquely, were woefully inadequate. Participatory democracy would make it possible that each "individual share in those social decisions determining the quality and direction of his life; that society be organized to encourage independence in men and provide the media for their common participation." All "decision-making of basic social consequence [would] be carried on by public groupings." Politics would create an "acceptable pattern of social relations" and draw "people out of isolation and into community."[1]

Participatory democracy represented the panacea for the country's social and political ills: it would lead to a world in which SDS's optimistic assumptions concerning human nature could be realized. Unlike political thinkers in the liberal tradition, the SDS activists believed humanity was nearly perfectible, a work in progress that could reach untold moral heights. In the manifesto they wrote:

> We regard men as infinitely precious and possessed of unfulfilled capacities for reason, freedom, and love. . . . We oppose, too, the doctrine of human incompetence because it rests essentially on the modern fact that men have been "competently" manipulated into incompetence—we see little reason why men cannot meet with increasing skill the complexities and responsibilities of their situation, if society is organized not for minority, but for majority, participation in decision-making.

Liberal doubts about the wisdom of the people and fears of majority tyranny, they believed, were unfounded and elitist. For them, every man possessed unfulfilled potential. If situated in the proper political and social context, with ample opportunity for for truly deliberative political participation, every person could cultivate an unlimited capacity for goodness, for empathy, for thinking beyond narrow self-interest. The students considered participatory democracy both educational and enlightening. They believed that deliberation with others within the community would lift the veil of ignorant selfishness, that it could reveal to man the experiences and needs of his fellow men. Participatory democracy was transformative, turning isolated and perpetually inward-looking souls into motivated citizens who considered the communal good over private interest.

This is not to suggest that people must surrender their individual identities to the collective. On the contrary, individuals, out of their political and social involvement, would find "meaning in personal life" and also a way to reach their "unrealized potential for self-cultivation, self-direction, self-understanding, and creativity."[2] The early SDS members—

although undoubtedly influenced by Marxist alienation theory—were not adherents of communism or any of its twentieth-century manifestations. Indeed, in their unwaveringly humanist judgment, the free individual was paramount.

However, they did consider the individual self both malleable and dependent on social relations. While the individual was not to be subordinate to society, he was a product of it and was thus in many ways accountable to it. To force the individual to submit to the general will, as in Rousseau's (and indeed Stalin's) chilling formulation, robbed him of his dignity and freedom. The win-win option was to place the individual in an ideal social and political context, where he could *of his own volition* arrive at certain ethical realizations about his role in the greater community. In this situation, the individual would maintain his personal dignity and freedom, and at the same time learn that he has the responsibility to help make a better, more just society. Participatory democracy would thus promote the general welfare and the moral development of each individual. Society would be more just, and each individual more fulfilled.

At this time a nascent student organization, with only eight hundred dues-paying members and a handful of functioning chapters in the North, the SDS had hubristic ambitions. Its leaders believed they could effect a radical transformation of American values. Only a few dozen student activists actually were in attendance at Port Huron for those five days in June 1962, most hailing from the University of Michigan and a few other colleges in the Midwest. Yet the *Port Huron Statement* has become legendary for defining the political values that animated 1960s activism—so much so that thousands claim to have been there. The Port Huron gathering represents an important moment in the history of American political thought: it gave voice to the idea of participatory democracy and captured the imagination of a generation of student activists.

Participatory democracy was no longer an empty intellectual concept, the lost relic of civic republicanism. Instead it galvanized a movement. One of the few at Port Huron, Sharon Jeffrey, said that "the key theme there was participatory democracy, and this was something that somehow had a resonance to it." According to another one there, Bob Ross, their "vision of participatory democracy" was that "people, separately and together, have the power to direct the key institutions of the society, power to control their own lives." This meant, said Steve Max, yet another attending activist, that

> democracy was something you go out and do everyday, and it wasn't merely voting for representatives every couple of years. . . . You found ways of implementing democracy every time you got up in the morning. You didn't wait for the government to pass a civil rights law if you couldn't get into the barber shop. You opened the doors and went in, and that was the essence of what participatory democracy was about.[3]

Members of SDS drew inspiration from the civil rights movement, and especially from the activities of the Student Non-Violent Coordinating Committee (SNCC), which organized peaceful sit-ins and demonstrations to protest racial segregation in the South. People had no choice but to take direct action, when social and political institutions controlled by elites not only failed to address their grievances but even went so far as to safeguard the practices of bigotry and hatred. Many SDS members became Freedom Riders and spent their summers in the South, to help organize voter registration drives and to participate in demonstrations, but their grievances extended far beyond racial injustice. In their view, the problems of race, poverty, social and economic inequality, and nuclear proliferation (to name but a few) were symptoms of the more fundamental issue of citizen complacency and apathy, the general population's mind-numbing acquiescence in a system controlled by self-regarding elites. Only direct political participation could awaken the American public from its dormant state. SDS activists were audacious enough to believe in their ability to make this happen.

Unlike the Old Left, inspired by the dogmatic assertions of Marx and Lenin, SDS members did not believe anyone should ever blindly embrace values or truths handed down by previous generations or venerated figures of the past. Although they shared many concerns with the Old Left, SDS members believed that communities had to arrive at truths and principles on their own, through a painstaking deliberative process. Each community, on its own, must construct values by which it would willingly abide, not await orders from a revolutionary vanguard. "The idea that you made your own values as a group was a new thing," said Steve Max. "That values weren't just inherited and just weren't transmitted from the older generation but that people could actually sit down and work out an ethical framework as an organization, and then go and try to live that way was not something that was popularly in the culture."[4]

Although Max characterized this faith in participatory democracy as a "new thing," it did not emerge in a vacuum. Tom Hayden was given the responsibility of writing an initial draft of the manifesto that would later become the *Port Huron Statement,* and he has cited a number of influences. Among the most important were New Left thinkers C. Wright Mills and Arnold Kaufman, along with the pragmatist philosopher John Dewey.[5]

Perhaps the most immediate inspiration for the *Port Huron Statement* was a short essay by C. Wright Mills published in the *New Left Review* in 1960.[6] Entitled "Letter to the New Left," this brief missive urged young intellectuals to undertake political radicalism, to reject the status quo and the prevailing liberal democratic ethos. Mills seemed to be speaking directly to the SDS activists. In his memoirs Hayden calls Mills "the oracle of the New Left," for the renegade professor of sociology at Columbia University offered a powerful critique of the establishment and its elite-driven institutions.[7]

In another work, *The Power Elite,* Mills argued that the real power in this country was vested in the hands of a small number of elites occupying the top positions in the corporate, political, and military worlds. The power elite was not a permanent ruling class such as an aristocracy but, rather, a loose network of corporate leaders and other high-level decision-makers. They might not work together in a conspiratorial fashion, but they shared common interests, one of which was to deny average citizens the power to effect social change.

Although Mills offered no easy solution to the problem, he insisted that the Old Leftist approach—the dictatorship of the proletariat—would do nothing more than replace one group of elites with another. Instead, he called for the radical democratization of society, in which "everyone vitally affected by a social decision, regardless of its sphere, would have a voice in that decision and a hand in its administration."[8] Mills hoped that America could recapture the intense level of public spirit it had once enjoyed in the eighteenth and early nineteenth centuries, the civic engagement praised so eloquently by Alexis de Tocqueville in *Democracy in America*. Sadly, Mills did not live to witness his profound influence on a generation of activists. He died in March 1962, three months before the SDS retreat in Port Huron.

Arnold Kaufman, a professor of philosophy at the University of Michigan who taught Tom Hayden and other SDS members and who shared their admiration for Mills, was also an important influence on the emerging New Left. He inspired many of his students with his lectures on "participatory democracy"—a term he often receives credit for coining.[9] Kaufman did not consider human beings incapable of assuming the responsibilities of self-governance. He maintained that democracy had the power to transform its participants, both morally and intellectually. "The main justifying function of participation," he argued, "is development of man's essential powers—inducing human dignity and respect, and making men responsible, by developing their powers of deliberate action."[10]

While Kaufman accepted the fallibility of the people, even going so far as to suggest that "men do not always know what is best for them," he did not accept that a coterie of experts would have superior knowledge or would rule more wisely. He thought it reasonable to assume that participatory democracy would provide citizens with the education necessary to "judge men and policies with reasonable intelligence, and also initiate policy in suitable spheres." He did not wish to dismantle traditional institutions in which bureaucrats and elites operated. Instead, he sought to "enrich the Welfare State by increasing the element of participatory democracy." He recognized the many achievements of the centralized bureaucratic state and argued that opportunities for citizen participation should supplement rather than replace it. His ultimate aim was to reconcile participatory democracy with New Deal liberalism.[11]

Unlike Mills, who died prematurely in 1962, Kaufman lived to experience the rise of 1960s campus activism. He accepted the invitation to participate at Port Huron, where he worked alongside many of his students and former students to create the founding document that echoed many of his ideas. A few years later he developed even more of a leadership role and organized teach-ins against the war in Vietnam, first at the University of Michigan in March 1965, and then nationwide two months later. These early groundbreaking teach-ins proved very successful, paving the way for more to proliferate on campuses throughout the country.

Kaufman saw the teach-in as a way to put participatory democracy in action, an opportunity for teachers, students, and members of the campus community at large to engage in fruitful discussion concerning vital issues that affected them all. In his view, intellectuals were particularly useful in creating a forum where citizens could acquire useful information, express opinions, relate experiences, and listen to the perspectives of others. He was careful to make sure that teachers limited their efforts to providing information and facilitating discussion, and that everyone in the community had an equal voice.

Exhibiting an immense reserve of energy, Kaufman devoted more and more time to political activism. He threw himself into the civil rights movement, helped to organize the New Democratic Coalition (NDC) in an attempt to move the Democratic Party leftward, and after moving to UCLA in 1969 became the president of his local American Federation of Teachers union. Unfortunately, he also died early, perishing in a plane crash in June 1971.[12]

Both Mills and Kaufman played important roles in shaping the participatory democratic ethos. As a prominent public intellectual and a prolific writer, Mills exercised widespread influence and animated a whole generation of student radicals. Kaufman's influence was more localized, limited primarily to the University of Michigan and its SDS members, and his writings were not so well known. His only book, *The Radical Liberal,* appeared in 1968, well after the New Left and student movement were already under way, and his criticism of the student movement was perhaps more pronounced than his call for greater citizen involvement in our democracy.[13]

Neither Mills nor Kaufman can claim credit as the originator of the idea of participatory democracy, however. Long before they or SDS came on the scene, John Dewey had espoused the kind of participatory democracy for which the New Left would have such boundless enthusiasm, and he often invoked pragmatist ideas in his efforts. In developing their radical conceptions of democracy, both Mills and Kaufman drew heavily on the pragmatist school, especially the work of Dewey, a towering figure in American philosophy through the first half of the twentieth century. They were both steeped in the pragmatist tradition and acknowledged their debt to it. Mills wrote his dissertation on pragmatism and read with particular interest Dewey's definitive statement on democratic theory, *The Public and Its Problems*. Kaufman also admired Dewey's works on political thought and argued that a defense of participatory democracy must rest, at least in part, on pragmatist grounds.[14]

::: **The first objective of this current work** is to *locate the origins* of participatory democracy in the pragmatist tradition, which began in the late nineteenth century with Charles Peirce and William James. I argue that pragmatism provided the necessary intellectual foundation for the democratic ideas advocated more than half a century later by SDS and the New Left. Often considered America's first and only native-born philosophy, pragmatism challenged current ideas about truth, human nature, and free will. Maintaining that truth is probabilistic and socially determined, that men are mutable and improvable, and that men are poised for willful action, pragmatism opened the doors for a radically different understanding of democracy. It suggested that human beings could no longer appeal to an established authority for political and ethical truths, that they must share the responsibility of creating values and solutions to social problems with their fellow citizens. Rejecting inherited dogmas and first principles, citizens must employ democratic methods to attain socially useful knowledge, and they must believe that they can always better themselves and meet the challenges of group deliberation and cooperation.

This does not mean that pragmatism leads inexorably to participatory democracy. A pragmatist is not necessarily a participatory democrat, and many pragmatists have taken other paths.[15] But any faith in participatory democracy requires unwavering acceptance of the pragmatist conceptions of truth, human nature, and freedom. Thus, pragmatism is a necessary precursor to—though hardly a sufficient cause of—an ardent faith in participatory democracy. In other words, pragmatism paved the road on which one had to travel to arrive at a participatory democratic ethos, but pragmatism did not require one to take this road.

The second objective of this work is to *assess the legacy* of the New Left enthusiasm for participatory democracy. More than forty years after Port Huron, the influence of participatory democratic thought appears limited, even nonexistent. Our formal political institutions have remained largely unchanged since Dewey began his crusade. The call for participatory democracy has created neither formal mechanisms nor public space for citizen deliberation and decision-making. Moreover, no democratic uprising has delivered a death blow to the prevailing system.

The American people show little interest in opportunities for political participation; the level of political ignorance, apathy, and complacency seems higher than ever. Studies show that citizens are less knowledgeable about—or interested in—public affairs than they were a generation ago. Voter turnout has reached all-time lows, barely exceeding 50 percent of the voting-age population in recent presidential election years.[16] The New England town meeting, one of the few shining examples of participatory democracy in the United States, has experienced decreased attendance.[17] Even Tom Hayden and Dick Flacks, two authors of the *Port Huron Statement,* admitted recently that their "dreams have hardly been realized."[18]

This said, we can find the legacy of the New Left most readily within the academy. Intellectual heavyweights such as Sheldon Wolin, C. B. Macpherson, Robert Dahl, Carole Pateman, Benjamin Barber, Jane Mansbridge, and Amy Gutmann (to name just a few) have all called for deepening democracy, arguing that liberalism and representative democracy have done more to protect the prerogatives of a bloated plutocracy than to safeguard the rights of the truly vulnerable, more to consolidate the power of an established elite than to promote political equality and fairness. Some of these thinkers regard all institutions and reform efforts with suspicion, while others believe it is possible to change the system from the inside without compromising oneself. But they all reject liberalism, share a concern about the political complacency and passivity of most American citizens today, and believe that our current crises demand a significant devolution of power into the hands of average citizens. Their influence, even if confined within academia, invites a careful analysis of the assumptions undergirding their thought and an assessment of thought's viability and theoretical coherence in twenty-first century America.

Once situated within the pragmatist tradition, participatory democratic thought reveals unresolved tensions and internal contradictions that challenge both its viability and its theoretical coherence. For one, the pragmatist assumptions about truth, human nature, and free will—on which participatory democratic thought rests—are contestable, to say the least. To embrace them blindly requires a leap of faith that most intellectually honest critics are not willing to take. Second, these assumptions stand in uneasy relation to each other. Finally, even the most enthusiastic supporters of participatory democracy have displayed ambivalence concerning some of these assumptions (especially the faith in free will), which thereby undermines the intellectual foundation of their political commitments. The irony is that, although pragmatism claims to be an anti-foundationalist philosophy that rejects first principles and fixed truths, it has introduced a set of contestable maxims on which participatory democracy rests ever so precariously. In other words, the rabid anti-foundationalists are, in fact, closet foundationalists. But, first, a critique of participatory democracy requires a full exploration of its intellectual origins—its pragmatist ancestry. What did the pragmatists say about truth, human nature, and free will that participatory democrats would find so appealing?

## American Pragmatism

William James introduced pragmatism to the world in an 1898 lecture at the University of California in Berkeley, but in fact the philosophy had emerged as early as 1872, when a number of young intellectuals at Harvard—including James, Charles Peirce, Chauncey Wright, and Oliver Wendell Holmes—met occasionally to discuss philosophy in the short-lived and ironically named Metaphysical Club. It was "ironically named" because pragmatism was a putative rejection of metaphysics, and of abstract sources of moral or intellectual authority. In the wake of Darwin and Nietzsche, modernity suffered from what historian John Diggins has called a "crisis of knowledge and authority," and pragmatism offered a solution without invoking old and outdated ideas.[19]

Any attempt to describe pragmatism in brief will undoubtedly be inadequate, as it embodies many variants and subtly different approaches. Louis Menand, whose Pulitzer Prize–winning *The Metaphysical Club* has revived popular and scholarly interest in pragmatism, has perhaps come the closest to capturing its essence in a few words:

> [The pragmatists] believed that ideas are not "out there" waiting to be discovered, but are tools—like forks and knives and microchips—that people devise to cope with the world in which they find themselves. They believed that ideas are produced not by individuals, but by groups of individuals—that ideas are social. They believed that ideas do not develop according to some inner logic of their own, but are entirely dependent, like germs, on their human carriers and the environment. And they believed that since ideas are provisional responses to particular and unreproducible circumstances, their survival depends not on their immutability but on their adaptability.[20]

Of course, to suggest there is an "essence" to pragmatism belies what it is trying to do, for its adherents reject essences; they reject the notion that there is an a priori truth or an objective reality, of which, if we work hard enough, our minds can produce a mirror image. A priori truth may in fact exist, but we do not have the capacity to attain it. No matter how much logic, reason, prayer, meditation, or study we devote to our quest for truth (a strategy metaphysicians and philosophers have relentlessly and fruitlessly pursued for centuries), we will never find it outside or independent of our earthly experience. For truth, according to pragmatist thought, does not exist prior to human experience; rather, truth is constituted by it. Thus "we don't act because we have ideas; we have ideas because we must act."[21]

James described ideas as "rules for action," which become true if they give us satisfactory results, if they have what he called "cash-value."[22] True ideas are those upon which we are prepared to act in our daily lives because of their proven usefulness. Truth, then, is embedded in life experience. Like scientists we must subject truth claims to a process of verification. Truths are always tentative and must continually undergo retesting as new experiential data arrives. "Intellectualists," as James calls anyone who is not a pragmatist, hold that a true idea must correspond with some immutable and independent reality. Pragmatists, on the other hand, argue that a true idea must correspond only with our *experience* of reality. A truth is an idea that works. I do not, for example, accuse my neighbors of being noisy because they have met some a priori condition of noisiness; rather, I make this accusation because their loud music and foot-stomping disrupted my concentration while reading William James. I experienced this disruption first, and afterward applied the term "noisy" to describe my neighbors. My subjective experience, not objective knowledge about the essence of noisiness, led me to make this particular truth claim about my neighbors. Their noisiness becomes true in the course of events. I may not consider my neighbors noisy if I am engaged in an activity that requires less concentration.

James claimed metaphysical truths can be put to this same test: if a particular religious belief works for me, if it gives me emotional satisfaction, then it is true. One would be hard-pressed to determine conclusively whether Jesus was actually the son of God, but so long as this belief has "cash-value," it is true. The problem is, this instrumental conception of truth may ultimately prove unsatisfactory. After all, Christianity may have emotional and psychological benefits, but we only enjoy them if we believe its principles are universal and timeless. If I observe Christianity in the pragmatic spirit, will it not fail to give me satisfaction and thus fail to meet the pragmatist test of truth? G. K. Chesterton suggested as much when he said, "Pragmatism is a matter of human needs, and one of the first of human needs is to be something more than a pragmatist."[23] In other words, one can and should reject pragmatism on pragmatist grounds. We all need to believe in a truth that exists outside our subjective experience.

This radical subjectivism has led critics to charge pragmatism with opening the floodgates to a dangerous relativism—or even a Nietzschean nihilism—where, as Dostoyevsky once described a world without god, everything is permissible. But the pragmatists were hardly Nietzscheans, for they remained optimistic about the possibility of acquiring truths that proved useful in our experience. Nietzsche rejected the quest for truth altogether, arguing that men "have no organ at all for knowledge, for 'truth'." In his view, even science was just another metaphysic, another religion that mistakenly put truth within man's grasp.[24]

Though far more sanguine than Nietzsche about man's capacity for acquiring truth, pragmatism embraced a dynamic of uncertainty that could not so easily escape charges of relativism. For the pragmatists put a great deal of emphasis on science and the scientific method, democratizing the latter by suggesting we all acquire knowledge just as a scientist does—by testing and retesting hypotheses with the empirical evidence at our disposal. We all generate truths through an endless process of verification and reverification. If at some point our truths fail to meet these tests, if they fail to work as they once did, we must at the very least adapt them, at most scrap them altogether. All truths are provisional, according to pragmatism, except perhaps for one—the method by which those truths are attained.

The English philosopher Bertrand Russell wrote some of the most scathing indictments of pragmatism. He was quick to detect a democratic spirit inhabiting the philosophy, but he believed that underneath all its impatience with authority, prejudice, and certitude lurked "the worship of force."[25] He found pragmatism objectionable because its rejection of any kind of absolute truth existing outside human experience led to a Nietzschean epistemology of power. Its fatal flaw was hubris—the belief in man's limitless capacity to improve himself and the world around him. In an astonishing reversal of the crude Machiavellian motto "The ends justify the means," and in their myopic focus on method, pragmatists actually suggested that the means justify the ends.[26]

The assumption was that concentrating on the correct means (the scientific method) would automatically yield a conformity of good ends—that we would all naturally come to an agreement on what is true and right. Russell considered this a naive and dangerous assumption. If taken seriously, this refusal to consider ends upfront uproots man from any moral foundation, leaving him free to define "the true" simply as that which he considers "expedient."[27] Truth becomes simply what works for me, period. And if what works for me clashes with what works for someone else, there is no impartial referee to arbitrate and help us settle our dispute. Russell colorfully described the problem: "In the absence of any standard of truth other than success, it seems evident that the familiar methods of the struggle for existence must be applied to the elucidation of difficult questions, and that ironclads and Maxim guns must be the ultimate arbiters of metaphysical truth."[28] Only through violent struggle and bloodshed will people arrive at an authoritative settlement between competing truths. The victors, those who have achieved power, will write history. The victors will determine truth.

Russell's argument proved so powerful that it resonated throughout the twentieth century in the writings of luminaries such as Randolph Bourne, Lewis Mumford, Mortimer Adler, Robert Hutchins, and Leo Strauss. These critics echoed Russell's discomfort with the pragmatist disavowal of objective truth. Especially in light of the devastation and atrocities that beset humanity during the twentieth century, the pragmatist abandonment of objective truth invited sharp criticism.

In the end, it seemed that this method-oriented philosophy could not even explain why Nazism was evil. After all, could not the most enthusiastic and horrifying participant in the Final Solution, Josef Mengele, have justified his actions on pragmatist grounds? Could he not have said that the mass destruction of the European Jewry was true and right because it "worked" for the Nazi cause? Because pragmatism "stands for no particular results . . . has no dogmas, and no doctrines save its method," it has no basis on which to criticize the Nazis. Because pragmatism rejects (to use James's words) "first things" or "principles," it can only assess the truth of an idea by the degree to which that idea fulfills the "last things, fruits, [or] consequences" one seeks, no matter how monstrous or sickening they may be to the rest of us.[29] When the means justify the ends, everything becomes permissible.

But these seemingly devastating criticisms in part betray a superficial understanding of pragmatism. It is true that pragmatism was instrumental and method-oriented, but its critics tended to overlook another essential characteristic of pragmatism: the quest for truth must be social and public. This fact might be lost on the critic who focuses on the work of James, whose individualist streak downplayed the social aspect of learning in pragmatist thought. Peirce and Dewey, however, could not stress this point enough. Indeed, Peirce warns his readers not to take the instrumental understanding of truth "in too individualistic a sense."[30]

Behind Peirce's epistemology was his concept of fallibilism. A real objective truth may exist out there, but none of us is likely to find it on our own. All truth claims and experiences are subject to the law of errors. Any individual truth claim, based on one person's subjective experience, is woefully fallible. But a collective, which draws on the experiences and perceptions of many people, is less fallible. An advanced student of mathematics and probability theory, Peirce developed an epistemology that was explicitly statistical: add more people to the inquiry (that is, increase the sample size), and you are likely to get closer to the truth (that is, reduce the amount of standard error).

Peirce believed induction—this very process of sampling specific facts from which one can infer generalizable truths—was the principal way people acquired reliable knowledge. Indeed, he was suspicious of deductive forms of reasoning. The problem with deductive logic, he believed, was that its conclusions rested on suspect and general postulates. Working from faulty assumptions, deduction could at the very start lead us astray in the pursuit of truth. Deduction moves from dubious general propositions to specific conclusions, whereas induction does the opposite. It begins with specific experiences from which one can draw general conclusions, and this was why Peirce considered it a superior form of logic or method of attaining knowledge. Any individual experience is certainly fallible, but a collection of experiences can begin to shed light on a subject through a process of verification and validation.

The scientific method involves the testing of hypotheses or beliefs, time and again, by a community of scientists who share information and review each other's work. Peirce suggested that all truth inquiries must apply the same rigorous method. That an idea works or has "cash-value" for one or two people hardly makes it true. An idea must work for a group of people, who, after exhaustive testing and deliberation, reach a consensus about the utility of an idea. Unlike our individual experiences, said Peirce, the "method of science" is a reliable arbiter of truth. While James agreed that the scientific method is vital, Peirce made a point of stressing that his "conception of truth" was "public." If only applied to "one individual" and not to "every man" that it "might affect," then the method fails to be scientific.[31] Peirce summarized his social and consensual conception of truth as follows: "The opinion which is fated to be ultimately agreed to by all who investigate, is what we mean by truth, and the object represented in this opinion is the real."[32] Pragmatic truth, then, is an agreement among a community of inquirers.

Also crucial to an adequate understanding of pragmatism is the concept of habit. Ideas and beliefs are "rules for action," according to the pragmatists, and when they work, these rules quickly become ingrained in us; they form into habits. James maintained that our ideas and beliefs, when acted upon repeatedly, become habits that are hardwired in our neural pathways, thus ensuring that certain stimuli will elicit predictable (or habitual) reactions. In a way, ideas that become habits cease even to be ideas because we do not think about them anymore. They are automatic. Before long these habits seem immutable and are often construed as human nature. But, although habits are indeed difficult to break and thus a "conservative agent," there is always the possibility that they can be changed. If a habit ceases to be useful, or a different rule for action proves more useful, individuals or groups can condition themselves to develop new habits. The extent to which a habit becomes ingrained or hardwired depends on its reliability, on how well it works—not just for the individual in question but for others in his community. Man is not rigid and uneducable; he is not fated by the laws of human nature. Rather, all men are "walking bundles of habits" and, brimming with unlimited potential, have the power to change when more useful ideas materialize.[33]

This power to change presupposes that people have a certain degree of agency or free will, a notion embraced wholeheartedly by Peirce and James. Both thinkers argued that ideas serve as guides or rules for action and that there is no reason for us to think that either ideas or actions are necessarily predetermined. They saw an element of chance or spontaneity in the universe that leaves considerable room for human freedom. The universe did not resemble a large, complex machine of which we were an integral part and whose immutable laws were slowly becoming known to us. Rather, it was an evolving system whose laws were subject to random mutation. Laws of causation do exist in the universe, said Peirce, but they are "not perfect, for an element of pure spontaneity or lawless originality mingles, or at least, must be supposed to mingle, with law everywhere." It is quite reasonable, then, to believe that human beings who act on their ideas often reflect this "pure spontaneity or lawless originality." The influence of Darwinism cannot be overestimated here, for the pragmatists rejected a mechanistic view of the universe in favor of chance variation.[34]

According to the pragmatists, however, chance variation does not suggest that the universe is a chaotic mess over which human beings can gain no measure of control, for the very process of ascribing meaning and finding truth in the world requires volition. Both Peirce and James argued that volition is fundamental to human experience and our ability to make sense of the world. We cannot interpret the world around us or be conscious of it without the power of volition. The general idea of an apple, for example, comes from the total sum of sensory experiences produced by our willful actions. We do not know a certain object is an apple until we look at it and notice it is red, pick it up and feel its smoothness, bite into it and taste its particular flavor, and so on. The idea of appleness exists within individual apples, but the idea will not become known until we exercise our will on those apples (that is, bite them, touch them, inspect them, and so on). Our willful actions test the veracity of our ideas—in this example, that this particular object is indeed an apple. While it has often been fashionable to believe that human beings are at the mercy of systems beyond their control (whether biological, social, or political), pragmatism subscribes to the view that we meet the world halfway and give it meaning through our actions, that we make the world and not vice versa. To believe otherwise is to deny us our humanity.

While Russell and other critics were right to associate pragmatism with power, it is wrong to argue that power was the arbiter of truth in the pragmatist conception. It would be more accurate to suggest that, for the pragmatist, power (or will) operates as the agent of action and freedom. People are free so long as they have the power to act on their ideas—to put them into practice.

The notion that freedom and power are in essence one and the same became especially manifest in John Dewey's work. Dewey represented the next generation of pragmatists and, unlike his predecessors, devoted a great deal of time and energy to political philosophy, advancing a theory of participatory democracy that anticipated the Port Huron Statement. He summarized his political philosophy most succinctly in *The Public and Its Problems* (1927), where he argued that "the cure for the ailments of democracy is more democracy."[35]

Whenever his contemporaries bemoaned the inadequacies of democracy in practice or warned against the tyrannical tendencies of democratic majorities, Dewey argued that these concerns did not reveal any problems inherent to democracy. Instead, any problems facing democracies today showed that our political institutions were not democratic enough. He rejected the purported tension between individual freedom and the social good, between liberty and democracy, that necessitated restraints on democratic institutions. All the "ailments" identified by Walter Lippmann and others—such as widespread popular ignorance about important public issues, or the inability of democratic governments to address social problems rationally and efficiently—were prima facie evidence that democracy had not fully set root in the American political soil. For Dewey, free elections were not sufficient grounds for true democracy. Only when the people played a direct role in political decision-making, when democratic participation became a way of life for all citizens, would America become a true democracy and a nation of free citizens.

Democracy was an ethical ideal in which each individual is given the opportunity to realize his potential for self-governance and his ability to work with his fellow men to build a community based on reciprocity and mutual respect. Like his intellectual descendants in the SDS, Dewey rested his democratic ideal on a "faith in the capacity of human beings for intelligent judgment and action if proper conditions are furnished."[36] He rejected the notion that individual genius or intelligence develops autonomously, for every person is socially constructed and thus can become only as brilliant or talented as his circumstances allow. Education and learning are inherently social processes, and democracy itself could become the school from which socially beneficial ideas emerged and in which individuals realized their potential, both intellectually and ethically.

For Dewey, participatory democracy represented the scientific method writ large, an ideal way of life. As James Kloppenberg suggested, the Deweyan "democratic community replicates the community of broadly conceived scientific enquiry. . . . Free and creative individuals, in democratic as in scientific communities, collectively test hypotheses to find out what works best."[37] Imitating the scientific community, minus the professional exclusion, participatory democracy was the best means of determining social truths, and an end in itself for those who wish to find self-fulfillment and happiness. The accusation that pragmatism sacrificed ends in its love affair with method was mistaken, Dewey believed, for pragmatism culminated in participatory democracy, which was both the means and ends of an improved humanity. Participatory democracy promoted the common good and empowered the individual.

## Democratic Faith

This Deweyan faith in participatory democracy—in its capacity both to promote the common good and to transform the individual—rests on three pragmatist tenets, so interconnected that they both build on and conflict with each other. The first is that truth is probabilistic and socially determined, never absolute. *Man* does not arrive at truth through the use of reason or the pious contemplation of god, nor does he arrive at truth within the confines of his scholarly hermitage. Instead, *men* arrive at truth socially, deliberatively, and experientially, and the more people involved in this rather unruly and messy process, the closer they get to truth.

Displacing Jehovah, Jesus, Muhammad and even human reason, statistics and the scientific method become the new gods, the arbiters of truth. By increasing the sample size of competent inquirers who rigorously apply the scientific method, by allowing more participants to bring their experiences and knowledge to the fore, we maximize statistical power, reduce the amount of standard error, and more accurately approximate the true answer. Put another way, we must attain truth inductively, sampling a large number of specific experiences from which we can infer generalizable truths, which then serve the interests of the entire collective. We can call this the *democratic epistemology*.[38]

The second tenet, which flows from the first, is that man himself is a social construct. In other words, there is no such thing as human nature, nothing in man's character that is static or fixed. What at first appears to be nature or law is merely habit (perhaps deeply entrenched habit), which can ultimately be changed. Man is eminently mutable and educable and therefore brimming with unlimited potential; he forever remains a soft piece of clay that can be wrought and rewrought into near perfection. Despite what pessimists say, man is not fatally flawed (or irredeemably wayward). He only awaits a proper education to fulfill his immense capacity for love, empathy, and moral strength. What constitutes a "proper" education becomes evident when we recall the first tenet, the democratic epistemology. As man arrives at truth socially and experientially, not autonomously and contemplatively, the best form of education must create opportunities for this kind of group-based and interactive education. We can call this the *democratic psychology*.

Given these assumptions (that humankind gains knowledge socially and that each man has nearly limitless potential to improve himself), participatory democracy appears to be the logical form of governance. Unlike any other conceivable political system, it rightly includes as many people as possible in the process of acquiring better truths; and these truths—along with the process of forming them—in turn educate, rehabituate, and transform the participants. Thus the democratic participant is both sculptor and sculpture, both artist and work of art, both Professor Higgins and Miss Doolittle.

The third pragmatist tenet upon which democratic faith rests is that people have free will and thus face no serious obstacles, either overt or subtle, that prevent them from devoting considerable time and energy to politics. This tenet conflicts with the previous one, for the belief that human beings are socially constructed creatures of habit may liberate them from their nature and suggest that they can evolve and improve themselves, but it may also mean they are severely circumscribed by the very society of which they are products. Although not bound by biology or instinct, they may be imprisoned by their own habits. Nevertheless, the third tenet is as indispensable to a participatory democratic faith as the other two: even if democratic participation has the aforementioned epistemological and psychological benefits, there is no guarantee that people will actually engage in politics in a serious way. Or, to put it bluntly, there is no telling whether people will actually go to all those darn meetings.

But participatory democratic theorists believe this argument betrays a liberal misunderstanding of the human condition. They claim that liberal theory rests on a fiction that man, completely rational and unencumbered by history or custom, contracts with others and willingly exchanges his natural liberty and his power for security, lest he should die violently and painfully. In the liberal conception each person is a self-contained atom, fearful of injurious contact with other equally self-contained atoms. Freedom means protection, guaranteeing safety and comfort in a stark world that promises only physical suffering and violent death. The political means by which this is accomplished is really beside the point.

Participatory democrats, on the other hand, understand that man is embedded in a complex web of history, traditions, and customs. His freedom does not depend on severing ties with this social and historical embeddedness: a goal as imprudent as it is impossible. On the contrary, his freedom depends on developing the power to share in the shaping of the history, traditions, and customs to which he is inextricably bound. From a Deweyan perspective, it is inconceivable that people prefer to exchange this freedom for security and material comfort. Vested with free will, people are poised for civic action. That people have this positive form of freedom and will embrace it unrelentingly—this is what we might call the *democratic metaphysics*.[39] It is the belief that, if given chisels, people will take hold of them and begin the long painstaking process of sculpting themselves and the world around them. It is the faith that, if given the opportunity, people will exercise this power and work collectively to put their ideas into action.

Of course, detractors of this democratic faith abound. Many thinkers —often referred to as democratic realists—find it implausible that citizens would ever devote considerable time and energy to civic life, or that, if they happened to, by chance, they would ever do so intelligently and judiciously. In the view of these detractors, democracy is not an unmitigated good; it can lead to ill-advised policies and, in the worst case scenario, majority tyranny. For this reason, democracy requires qualification —institutional safeguards to curb its excesses and protect individual rights. Realists praise the Founding Fathers for devising a system of government that frustrates the momentary whims of the people and promotes incrementalism, deliberation, and compromise. The constitutional convention in 1787 produced a system that places little responsibility on the shoulders of the average citizen, and democratic realists think it should stay that way. In the end, most of them are quite content with the pluralist conception of democracy as a competition among elites or groups for influence over government.[40]

Despite these sobering reflections from the realist camp, contemporary proponents of participatory democracy continue to embrace the Deweyan faith, because they cannot ignore the inadequacy of guaranteeing only formal liberty or abstract rights. To be sure, the existence of property rights has little value for people who have few possessions; and the abstract right to life means nothing to a person with no health insurance who suffers from a life-threatening illness. In reality, some people enjoy more freedoms and privileges than others, and these inequalities are not merely the result of individual choice. They often have structural causes that liberals are too prone to dismiss out-of-hand. Many democratic theorists criticize liberals for failing to acknowledge that asymmetries of power and resources give some groups systematic advantages—social, economic, and political—over others.[41] These advantaged groups can quickly mobilize and attain better access to liberal government institutions; accordingly, they have a preponderant influence on public policy and enjoy a disproportionate share of the benefits.

Furthermore, the assumption that the liberal state is separate from civil society is clearly wrong. Despite the liberal insistence that the state should refrain from meddling in civil society, the state and civil society will always intermingle in some way; thus the state itself is often culpable of perpetuating social inequalities.[42] The liberal state claims to be neutral on questions of the good life and on group conflicts in civil society, but its actions (or, in many cases, inaction) undoubtedly privilege certain groups over others and uphold a particular value system.

This is where participatory democracy comes in. Its proponents argue that, until everyone has the opportunity to make his voice heard, the chorus of democracy is incomplete. The goal is to empower those people who have been effectively disenfranchised in liberal democratic society, to give them the opportunity to participate directly in politics. Each individual must have what Isaiah Berlin called positive freedom—the freedom to lead one's own life and to be the author and definer of one's own existence. Proponents of positive freedom contend that, in concentrating on "freedom from" intrusion on the individual's private sphere, liberalism fails to address the fundamental question, "What am I free to do or be?"[43]

Positive freedom affirms a person's right to self-determination, his "freedom to" be his own master. Participatory democrats maintain that civic engagement, direct involvement in the political process, is the principal way a person can exercise his positive freedom and control his own destiny.

Liberal warnings about threats to negative freedom in an unrestrained democracy are unwarranted because political participation enlarges man's thinking and transforms him into an enlightened citizen who, while seeking the common good, always remains mindful of individual rights.

Participatory democrats have been vague about the practicalities, but many of them, including political theorist Benjamin Barber, agree that it would be unwise (and impracticable) to discard many of the central institutions of liberal democracy such as competitive parties, political representatives, an independent judiciary, and periodic elections. Often called proponents of *deliberative democracy,* they acknowledge that civic participation will work best with those issues that affect people directly. More complex or remote national issues are less likely to attract the interest of average citizens; simpler and more salient issues with an immediate and discernible impact would probably draw more people to the political process.[44] Thus participatory institutions would complement, rather than replace, many liberal democratic institutions and would have a limited role in the political process.

That said, deliberative democrats believe it is important to underscore how vital these participatory institutions could still be at a broader level. If people are made to understand that their participation will produce tangible results, that their participation will make a difference in their lives, their faith in political institutions and in their own political efficacy will be restored. Their participation will elevate government accountability and ensure that, in listening to all the voices in the democratic chorus, the government will serve the public good, not just privileged interests. And, perhaps more important, participation will have a transformative effect: people who engage in public affairs will learn the nuts and bolts of democratic procedures, the painstaking nature of deliberation, the necessity of compromise, and the virtue of thinking beyond one's own interests. Barber is not atypical when he suggests that man is a "mutable" creature whose capacity for "self-transformation" stems from deliberation and interaction with his fellow men. Democratic participation, he claims, changes both "the community" and "the participating member."[45]

Some participatory democrats uphold a more radical and uncompromising vision of democracy, to which they compare the existing system of centralized power. Nothing short of a total subversion of the system will bring an end to what they see as a crisis in American politics. Sheldon Wolin, often considered the patriarch of political theory in the American academy, has been a forceful advocate of so-called *radical democracy.* Through his reputation as an august and unassailable scholar, he has given credence and intellectual gravitas to the New Left ethos.[46]

For Wolin, the term "democratic state" is an oxymoron. The rise of the megastate (the sinister cooperation of big government and big business) is the tragic story of modernity and signifies the beginning of a Kafkaesque nightmare from which no one can easily escape. In Wolin's view, until power is reconstituted in such a way as to remain decentralized and resistant to co-optation by the state, until democracy can flourish and remain immune to systemization and institutionalization, a quiet despotism will continue to loom ominously in our lives. Forever dour and intellectually honest, he concedes that real democracy is probably not sustainable in the postmodern world.

Wolin offers no clear remedy to the problem, and it is quite clear he considers reform efforts insufficient. Only in episodic democratic uprisings—or what he calls "fugitive democracy"—does he find hope. Empowering communities to redress social injustices and to promote the commonweal, participatory democracy in its purest form remains spontaneous and unencumbered by plans, rules, and institutional norms. Blueprints are anathema to democracy because they immediately place limits on the possible and necessarily guide politics in particular directions.

Radical democrats have been so bold (or foolhardy) as to take pragmatism to its logical extreme. By insisting that democracy remain pure, they keep open all horizons and search endlessly for truth. Without a form or blueprint, however, democracy remains an elusive (and perhaps illusive) political form that can surface only, if at all, in brief moments before it is domesticated by the state. What emerges from Wolin's writings is a blurred line between "pure" democracy and anarchic social movements. Although representing a more radical vision than his counterparts in the deliberative camp, he also sees democracy as a transformative process that can not only bring about positive change for the community but can also develop "the capacities of ordinary persons."[47]

## The Pragmatist Connection

Locating participatory democratic thought in the pragmatist tradition may raise some eyebrows. After all, the idea that civic participation can promote the general welfare and transform self-absorbed individualists into other-regarding citizens would seem to fall more within the civic republican tradition, which had begun with the proclamation by Aristotle that man is a political animal. Republican thought has enjoyed some continuity over the centuries, in the ideas of Niccolo Machiavelli, Jean-Jacques Rousseau, James Harrington, and the Anti-Federalists, for example. It also can be seen in the writings of contemporary communitarian thinkers such as Michael Sandel, Michael Walzer, and Alisdair MacIntyre. Although participatory democracy shares similarities with—and certainly draws on—this tradition, there are sound reasons for understanding it as a more direct descendant of American pragmatism than of republicanism.

Civic republicans place considerable emphasis on the importance of virtue and the cultivation of this quality in the citizenry. Participationists such as Wolin and Barber shy away from discussing virtue, mostly because virtue smacks of foundationalism, the belief in the existence of fixed truths prior to human experience. Foundationalism is anathema to widespread democratic participation, for it implies that we must rely on elites with the authority or expertise to attain truth—and that we must defer to their judgments about how to live by these truths and act virtuously. As anti-foundationalists, participatory democrats believe that politics is an ongoing process of discovery that must include every person with relevant experiences to share. Participatory democrats embrace the democratic epistemology, while civic republicans often do not.

There is an element of elitism in the republican tradition for which participationists have great contempt. Republicans have accepted the belief that only a select few, perhaps a certain class, have the natural endowment to attain truth and to bear the responsibility of citizenship. As a result, the republican tradition has never demanded full inclusion in the political process. Indeed, over the centuries, it has been comfortable with excluding certain segments of society—slaves, women, peasants, the working class, "barbarians," or "savages"—on the grounds that nature places limits on their abilities. Participatory democrats have been uncompromising on this point: in their view, *all* people have the capacity for citizenship and must be given the opportunity to engage fully in politics, for participation is the road to self-realization. While participationists subscribe wholeheartedly to the democratic psychology, civic republicans have betrayed a distrust of human nature.

Finally, civic republicans are prepared to subordinate individual freedom and happiness to the common good.[48] Although committed to the commonweal, participationists refuse to compromise individual dignity and development. In an attempt to reconcile individualism and communalism, they insist that civic participation must be voluntary. Hardly subsumed by the collective, the citizen elects to engage with it and is transformed in the process. He is not forced to be free; he chooses to become free. The democratic metaphysics of participationists remains intact. The same cannot be said of civic republicans.

:::  **To convince readers** that participatory democratic theory has pragmatist roots, this work must by necessity be an intellectual history. Chapters 1 and 2 begin with the founders of American pragmatism, Charles Peirce and William James, who laid the intellectual groundwork for participatory democratic thought. The story continues in Chapter 3 with John Dewey, a pivotal figure who saw clearly the political implications of pragmatism, from which he forged a participatory democratic ethos. In Chapter 4 the reader is introduced to C. Wright Mills, who carried the torch of Dewey's democratic faith and inspired the New Left in the early 1960s. The story comes to a conclusion in Chapters 5 and 6, with contemporary democratic theorists Benjamin Barber and Sheldon Wolin, who in many ways deserve to be called the political descendants of the early pragmatists. They represent the intellectual legacy of participatory democracy, which has split into mainstream and radical camps. In Chapter 7 and the Epilogue, I elaborate on the implications of this story.

The story may be illuminating in its own right, but this work is hardly history for history's sake. Indeed, I hope to shed light on participatory democratic thought by examining it through the lens of pragmatism. I try to show that participatory democratic theory—of all kinds, whether institution-friendly or radical—rests on three pragmatist tenets: that truth is probabilistic and socially determined (democratic epistemology); that man is malleable and educable (democratic psychology); and that, vested with free will, man is poised for civic action (democratic metaphysics). Taken together, these tenets suggest that democracy is a transformative experience for both individuals and communities, and that people have the freedom to partake in the experience once they become aware of its benefits. In the view of participatory democrats, political man learns best in the school of democracy, where a community of competent inquirers can devise the best policies for their community and where each participant can grow and mature into a broad-minded citizen. Unfettered by biological determinism or the uncompromising logic of historical or social forces, man has the freedom to enter that school of democracy, and he will certainly do so once he discovers the transformative effects of democratic participation.

Should any of the three tenets prove untenable, however, participatory democracy rests on shaky ground. As we shall see, there is every reason to call all three tenets into question, especially when applied to democratic politics. In addition, the tenets stand in uneasy relation to each other, revealing an inner tension within participatory democratic thought. Viewed in this harsh pragmatist light, participatory democracy reveals itself as a controvertible faith, not a rigorous theory.

# Charles Peirce

*The Joyful Nirvana of the Unlimited Community*

Underappreciated and misunderstood in his own time, Charles Sanders Peirce (1838–1914) has in recent years been called the most important philosopher in the American canon. Although his erudition was undoubtedly impressive, with his studies ranging from mathematics and astronomy to formal logic and semiotics, he probably is best known as the founder (or one of the founders) of pragmatism. Peirce hardly devoted any systematic study to political philosophy or showed any serious interest in democratic politics, but his pragmatism helped lay the philosophical foundation for the rise of participatory democratic thought in America.

Peirce's philosophy evoked a democratic temperament of which he may have been only partly aware but which nonetheless should not be overlooked, for one can identify all three pragmatist tenets in Peirce's thought. Endorsing a democratic epistemology, he maintained that people can acquire knowledge only socially and deliberatively, and that they should always keep an open mind and accept the provisional status of all human knowledge. He also embraced an unquestionable democratic psychology, asserting that human nature is malleable and socially determined, that people have the capacity to learn new habits and, drawing on the spirit of social cooperation, transform themselves for the better. Finally, he revealed a democratic metaphysics in his belief that human beings enjoy the freedom—albeit limited—to choose their social destiny.

It seems never to have occurred to Peirce to derive political lessons from these ideas (as Dewey would begin to do in the 1920s), in large part because he understood the pursuit of knowledge as primarily a scientific endeavor in which only an educated elite could participate. But Peirce's epistemology does strike a democratic tenor when he suggests that the scientific method should and could be applied more broadly—both inside and outside the laboratory and by scientists and laymen alike.[1] Accordingly, Peirce planted the seeds for a democratic theory that would grow in importance and influence throughout the twentieth century in America, culminating perhaps with the New Left in the 1960s but continuing to have its voice heard in academic circles to this day. The story of participatory democratic thought in America begins with pragmatism and with its founders, especially Charles Peirce.

Having devoted two years of his early years to daily study of Immanuel Kant's *Critique of Pure Reason,* the young Peirce was particularly struck by the German philosopher's notion of "pragmatic belief." Kant provided the example of a physician who observes the symptoms of a dangerously ill patient and makes a provisional diagnosis to the best of his ability. Quite aware that "his belief is contingent only," the doctor understands that "another observer might perhaps come to a sounder conclusion." Nevertheless, this "contingent belief" (his diagnosis) will guide the doctor's action, his particular course of medical treatment. He does not know for sure that the patient suffers from jaundice, say, but the symptoms indicate he probably does. Betting that the patient has jaundice, the doctor acts accordingly.[2]

Whereas Kant considered "pragmatic belief" to be one of many kinds of belief, Peirce considered it the only kind. Ideas or beliefs of any kind, said Peirce, are just rules for action that we are betting will work in our experience. We can thank Kant for inspiring Peirce to coin the term "pragmatism" in the early 1870s (even though the world did not hear the term until William James introduced it nearly twenty-five years later) and also for planting the germ of a new and fecund idea.

Alexander Bain, whose *Emotions and the Will* was published in 1859, also had a profound influence on Peirce and the other participants of the Metaphysical Club. Bain called their attention to the practical importance of ideas. The Scottish philosopher defined a belief as "that upon which a man is prepared to act," and Peirce and his fellow club members found this an exciting proposition.

Drawing on Kant, Bain, and the intellectual ferment at Harvard, Peirce wrote a paper that he delivered in the summer of 1872, at the last meeting of the Metaphysical Club, where, according to James, he first introduced the idea of pragmatism. Six years later he published a version of the paper as an article entitled "How to Make Our Ideas Clear" in the *Popular Science Monthly.* Although Peirce does not use the term "pragmatism" in his article, he does clearly articulate a pragmatist creed—the idea that beliefs involve "the establishment in our nature of a rule of action, or, say for short, a *habit*."[3] Acting on our beliefs habitually is our modus operandi, but when these beliefs suddenly cease to work for us we are irritated by doubt. Seeking to alleviate this irritation and return to our contented state of belief, we investigate the problem immediately. By trial and error we discover what went wrong, and accordingly we modify our habits or develop entirely new ones. Whatever ultimately works after repeated tries becomes the modified or new habit.

This fairly simple idea constitutes the core of Peirce's thought. His ideas matured considerably over the next forty years or so, but the beginnings of his complex and comprehensive philosophical system can be traced back to those rudimentary ideas formed during his early years in Cambridge.[4] Without a doubt Peirce was indebted to a number of philosophers and thinkers (including Duns Scotus, Ockham, Hume, Kant, Bain, and many of his peers in Cambridge), but it is important to note that his ideas grew far beyond his influences and into something quite original.

Peirce was attracted to pragmatism in large part because he believed it helped settle the centuries-long debate between realism and nominalism. A dyed-in-the-wool realist, he believed that the regularities or uniformities we observe in our experience, and then give a name or label to, reflect a reality independent of what anybody thinks of them. In other words, mental ideas or general concepts are real. Newton introduced the concept of gravity, for example, when he observed that objects consistently fall to the ground when we let go of them. According to Peirce, this concept is "real" in the sense that it tells us something essential about how objects in the universe behave, and about how the universe in general operates.

Nominalists, on the other hand, maintain that general concepts are not real. Instead they are convenient fictions that help us negotiate the world around us but tell us nothing about the reality of the universe. The only real things in the universe of which we can be certain are particulars, individual events or objects. Peirce characterizes nominalism as the view "that the facts are, in themselves, entirely disconnected, and that it is the mind alone which unites them. One stone dropping to the earth has no real connection with another stone dropping to the earth."[5] Any connection between these similar events exists only in our minds, not in the objects themselves. I observe something real when I drop my fork to the ground, and I observe something real again when immediately afterward I drop my spoon. Each discrete event and the objects involved are real, but any general or universal concept that attempts to explain this regularity or commonality can never be real, for there is no telling whether the fork or spoon will drop to the ground tomorrow. At most, the concept of gravity has proved convenient to us so far, but we do not know what the future holds.

While it might be true that the spoon will not drop to the floor when I let go of it tomorrow, the realist believes there is something real about the strong likelihood of the spoon falling to the floor again—and again. Concepts like gravity may not tell us what will occur in the future, but they do tell us something about what is likely to occur. Peirce maintained that this potential, this statistical likelihood, that we gauge from past experience tells us something real about the universe. The whole point of scientific investigation, Peirce argued, is not merely to construct associations in our minds but rather to establish laws that tell us something about the objective world and that predict what is likely to occur in the future under similar circumstances. While not infallibly predictive, scientific laws generally work for us time and again. Having demonstrated a high degree of reliability in the past, these laws are real, according to Peirce, even when instances of them are not currently being exemplified, for we know we could put any of these laws on display at a moment's notice if we desired.

That many of his contemporaries in the scientific community subscribed to nominalism was a considerable source of frustration for Peirce. An unwillingness to believe in the reality of generalizable experiences (or "generals") belies what they were trying to accomplish—namely, to explain why the universe operates in certain ways. Said Peirce: "Uniformities are precisely the sorts of facts that need to be accounted for. That a pitched coin should sometimes turn up heads and sometimes tails calls for no particular explanation; but if it shows heads every time, we wish to know how this result has been brought about. Law is *par excellence* the thing that wants a reason."[6] The scientist always seeks an explanation behind observed regularities and believes his analysis can reveal something real and general about the objective world.

The nominalist-versus-realist debate extends beyond the realm of scientific laws and into everyday experience, such as when we consider the general concept of an object—say, an apple. The realist would have us believe there is something real about this concept, whereas the nominalist would say it is a linguistic construction, a grouping together of individual objects that we call "apples" out of convenience. As the nominalists would suggest, to assert that a general idea of "appleness" exists in the universe is almost laughable, echoing the Platonic forms that exist in some transcendent realm outside our corporeal experience. But Peirce was no Platonist. He argued that the meaning of our ideas inhere in our particular experiences. Those objects we call "apples" have a set of "conceivable practical effects" that constitute appleness.

In "How to Make Our Ideas Clear," Peirce articulated what is commonly called the "pragmatic maxim" in famously tortured prose: "Consider what effects, that might conceivably have practical bearings, we conceive the object of our conception to have. Then, our conception of these effects is the whole of our conception of the object."[7] In other words, our conception of an object or idea stems from the sum total of its conceivable effects on us. It is worth noting that Peirce used the qualifier "conceivable" because "[i]f pragmatism is the doctrine that every conception is a conception of conceivable practical effects, it makes conception reach far beyond the practical. It allows any flight of imagination, provided this imagination ultimately alights upon a possible practical effect."[8] This means that we derive our general conception of an apple from our actual and our imaginable experiences with those objects to which we eventually attribute the name "apple."

The entire set of conceivable practical effects from an apple is infinitely long, of course, but listing a few will be illustrative: if I look at an apple, I will see the color red or green; if I bite into it, I will taste its unique flavor and juiciness; if I hold it, it will feel smooth and spherical; if I throw it, it will fly fairly far; and so on. Peirce the realist maintained that the experiences we have with apples—their color, taste, texture, throwability, and so on—exist independently of what any of us may think of them, forcing themselves into our consciousness through their brute reality.[9] "The real," he claimed, "is that which insists upon forcing its way to recognition as something other than the mind's creation."[10] The meaning of appleness inheres in those very real experiences we have or could conceivably have with apples.

A closer examination of the pragmatic maxim requires a discussion of Peirce's three phenomenological categories. Perhaps his most original and provocative contribution to pragmatist thought was his reduction of all human experience (the entire cosmos, for that matter) to three "indecomposable concepts."[11] His extensive study in logic led him to the conclusion that any experience in the universe could be broken down, like a chemical compound, into its constitutive elemental parts. The chemistry analogy is apt, although the periodic table has 112 elements, whereas Peirce's phenomenology has only three—which he called firstness, secondness, and thirdness. An explication of these categories will eventually shed light on his theories about knowledge, human nature, and free will (that is, his democratic epistemology, psychology, and metaphysics). As Peirce put it, "pragmatism cannot be understood without [the categories]."[12]

Firstness is difficult to describe or conceptualize because we are not exactly conscious of it. Peirce often characterized firstness as the possibility of an idea, something that enters the mind as pure sensation but is never fully cognized, reflected upon, or compared to anything else. He wrote:

> Imagine, if you will, a consciousness in which there is no comparison, no relation, no recognized multiplicity (since parts would be other than the whole), no change, no imagination of any modification of what is positively there, no reflexion—nothing but a simple positive character. Such a consciousness might be just an odour, say a smell of attar, or it might be an infinite dead

ache; it might be the hearing of a piercing eternal whistle. In short, any simple and positive quality of feeling would be something our description fits that it is such as it is quite regardless of anything else.[13]

Firstness is a decidedly noncognitive quality, a "purely monadic state of feeling" that has no attributable source or opposing point of comparison.[14] It is a prelinguistic, nonrelational experience of the senses. It is the kind of feeling that "retains its positive character but absolutely loses all relation (and thereby all vividness, which is only the sense of shock)."[15]

While Peirce's comparison of firstness to "an *infinite* dead ache" or "a piercing *eternal* whistle" (my emphasis) captures the sensory monotony of firstness, we should not mistake firstness as an experience to whose dullness we become too accustomed from long-term exposure. On the contrary, we experience firstness at the very beginning when a percept first imposes itself on us, representing mere possibility in its immediate state of indeterminacy. In his mind-bending cosmological speculations, Peirce characterized firstness, that time in "the infinitely distant past" when the universe began, as a "confused dream," a state of "original chaos" in which there was no persistent regularity. And because the "reality of things consists in their persistent forcing themselves upon recognition"—in their "regularity"—the immediate and original experience of firstness does not leave a marked impression on our consciousness.[16] Consider the hum of an alarm clock in the early morning when we have entered that state of semiconsciousness in which we can hear the sound but cannot yet recognize its significance or source. It has yet to acquire any meaning for us. We hear the noise but have become aware of nothing but its being present.

Like firstness, secondness is also an experience of which we are not fully conscious but, unlike firstness, it is relational, involving two objects that resist or oppose each other in some fashion. It is the often startling confrontation with brute fact, the experience of acting or being acted upon. Peirce also used the ideas of volition or struggle as synonyms for secondness.

The experience of secondness in these physical terms is fairly easy to comprehend. In pushing against a door, I exercise volition and apply force, and the door, successfully or not, resists my efforts. I do not recognize the door or my actions upon it in general terms; rather, I experience this interplay between "effort and resistance" as an individual and isolated event. The psychological manifestations of secondness are a bit different, typically evoking "shock" or "surprise" in the subject when he is acted upon. Although it "is something which cannot properly be conceived," secondness can often be characterized as the "shock of reaction between ego and non-ego."[17]

If the eternal whistle, for instance, should suddenly stop, we would be surprised by the unprecedented experience of silence. Again, we would not attribute the sudden silence to a particular event or meaning, but we would nevertheless notice its particular effect on us. The moment we identify a reason for the abrupt cessation of the whistle, once a general conception of the whistle and the silence that follows enters our minds, we have moved beyond the initial experience of shock and entered the realm of thirdness.

Thirdness can be distinguished from the first two categories as follows: whereas firstness and secondness are not cognitive and can only be experienced, thirdness *is* cognitive, giving our raw experiences, the various instances of firstness and secondness, meaning. To be more specific, thirdness entails explaining the relationship between firsts and seconds, identifying regularities on which we can rely in our daily experience, and conceiving general laws that become rules for action (or habits).[18] In establishing conceptions that link firsts and seconds together, thirdness introduces a third object to the relationship.[19]

Thirdness establishes a relationship between two objects by way of a third. When person A acts on object B, it will yield the set of practical effects C. If I come across an object that is unknown to me, I will act upon the object in various ways (seconds) to gain sensory information (firsts). Eventually I will develop a general idea (third) about the object as I learn that certain acts of volition will regularly produce certain perceptions.

The experience of thirdness is what we often characterize as consciousness, the awareness of general concepts or relationships in the world we negotiate. As demonstrated in the example of the piercing whistle, sometimes secondness involves the subject being acted upon. And when we awake from our foggy slumber, our dawning consciousness of its meaning (thirdness) will not require us to act physically. We will consider the relationship between the piercing sound and the ensuing silence and eventually realize that the passing of a train probably accounts for the practical consequences. According to Peirce: "The elements of every concept enter in logical thought at the gate of perception and make their exit at the gate of purposive action; and whatever cannot show its passports at both these two gates is to be arrested as unauthorized by reason."[20] Only by interacting with the world around us, either by our acting on it or by its acting on us, and then by learning from these experiences do we develop ideas and beliefs on which we are prepared to act habitually. Once we comprehend the meaning of the piercing whistle, we will automatically attribute this experience to the passing train and will continue to bet that this is the case unless new information casts doubt on our belief.

Peirce's categories were the core elements of his philosophy, the building blocks for nearly everything else he had to say in his philosophical writings. He insisted that this triadic analysis could be applied to any kind of human experience. Hardly just figments of the mind, laws and generals impose themselves on us in our experience, as if demanding that we become aware of them. Whether we know about these generals or not, they are real nonetheless.

To assume they are not, that instead all generals are just convenient fictions or the mental groupings of individual events, is analogous to having a "court without a sheriff." If the law of gravity, for example, is a "mere uniformity" (a verbal construct that serves only as a testament to "the perfection of human reason"), then "what in the world would induce a stone, which is not a term nor a concept but just a plain thing, to act in conformity to that uniformity?" The answer, said Peirce, is nothing. "There is no use talking reason to a stone."[21] In reality, stones have no choice but to fall to the ground because the sheriff (in this case, gravity) compels them.

Our awareness of this concept (or sheriff) stems from its practical effects, which we have observed for many years, but it indeed existed before Newton discovered it and gave it a name. No doubt, human beings have long noticed the effects of gravity and have developed habits from their observations that unsupported objects always fall to the earth. We do not see gravity per se, just like we do not really see electricity or ultraviolet rays in and of themselves, but we know they exist chiefly by their effects. Similarly, we know the sheriff is in town not when we see someone walking down the street with a star pinned to his vest but when we notice that lawbreakers are arrested and brought to justice. In fact, we may never meet the sheriff in person, but this does not prevent us from knowing he is real. For we know he is real when we observe the practical effects of his regularly performing sheriff duties—safer streets and crowded jails, perhaps.

Representing the irreducible elements of experience, the Peircean categories show how each of us applies the pragmatic maxim in our search to make sense of the world around us. Now let us turn to Peirce's epistemology, his ideas about how people can collectively acquire reliable, if not infallible, knowledge about reality. An independent reality may indeed exist, but Peirce reminded us that man can never know for certain that he has grasped this reality. But, as we shall see, there are ways to reduce the degree of uncertainty.

## The Unlimited Community

At the heart of Peirce's epistemology is the idea of fallibilism—the idea that no individual or group of individuals can assert with complete confidence that they have an accurate knowledge of reality or a firm grasp of the truth. "[It] is the doctrine that our knowledge is never absolute but always swims, as it were, in a continuum of uncertainty and indeterminacy."[22] While he can generally trust the ideas on which he acts in his daily life, the fallibilist is always prepared to "dump his whole cart-load of his beliefs, the moment experience is against them."[23] Even the "accepted propositions" of science are "but opinions at most, and the whole list is provisional." Perhaps representing the fallibilist par excellence in Peirce's estimation, the "scientific man is not in the least wedded to his conclu-sions. He risks nothing upon them. He stands ready to abandon one or all as soon as experience opposes them."[24]

As a realist Peirce argued that there is an objective reality about which all human beings, especially scientists, busied themselves trying to learn, but he also maintained that we were poorly equipped for attaining truth. He never suggested, however, that our deficiencies should prevent us from engaging in this most noble of enterprises. On the contrary, he is famous for admonishing, "Do not block the way of inquiry."[25]

The fallibilist always searches relentlessly for truth, acknowledging at every point along the road that his beliefs, no matter how satisfactory they appear to us, may be entirely wrong. He accepts neither the rigidity of absolutism nor the hopelessness of skepticism. Falling quite comfort-ably between these two extremes, the fallibilist is sanguine about the pos-sibility of attaining knowledge about reality but remains forever open to new ideas and humble about what he alone can achieve. Unlike the abso-lutist, he is always willing to reassess his beliefs and revise them as new in-formation is brought to light. Unlike the skeptic, he believes humanity has both the capacity and the responsibility to seek out the truth, even though we will never know for sure when we have found it.

Implicit in Peirce's discussion of fallibilism is the idea that truth is prob-abilistic. One man can never know for sure that his perception of reality corresponds with objective reality, so he instinctively applies "tests of ex-ternality," the most important of which is to call in other observers from his community.[26] If upon walking into my apartment, for example, I expe-rience something out of the ordinary, I immediately call my friends and family and ask them to verify that I have not imagined this strange event or somehow perceived it incorrectly. As the community of inquirers grows, presumably confirming my perception of the extraordinary experi-ence, I become more certain that I am right and will eventually be willing to bet on it.

According to Peirce, logic dictates that we operate this way, for his analysis of the three categories shows that we develop thirds by identify-ing persistent relationships between firsts and seconds. Or, in other words, we arrive at general conceptions or truths by observing uniformities in our experience, the unfailing connections between our sense percepts and our actions. This means that limiting ourselves to only our own subjective ex-periences, as we try to identify these uniformities, defies logic. We must draw on the experiences of other people in our community before we can embrace any general concept with confidence.

Peirce invoked lessons drawn from astronomy, in which a community of scientists pooled their observations to determine the most probable loca-tions of stars. No single telescopic observation can locate a star reliably be-cause it is prone to subjective error, but a sample of observations measured by different people working in different observatories can reveal the most likely location. Astronomers in the eighteenth century realized that a graphical distribution of every observed location always took the shape of a bell-shaped curve. Then, drawing on statistical theory, they concluded that the arithmetic mean, around which this curve converged, represented the most probable real location of the star. This solution became known as the method of least squares, whereby the most likely location was determined by minimizing the sum of the squared differences between it and each of the observed locations. When an object is at rest, calculating the arithmetic mean accomplishes this task. Applying the method of least squares to estimate the location of a moving celestial object, such as a comet, was discovered at the end of the eighteenth century and involved far more sophisticated computational techniques. But the principle remained the same, pinpointing the location "around which repeated observations ineluctably converge."[27] The idea here is that individual knowledge is fallible but that collective knowledge is less so.

The method of least squares is a prime example of what Peirce called inductive logic, and he argued that this is the only way in which a community of inquirers can infer general truths. An accomplished student of logic, Peirce wrote extensively on the subject, parsing it into its three main types—abduction, deduction, and induction. To differentiate them succinctly, Peirce wrote: "Deduction proves that something *must* be; Induction shows that something *actually is* operative; Abduction merely suggests something *may be*."[28]

Almost all truth inquiries begin with abduction, generating a hypothesis or guess that could possibly explain the occurrence of a surprising event. We then turn to deduction to infer particular conclusions that necessarily follow from that hypothesis. Finally, the purpose of induction is to test these conclusions, to determine whether the hypothesis and the conclusions that necessarily follow from it are empirically true. The process of induction involves drawing on a set of specific examples from which one can infer general truths—truths that are "operative" in the real world. The final step, the actual test, is to compare these general and operative truths inferred by induction with the initial hypothesis and the deduced conclusions.

While all three types of logic have an important role to play in the search for truth, Peirce placed particular emphasis on induction, for it is the only one that can tell us what really is true, not just what may be true or what must be true if we accept some dubious premises. Peirce identified three kinds of induction—crude, qualitative, and quantitative—and clearly found the latter the most reliable. He defined induction as "an argument which proceeds upon the assumption that all the members of a class or aggregate have all the characters which are common to all those members of this class concerning which it is known." Induction assumes that what "is true of a whole collection" is also "true of a number of instances taken from it at random. This might be called statistical argument."[29]

No matter what kind of induction one may apply, it always involves at some level taking a random sample of cases from a defined population, observing certain characteristics in that sample, and inferring that the whole population has the same characteristics. In other words, induction assumes that the sample is an adequate reflection of the whole. While both crude induction and qualitative induction draw on a limited number of cases, quantitative induction involves taking a large enough sample to infer general truths with a certain level of statistical confidence. Our confidence grows along with the size of the sample: as it approaches infinity, our degree of doubt approaches zero. Peirce provided the following example to illustrate the logic of induction:

> Case.—These beans are from this bag.
> Result.—These beans are white.
> Therefore, Rule.—All the beans in this bag are white.[30]

We cannot be entirely certain about the inferred rule, but as the sample of beans increases in size, we become more confident that it is representative of all the beans in the bag. With an infinite sample, we can be completely sure.

This preference for inductive logic, especially the quantitative variety, led Peirce to make his famous formulation: "The opinion which is fated to be ultimately agreed to by all who investigate, is what we mean by the truth, and the object represented in this opinion is the real."[31] Fate was a statistical concept for Peirce. It represented a kind of destiny, "which is sure to come about although there is no necessitating reason for it. Thus, a pair of dice, thrown often enough, will turn up sixes some time, although there is no necessity that they should. The probability that they will is 1: that is all."[32] Just as sixes are destined to come up at some point if you throw a pair of dice an infinite number of times, the final opinion of an infinitely large community is destined to represent the truth. In both cases, said Peirce, the probability is 1.

Once understood in these statistical terms, Peirce's famous formulation cannot mean (as some have suggested) that truth is merely a social construction, whatever the community of inquirers arbitrarily opine. Peirce did not claim that truth is subjective, but rather that a community of inquirers is destined to formulate a final opinion that corresponds with the objective truth—that is, if they pursue their investigation into the infinite future.

> The real, then, is that which, sooner or later, information and reasoning would finally result in, and which is therefore independent of the vagaries of me and you. Thus, the very origin of the conception of reality shows that this conception essentially involves the notion of a COMMUNITY, without definite limits, and capable of a definite increase of knowledge.[33]

As Peirce saw it, reality is indeed independent of what you or I or some finite number of people may think about it; and an infinite quest conducted by an unlimited community is "destined to lead, at last, if continued long enough to a belief" in that independent reality—in the truth.[34] This is an explicitly statistical epistemology: as the size of the community approaches infinity, its opinion converges asymptotically on the truth. This unlimited or infinite community whose opinion merges with the truth is a hypothetical, an unreachable endpoint for which we should nevertheless always strive in hopes of reducing subjective error as much as possible.

It is important to note, however, that this does not imply that only an infinite community can know the truth, for even one man may be fortunate enough to find it. But an infinite investigation is necessary "to know *that* we know the real object."[35] In practical terms, this means we can never be certain we are right, even when we are, for infinite investigations are unattainable. Peirce's fallibilism drew explicitly on this notion of statistical error.

This statistical logic led Peirce to believe that the search for truth is a social endeavor, which filters out the idiosyncrasies and peculiarities of individual observers and corrects the "limitations in circumstances, power, and bent" of each human being, who cannot help but perceive the objective world through a radically subjective lens. Peirce gave an example of a deaf man and a blind man who both witness a murder. "One hears a man declare he means to kill another, hears the report of the pistol, and hears the victim cry; the other sees the murder done." Each witness has an incomplete understanding of the event, but should they talk with one another and share their subjective information, "their final conclusions, the thought the remotest from sense, will be identical and free from the one-sidedness of their idiosyncrasies."[36] Peirce suggested here that if the community of investigators—in this case, the deaf man and the blind man—deliberate long enough, their disparate individual beliefs will eventually converge around one shared belief. As he saw it, this is the way scientific inquiry works, with investigators searching collectively for solutions from different angles and then ultimately gravitating toward one "destined center" upon which they will all agree.[37]

While this reasoning draws on statistical logic, it also speaks to the public and deliberative quality of the scientific method, where scientists openly share information with other inquirers in the community and build on earlier work. According to Peirce, the selfless devotion with which scientists pursue knowledge leads "to their unreserved discussions with one another, to each being fully informed about the work of his neighbor, and availing himself of that neighbor's results." Thus, said Peirce, "in storming the stronghold of truth one mounts upon the shoulders of another who has to ordinary apprehension failed, but has in truth succeeded by virtue of the lessons of his failure. This is the veritable essence of science."[38] In other words, the community of inquirers is just that: a community, not a collection of independent agents who pursue the truth alone and contribute their data to some repository where final results are tallied and released to the world. The scientific method settles belief more satisfactorily than other approaches because it is self-corrective, incrementally improving on the failures and successes of others and creating consensus along the way.

Tying in both the logic of statistics and the virtues of deliberation, Edward C. Moore has given a wonderful description of this "self-corrective" element of Peirce's epistemology:

> The method is self-corrective because, although one observer, or a large group of observers, may examine an object and come to a false conclusion about it, the object continually constrains each successive observer to see it as it really is, and if this process is continued over an infinite period of time the method will correct the error, since, by continually referring back to the object, an infinite number of observers must sooner or later discover and remove any subjective elements in the conception of the object and eventually perceive the object as it really is.[39]

A successful application of the scientific method never ends, pushing each investigator to build on the work of his predecessors and to get that much closer to the truth.

But Peirce acknowledged that, realistically, a community of inquirers, whose size and time is decidedly finite, may not correct itself and may remain divided on many questions. No matter how hard they try, participants will often not be able to make significant progress or reach any kind of consensus on a particularly difficult question. Nevertheless, this reality check should not dash all hope that we can collectively find answers to those "particular questions with which our inquiries are busied."[40] What mattered most to Peirce was the process—striving for consensus through painstaking deliberation and cooperation, even when the fruits of this labor are not immediately evident.

The importance of community for Peirce cannot be overstated. His aversion to nominalism in large part stemmed from its assumption that reality can be experienced only on a particular basis, that the acquisition of any kind of truth is an individual endeavor. But no one can determine what is right on his own. The certainty of death, said Peirce, limits the number of experiences from which any one person can infer any kind of general truths. Because the "very idea of probability and of reasoning rests on the assumption that this number [of experiences] is indefinitely great," logic dictates that our interests shall *not* be limited. They must not stop at our own fate, but must embrace the whole community. This community, again, must not be limited, but must extend to all races of beings with whom we can come into immediate or mediate intellectual relation. It must reach, however vaguely, beyond this geological epoch, beyond all bounds. He who would not sacrifice his own soul to save the whole world, is, as it seems to me, illogical in all his inferences, collectively. Logic is rooted in the social principle.[41]

Peirce was a great critic of individualism, believing that it blocked the road not only of inquiry but also of human progress. To assume that one can learn autonomously, by solely looking into the dark recesses of the self in the Cartesian fashion, was the "vulgarest delusion of vanity."[42] To suggest that "progress takes place by virtue of every individual's striving for himself with all his might and trampling his neighbor under foot whenever he gets a chance to do so . . . may accurately be called the Gospel of Greed."[43] Peirce called for a return to the gospel of Christ, which states that "progress comes from every individual merging his individuality in sympathy with his neighbors."[44] No doubt, he believed that the widespread practice of the scientific method constitutes this return.

## Man's Transmutation into a New Form of Life

Peirce embraced fallibilism not only because he thought that man has a native inability to know anything with absolute certainty but also because the natural world man seeks to understand is always changing. In other words, nature itself is just as unreliable as man's perception of it. The problem with infallibilism is that it cannot accommodate this growing and evolving world—events occur spontaneously and unexpectedly, and nature and its laws are never stable.

> The infallibilist naturally thinks that everything was substantially as it is now. Laws at any rate being absolute could not grow. They either always were, or they sprang instantaneously into being by a sudden fiat like the drill of a company of soldiers. This makes the laws of nature absolutely blind and inexplicable. Their why and wherefore can't be asked. This absolutely blocks the road of inquiry. The fallibilist won't do this. He asks may these forces of nature not be somehow amenable to reason? May they not have naturally grown up? After all, there is no reason to think they are absolute. If all things are continuous, the universe must be undergoing a continuous growth from non-existence to existence.[45]

We can never pursue the meaning of law if we simply assert either that it has always existed or that it appeared one day in its fixed condition out of nothing. Either supposition "blocks the road of inquiry," according to Peirce, because it does not offer any kind of explanation for the existence of laws.

Instead of defining law in dichotomous terms (as either absolute or nonexistent), Peirce found it more reasonable to understand law in dynamic terms, as moving along a continuum that ranges between two asymptotic poles. Law begins at a point of complete indeterminacy in the infinitely distant past and ends at a point of absolute certainty in the infinitely distant future. "[C]onformity with law," Peirce concluded, "is a fact requiring to be explained; and since law in general cannot be explained by any law in particular, the explanation must consist in showing how law is developed out of pure chance, irregularity, and indeterminacy."[46] This is not much of an argument, but Peirce did not contend that this dynamic view of the universe unfolding from chaos to regularity is absolutely true. He only suggested that it is a more reasonable hypothesis, whose conformity with our experiences can actually be tested.

A belief in the immutability of natural law presupposes that instances of cause and effect will occur with exact precision and infallible regularity. If we observe imprecision or irregularity in our laws, we have reason to believe that they are not the product of a vast unchanging mechanism but are instead subject to spontaneous deviation or chance variation—or what he called tychism. Peirce contended that there are many examples of tychism of which scientists are particularly aware. The inexactitude of empirical observations in the laboratory, for example, confirms the hypothesis that the universe and its laws are evolving. To those with intimate knowledge of the scientific enterprise, said Peirce, "the idea of mathematical exactitude being demonstrated in the laboratory will appear simply ridiculous." For even the "most refined comparisons of masses, lengths, and angles, far surpassing in precision all other measurements . . . are about on a par with an upholsterer's measurements of carpets and curtains."[47]

Some scientists would attribute these variations and imprecisions in measurement completely to human error, but Peirce considered this a quixotic attempt to defend a mechanistic view of the universe, the notion that events unfold in a necessary and logical sequence. We have no way of knowing whether events are determined in this way, and we should not make this assumption when our experiences seem to belie such a hypothesis. Men of science usually have the sense to remain more humble than those crude mechanists who believe they hold the secret of the universe. Peirce wrote: "I have not found that it is the men whose lives are mostly passed within the four walls of a physical laboratory who are most inclined to be satisfied with a purely mechanical metaphysics."[48]

Scientists know from empirical observation that, although the world may appear mechanical to the untrained eye, it is in fact teeming with chance occurrences and irregularity. Peirce argued that tychism is the only reasonable explanation not only for observable imprecision in the laboratory but also for the growth toward increasing complexity and variety in the universe. Mechanism cannot account for the observable increase of diversity in our world, and "wherever diversity is increasing, there chance must be operative."[49]

Peirce drew explicitly on Darwinism to make this argument. Darwin contended that evolution begins with chance variation, the random change in the traits of an individual, which then gets passed on to future generations. Of course, anyone with a passing knowledge of Darwinism knows that sometimes this trait may either prove conducive to the survival of a particular species or spell its future doom. But Peirce was more interested in how tychism, unlike mechanism, can explain both the increase in variety within a species and, on rarer occasions, the creation of new species.

Although tychism introduces this element of spontaneity to the universe, adding to its richness and variety, this does not mean that the universe has no order or regularity at all. To the contrary, laws always constrain chance variation "within narrow bounds." Tychism merely suggests that the universe produces innumerable "departures from the law," most of which are "infinitesimal"—such as those small but measurable inexactitudes observed in the laboratory—but some of which, on extremely rare occasions, prove "great" and monumental.[50] This means that laws have a certain uniformity and order to them but that they are always subject to the possibility of variation.

Just as fallibilism rests on the notion of probability, so does tychism. We can think of law as a statistical mean around which a distribution of events, shaped like a bell-curve, can be drawn. While large-scale (or "great") deviations are statistical outliers and thus will occur infrequently, minor (or "infinitesimal") deviations are quite common and will occur frequently. Understood in statistical terms, laws are variable, giving us predictions that are likely but never precise. While Peirce speculated that laws are becoming less variable over time and will become absolutely certain and mechanistic in the infinite future, this means that for all practical purposes he had to replace the mechanical metaphor with an organic one. The Peircean universe is not a machine but a conscious organism or a living mind. This organism, born in a state of utter confusion and indeterminacy, must develop modes of behavior in order to establish a sense of order.

Laws, then, do not follow the unalterable logic of machines but instead resemble habits, those patterns of behavior that any life form develops over time after countless repetitions. Laws and habits were actually the same thing in Peirce's estimation. As the universe evolves over time, it develops laws or habits that give it an increasingly recognizable and predictable form. Habit is responsible for creating any kind of intelligibility in the universe, endowing it with a predictability and coherence with which it did not start. Nevertheless, until that day in the infinite future, habits have that peculiar quality of "not acting with exactitude," of responding to certain circumstances in generally reliable, but never precisely uniform, ways.[51]

Peirce's discussion of habit had important implications for his ideas about human nature. Because laws were not immutable in Peirce's view, neither were human beings. In his search for ideas and beliefs that serve as "rules for action," man develops habits, modes of behavior that in his experience prove useful time and again. Eventually, he employs these habits without thinking about them too much, and they come to define him. But no matter how mechanical his habits may appear, they are not hardwired irrevocably. Indeed, "no mental action seems to be necessary or invariable in its character. In whatever manner the mind has reacted under a given sensation, in that manner it is more likely to react again," said Peirce. But if this were "an absolute necessity, habits would become wooden and ineradicable and, no room being left for the formation of new habits, intellectual life would come to a speedy close." Like natural laws, which provide form to the universe, mental habits are variable. In fact, mental habits are even more uncertain than natural laws, for they are only under the influence of "gentle forces" that guide our actions in certain directions without ever removing an element of "arbitrary spontaneity."[52] We may be creatures of habit, but these habits can always be altered.

A believer in the epistemological superiority of the unlimited community, Peirce believed that human beings could only develop good habits—or habits that accord with the truth—in a social context. He was a great critic of nominalism in large part because he believed that, in denying the existence of universal truth, it promoted an ethos of individualism, selfishness, and greed. Peirce's realism, on the other hand, teaches people that universal truth actually exists and that a community of inquirers can become quite confident, though not completely certain, of having attained it.

That said, people have to adopt the right social habits to form such a community and become productive members of it. We have the choice, said Peirce, between two real options. We can either embrace "Americanism, the worship of business, the life in which the fertilizing stream of genial sentiment dries up or shrinks to a rill of comic tit-bits," or we can come to terms with our "own insignificance" as "mere cells of the social organism" and "recognize a higher business than [our own] . . . a generalized conception of duty which completes [one's] personality by melting it into the neighboring parts of the universal cosmos." If he chooses the latter, "man prepares himself for transmutation into a new form of life, the joyful Nirvana in which the discontinuities of his will shall have all but disappeared."[53] The suggestion here is that man has the freedom to choose between subjective individualism and objective truth, between the habits of greed and the habits of social cooperation. In recognizing his duty to something larger than himself and becoming an integral part of the unlimited community, man has the power to transform himself, both intellectually and morally, and to make his personality complete.

## The Freedom of Choice

The mutability of law and human nature may seem to imply that men have free will. But Peirce claimed that this is not necessarily the case:

> The propositions that laws of nature are not absolute and that important physical events are due to human reasoning are far from proving that human action is (in any important degree) free, except in the sense that a man is a machine with automatic controls, one over another, for five or six grades, at least. I, for my part, am very dubious as to man's having more freedom than that.[54]

This passage, taken from a letter to British pragmatist F. C. S. Schiller, seems to suggests that Peirce was actually a determinist. Indeed, in a letter to William James, Peirce also said that he did not think "the will is free in any appreciable measure," because occurrences of chance variation or spontaneity "can only amount to much in a state of things closely approximating to unstable equilibrium"—as when our habits cease to work and we are irritated with doubt. The exercise of will, on the other hand, occurs in a state of stable equilibrium, long after we have alleviated any doubts. In other words, we exercise will in a largely mechanical or habitual way. That said, Peirce still upheld a doctrine of limited freedom. In his letter to James he continued: "The freedom lies in the *choice* which long antecedes the will. *There* a state of nearly unstable equilibrium is found."[55]

We exercise freedom during those moments of doubt when we must make conscious choices in our struggle to develop new habits. Peirce suggested here that the term "free will" is a misnomer and should be replaced with "free choice." In his understanding, the will actualizes those choices we made at an earlier time. These actualizations do not always reflect our earlier choices perfectly, in large part because habit often gets in the way. There is no avoiding the ongoing battle between conscious choice and preestablished habits—hence, Peirce's doctrine of limited freedom.

A discussion of Peirce's three categories and their relation to his ethics may shed more light on the subject of freedom. Ultimately concerned with human action or volition, ethics first turns to aesthetics to identify "what state of the world [is] most admirable" and then investigates how we should bring this ideal world about.[56] Logic, the study of how to reason correctly, emerges out of ethics. This last point may strike one as counterintuitive, but we must recall that, according to Peirce, we only think because we must act. This becomes clear when we recall the three categories. The creation of any general idea requires that we first experience sense perceptions (firsts) and then react in particular ways (seconds). As we make sense of the world around us by perceiving and acting, we grow aware of connections between the two and eventually arrive at general ideas (thirds), out of which habits emerge. At that moment when our habits have not yet been established, we have a choice to make. We are free to decide which firsts we would like to experience, and free to choose which seconds we will employ to bring about those firsts. Our choices have important ethical implications because they ultimately shape our ideas and beliefs, which in turn become rules (or habits) for future actions.

According to Peirce, there are such things as good and bad habits. Just as the person who practices good logic must engage with the "unlimited community," so must the ethical person. The ethical person will exercise self-control and develop good habits that promote social cooperation and deliberation. As these good social habits are vital to good reasoning, the suggestion here is that the logical person is by definition an ethical person. "A logical reasoner," said Peirce, "is a reasoner who exercises great self-control in his intellectual operations; and therefore the logically good is simply a particular species of the morally good."[57] Critics have often assailed pragmatism for promoting moral relativism, but they have obviously misread or overlooked the work of Peirce.

Doing the right thing, acting morally, was not a matter of subjective opinion for Peirce. He rejected subjectivist morality, such as the ethos of hedonism, on the basis that there are many times in our lives when simply satiating our instinctive desire for sensual pleasure is not what we really desire to do—and certainly not what we ought to do. Acting solely on the basis of sensual instinct will often make us very dissatisfied, which is why we must turn to reason or logic to ascertain what is morally right. The ethical person "deliberately . . . controls his passions, and makes them conform to such ends as he is prepared to adopt as *ultimate*."[58] The goal here is not to satisfy temporary passions but to find an objective morality that exists independently of individual gratification.

Ethics teaches us how we can do this. It "tells us that we can have a power of self-control, that no narrow or selfish aim can ever prove satisfactory, that the only satisfactory aim is the broadest, highest, and most general possible aim."[59] To do right in this world, we must control our individualistic habits and cultivate a sense of community and wider social responsibility. It is well within our power to achieve this highest of aims.

Although human beings do not enjoy radical freedom in Peirce's estimation, they do have the capacity to make choices and alter their habits. He firmly believed that men can find greater happiness and wisdom if they can only learn the virtues of thoughtful reflection and public deliberation, engaging with the larger community to solve problems. Whether they would ever learn these virtues is another question to which he conceded there was no easy answer:

The question whether the *genus homo* has any existence except as individuals is the question whether there is anything of any more dignity, worth, and importance than individual happiness, individual aspirations, and individual life. Whether men really have anything in common, so that the *community* is to be considered an end in itself . . . is the most fundamental practical question in regard to every public institution the constitution of which we have it in our power to influence.[60]

Even if Peirce never fully considered the political implications of his philosophy, the democratic tone of his hopes is unmistakable. He was committed to the idea that people can come together and achieve a higher ideal than American individualism. While the house of participatory democracy had yet to be built, Peirce most certainly helped to lay down its foundation.

# 2

# The Lonely Courage of William James

In 1898 William James (1842–1910) delivered a paper at the University of California at Berkeley, in which he credited his friend Charles Peirce for introducing pragmatism to the world over twenty years before. Peirce's difficult personality and untoward lifestyle prevented him from ever landing a permanent academic position, and his inability to finish most of the projects on which he worked tirelessly left his philosophical contributions largely unnoticed.[1] James, whose professorship at Harvard and well-received publications gave him a celebrity status in academic circles, never forgot his friend and tried many times to lift him out of philosophical obscurity.

Although certainly appreciative of his friend's generous efforts, Peirce did not treat James's philosophical works with equal kindness. He faulted James for being imprecise and unsystematic—relying too heavily on psychology and not enough on logic in his formulation of pragmatism. In fact, Peirce was so dismayed by the direction in which James and others were taking pragmatism that he sought to distance himself from them by naming his philosophy "pragmaticism," a term "ugly enough to be safe from kidnappers."[2]

Without a doubt, James's version of pragmatism differed considerably from that of Peirce. James initially turned to pragmatism as a means to justify faith in god and free will, and he often presented this school of thought as a way for individuals to avert metaphysical crises, as, in fact, he did for himself. The virtue of pragmatism, as he saw it, was that it provided a harmonious balance between the "tough-mindedness" of materialism and empiricism and the "tender-mindedness" of spiritualism and rationalism.[3] It could meet the factual and methodological rigors of science and at the same time appeal to our subjective need for something more meaningful and permanent in our lives. The end result was a philosophy that placed considerable emphasis on the dignity of the individual and his freedom to change himself and the world around him.

At times James seemed to neglect the importance of community in the search for truth, and his philosophy seemed to languish in radical subjectivism and relativism, where truth amounted to nothing more than the desires of each individual. But critics of James have overstated his individualism. He did not subscribe to liberal dogma that delineated a clear divide between the individual and the collective; he understood that they shared a symbiotic relationship. James's philosophy proved friendly to democratic principles, for which he often showed public support, and his work helped lay the groundwork for participatory democratic theory.

It is not surprising, then, that all three pragmatist tenets are recognizable in his writings. In arguing that people can acquire knowledge only experientially and socially, that their truth claims are always working hypotheses, James espoused a democratic epistemology. He also revealed a democratic psychology when he maintained that human nature is flexible and subject to social construction and that, as mere bundles of habits, people are transformable. Finally, he held faithfully to a democratic metaphysics, the belief that human beings have free will and can thus choose their destiny.

Unlike Peirce, James understood clearly that political lessons could be derived from pragmatism. Although he did not match Dewey in calling for a participatory democracy, James struck a decidedly democratic tenor not only in his philosophical writings but also in his approach to teaching, his personal relationships, and his political commitments. He was an exceedingly magnanimous and tolerant man, whose reputation for open-mindedness attracted the more unorthodox students at Harvard. W. E. B. Dubois, Alain Locke (the first African American Rhodes scholar), and Gertrude Stein were among his most enthusiastic students.

James was a champion of the underdog, the lost soul and the nonconformist, and he held large elite institutions in contempt for trampling on even the most unconventional expressions of individual genius. It should come as no surprise that James was one of the few who were able to overlook the eccentricities and appreciate the mind of Charles Peirce. Just a few months after James's death, Walter Lippmann called his former professor "so very much of a democrat" and said that "[i]t is an encouraging thought that America should have produced perhaps the most tolerant man of our generation."[4]

Forever concerned with the plight of others, James ardently opposed reckless American intervention abroad and saw the moral bankruptcy of colonialism, imperialism, and excessive militarism. In the wake of the Spanish-American War and the occupation of the Philippines, he became the vice president of the Anti-Imperialist League and wrote countless letters to the editor denouncing American foreign policy. His opposition rested primarily on his belief that American imperialism betrayed a blindness to alternative perspectives and ways of life.

He was just as critical of excessive greed and materialism at home, blaming luxuriant living and "the exclusive worship of the bitch-goddess SUCCESS" for our "moral flabbiness."[5] Striking almost a Marxist tone, James claimed that men enthralled by luxury are corrupt, cowardly, and morally lethargic. He felt that only a "man for whom poverty has no terrors becomes a freeman"; his sympathy for the poor led him to support the redistribution of wealth and moving toward a "socialist equilibrium," but he adamantly opposed all things big, including big government.[6] Indeed, his political philosophy grew increasingly anarchistic, and he came to believe that only small communities could govern themselves in a manner both just and sane and provide ample opportunity for the exercise of civic courage.

While Peirce's democratic temperament appeared most strongly in his epistemology, James displayed his democratic colors brightly in all three tenets. Peirce placed a great deal of weight on his belief that truth is probabilistic, best approximated by deliberative communities. James agreed with Peircean epistemology, but his individualistic streak tended to overshadow the importance of communal learning in his thought. With far more pomp than Peirce, James stressed an ardent faith in the educability of all men (not just members of the elite) and in their immense capacity for strenuous action and control of their destinies. The heart of James's democratic thought lies in his call for civic action. An examination of James's pragmatist philosophy will identify the origins of his political orientation and show how he played a crucial role in the story of participatory democratic thought in America.

## Finding Hope in the Melioristic Universe

James's part in the story begins with a metaphysical crisis. Throughout the 1860s and early 1870s, he suffered from intermittent bouts of depression. Some evidence suggests that these dark periods may have stemmed in part from his upbringing or a genetic predisposition for melancholia, but the prevailing philosophical doctrines of the Victorian age, determinism and materialism, seem to be the primary culprits.[7]

As a young man trying to choose a vocation in life, James proved frustratingly indecisive. The prospect of living in either a preordained or a nihilistic universe (or both) made choosing a vocation seem pointless to him. He finally settled on teaching psychology and philosophy, almost accidentally, after dabbling for many years in chemistry, anatomy, medicine, and even art. A temporary teaching appointment at Harvard in 1872 awoke within him unknown reserves of energy and confidence. But his experience did not lift him miraculously out of his crisis; throughout his life he would suffer from periodic relapses of paralyzing self-doubt.

Teaching represented James's way out of his funk, perhaps not a calling so much as a respectable career for which he happened to have a particular talent and also received just compensation. But finding a fairly rewarding and lucrative vocation was not sufficient to prevent those nagging specters—determinism and materialism—from haunting him. James gravitated to psychology and philosophy in particular because they helped him challenge these paralyzing doctrines, gave him the resolve to fight back and find meaning in life, and ultimately turned him into a vigorous and admirably productive person. But before he could become that man, James had to contend with determinism, which "professes that those parts of the universe already laid down absolutely appoint and decree what the other parts shall be. The future has no ambiguous possibilities hidden in its womb. . . . Any other future complement than the one fixed from eternity is impossible."[8]

Determinism comes in two forms, material and spiritual, neither of which was satisfactory to James. In 1869 he wrote his old friend Tom Ward in despair over the bleakness of materialistic (or mechanistic) determinism. If this vision were true, he observed, we inhabit a universe of "instable molecules trembling in their own preappointed way. . . . I feel," he continued, "that we are Nature through and through, that we are wholly conditioned, that not a wiggle of our will happens save as the result of physical laws."[9] While this vision was hardly uplifting, neither was a Calvinist or Hegelian universe, in which our lives were preordained by an all-powerful Absolute. Spiritual determinism provided no comfort for James. Given the cruel realities of life, he could not envision "the old warm notion of a man-loving Deity." Instead, he saw "an awful power that neither hates nor loves, but rolls all things together meaninglessly to a common doom. This is an uncanny, a sinister, a nightmare view of life."[10] Whatever its form, determinism suggested a chillingly amoral universe, where man was powerless to control his own destiny and was subject to the caprice of matter or god, each equally insensitive to man's plight and the evils he endured.

The problem of evil was a particular sticking point for James. In the throes of his metaphysical crisis in February 1870, he wrote in his diary: "Can one with full knowledge and sincerity ever bring one's self so to sympathize with the total process of the universe as heartily to assent to the evil that seems inherent in its details?"[11] James could not passively accept the existence of evil in the universe. Nor could he fathom a benevolent and loving god who would abide the many evils that befell humankind if he had the power and knowledge to prevent them. God as traditionally understood, both omniscient and omnipotent, could include evil in his plan of the universe only if he were profoundly indifferent to our pain and suffering.[12]

Many absolutist philosophers—including James's eventual colleague and rival at Harvard, Josiah Royce—posited a higher truth that mattered far more than our temporal experience and that, if made known to us, could explain how evil fit into god's scheme. But the only explanation open to them, according to James, was an unsatisfying form of subjectivism, in which the preordained unfolding of the universe is understood as "a contrivance for deepening the theoretic consciousness of what goodness and evil in their intrinsic natures are. Not the doing either of good or of evil is what natures cares for, but the knowing of them." James thought this explanation trivialized earthly experience and reduced it to mere theater. Such an unconscionable philosophy "wrenches my personal instincts," he wrote. "It transforms life from a tragic reality into an insincere melodramatic exhibition."[13] It has the audacity to suggest that the world we experience day to day, with its many trials and miseries, is not real, when it is the only reality we can be sure of:

> While Professors Royce and Bradley and a whole host of guileless thoroughfed thinkers are unveiling Reality and the Absolute and explaining away evil and pain, this is the condition of the only beings known to us anywhere in the universe with a developed consciousness of what the universe is. What these people experience *is* Reality. It gives us an absolute phase of the universe. It is the personal experience of those best qualified in our circle of knowledge to *have* experience, to tell us *what is*. Now what does *thinking about* the experience of these persons come to, compared to directly and personally feeling it as they feel it? The philosophers are dealing in shades, while those who live and feel know truth.[14]

As James saw it, the world we experience, with all its evil and pain, is the reality we are dealt. Our job here on earth, however brief our time might be, is not to acquiesce quietly but to fight evil and injustice with every ounce of energy we can muster.

The problem, however, was that a deterministic universe does not endow men with the free will to engage in this fight. Passive acceptance seems our only option. James found this worldview profoundly pessimistic because it at once reduces man to an ineffectual spectator, eliminating the possibility of hope or redemption, and making ethics irrelevant. As mere spectators, men do not have the capacity to reshape the world around them or to ameliorate the problems and evils they face. "Determinists, who deny [free will], who say that individual men originate nothing, but merely transmit to the future the whole push of the past cosmos of which they are so small an expression, diminish man. He is less admirable, stripped of this creative principle."[15] Without this creative capacity, man can find no hope in the dawning of a better day and must resign himself to the inevitability of what the future holds.

Perhaps the most disturbing point is that a universe devoid of free will requires us to reserve moral judgment, no matter how repugnant and hideous the behavior we observe may be. In James's view, we cannot pass judgment on a person and hold him accountable for his behavior if he could not have chosen to act differently. Although Royceans would suggest that even a predetermined universe should awaken our moral sympathies and deepen our knowledge of good and evil, James simply could not reconcile determinism with ethics, for determinism means that human effort does not make an ounce of difference in the future.

While determinism made James increasingly despondent as a young man, he also had difficulties grappling with materialism.[16] Some of James's contemporaries, including the English philosopher Herbert Spencer, claimed that materialism can still inspire one to appreciate, even worship, the sublime and wondrous creations of nature. The fact that these creations originate from blind physical forces and not a grand designer makes no difference, they said, for nature remains just as fascinating and refined.

But James understood intuitively that a universe composed solely of matter had no intrinsic meaning or moral structure. As a seasoned philosopher, many years later, he was able to articulate quite succinctly what was at stake in this debate: "Materialism means simply the denial that the moral order is eternal, and the cutting off of ultimate hopes; spiritualism means the affirmation of an eternal moral order and the letting loose of hope . . . spiritualistic faith in all its forms deals with a world of promise, while materialism's sun sets in a sea of disappointment." In a number of publications, James found occasion to offer a materialist "picture of the last state of the universe" by quoting Arthur James Balfour, an English philosopher and politician who became prime minister in 1902.[17] Balfour's *Foundations of Belief* (1895), an introduction to the study of theology, pulled no punches in its portrayal of the materialist abyss:

> The energies of our system will decay, the glory of the sun will be dimmed, and the earth, tideless and inert, will no longer tolerate the race which has for a moment disturbed its solitude. Man will go down into the pit, and all his thoughts will perish. The uneasy consciousness which in this obscure corner has for a brief space broken the contented silence of the universe, will be at rest. Matter will know itself no longer. "Imperishable monuments" and "immortal deeds," death itself, and love stronger than death, will be as if they had not been seen. Nor will anything that is, be better or worse for all that the labor, genius, devotion, and suffering of man have striven through countless ages to effect.[18]

For James, Balfour captured what is so unsettling about materialism: it implies that man is but an accidental interruption, a momentary flicker of consciousness in an otherwise cold and indifferent universe. When the last light of humanity is extinguished, all our triumphs and ideals, the many evils we endured and inflicted, will disappear unremembered, as if we never were. Evoking a universe devoid of morality and meaning, this image proved intolerable for James.

It is ironic that critics of James have accused him of flirting with nihilism: he devoted his career to constructing a philosophy that would enable men in a scientific age to reconcile their empirical impulses with their need for something more meaningful and permanent in life. James scholar George Cotkin argues that the philosopher "was convinced that the failure of individuals to believe in either God or their own free will confined them to lives of depression and debility, doubt and ennui. James wanted to reach the hearts of this class of thinkers."[19] Certainly identifying with those thoughtful men who had trouble making their way out of this philosophical thicket, James felt it was incumbent upon him and any philosopher to restore their faith in free will and god, and at the same time to remain in accord with science. It was for this reason that James was drawn to pragmatism, which he saw as a method of finding truths both intellectually and emotionally satisfactory. Whereas Peirce saw the pragmatist method as an outgrowth of logic, James tapped into its psychological roots.

Although at the time the young angst-ridden James was unaware of it, his first experience with the pragmatist method occurred in 1870, when he read the second volume of Charles Renouvier's *Essais de critique générale*. Renouvier argued that, although we may indeed inhabit a determined universe, to embrace it would be absurd given its implications. The only rational choice is to believe in our free will and act accordingly. In Renouvier's reasoning, although we can never know for sure that our belief is true, we should not despair from our doubt, for "[c]ertainty is not and cannot be absolute."[20]

Renouvier's defense of free will was a revelation to James, who overnight became a believer in free will even though there was no definitive proof of its existence. On April 30, 1870, he wrote in his diary:

> I finished the first part of Renouvier's 2nd Essays and see no reason why his definition of free will—the sustaining of a thought *because I choose to* when I might have other thoughts—need be the definition of an illusion. At any rate I will assume for the present—until next year—that it is no illusion. My first act of free will shall be to believe in free will.[21]

Going far beyond "next year," James would sustain his belief in free will for a lifetime.

This affirmation helped James ascend from the depths of his depression and, though he would continue to suffer from melancholy and doubt periodically throughout his life, planted the seeds of an idea that would serve as both a personal coping mechanism and a philosophical method. James learned from this experience that we have every right to embrace beliefs for which there are no definitive proofs, so long as they are reasonable, given what we do know, and more satisfactory to us than the alternatives. It was an object lesson on which he would draw for the rest of his life. More than twenty-five years after James experienced his revelation, he still justified the belief in free will as he did in his 1870 diary entry. In *The Principles of Psychology* (1890) he wrote: "If, meanwhile, the will be undetermined, it would seem only fitting that the belief in its indetermination should be voluntarily chosen from amongst other possible beliefs. Freedom's first deed should be to affirm itself."[22] In the "Dilemma of Determinism," an article published in his book *The Will to Believe* (1895), James reiterated this sentiment when he maintained that "our first act of freedom, if we are free, ought in all inward propriety to be to affirm that we are free."[23]

James was well aware of the empiricist dictate that a rigorous thinker should never accept a belief based on insufficient evidence. A contemporary of his, William Kingdon Clifford, even called it "sinful."[24] But James argued that when faced with a "living option" (an inescapable choice between two or more beliefs that intellect alone cannot resolve), we have the right to accept the most satisfying one as true without sufficient evidence.[25]

In reality, we all make assumptions and accept beliefs for which we have not received conclusive evidence. The empiricist, for example, assumes there are truths and realities that we can discover by testing hypotheses with data collected from our experience. His life's work rests on an unprovable belief in the existence of objective reality. As James saw it, we all exist on "'dogmatic' ground," embracing those belief systems that we find intuitively appealing and vital to our way of life.[26] The scientist, just as much as the believer in free will or god, believes certain foundational ideas that can be neither proved nor disproved. The intellectually honest thing to do is to admit as much and come clean about those unsubstantiated beliefs—our dogmas—to which we all cling at certain pivotal moments in our lives.

The free will dogma was especially important for James, for it functioned as the basis of his philosophical system and a worldview that was satisfying on a personal level. It was a platform from which everything else would spring, a liberating belief opening the universe to infinite possibilities and unseen vistas that in a deterministic universe remained forever closed. Free will implies that the universe is subject to novelty and spontaneous change, that we can expect the unexpected, including valiant efforts on our part to ameliorate the many problems and evils we face in this world. It means that life is a "real fight, in which something is eternally gained for the universe by success," not a "game of private theatricals from which one may withdraw at will."[27]

In *Pragmatism,* James made the distinction between pessimists and optimists—the former believing the world's salvation is impossible and the latter believing it is inevitable—and found neither one satisfactory. This may be surprising to those who assume that when James's belief in free will unshackled him from the dark dungeon of pessimism, he ran straight to the sunny valley of optimism. But, for James, each option represented a closed system, a "block universe" whose story is foretold from the beginning of time. Optimism, like pessimism, means a predetermined world; even if salvation awaits us, there arise the same old questions about the existence of evil and the dignity of man. The only remaining alternative, according to James, is the doctrine of meliorism, which "treats salvation as neither inevitable nor impossible. It treats it as a possibility."[28] Meliorism means that the world's salvation ultimately depends on us, on the free choices we make, on the amount of grit we bring to the struggle.

James found a melioristic universe, in which humanity can play an active role in its salvation, far more comforting than the alternatives, for it meant that the universe was not a block, a pristine geometric shape with all the parts interconnected and unified. Embracing chance and spontaneity, James envisioned a universe with many uncertainties and disjointed parts, with many unpredictable, even thrilling, stories that bear no particular relation to each other. His was a Darwinian universe with no Author or Designer; we the actors wrote the stories willy-nilly as we went along, never sure of the outcome but determined to make our mark.

James understood that faith in free will and meliorism led inexorably to the conclusion that the universe was pluralistic. "Indeterminism thus denies the world to be one unbending unit of fact. It says there is a certain ultimate pluralism in it; and, so saying, it corroborates our ordinary unsophisticated view of things," he wrote. "To that view, actualities seem to float in a wider sea of possibilities from out of which they are chosen; and, somewhere, indeterminism says, such possibilities exist, and form a part of truth."[29] A pluralistic universe does not accept the possibility of absolute truth, because what may be true in one part of the universe may be decidedly false in another. Instead, many truths are being created independently in various segments of the universe, and we have no way of reconciling them in a neat and universal way. "All that *my* pluralism contends for," James wrote in a letter to a friend, "is that there is nowhere extant a *complete* gathering up of the universe in *one* focus, either of knowledge, power or purpose."[30] In keeping with this spirit, James often said that the terms "multiverse" or "pluriverse" were more precise reflections of the diverse and complex world in which we lived than the term "universe."

Unfortunately, solving the "dilemma of determinism" in this manner opened the door to his fear of nihilism and godlessness. It seemed to invite a Balfourian view of the world. But James found a way out of this conundrum by once again exercising his right to believe in god—but a god that could be accommodated within his pluralistic universe. Although pluralism cannot make sense of a traditionally understood god—all-knowing, all-powerful, and all-loving—it can certainly make room for a god that "works under some dark and inscrutable limitations."[31] As James saw it, "the only way to escape" the stark choice between complete determinism (or monism) and indeterminism (or nihilism) was "to be frankly pluralistic and assume that the superhuman consciousness, however vast it may be, has itself an external environment, and consequently is finite . . . that there is a God, but that he is finite, either in power, in knowledge, or in both at once."[32] James believed that an all-powerful god could abide evil and human misery only if he were amoral, completely unmoved by our experiences. This god does not deserve our reverence.

A "finite God," on the other hand, does not have to be tolerant of evil or its creator; in fact, we can imagine him working tirelessly, if not always successfully, to defeat it. "If there be a God," remarked James, "he is no absolute all-experiencer, but simply the experiencer of the widest conscious span."[33] This is undoubtedly a wise and just god to whom we must often turn for strength and guidance. But, for some unknown reason, he also requires our assistance, the human exercise of free will to "strengthen his hands" in the battle against evil.[34] James described our relationship with god quite succinctly: "He helps us and we can help him."[35] This higher being, whose finitude makes our role in the universe far more crucial, is the only kind of "God worthy of the name."[36]

Of course, James could never demonstrate that god has limited powers, or that there is a god in the first place. He was once again faced with a "living option," this time a choice between three reasonable but unprovable beliefs—that there is no god, that there is an all-powerful god, and that there is a finite god—and, in accordance with what he considered to be his right, he embraced the most satisfying belief as true. While James could quite comfortably justify his faith in this way, he knew that persuading a larger audience would require him to develop his idea further and engage in a systematic study of the nature of truth.

Hoping to reconcile the age-old tension between science and religion, James devoted the last decade of his life to developing his pragmatic conception of truth. He asserted that ideas or beliefs are true only insofar as they work for us in our concrete experience. Even our unsubstantiated beliefs, including faith in god and free will, are true if they work for us, if they prove somehow beneficial in our day-to-day lives. After the release of his book *Pragmatism* in 1907, James would have to endure an onslaught of criticism from a wide range of philosophers and intellectuals—including even the friend from whom he borrowed most heavily, Charles Peirce. He would spend the rest of his life defending this rather curious understanding of truth.

## Truth on the Credit System

In 1898 James introduced pragmatism to the world in a paper entitled "Philosophical Conceptions and Practical Results." In this paper he credited Peirce for making a simple but profound formulation: ideas are really just rules for action. But Peirce's particular interest was in how we derive the meaning of an object. Our concept of an object is nothing more than the total sum of the practical consequences of our experiences with it, both real and imagined. Take a pear, for example. We act on the pear in a variety of ways in order to gain a large quantity of sensory information about it. Our preliminary idea of it will be tantamount to the percepts our actions produce. Some of these sensory experiences, especially the more satisfying ones, may inspire habitual action. Tasting the pear may produce such a pleasurable experience in our mouths that we are inclined to taste it again. Eventually, every time we are hungry and see a pear, we will automatically take a bite. Our final idea of a pear, then, points to both the sensory experiences we associate with it and the habitual actions it induces in us. A pear will have a particular feel and appearance, and we will eat it in a certain manner and on certain occasions. If we believe that a pear is indeed before us, we will obey those habits and act accordingly.

In other words, the idea of a pear sitting before us, our belief in its existence, will evoke certain rules for action. James called this "the principle of Peirce, the principle of pragmatism." In his paper from 1898, he wrote:

> Beliefs, in short are really rules for action; and the whole function of thinking is but one step in the production of habits of action. If there were any part of a thought that made no difference in the thought's practical consequences, then that part would be no proper element of the thought's significance. . . . Thus to develop a thought's meaning we need only determine what conduct it is fitted to produce; that conduct is for us its sole significance. . . . To attain perfect clearness in our thoughts of an object, then, we need only consider what effects of a conceivably practical kind the object may involve—what sensations we are to expect from it, and what reactions we must prepare.[37]

Ideas or beliefs are significant only insofar as they have concrete and perceptible consequences. This is why James maintained that "there can *be* no difference which doesn't *make* a difference—no difference in the abstract which does not express itself in a difference of concrete fact, and of conduct consequent upon the fact, imposed on somebody, somehow, somewhere, and somewhen."[38] I may refer to a particular object as a wrench while my less verbal friend calls it a thingamajig, but if we both use the object in precisely the same way, to tighten loose bolts and assemble bicycles and futon frames, our ideas of the object are identical. The abstract distinction is nominal and has no bearing on how we relate to the object, on what it really means to us in practical terms.

To this point James and Peirce had shared similar ground. But James began to diverge from his friend when he derived meaning not only from our percepts and actions but also from our subjective feelings and emotional responses. James found this to be perfectly justifiable, arguing in his 1884 essay "What Is an Emotion?" and developing the thought further in his two-volume opus, *The Principles of Psychology*, that our emotions consist of nothing more than the physical changes or responses that may be induced by a particular stimulus.

Often called the James-Lange Theory of Emotion (named after William James himself and another psychologist, Carl G. Lange, both of whom formulated this theory, around the same time and independently of each other), the idea was startlingly simple yet difficult to accept. It stated that emotions do not trigger a physical response; they *are* the physical response. Take the emotion of sadness as an example. We do not cry because we are sad; we are sad because we cry. We cry and feel a constriction in our throats not because we are in a state of sadness beforehand but rather because, for some unknown reason, we have developed the habit of producing these physiological responses in certain instances.[39] All this implies that emotions and feelings are merely percepts, awakened when we confront certain objects. A tulip may evoke joy in the same way that it evokes the color red; the full meaning of a tulip has to include both these sensory experiences. Once he equated emotional experiences with percepts, James steered his version of pragmatism down a more subjective path, for emotions are variable, unique to each individual. But James believed that introducing this element of subjectivism to the pragmatic method sometimes helps us understand what an object really means to us.

Consider the idea of god. The difference between materialism and theism, according to James, is practical: the former denies the existence of an eternal moral order and makes us feel depressed or anxious, while the latter gives us hope and gives us joy. For many of us, the idea of god becomes tied up with the emotional feeling of joy, which is why so many people have embraced it for millennia. Indeed, its meaning has generated such a wellspring of good feeling that people have naturally taken the next step and come to believe it is in fact true.[40] The subjective element in James's pragmatism led him to declare, much to his friend Peirce's chagrin, that "the truth of an idea is determined by its satisfactoriness."[41] Our belief in god, then, can be true if it satisfies us emotionally.[42]

It should come as no surprise that James's harshest critics accused him of radical relativism or subjectivism, of suggesting that truth is whatever we want it to be. This criticism betrays a superficial understanding of James's pragmatic conception of truth. James never said that we can assert any truth that suits our fancy. He subscribed in part to what philosophers call a coherence theory of truth, the notion that new truths must accommodate as many old truths as possible. This means that our belief in god is true not just because it is satisfactory emotionally but also in every other aspect of our lives. The "hypothesis of God" is only true if it can "combine satisfactorily with all the other working truths" to which we adhere.[43]

This is why James maintained that "the greatest enemy of any one of our truths may be the rest of our truths. Truths have once for all this desperate instinct of self-preservation and of desire to extinguish whatever contradicts them. My belief in the Absolute, based on the good it does me, must run the gauntlet of all my other beliefs."[44] The belief in God may do me good emotionally but may prove unsatisfactory as a whole because it fails to appeal on an intellectual level. James could never accept the conventional understanding of God, either emotionally or intellectually, but he eventually arrived at a theistic truth—the existence of a finite god— that could "run the gauntlet" of all his other beliefs and values. We are all "extreme conservatives" at heart, only adopting new truths that preserve "the older stock of truths with a minimum of modification."[45] Failure to understand this, said James, accounted for a large portion of the criticism leveled against pragmatism.[46]

It is important to note that James combined his coherence theory with a correspondence theory of truth. His correspondence theory did not suggest, as some philosophers do, that truth is a mere copy of the object under consideration, but rather that it is an ongoing verification process to test whether our idea agrees with both sensory and intellectual experiences. James liked to describe pragmatic truth in metaphorical terms, sometimes calling it an idea that "works" or proves "useful," other times an idea that has "profitability" or "cash-value." Although his metaphors were sometimes vague and open to misinterpretation, James was actually expressing a fairly simple concept: all truths have specific consequences that can be verified experientially. While "intellectualists" regarded "truth" as "an inert static relation," a "stable equilibrium" that remains immutable ad infinitum, the pragmatist asks whether this supposedly true idea makes a "concrete difference" in "one's actual life" and whether it has "cash-value in experiential terms." James continued: "The moment pragmatism asks this question, it sees the answer: *True ideas are those that we can assimilate, validate, corroborate and verify. False ideas are those that we can not.* That is the practical difference it makes to us to have true ideas; that, therefore, is the meaning of truth, for it is all that truth is known-as."[47]

James's pragmatism drew heavily on science and the scientific method and at times sounds a lot like positivism, as indeed it does in the preceding passage. From a positivist perspective, the virtue of pragmatism is that it resists excessive abstraction and never deduces truths from dogmatic assertions or immutable first principles. Instead pragmatism asserts that we only know what we can verify factually; it has the additional virtue, according to positivists, of not standing for any particular results, of being "a method only."[48]

But unlike positivists, James (and his fellow pragmatists Peirce and Dewey) believed that truth acquisition involves projecting observations of past experiences into the future and making predictions based on that information. In other words, truth is prospective rather than retrospective. For James, a true idea was simply a successful prediction, a belief that turns out to be right some time in the future. It escorts us directly to those sense experiences we believed our actions would produce. This means that we cannot passively observe the world around us and absorb its many truths; we must actively test whether our predictions are correct.

Based on my observations of how meter maids on campus go about their business, for example, I may have good reason to believe that unpermitted cars parked in the lot near my building never receive tickets after 2:30 p.m., but the verification of this hypothesis, of this prediction, demands action on my part. I need to park in the lot at 2:31 p.m. for several days in a row, and each time I leave the lot in the evening without a ticket, I reconfirm my hypothesis. After a month or two of success, I may begin to park in the lot after 2:30 p.m. without even thinking and thus make my initial hypothesis a true idea, a rule for habitual action. This example illustrates what James meant when he said, "The truth of an idea is not a stagnant property inherent in it. Truth *happens* to an idea. It *becomes* true, is *made* true by events. Its verity *is* in fact an event, a process: the process namely of its verifying itself, its veri-*fication*."[49]

It is important to stress that, for the pragmatist, truth is that which tells us something about what the future holds. Never entirely certain about the future, he accepts that his truths are fallible—always probabilistic affairs. It is always possible, for example, that parking services will instruct meter maids to alter their routes so as to bring them to my lot later in the day. Because truths always have a provisional status, they must be constantly verified and re-verified. Truth cannot abide a hiatus in the verification process; it demands vigilance on our part and will quickly dissipate without our active and persistent participation. If I stop parking in the lot for a while, I will not know whether my truth still holds.

James blamed the peculiarities of our language for the conventional, and mistaken, view that truth is a static entity preceding our experience. He saw the word "truth" as the noun form of the verb "verify"—as another word for the process of verification—and he compared it to other nouns ending in "th"—which describe processes rather than entities. "Truth for us is simply a collective name for verification processes, just as health, wealth, strength, etc. are names for other processes connected with life. . . . Truth is *made,* just as health, wealth and strength are made, in the course of experience." Although we sometimes make the mistake of thinking that health is an abstract concept or an a priori condition that precedes life experience, we have an intuitive sense that health is a process, a way of life that requires eating right, taking regular exercise, and getting an adequate amount of sleep.[50] Quite similarly, Jamesian truth is a way of life, a process that continues to grow throughout our lives, so long as we actively nurture it.

This notion of truth as growing toward the future, always becoming and never just being, is what separates pragmatism from positivism and empiricism. In 1875, long before he fully developed his pragmatist philosophy, James scratched out a note in which he defined truth along these lines: "The truth of a thing or idea is its meaning, or its destiny, that which grows out of it. This would be a doctrine reversing the opinion of the empiricists that the meaning of an idea is that which it has grown from."[51] This implies that the truth is not only prospective but also dynamic. This was why James believed that truth-building sometimes requires leaps of faith, exercising our will to believe in unverified truths and acting on them.

The very act of believing could be the first and most crucial step in making that belief come true. Such beliefs "cannot become true till our faith has made them so," wrote James, citing the example of a trapped mountain climber who must believe he can make a dangerous leap to safety if he ever wants to do so successfully and avert his imminent doom. This example illustrates perfectly that there are *"cases where faith creates its own verification."*[52]

Critics of James were especially troubled by the dynamism of his truth. They made the familiar accusation that a changing and man-made truth gives us license to believe whatever we want. In addition, they detected a Nietzschean moral relativism in which truth-making becomes a blood sport. Rather than a noble quest for something higher and more permanent than ourselves, James's search for truth seems to devolve into a violent struggle for power, the victor rising from the ashes as the final arbiter of truth.[53] James certainly did not help his case when he said that the pragmatist eschews "first principles" and "turns towards concreteness and adequacy, towards facts, towards action and towards power."[54] Nor did he make things better when he equated truth with expediency.[55] But James thought the charges leveled against him were baseless. He blamed his critics for both misreading his work and conflating the concepts of truth and reality, which in turn gave them the fodder for their accusations.

In a seemingly willful misrepresentation of his work, critics mistakenly charged James with nominalism, denying the existence of a reality independent of human experience. But he was most assuredly a realist, and he took pains to clarify his position on countless occasions.[56] Like Peirce, James accepted fully that the universe is full of external realities, including objects and relations between objects, that exist whether human beings come in contact with them or not. When we do confront these realities, they force themselves upon us through our sensory experiences. Our percepts open a window to this brute reality, and then our concepts bring us even closer. Unfortunately, however, we cannot know any reality directly. All we ever really know are our percepts and concepts, not the reality underlying them. Still, our inability to experience reality directly does not change the fact that it exists independently of us and, as a result, places significant constraints on the truths we can create.

This last point leads to the other mistake of which James accused his critics: conflating the concepts of reality and truth. In James's view, reality was simply an irrefutable fact, something with which we must contend, whether or not we like it, not something that can be true or false. Only our ideas about it are true or false. In *The Meaning of Truth,* James made the distinction as simple as possible: "Realities are not *true*; they *are*; and beliefs are true *of* them."[57] The "useful" ideas we have about reality, those ideas that prove satisfactory in our experience, are our truths, and these evolve over time. Reality itself remains what it is, no matter what we may know or think about it.

> All our truths are beliefs about "Reality"; and in any particular belief the reality acts as something independent, as a thing *found*, not manufactured. . . . *"Reality" is in general what truths have to take account of*; and the *first* part of reality from this point of view is the flux of our sensations. Sensations are forced upon us, coming we know not whence. Over their nature, order and quantity we have as good as no control. *They* are neither true nor false; they simply *are*. It is only what we say about them, only the names we give them, our theories of their source and nature and remote relations, that may be true or not.[58]

Arriving at useful or satisfactory truths demands that we "take account of" reality, that we take it seriously. We ignore it at our peril. "Woe to him whose beliefs play fast and loose with the order which realities follow in his experience; they will lead him nowhere or else make false connexions."[59] We cannot avoid the effects of reality; we can neither wish them away nor make them different. With such constraints imposed on us by reality, not to mention those enforced by our old truths, "we can not be capricious with impunity" when constructing our beliefs.[60] Our hypotheses must pass through countless checkpoints before they can ever reach the kingdom of truth—and even when they have reached that glorious land, they always face the possibility of deportation if their papers do not remain in order. Every truth requires periodic reality checks. All this goes to show that Jamesian truth is not whatever we want it to be, for it must accommodate both our prior truths and the oblique but unmistakable realities we continually experience. Although truth is both man-made and dynamic, reality is independent of us, a given fact.

This distinction can help us solve, at least provisionally, any number of epistemological puzzles. Take, for example, the problem of god. Our given reality, which we experience indirectly through our sensory and conceptual experiences, provides no definitive evidence of god's *existence*. Some people point to nature and see evidence of design, while others see only blind chance. But the satisfaction many people get from believing in him—after they have run the "god hypothesis" through the gauntlet of old truths and reality as they know it—makes their belief in god a legitimate *truth*. Obviously, this does not mean that our believing in god makes him pop into existence. Pragmatists acknowledge that god may or may not be real, but this unsettled issue should not prohibit us from embracing a belief that may enrich our lives substantially and may also become the first step in reaching out to a god who may some day reveal himself to us. To deny the truth of god outright will only "block the road of inquiry." As truth-makers, James often said, we must meet the universe halfway. Truths will slowly unveil themselves if we seek them out, cajole and badger them, and continually test their usefulness in our own lives. Otherwise, they will remain forever hidden.

Another way to look at the distinction between truth and reality is to consider James's stream of consciousness, a concept he first devised in the 1880s when he was writing *The Principles of Psychology*. Although he admired the great British empiricists, including John Locke and David Hume, he did not much like their account of human consciousness. Both Locke and Hume argued that we experience the world in fragments, which our minds then link together so that our consciousness of the world appears continuous. James rejected this thesis, because it leaves unexplained how the mind performs this linking function, how it can unify a world initially sliced into little bits.[61]

James's solution to the problem of consciousness was ingenious. He argued that we initially experience consciousness not in fragments but in a confusing flux or a rushing stream of percepts. This initial (or pure) experience resembles that "immediate flux of life" known only to "newborn babes, or men in semi-coma from sleep, drugs, illnesses, or blows."[62] Now, the trick was to explain not how we get from fragments to unity but how we get from this confusing flux to a coherent continuity. James maintained that making sense of this "blooming buzzing confusion" required only that we select, or focus our attention on, those things in our experience that interest us most.⁶³ In so doing, we turn that "buzzing confusion" into a coherent world consisting of recognizable objects and relations to which we attach names.

James enjoyed comparing this process to carving a statue out of a block of marble. The block represents the rush of pure experiences out of which we as sculptors proceed to make successive cuts until the marble becomes something recognizable. The world of pure experiences stands before us, monolithic and inscrutable; we then take our chisels and go to work, carving out shapes that prove most pleasing to us. Out of these shapes we forge our conceptions and ideas, even our truths.⁶⁴ The marble block represents a given reality that will remain forever enigmatic to us. We look upon the block, perhaps even touch and smell it, and these initial sensory experiences constitute our first brush with reality, but it has no intrinsic meaning for us. In order to acquire more knowledge of reality, we cut into it and divide it into manageable chunks.

Soon we become aware that knowing this reality better requires making choices, discarding those parts of our experience for which we have no use and focusing our attention on the interesting sections. In order to get closer to reality, we must not only let it act on us, we must also act on it. We create conceptions and truths so that we can understand this reality better. The truths are always ours—indeed, they are the shapes we carve out of the block—but they always serve to increase our knowledge of a given reality, the enigmatic block of marble. In James's view, to know reality ultimately meant making creative use of it for our own lives, standing in satisfactory and harmonious relation with it. "In our cognitive as well as in our active life we are creative," said James. "We *add*, both to the subject and to the predicate part of reality. The world stands really malleable, waiting to receive its final touches at our hands. Like the kingdom of heaven, it suffers human violence willingly. Man *engenders* truth upon it."⁶⁵

James found this an exciting proposition, endowing people with the freedom to construct truths that would give them more useful knowledge of reality. But his critics still only saw danger in James's epistemology, wherein truth was subject to the whims of each individual. He may have posited a given reality, but he rejected the possibility of our ever acquiring direct knowledge of it. Truth, for James, would always be "a human device and not a literal transcript" of reality.⁶⁶

His critics believed that so crudely portraying truth as a mere "human device" turned reality into a plaything, a world that must endure "human violence willingly," no matter the cost. After all, pragmatism could only offer a "method" for ascertaining truth and, though results-oriented, had no way of distinguishing good ends from bad. Deciding on ends seemed to remain solely within the purview of each individual, who alone settled on ends that his truths would then dutifully serve. Woefully subjective and instrumental, Jamesian truth could not provide a higher or independent standard to which we all must adhere. There may have been an independent reality in James's pluriverse, but there was no given truth telling us right from wrong, instructing us how to behave toward our fellow man.

James's realism could not deflect all charges that his philosophy invited moral relativism and radical subjectivism. But to a large extent critics have overstated James's emphasis on the individual's subjective choice in truth matters. Although it is true that James devoted much of his philosophical energy to extolling the dignity of individuals, his epistemology is in fact more Peircean—more democratic—than it may appear at first glance.[67]

In part we can blame James for this misunderstanding. An enviably gifted writer, he cultivated a graceful and accessible style and illustrated his ideas with powerful metaphors. While this made for more enjoyable reading, it sometimes compromised precision and clarity. On the other hand, had critics given James's work the close reading it deserved, they might have seen the social aspect of his epistemology. They would have found that James considered truth-making a probabilistic, social, and moral enterprise, a process that must draw on a large number of verification experiences in the community, involve ongoing discussion and persuasion, and require an enlarged capacity for tolerance, social inclusion, and sympathy for others.

In *The Will to Believe*, James revealed as much in an often overlooked caveat. After arguing that truth is an ongoing verification process, he wrote:

> For the sake of simplicity I have written as if the verification might occur in the life of a single philosopher—which is manifestly untrue, since the theories still face each other, and the facts of the world give countenance to both. Rather should we expect, that, in a question of this scope, the experience of the entire human race must make the verification, and that all the evidence will not be "in" till the final integration of things, when the last man has had his say and contributed his share to the still unfinished *x*. Then the proof will be complete.[68]

James said quite clearly here that the verification of a hypothesis is not a solitary activity, as some of his more simplified examples may imply. It is a complex process that must draw on "the experience of the entire human race." Undoubtedly echoing Peirce here, he argued that verification must continue indefinitely, that we must collect evidence until "the last man has had his say and contributed his share to the still unfinished *x*." While James did not pursue this theme to the same depth as Peirce, the implication is that truth-making is an inductive process, drawing on a number of particular concrete experiences to arrive at general and more abstract principles.

The other implication, equally Peircean, is that truth is probabilistic, a working hypothesis about which we should have some doubt until every man has contributed his experiences. A particular truth may work for you and me, and perhaps hundreds of others, but we cannot be completely certain it will work for everyone, not, at least, until everyone has shared their experience. Consider once again the parking lot example. I can be more certain of my truth claim—that parking services does not ticket in the lot near my building after 2:30 p.m.—if I draw on the experiences of other people who park there without a permit. And only when "the last man" has had his say, when my sample encompasses the entire population of illegal parkers, can I be certain of my truth. The failure of this truth to work for some people will compel me to refine my truth. Perhaps further investigation and verification will reveal that my truth works only on certain days, or only if one already has a permit for another lot.

James also suggested that truth acquisition involves social interaction and trust. In reality, we do not have the time to personally verify every truth claim we put to use. We often trade verifications with other people whose claims have proven useful to us in the past. We know intuitively that other people have verified this truth in a more systematic way, so we accept it as long as it works for us in our lives. "Truth lives," said James, "for the most part on a credit system." He continued:

> Our thoughts and beliefs "pass," so long as nothing challenges them, just as bank-notes pass so long as nobody refuses them. But all this points to direct face-to-face verifications somewhere, without which the fabric of truth collapses like a financial system with no cash-basis whatever. You accept my verification of one thing, I yours of another. We trade on each other's truth. But beliefs verified concretely by *somebody* are the posts of the whole superstructure.[69]

While this "credit system" does not completely resemble a deliberative scientific community, which was the core of Peirce's epistemology, they do share some important elements. Both Peirce and James argued that our systems of truth rely on accepting precedents established by the verifications of others. The element of trading truths in James's epistemology suggests that truth acquisition involves ongoing discussion with others in our community—convincing each other that one's verifications will work for the others as well. A self-proclaimed expert on the parking situation on campus, I may have collected a sufficient amount of evidence to be confident about my truth claim and to share it with my colleagues. In turn, they may supply me with much needed information about the placement of radar traps in our town. The scientific community operates in a similar way: confined to a narrowly specialized area of expertise, each scientist contributes modestly to a large body of research that he or she is convinced is the product of proper verification procedures—that is, the scientific method.

James maintained that scientific and ethical beliefs alike require contributions from every person in the community before one can be certain of their truth. Utterly useless are those abstract ethical principles emanating from the scholarly chambers of a great philosopher. As if channeling Peirce once again, James argued that we can arrive at ethical beliefs only inductively and socially. He argued in "The Moral Philosopher and the Moral Life," that "there is no such thing possible as an ethical philosophy dogmatically made up in advance. We all help to determine the content of ethical philosophy so far as we contribute to the race's moral life. In other words, there can be no final truth in ethics any more than in physics, until the last man has had his experience and said his say."[70] Like science or any other area of inquiry, ethics must draw on the experience of the entire human race before it can arrive at robust truths. Notions of good and bad cannot precede our life experiences. After all, said James, a universe devoid of sentient life has no need for ethics. Only in a world comprised of sentient beings, with real feelings and experiences, do ethics become necessary.

According to James, a universe with only one sentient being would have the beginnings of an ethical system: anything that person wants is good, and anything he does not want is bad. But a world inhabited by many people with competing demands faces a far more difficult situation. It would be impossible to devise a system that could satisfy all the demands of every person; satisfying some demands will most certainly leave others unfulfilled. In the end, an ethical system must satisfy as many demands as possible. James posed the question: "Since everything which is demanded is by that fact a good, must not the guiding principle for ethical philosophy (since all demands conjointly cannot be satisfied in this poor world) be simply to satisfy at all times *as many demands as we can*?" The most ethical act, said James, was that which "makes for the best whole, in the sense of awakening the least sum of dissatisfactions" and which destroys "the least possible number of other ideals."[71]

This formulation may sound a lot like Bentham's utilitarianism, but James took pains to differentiate between the two. Bentham and his followers equated the good with pleasure and then claimed that the most ethical system is that which provides the greatest good for the greatest number of people. James rejected hedonism as the basis for an ethical system and focused instead on satisfying demands, a broader term that can include pleasure but also other ideals that may not be pleasurable in any immediate sense. He was also loath to reduce his ethics to a simple formula that might maximize the amount of good but at the cost of a minority's enslavement.

For James, ethics involved a delicate balance, satisfying as many demands as possible while making sure that the interests of the losing party are not completely ignored. The operating principle here is inclusion, creating an ideal that appeals to everyone at some basic level. The goal is not to maximize the amount of pleasure in society but rather to give everyone an opportunity to have their voice heard. "Since victory and defeat there must be," said James, "the victory to be philosophically prayed for is that of the more inclusive side—of the side which even in the hour of triumph will to some degree do justice to the ideals in which the vanquished party's interests lay."[72] Ethics cannot be reduced to a mere calculation because it is an ongoing process, a drama that has unfolded throughout history and will continue to reveal new insights as more people contribute their perspectives. "The course of history is nothing but the story of men's struggles from generation to generation to find the more and more inclusive order," said James. "*Invent some manner* of realizing your own ideals which will also satisfy the alien demands—that and that only is the path of peace!"[73]

James envisioned the creation of a social order that may realize my particular ideals while it also strives to accommodate the demands of others. For this to happen, every person must have the chance to challenge the ethical hypotheses of others by sharing his or her experiences. We must pay heed to every voice in the social chorus and listen attentively for the discordant sounds of complaint. That our civilization has made any moral progress at all has been the result of our ability to remain sympathetic to the voice of complaint—even when reactionary forces sought to mute them. Someday, when the voice of "the last man" is finally heard, the social order will have reached that inclusive ideal.

What becomes clear in James's work is that his ethics were closely tied to his epistemology. In his view, learning the truth required individuals to enlarge their capacities for sympathy and to see the world from varying perspectives, even in the most unlikely places. In "On a Certain Blindness in Human Beings," he warned his readers that the inability to feel for the plight of others, to truly appreciate what they are going through, accounts for ethical shortcomings. He was quite aware that most people are preoccupied with practical affairs, that our lives, often manic, do not afford us the time to ponder deeply the experiences of others and to derive any meaningful insights from these reflections. Indeed, he conceded that only "your mystic, your dreamer, or your insolvent tramp or loafer, can afford so sympathetic an occupation." A lifetime dedicated to these profound musings may make someone a "prophet" but certainly not a "worldly success."[74]

James cited Walt Whitman as one of those rare men whose heart felt with acute sensitivity the joys and sufferings of his fellow men. The great poet could spend an entire day observing with indolent rapture the mundane activities of his Brooklyn neighbors. What most would consider time wasted was a sublime and treasured afternoon for Whitman. For the rest of us, James requested that we make do with less worldly success. Cultivating a poetic consciousness, an ability to reflect with great sympathy on the human condition and to love humanity in its most glorious and its most abject moments, paved the road to truth.[75] James was most likely thinking of Whitman when he wrote: "If you say that this is absurd, and that we cannot be in love with everyone at once, I merely point out to you that, as a matter of fact, certain persons do exist with an enormous capacity for friendship and for taking delight in other people's lives; and that such persons know more of truth than if their hearts were not so big."[76]

People with bigger hearts know more of truth simply because they look beyond their own narrow lives and tap into a larger set of experiences to glean knowledge and understanding. Selfish and uncaring people will have knowledge only of their limited experience. Thus, James admonished his readers "to tolerate, respect, and indulge those whom we see harmlessly interested and happy in their own ways, however unintelligible these may be to us. Hands off: neither the whole truth, nor the whole of good, is revealed to any single observer. . . . Even prisons and sick-rooms have their special revelations."[77] People in even the most dire or peculiar situations can provide invaluable insights from which we can all learn. The single observer must never think he has a monopoly on the truth.

## Launching New Habits

While James held to a democratic epistemology, arguing that men acquire provisional truths best in a social context, he also subscribed to a democratic psychology. As did Peirce, he maintained that man was hardly a finished product but rather a lump of clay, malleable and moldable: "He is, *par excellence,* the *educable* animal." It is more accurate to speak of human habit than of human nature. We all can be described as "bundles of habits," mere collections of learned behaviors that we can execute without conscious thought.[78] Our verified truths eventually translate into rules for action; if these actions continue to work for us, we will perform them repeatedly until they become habits. Habits, then, are time-tested truths, hardened rules for action that have proven to work many times. James maintained that it is impossible to overstate the significance of habit in our daily lives. Our ability to function at a most basic level demands that we cultivate habits, for those things we do most efficiently and competently are automatic. Said James:

> The great thing, then, in all education, is to *make our nervous system our ally instead of our enemy*. It is to fund and capitalize our acquisitions, and live at ease upon the interest of the fund. *For this we must make automatic and habitual, as early as possible, as many useful actions as we can,* and guard against the growing into ways that are likely to be disadvantageous to us, as we should guard against the plague. The more of the details of our daily life we can hand over to the effortless custody of automatism, the more our higher powers of mind will be set free for their own proper work.[79]

The implication here is that education is really just the process of habit formation, repeating a practice until it becomes second nature. That which we do "with difficulty the first time" will, "with sufficient practice," be accomplished "semi-mechanically, or with hardly any consciousness at all."[80] These habits ultimately define us: they manifest the ideas, or rules for action, that help us cope with life.

This process of defining ourselves through repetition applies to both good and bad habits. Whether we are taking up smoking or flossing, our first forays into these activities are typically fraught with awkwardness and halting movement. The novice smoker fumbles with the lighter and coughs violently after inhaling, while the unpracticed flosser will feel like he is all thumbs and will find the whole process exceedingly frustrating. But before long the novice achieves fluency, whether in lighting cigarettes and inhaling smoke with the grace of a 1950s movie star, or in dexterously wedging the floss between his teeth on a nightly basis. Save for those occasions when we are introduced to something new in our lives, almost everything we do is habitual. "All our life, so far as it has definite form, is but a mass of habits—practical, emotional, and intellectual—systematically organized for our weal or woe."[81] Even though some of our habits are bad for us, we still become attached to them and find it increasingly difficult over time to renounce them.

The moment our habits cease to work for us, however, when we become acutely conscious that they contribute in some way to our "woe," we immediately search for new habits that will restore our ability to function in the world around us. Although hardwired into us after years of repetition, our old habits always remain vulnerable to erasure. "New habits *can* be launched," said James, "on condition of there being new stimuli and excitements." During those "critical and revolutionary" moments in his life, man can "change" his "whole scale of values and system of ideas. In such cases, the old order of his habits will be ruptured; and if the new motives are lasting, new habits will be formed."[82] While James conceded that habit often serves as a "conservative agent," preventing people from recklessly changing course when their current behavior seems to work well enough, he believed that the "plasticity" of the "nervous system" allows them to change their modes of behavior in accordance with the demands of experience.[83]

The plasticity of man notwithstanding, James also claimed that human beings inherit certain instincts at birth. Within every man dwell impulses or tendencies that undoubtedly influence his behavior, but he is never a slave to them. Our learned behavior can always work to counteract these impulses, either inhibiting them completely or, at the very least, restricting their range of influence. In most cases nature endows man with "contrary impulses"—such as friendliness and belligerence—between which our habits ultimately mediate. I may be inclined to both friendliness and belligerence, but my habits will determine which impulse emerges victorious in a given circumstance. As reflective creatures with the power of memory and inference, we remember the consequences of our having acted on our impulses the first time. Depending on what we thought of these consequences, we cultivate habits that either inhibit or reinforce these impulses. In other words, our habits can strengthen our more laudable instincts and weaken the more shameful ones.[84]

James also pointed out that many instincts are transitory. They may figure prominently at an early stage in a person's life and then slowly wane in potency over time—or the reverse. The transitoriness of some instincts only adds to the variability of human nature.[85]

But, according to James, human nature is not always so variable. Some instincts are neither transitory nor easily contained. No matter what inhibitive habits we unleash on them, they prove alarmingly recalcitrant. Especially troublesome to James was the imperial impulse of man, the "bellicose constitution of human nature" which makes "people *want* war." In a letter to a friend James declared, "Human nature is everywhere the same; and at the least temptation all the old military passions rise, and sweep everything before them." He asserted in a letter to another friend that man "is essentially an adventurous and warlike animal."[86] According to James, human beings inherited these warlike characteristics through the evolutionary process. At one time in man's evolutionary development, bloodlust was a necessary trait for survival. Civilized man, however, has no use for this ancient instinct; he has reached the point, both technologically and socially, where it can lead only to his destruction.

Fortunately, James saw a way out of this dangerous predicament and suggested that the first step was to be realistic. We should acknowledge that the imperial impulse is a deep-seated part of human nature, an evolutionary characteristic that has taken root in the heart of man. In a number of talks, including his famous "The Moral Equivalent of War," James ridiculed pacifists for dreaming that men will change and renounce their imperial impulses. "Our ancestors have bred pugnacity into our bone and marrow, and thousands of years of peace won't breed it out of us." Dashing these naive hopes once and for all, James argued that we should embrace the bellicose and aggressive nature of man and find ways to channel this energy in socially constructive ways. The problem with the pacifists, according to James, was that they refused to see any virtue in man's martial spirit. They saw only death and destruction, while James understood that this was the same instinct that fostered heroic action— "intrepidity, contempt of softness, surrender of private interest, obedience to command."[87] Abolishing the martial spirit, if it were at all possible, would mean the elimination of these virtues without which humankind would never achieve anything noble or heroic. The pacifist's utopia championed mediocrity.

To the contrary, James envisioned a society in which martial virtues were reaffirmed as "absolute and permanent human goods" but were expressed in something other than a warlike form. "Patriotic pride and ambition in their military form are, after all, only specifications of a more general competitive passion. They are its first form, but that is no reason for supposing them to be its last form." While men may be "proud of belonging to a conquering nation" for which they will shed blood without question, they could learn to appreciate other characteristics of their country. "The war-function has graspt us so far; but constructive interests may some day seem no less imperative, and impose on the individual a hardly lighter burden."[88] Until now, men had committed the martial virtues to war, but this did not have to be the case forever. James suggested that men can sublimate their warlike instincts and redirect them toward more constructive ends. This process of rechanneling our martial spirit involves the formation of new habits, requiring "time and education and suggestion," that would "inflame the civic temper as past history has inflamed the military temper."[89]

He called for the creation of a mandatory national service program, which would promote the "manly virtues" in the country's youth but would enlist their energies for a war "against *Nature*" rather than other men. He hoped this program would be the first step in redefining the civic virtues that animate heroic action, summoning our young not to battlefields but to the sites of working-class toil—our "coal and iron mines, to freight trains, to fishing fleets in December, to dish-washing, clothes-washing, and window-washing, to road-building and tunnel-making, to foundries and stoke-holes, and to the frames of skyscrapers." Having "done their own part in the immemorial human warfare against nature," our young men would return to society like the soldiers of yore, proud and strong, but also "with healthier sympathies" for their fellow men from other walks of life.[90] Through hard and painstaking labor our young men would become heroes and learn to appreciate the many unsung heroes already walking among us. These experiences would be transformative—toughening our young men to face life's many challenges with silent courage, instilling in them a strong sense of moral and civic responsibility at home, and providing them an invaluable education in the hardships with which working-class people struggle on a daily basis.

James's "moral equivalent of war" resembles programs organized by the federal government many years after his death, including the Civilian Conservation Corp of the New Deal and the Peace Corps and AmeriCorps of today. Granted, none of these programs has done much to abate the lust for war or to broaden our sense of civic virtue, but James envisioned something far more ambitious in scope and still untried. Besides, the viability of his specific program is less important than the idea he sought to express: man's pugnacious instincts need not always manifest themselves so destructively. Man can harness those energies and dedicate them to a new set of civic and patriotic principles that strengthen human ties rather than tear them asunder. Despite all evidence to the contrary, we should never resign ourselves to the idea that man is a slave to his wretched nature; instead we should rejoice in his unlimited potential for transformation.

## Summoning Civic Courage

The fact that man is a mutable mass of habits does not necessarily mean he has the free will to adopt (or refuse to adopt) new habits himself. It is always possible that his habits are the product of invisible forces, either material or spiritual, in a preordained universe. But, as we have already seen, James supported indeterminism and free will, on faith alone, revealing a robust democratic metaphysics. He exercised his right to believe in an idea that provided more satisfaction and relief than the determinist alternative. The overriding concern for James was ethical: we cannot hold people accountable for wrongful action if we think they had no control over what they did, and life becomes rather bleak and meaningless if we have no chance of altering the course of events through our willful actions.

Positing a world full of possibility, where individual choices have a significant impact on future events, made life worth living for James. It vested in man a creative power to perform either wonderful acts of beneficence or the most dastardly of deeds, the world becoming decidedly better or worse as a result. The only trick, for James, was to make sure that he could firmly situate this belief within the constellation of other truths he held dear. He found this quite easy to do. His reading of Darwin and study of human psychology and cognition provided useful insights that fit quite comfortably with, and even supported, his faith in free will.

Initially, Darwin's *The Origin of Species* contributed to the younger James's metaphysical crisis. Depending on how one looks at it, a Darwinian universe could accommodate either the doctrine of complete randomness, where events were determined by a cosmic roll of the dice, or the doctrine of materialistic determinism, where Homo sapiens represent just another species in the chain of life that began aeons ago in a pond of primordial slime. While the former gives life neither form nor meaning, the latter denies human beings their freedom. Eventually, James saw that he could appropriate Darwin to support his faith in a finite god and free will.[91]

What most excited James about Darwinism was that it welcomed indeterminism and novelty and lent credence to the notion that the universe is teeming with possibility. Spencer and other determinists argued that human beings, great and small, are the product of their environment and biology and, thus, are not free to defy the inevitable sweep of history. Drawing on Darwinian logic, James believed that the universe supplies an array of evidence to the contrary. Constantly observing physical events that occur without warning or explanation, scientists must modify their theories and laws in compliance with these unexpected findings. The spontaneity of events seems to suggest that we inhabit an evolving universe where things are probable but never certain. In a Peircean spirit, James said: "It is folly, then, to speak of the 'laws of history,' as of something inevitable, which science has only to discover, and whose consequences any one can then foretell but do nothing to alter or avert. Why, the very laws of physics are conditional, and deal with *ifs*."[92] If even the laws of physics are not subject to the doctrine of necessity, there is little reason to believe that conscious human beings, who often agonize over the decisions they must make and then feel deeply regretful about choices that yield bad results, cannot act with spontaneity and inspiration.

According to James, chance variation can account for the emergence of "great men" whose actions have a profound impact on history and the development of humankind. People of all stripes—rich and poor, brilliant and slow-witted, young and old—perform novel acts every day, and those elect few who are selected by their social environment will have the opportunity to put their individual genius to significant use. This means that so-called great men are merely fortunate enough to possess certain qualities that their society finds important; accordingly, they are catapulted into positions of authority and prestige with which they can influence generations of their fellow men. "I affirm that the relation of the visible environment to the great man is in the main exactly what it is to be 'variation' in the Darwinian philosophy. It chiefly adopts or rejects, preserves or destroys, in short *selects* him," said James. "And whenever it adopts and preserves the great man, it becomes modified by his influence in an entirely original and peculiar way." In James's mind, the individual and society share a symbiotic tension. Society could not progress without the input of great individuals, and great individuals could not emerge without the sympathies of their community to make their genius known. It is important to note that, for James, the individual drives social progress, while society merely serves as the vehicle.[93]

The expression of individual genius, whether selected by the community or not, begins with man's ability to pay attention to the world around him. James believed that people make sense of the rushing stream of sensory experiences with which they are deluged by focusing their attention on what interests them and ignoring the rest. Or to draw on the now familiar metaphor, we each play the part of a sculptor, cutting away the irrelevant chunks of the block and preserving those sections that are more meaningful and useful to us.

In many cases, this process of selection, attending to that which interests us, will lead to an idea of movement on our part. If the anticipated consequences of this movement are to our liking, we will act without pause. James called this process ideo-motor action: "Wherever a movement *unhesitatingly and immediately* follows upon the idea of it, we have ideo-motor action. We are then aware of nothing between the conception and execution. . . . We think the act, and it is done."[94] For instance, I see my cup of freshly brewed coffee on my desk, contemplate enjoying its warmth and deliciousness, and then reflexively pick it up and take a sip. These reflexive actions, which can be instinctive or habitual, represent the normal state of affairs.

But on those occasions when we turn our attention to two or more competing ideas, we cannot act automatically because we are undecided about which idea is best. So long as we continue to entertain two or more of these conflicting ideas, we will be paralyzed with indecision; once we are able to focus our attention on only one of these ideas, we will act accordingly. At some point, one idea will prevail over the others, usually because we succumb to habit and focus our attention on the idea with which we are most familiar, but sometimes we must make a difficult choice. This process of choosing among many ideas, attending to one at the expense of the others, is what James called "voluntary attending"— and it is the very basis of free will.

There are times when focusing our attention on a particularly difficult object, such as a book manuscript, requires us to summon reserves of mental energy dwelling deep within us. While I savor the thought of watching the Red Sox–Yankees game tonight, I also know that an unfinished manuscript awaits me and will continue to await me, looming ominously in my life until I finish it. In this case attending to my manuscript is especially difficult because it does not provide immediate gratification as a baseball game does. According to James, the ability to focus my attention on a difficult object such as my work is the essence of free will. In *The Principles of Psychology,* James wrote: "*The essential achievement of the will, in short, when it is most 'voluntary,' is to attend to a difficult object and hold it fast before the mind. . . . Effort of attention is thus the essential phenomenon of will.*" The exercise of will is a psychological affair, a struggle that must be resolved in the mind. "The whole drama," said James, "is a mental drama. The whole difficulty is a mental difficulty, a difficulty with an ideal object of our thought. It is, in one word, an idea to which our will applies itself, an idea which if we let it go would slip away, but which we will not let go." The exercise of will occurs in the mind, before any actions are performed. In fact, James argued, "whether the act then follows or not is a matter quite immaterial," citing the example of a paralyzed man who tries to move his leg but never succeeds in doing so.[95]

In most cases, however, if we can attend to this elusive object long enough, hold it firmly in our minds and drive out any competing ideas, the ensuing action is a foregone conclusion. Despite the strong appeal of watching a baseball game between the historic rivals, I focus my attention on the task at hand and here I am, organizing my thoughts and typing these words into the computer. Exercising free will always involves attending to an idea that is less agreeable than some alternative. Sometimes the idea is far more hazardous than writing a book. The extraordinarily strong-willed man, said James, will cling to the idea of his duty, even when he knows that death is imminent. Despite "the host of exciting mental images [of death] which rise in revolt against" his acting bravely, the "strong-willed man" will focus his attention on the "difficult object" until he experiences a change of "consciousness," which "infallibly produces" the desired "motor effects."[96] The average person will not be able to expel terrifying images of a painful death and other unpleasantries, but the strong-willed person will overcome this instinctive reaction and, focusing his mind on a courageous act, stamp out his fear. Then, before he knows it, he will perform the courageous feat to which he put his mind.

James argued that a direct corollary of his theory of emotion was that we can control our emotions by changing our behavior, and the implication in this example is that the man who can ignore his fears and act bravely has successfully changed how he feels. The reader will recall that, according to James, our emotions do not lead to certain physiological responses; our physiological responses in fact *are* our emotions. Our emotions are merely habitualized physiological responses to certain objects or events, which means we can always change our emotions by cultivating new habits. "Action seems to follow feeling, but really action and feeling go together; and by regulating the action, which is under the more direct control of the will, we can indirectly regulate the feeling, which is not." By refusing to run away from pernicious situations, by facing them with equanimity, a man consumed with fear and trembling can transform himself into a man who embodies daring and courage. In other words, he can exercise his will to change his habitual response to these situations, and instead of acting cowardly, he can act bravely and thereby become a brave and fearless man. Said James: "So to feel brave, act as if we *were* brave, use all our will to that end, and courage-fit will very likely replace the fit of fear."[97] After acting bravely a few times, the former coward will find that courage comes more easily to him. What at first required a resolute concentration of will can become automatic.

According to James, this was the essence of free will: to dedicate enough thought and effort to an idea that it yields the desired response on our part and to continue to do so until the response becomes habitual. Forming habits is vital not only because they change our emotional responses but because they also determine who we are on a deeper level. At the head of the chapter on habit in his personal copy of *Psychology: Brief Course,* James wrote in his own hand the old adage: "Sow an action, and you reap a habit; sow a habit and you reap a character; sow a character and you reap a destiny."[98] When a man exercises his free will to develop habits, he has taken the first step toward forming his character and ultimately sealing his fate. Although habit implies reflex and will implies freedom, James could never easily separate his discussions of the two concepts because they represented opposite sides of the same coin. Man has the free will to formulate new habits, which in turn liberate him further to focus more attention on other concerns.

James expressed particular disdain for the "miserable human being" who fails to form any useful habits in life and whose every action is the result of "express volitional deliberation." Perhaps James was alluding to himself as a younger man. His years of acute depression were accompanied by periods of abulia—or "obstructed will"—which rendered him unable to make choices without hesitation or painful deliberation. As James learned from personal experience, the man without habits is enthralled to either his instincts or his indecision, and the only way out of this prison is to develop his atrophied will and to make a habit of using this faculty. Once a person has developed a sufficiently robust will and made a habit of exercising it regularly, he can then devote his attention to forming other useful habits.[99]

Toward the end of his chapter entitled "Habit" in *The Principles of Psychology,* James discussed how to cultivate good habits, laying down a number of maxims he thought would help the reader to do so. He maintained that turning an idea into a reflex action requires one to initiate what Cotkin describes as a training "regimen whereby, through an initial effort of attention and repetition, a new, more efficacious habit might become ingrained."[100] The degree to which we perform our action with uninterrupted frequency determines how deeply the tendency becomes ingrained in us. Each one of us embodies these ingrained habits, and they in turn define who we are. If we do not cultivate our own habits willfully and instead let them grow willy-nilly or leave them to wilt and die, we fail to live up to our capacity as human beings. Instead, we exist at the mercy of our physical and social environment or our biology—for James, an unacceptable option.

In his essay entitled "What Makes a Life Significant," James revealed his distaste for a life devoid of vigorous and willful action in his description of Chautauqua, New York, a small town he visited on his "Talks to Teachers" lecture tour in 1894. A model utopia with not even a hint of squalor or injustice evident, Chautauqua represented a "foretaste of what human society might be, were it all in the light, with no suffering and no dark corners." To his own astonishment, however, James found this "middle-class paradise, without a sin, without a victim, without a blot, without a tear," so stifling that he longed to escape and return to "the dark and wicked world again." After just a week of enjoying the many pleasantries and wholesome activities the town had to offer, James could no longer abide the "atrocious harmlessness" of it all and caught himself desiring something "primordial and savage, even though it were as bad as an Armenian massacre." He preferred to take his chances in the wicked world, replete with "the heights and the depths, the precipices and the steep ideals, the gleams of the awful and the infinite," than to spend another minute in "this dead level and quintessence of every mediocrity." In a letter to his wife, he revealed an even darker side of his reflections, wishing for the "flash of a pistol, a dagger, or a devilish eye, anything to break the unlovely level of 10,000 good people, a crime, a murder, rape, elopement, anything would do."[101]

What Chautauqua lacked was drama, the extremes that indeed make life painful and treacherous, but also exhilarating and invigorating. Supposedly a friend of civilization and social progress, James was profoundly disturbed by his visceral reaction. Why could he not appreciate the social harmony on display before him? Did he really need exposure to the violence and savagery of life to feel alive, even if it came at the expense of human suffering?

After meditating on his Chautauquan experience for a while, he realized what was missing there. This idyllic town seemed to provide no opportunities for strenuous action against the forces of evil, and it thus deprived its inhabitants of a meaningful life. "What excites and interests the looker-on at life, what the romances and the statues celebrate and the grim civic monuments remind us of, is the everlasting battle of the powers of light with those of darkness." The "struggle" against evil—with "human nature strained to its uttermost"—is what ultimately "inspires us."[102] For James, Chautauqua represented a world in which men had already defeated the forces of evil and were free to enjoy the fruits of heroics long past.

At first it may have sounded delightful, that the very image of justice and harmony emerged from the efforts of great men in an earlier age, but a closer look revealed a sickening, insipid world, so complete that it no longer demanded vigorous action to ward off dangers or even to remedy the most minor social ills. This a world without heroes, without even the need for heroes. James feared that Chautauqua foretold the future for all humanity, that its bourgeois mediocrity and blandness would creep slowly into every corner of the world, eventually turning it into "a mere Chautauqua Assembly on an enormous scale." Much to his alarm, an "irremediable flatness is coming over the world. Bourgeoisie and mediocrity, church sociables and teachers' conventions, are taking the place of the old heights and depths and romantic chiaroscuro." Observing the eagerness for fairness and compromise within his own country, James lamented that the "higher heroisms and the old rare flavors are passing out of life."[103] What James witnessed during his brief stay in Chautauqua was the dawning of modernity, a new world order that would foreclose opportunities for heroism and vigorous action, a time when the exercise of free will would become increasingly scarce.

An eternal optimist, James could not despair for long over these modern trends, and on the train heading toward Buffalo he experienced a revelation. He realized that true acts of heroism actually occur all the time and in every town and city in America. Looking for heroism in its traditional forms, James had failed to see the wonderful displays of it exhibited right before his eyes in the "daily lives of the laboring classes. Not in clanging fights and desperate marches only is heroism to be looked for, but on every railway bridge and fire-proof building that is going up today." It had dawned on James that the "demand for courage" can be found everywhere and that "the supply never fails. There, every day of the year somewhere, is human nature *in extremis* for you."[104] His earlier observations notwithstanding, James came to realize that working-class heroics abound in this world, even in Chautauqua. We so often overlook these daily displays of heroism, he said, because they do not follow an articulated ideal, as a soldier's sacrifice so clearly does. The laboring hero wields his shovel or axe to earn a wage, not to realize a larger vision, for he lacks the imagination and the education to devote arduous action to something higher.

On the other end of the spectrum is the educated man, refined and effete, who has plenty of ideals but fails to support them with the manly vigor performed regularly by the laboring class. A truly significant life, according to James, must achieve a marriage between our strenuous actions and our ideals. "Ideal aspirations are not enough, when uncombined with pluck and will. But neither are pluck and will, dogged endurance and insensibility to danger enough, when taken alone. There must be some sort of fusion . . . for a life objectively and thoroughly significant to result." The hero always acts with "pluck and will" but never for his own sake. He adheres to an "intellectually conceived" ideal that challenges preconceived notions, routines, or conventions.[105] James championed a mandatory national service program because it represented this fusion of manly action and ideals.

Unfortunately, the most common display of ostensible heroism in our world involves ill-advised and unconscionable acts of imperialism by modern states. A great opponent of American imperialism, James considered it a modern expression of our ancient impulse for war, not a true display of heroism. True heroism could not rest on outdated ideals about martial valor, national glory, or Manifest Destiny, and it required something other than the courage to face mortal danger with vigorous action. Indeed, the Jamesian hero had to resist the prevailing social order in the name of a higher ideal.

James expressed this idea most eloquently in May 1897 when he delivered an oration at the unveiling of a war monument dedicated to the slain Civil War hero Robert Gould Shaw who led the famous black Fifty-Fourth Regiment. Before a large crowd assembled at the Boston Music Hall, James

declared that we should not honor Shaw for his military valor on the bat-
tlefield—especially since "man is once for all a fighting animal" with an
incorrigible "battle-instinct." Instead we should honor him for the

> lonely courage which he showed when he dropped his warm commission in
> the glorious Second to head your dubious fortunes, negroes of the Fifty-
> Fourth. That lonely kind of courage (civic courage as we call it in peace-times)
> is the kind of valor to which the monuments of nations should most of all be
> reared, for the survival of the fittest has not bred it into the bone of human be-
> ings as it has bred military valor; and of five hundred of us who could storm a
> battery side by side with others, perhaps not one could be found who would
> risk his worldly fortunes all alone in resisting an enthroned abuse.

We should exalt and admire Shaw because he resisted conventional practices and gave up his comfortable commission for an ideal—that black
Americans should enjoy the same opportunities as their white brethren
and not be denied the honor of serving in the war against slavery. In
many cases, the most heroic actions will not be recognized as such in their
own time because they cut against the grain of popular opinion, but we
should do our best to lionize those who perform them, even if posthumously.

While Shaw was immortalized for his martial feats and his untimely death
at Fort Wagner, his most significant achievement resembled what the many
heroes in our midst do every day. Great nations are saved not by martial
valor, a common trait that has been bred "into the bone of human beings,"
but rather by lonely acts of "civic courage" performed with little fanfare:

> The nation blest above all nations is she in whom the civic genius of the peo-
> ple does the saving day by day, by acts without external picturesqueness; by
> speaking, writing, voting reasonably; by smiting corruption swiftly; by good
> temper between parties; by the people knowing true men when they see
> them, and preferring them as leaders to rabid partisans or empty quacks.
> Such nations have no need of wars to save them.[106]

We should always lavish men like Shaw with everlasting praise, said
James, because they do not seek publicity for their actions but instead quietly perform their duties as citizens of a democracy. Shaw stood for what
James called "the American religion"—the democratic "faith that a man
requires no master to take care of him, and that common people can work
out their salvation well enough together if left free to try." We honor him
and his compatriots in the Fifty-Fourth for fulfilling the democratic ideals
of participation and brotherhood, reminding us "that in such an emer-
gency Americans of all complexions and conditions can go forth like
brothers, and meet death cheerfully if need be, in order that this religion
of our native land shall not become a failure on earth."[107] From James's

point of view, we diminish Shaw and his comrades in arms if we understand them as mere pawns in the grand sweep of history. For there was nothing necessary or inevitable about what they did. Their deeds exemplified the great extent to which men can transcend social and political norms—and, through their heroic actions, redefine them.

## James's Democratic Soul

James's personal and philosophical travails led him to embrace a strong democratic ethos. He believed that all men must participate in the process of acquiring truths and remaking the world in accord with their ideals, and he had great disdain for stultifying institutions and self-proclaimed experts who claimed to have a monopoly on truth and method. He was especially disdainful of the modern trend toward the large bureaucratic organization, which he believed undermined the open search for truth and individual autonomy:

> I am against bigness and greatness in all their forms, and with the invisible molecular forces that work from individual to individual. . . . The bigger the unit you deal with, the hollower, the more brutal, the more mendacious is the life displayed. So I am against all big organizations as such, national ones first and foremost; against all big successes and big results; and in favor of the eternal forces of truth which always work in the individual and immediately unsuccessful way, under-dogs always, till history comes, after they are long dead, and puts them on the top.[108]

James found such large organizations to be hopelessly "mendacious" because they worked against the "eternal forces of truth," subjecting individuals to rigid procedures that prevented them from expressing their genius.

Instead, he favored small democratic communities in which all people —including the unassuming "under-dogs"—were free from the dominating forces of government and business and were empowered to contribute to the commonweal themselves. In a letter to a friend, he admitted to sharing affinities with "lovers of the ideal [of freedom] to found smaller communities." After all, "through small systems, kept pure, lies one most promising line of betterment and salvation."[109]

It is important to note that James did not see an inherent tension between the individual and his community, as liberals often do. His enthusiasm for individualism was often mistaken for a de facto contempt for groups and communities, but, rather, he believed that individual freedoms were best protected within a nurturing community that gave people the opportunity to exercise civic courage and to work to put their ideals into practice. Indeed, only a small community that tolerated—even welcomed—

eccentricity, diversity, and a certain amount of chaos could provide the right atmosphere for the incessant challenging of all truth claims and social conventions. It might be fair, if not paradoxical, to characterize James's political philosophy as "individualistic communitarianism" for its antipathy toward centralized bureaucratic organizations, its friendliness toward the small and motley community, and its ultimate championing of the individual.[110] Providing a method for arriving at useful truths socially, and a supportive environment for the exercise of civic courage, individualistic communitarianism would pave the way for a considerably deepened democracy where citizens could engage freely in an ongoing process of social experimentation and verification.

James hoped that these self-governing communities, equipped to make wise decisions, would move toward a "socialist equilibrium."[111] A contemporary critic of the Gilded Age, he was acutely aware of the "abuses which the institution of private property covers" and lamented "that one of the prime functions of the national government is to help the adroiter citizens to grow rich." He understood that social progress demanded our accepting the provisionality of all sacred truths (such as the right to property) and our recognizing that "there is nothing final in any actually given equilibrium of human ideals," for our "present laws and customs have fought and conquered other past ones," and "they will in their turn be overthrown by any newly discovered order."[112] If we were to challenge dogmas such as the right to property, it would only be a matter of time for the capitalist equilibrium to make way for a socialist equilibrium. In all likelihood, this new equilibrium would not be the final word on social justice; but at the very least it would take us one step closer to that truth that emerges when the last man has his say.

There is a distinct element of participationism in James's democratic ethos, an antielitist claim that the people are capable of governing themselves without the assistance of technical expertise and bureaucratic institutions, but he did not go so far as to formulate a theory of participatory democracy per se. Unlike participatory democrats today, he maintained a strong belief in the importance of wise leadership in a democracy. In his essay entitled the "Social Value of the College-Bred," he argued that the main purpose of a college education is to prepare students to judge the character and competence of other men. Our colleges become especially vital in a democracy, in which citizens must "be able to divine the worthier and better leaders." The clear implication is that, if our democracy is to succeed in choosing the best leaders, its citizens must either be college-educated or persuaded by those who enjoyed this educational advantage. By drawing a line between the college-educated and the rest of society, even suggesting that the former provided the "only permanent presence that corresponds to aristocracy in older countries," James seemed to accept the notion of class difference.[113] The college-bred, he insisted, must make their influence felt for democracy to prevail.

On the other hand, he also contended that the college-bred must broaden their outlook and embrace a larger number of perspectives. For this to occur, James said, our colleges and their progeny must adopt a message with a broad-based appeal and become "the yeast-cake for democracy's dough."[114] Calling on colleges to embrace a wider, more democratic vision, James suggested, without saying so explicitly, that they must open their doors to more than just children of the elite, and they must produce graduates who can persuasively communicate their ideals to the broader public. In short, democracy can work only if its institutions, educational and otherwise, move toward a "more inclusive order."[115] This requires the gap between the college-bred and the laboring class to narrow. As the college-bred are introduced to the hardships and heroics of physically demanding work through a national service program, members of the laboring class will broaden their horizons educationally and become more idealistic. The former will learn to back up their ideals with manly action; the latter will see that their hard work can achieve something far higher than a meager wage.

What becomes clear from a close reading of James is that inclusion is at the heart of his political philosophy, for it removes all barriers to the road of inquiry. An inclusive society promotes the fluid exchange of information among people with a diverse range of perspectives and, arousing our sympathies for others and their points of view, enhances our knowledge about each other and the world around us. At the same time, a more inclusive order provides its citizens the ever-important opportunity to exercise free will, to engage in the process of truth acquisition and to act decisively on those truths. The final result is the creation of a citizenry engaged in strenuous but enlightened action—or what James called civic courage.

These civically engaged citizens constitute a happy medium between an obstructed will (or abulia) and an overactive will, between effete intellectualism and blind imperialism. James often praised religion for being especially effective at inspiring men to act strenuously, but he understood that its more traditional forms often led to chauvinism and foreign aggression. His alternative was the religion of democracy, whose future was uncertain but held great promise:

> Democracy is a kind of religion, and we are bound not to admit its failure. Faiths and utopias are the noblest exercise of human reason, and no one with a spark of reason in him will sit down fatalistically before the croaker's picture. The best of us are filled with the contrary vision of a democracy stumbling through every error till its institutions glow with justice and its customs shine with beauty.[116]

Although we may not call James a participatory democrat, we can certainly credit him for building on the foundation laid down by Peirce, and for erecting a skeletal structure with which Dewey would proceed to flesh out a full-fledged theory of participatory democracy.

# 3

# The John Dewey School of Democracy

William James boasted that pragmatism would rival the Protestant Reformation in its impact on the way people think and understand their place in the world. Peirce and James taught that pragmatism gave humankind a method of solving problems in the absence of a universally accepted authority. By the first decade of the twentieth century, they both were reaching the twilight of their careers, and although they deserve much of the credit for putting pragmatism on the map, the nascent "school of thought" (as James enthusiastically hailed it in 1903) would come to achieve universal recognition—or notoriety—largely under the labors of John Dewey (1859–1952), heir apparent. Perhaps the most renowned and important philosopher in American history, Dewey enjoyed an extraordinarily long and illustrious career, writing voluminously for a stretch of nearly seventy years.[1]

Dewey owed a serious intellectual debt to his pragmatist forebears; much of his scholarly work restates or expands on what they said before him. He readily embraced their ideas about the fallibility of truth claims and the malleability of human nature; he was equally optimistic about the potential application of scientific method to promote social progress. They convinced him that we do not uncover preexisting absolute truths so much as we make and remake provisional truths, or what Dewey called "warranted assertions," through the ongoing process of experimentation and deliberation; and that this process, to work effectively, must involve every competent person in the community whose experiences prove relevant to the particular question or problem.

What distinguished Dewey from his predecessors was his ability to make good on the pragmatist promise by taking philosophy down from the clouds and applying it to concrete political and social problems. He undoubtedly made important and original contributions to more traditional subfields of philosophy, especially epistemology, metaphysics, and ethics, but the true significance of his work lies in its relevance to those enduring political questions that have continued to vex humanity. Peirce and James, the classical pragmatists, laid the philosophical foundation for a strong, if somewhat inchoate, democratic ethos in American thought. Both subscribed to what I call the three pragmatist tenets. Peirce was especially instrumental in laying the epistemological groundwork of democracy by arguing that communities can arrive at better truths through a deliberative and inclusive process of inquiry. James can be credited with highlighting the transformative powers of willful participation in the community. But neither of them fully explored the political implications of their ideas.

Dewey, on the other hand, was the first to see the logical connection between pragmatism and democracy. He recognized that pragmatism called for a widespread application of scientific method, and that democracy represented nothing other than the scientific method writ large, the ongoing social experiment conducted not only by scientists and other experts but by everyone in the community. For Dewey, the pragmatic approach culminated in participatory democracy.[2]

Dewey believed it was incumbent on him to live up to the pragmatist ideal and participate in the ongoing social experiment, not merely observe it from a safe distance. Writing prodigiously on a wide range of topics that had a direct impact on the lives of average Americans, and devoting considerable time and energy to social and political causes, Dewey came to personify the term "public intellectual." Of Dewey's importance in the American intellectual and cultural landscape, historian Henry Steele Commager wrote: "So faithfully did Dewey live up to his own philosophical creed that he became the guide, the mentor, and the conscience of the American people; it is scarcely an exaggeration to say that for a generation no issue was clarified until Dewey had spoken."[3]

Indeed, Dewey voiced opinions on nearly every important issue of the day, publishing hundreds of articles in mainstream periodicals such as the *New Republic* (of which he was cofounder) and giving public lectures throughout the country—and the world. He became immensely active in a number of political organizations and social causes, even helping to found the American Association of University Professors (for which he served as president for a time), the American Civil Liberties Union, the National Association for the Advancement of Colored People, and the New School. He was involved with so many organizations, one wonders how he could possibly have found time to fulfill his teaching obligations and write so many scholarly books.

Dewey's social and political commitments were many, usually putting his progressive propensities on display. This is not the place for a detailed account of his civic activity, but a few examples will give a sense of the kinds of issues he found compelling. He dedicated himself tirelessly to education reform throughout his career, beginning in his days at the University of Chicago where he founded a laboratory school, and continuing during his long tenure at Columbia University, where he influenced generations of scholars at Teachers' College. He firmly believed that the future of American democracy depended on significant educational reform: schools must stop treating students as empty vessels passively waiting to be filled with knowledge and should, instead, sharpen their critical thinking and problem-solving skills and promote learning by doing, not just memorizing. Deeply affected by the Pullman strike when he first moved to Chicago in the summer of 1894, Dewey became sympathetic with the labor movement in America and would champion its causes publicly for the rest of his life.[4] The growing inequality in America during the Gilded Age alarmed him greatly, and he not only advocated greater government involvement to alleviate poverty but also became involved in efforts to educate the lower classes and help them become self-reliant.[5] His sympathy for the downtrodden notwithstanding, he actively opposed communism for its ideological rigidity. Nor was he an advocate of New Deal liberalism, for he believed it undermined democracy by promoting the growth of an administrative state where bureaucrats and experts, with little or no accountability, would make crucial decisions on behalf of the country's citizens. He never endorsed the candidacy of Franklin Delano Roosevelt in his four presidential election bids but threw his support behind the socialist candidate Norman Thomas instead.

Dewey's civic engagement extended beyond domestic concerns. When America's involvement in World War I seemed a foregone conclusion, Dewey jumped on the bandwagon, justifying his position on the grounds that the war could provide an effective means to spread the cause of democracy abroad and to galvanize civic engagement and democratic sympathies at home. But the overly punitive Versailles Treaty, which merely handed the spoils of war to the victors, and the violations of civil liberties in the United States during and after the war, often inflamed by nativist reactions against immigrants, proved bitterly disillusioning for Dewey. This disappointment convinced him that war could never be a means to foster peace, understanding, and democracy but, instead, would serve only to encourage narrow-mindedness and reactionary politics. Accordingly, he took a leading role in the Outlawry of War movement in the 1920s, for which he received much (probably justified) criticism. He stayed true to this cause for the rest of his life, even opposing American entry into World War II because he feared, as he expressed in an op-ed article, that "if the United States is drawn into the next war, we shall have in effect if not in name a fascist government in this country."[6]

Some traditionalists may have seen his many extracurricular activities as diversions from his scholarly work, but Dewey saw them as natural, logical extensions of pragmatism, the truly democratic philosophy. The pragmatist understands that truth emerges not from the scholarly hermitage of a great philosopher but rather from spirited public debate and social inquiry. To be true to his creed, the pragmatist must participate in that conversation and do anything he can to keep it going. Because the professional philosopher does not have the capacity to discover or unveil a priori truths, Dewey thought his chief purpose, besides acting as just another participant, was to guide and facilitate the social pursuit of knowledge.

The philosopher's role was more critical than revelatory, explaining how and why our society failed to meet the standards of scientific method, and delineating those standards more precisely. This role as social critic became an invitation to engage in political theory, and most of Dewey's work, even his writings on education and on more esoteric philosophical topics, can be read in this way. They offered philosophical support for his participatory democratic enterprise and penetrating critiques of the current political system and liberalism. Dewey understood that the democratic enterprise was difficult to achieve, perhaps more an ideal for which we should strive forever than an attainable goal. Democracy, he said, "is an ideal in the only intelligible sense of an ideal: namely, the tendency and movement of some thing which exists carried to its final limit, viewed as completed, perfected. Since things do not attain such fulfillment but are in actuality distracted and interfered with, democracy in this sense is not a fact and never will be."[7]

Unfortunately, the current political and social system came nowhere near this ideal, and Dewey feared that the failure to approximate it could have grave consequences. In *The Republic,* Plato compared the polis to a sailing vessel whose "true captain" (the philosopher king) would possess superior navigational skills to lead his men safely to their destination. On Dewey's ship, there is no "true captain." No one person can choose the destination or the best way to get there, for there are no preexisting maps to consult, no stars or compasses to guide us. Together we are cast adrift in the vast ocean of modernity. The philosopher's job is to remind us of the democratic ideal—that only by working together and acquiring knowledge from our shared experience can we possibly avert catastrophe. But if there were any doubts at the beginning of the twentieth century about the predicament man faced in the modern world, World War I would dispel them for good. The crisis of modernity was upon us: our knowledge of ourselves lagged far behind our knowledge of nature and technology, and this was like putting a lighter and a stick of dynamite in the hands of a child—or giving a child sole control over the rudder and throttle of a powerful speedboat.

Many critics blamed science for our plight and called for an ethics and politics that would stem the tide of modernity by invoking traditional values and ancient truths. But Dewey argued this solution would only exacerbate the modern predicament, that the only way to close the gap between our knowledge of ourselves and our knowledge of nature was to understand human experience as being a part of nature. This required a radical expansion and redefinition of what he called the "scientific attitude," applying its methods of inquiry to social, political, and ethical problems. Dewey's solution means that we must reject all foundational truths, sacred myths, and dogmatic assertions and put our trust only in truth claims that hold up to the rigors of empirical testing.

More important, Dewey's solution also means we have to reconceptualize our notion of scientific method as the very definition of community, as the embodiment of social cooperation and intercourse, open-mindedness and tolerance, mutual sympathy and compassion. Dewey insisted that scientific method is not an esoteric art that is impossible for the average person to master. It merely refines the fruitful ways in which we already think, solve problems, and associate with our fellow man on a daily basis.[8] Hardly cold-blooded or Vulcan-like, Dewey's notion of scientific method evoked the spirit of community life and shared values. Both Peirce and James had hinted at the connection between science and ethics, but Dewey explicitly advocated a value-laden understanding of science.

Indeed, Dewey assailed positivism for endorsing the specious distinction between facts and values, for equating any ethical or political position with mere subjective opinion or desire. He argued that we must not separate the world into simplistic, ready-made dualisms. Values have no existence independent of the facts; instead they grow out of the facts and out of our concrete experiences. Social scientific inquiry can yield reasonable ethical positions and political solutions so long as the process remains deeply democratic, both inclusive and fraternal. It is for this reason that Dewey constantly referred to democracy as a "way of life."

To insist on the distinction between facts and values meant that all ethical and political systems were arbitrary, that humankind had no method of intelligence with which it could address ethical and political questions objectively. Dewey believed he had found this method in participatory democracy, and he sought to defend it on philosophical grounds. More than a form of government, Deweyan democracy aimed to penetrate the very fabric of our culture, tap into the experiences of everyone in the community, reshape our habits, and transform the way we understand ourselves, our social relationships, and our obligations to the community. This democratic faith allowed Dewey to maintain an unflagging optimism even in the face of modern bleakness. He saw the carnage and destruction, the ennui and alienation, that afflicted man in the twentieth century as problems to be solved in a communal spirit, not as the inevitable consequence of modernity.

Dewey's philosophical defense of democracy relied heavily on the three pragmatist tenets, which he was able to bring together in a more cohesive whole than his pragmatist predecessors had done before. Like Peirce and James, he believed that truth was both probabilistic and socially constructed, that human nature was malleable, and that man enjoyed the freedom, at least some of the time, to exert his will independently of social and biological forces. Nurturing these tenets with far more passion and ardent faith than his predecessors, Dewey would construct his participatory democratic theory.

He argued that participatory democracy served both as a method by which the most useful truths could emerge and as a school in which students could best learn these truths through a rigorous and endless process of verification. He maintained that this democratic education would not only produce more learned individuals but also transform its participants: instilling in them the value of scientific inquiry and of communicating and deliberating thoughtfully with one's peers. Finally, Dewey insisted that human beings enjoyed the freedom to choose a democratic way of life, and that they would undoubtedly do so if they were exposed to its many delights, for collaborative and intelligent effort liberated individuals further to act in useful and productive ways.

Before discussing Dewey's reliance on the pragmatist tenets, it is useful to lay out a succinct exegesis of his political theory—his criticism of the assumptions underlying individualism and of the inadequacy of merely safeguarding negative liberties, his conception of a positive liberty, his search for a coherent public and the state, and finally, his participatory democratic solution. After examining the house of Dewey's political thought, we may then descend into the cellar to inspect the foundation upon which it was built.

## Liberalism, Old and New

Like many of the participatory democrats who came after him, Dewey was a great critic of liberalism, exposing its specious assumptions about humankind and nature. He often called himself a liberal, but it would be difficult to find a liberal with whom he could have allied himself completely. He had great contempt for the classical liberalism of John Locke and Adam Smith, recognized the deficiencies in the utilitarian liberalism of Jeremy Bentham and John Stuart Mill, and greatly admired the idealist liberalism of T. H. Green but could not abide its Hegelian overtones.

If Dewey was a liberal, he represented a curious variant: one who tried to demystify the traditions of liberalism by placing them under the glaring light of historical context. As he saw it, the history of freedom illustrated that we could not say someone was free just because the state successfully protected an a priori list of rights. He agreed with traditional liberals that we could indeed locate freedom in the individual, but the nature or quality of that freedom depended on the kinds of associations or relationships in which that individual was engaged, and on the very consequences of those associations. Testing these consequences meant constantly redefining freedom, which in turn required constant vigilance and a supple intelligence on the part of the state.

Dewey's radical conception of freedom began with a critique of liberal assumptions that he considered woefully ahistorical and insensitive to social realities. To him, liberal thought first went astray in its specious assumptions about the human condition, when it posited each individual in his natural state as an isolated and autonomous creature with little need or desire for contact with other human beings. Liberals would have us believe that this solitary creature only associates with others in a larger social sphere because he fears he cannot protect himself on his own from those who may threaten his life or encroach upon the "natural" means of sustaining his own life (that is, private property). We have every reason to suspect others of such treachery, for men are vainglorious, acquisitive, aggressive, despicable creatures who, if they saw profit in it and thought they could get away with it, would stab you in the back as soon as look at you. We associate with others by means of a social contract, agreeing to respect the life and property of everyone in society, and creating a limited government whose sole function is to ensure that no one violates this agreement. Eventually, we come to recognize life and property as natural "rights" or liberties upon which nothing, not even the sovereign state, can rightfully impinge, and we consider society an artificial construct, a necessary evil, from which the individual will naturally withdraw whenever he can. Invoking nature once again for infallible guidance, we grow to believe an overactive state saps man's competitive and acquisitive impulses, which unleash his innovative energies and, in turn, fuel economic gain and prosperity for all.

Having experienced, or at least heard about, state abuse of power in the past (including arbitrary executions, torture, and expropriation of land), we regard warily any government or social movement whose designs grow beyond the modest function of securing our rights. Not surprisingly, we are suspicious of nearly all meliorative action by the state and seek to limit its role to the protection of negative freedom—freedom from bodily harm, intrusions on our property, and constraints on our activity. With the state held in check, we unleash the hounds of radical individualism, self-interest run amok, the dogged pursuit of material wealth no matter the social costs. The principal flaw in this liberal model, according to Dewey, is that it always searches, within nature, for universal causal forces or truths from which to derive political principles, and it fails to acknowledge the varieties of human experience throughout history.

Liberalism would have fared much better, said Dewey, if it had eschewed abstract conceptions of man leading a solitary life in a state of nature and, instead, sought to understand him in his actual social context. Dewey thought we are literally born into associated life, immediately dependent on other human beings for succor and love, and our relationships continue to nurture us and shape who we are for the rest of our lives. Likewise, our behavior has a profound effect on the lives of others. The solitary individual imagined by liberals is a complete fiction:

> Such thinking treats individualism as if it were something static, having a uniform content. It ignores the fact that the mental and moral structure of individuals, the pattern of their desires and purposes, change with every great change in social constitution. Individuals who are not bound together in associations, whether domestic, economic, religious, political, artistic or educational, are monstrosities. It is absurd to suppose that the ties which hold them together are merely external and do not react into mentality and character, producing the framework of personal disposition.[9]

To make his point clear and unmistakable, Dewey described the individual unencumbered by any form of association as a "monstrosity." The notion of a solitary human being is absurd. Despite idyllic descriptions by Locke of man subsisting quite contentedly in a state of nature (not to mention Rousseau's primitivist delusions), such a creature does not and cannot exist, and if it did, it would not be human. Ever smitten with organic metaphors, Dewey compared an individual human being to an individual cell in the body. Just "as the activity of each cell is conditioned and directed by those with which it interacts, so the human being . . . is moved and regulated by his associations with others; what he does and what the consequences of his behavior are, what his experience consists of, cannot even be described, much less accounted for, in isolation."[10]

It is important to note here that, organic metaphors notwithstanding, Dewey did not swing too far the other way. He did not argue that the individual was a fiction, shaped by external social and historical forces over which he had no control. This would have made Dewey guilty of embracing another abstraction, "society" or "history" rather than "the individual."

Dewey identified two types of political theories—those that exaggerated the importance of forces derived from the native capacities of individuals, and those that exaggerated the "conditions provided by the environment" in which individuals are situated—and he found both inadequate and far too simplistic.[11] Classical liberalism represented an example of the former, assuming that each individual human being was a completely self-contained, self-activating unit whose achievements did not require nurturing from society. The best example of the latter, exaggerating environmental conditions, can be found in Marxism, which, in its most horrifying manifestations, regarded individuals as insignificant and dispensable components of a collective and inexorable march toward the end of history. Between these two extremes Dewey offered a via media, or middle way, that he considered a more accurate understanding of the human condition. In his view, both the individual and society are real, each sustaining the other in a never-ending series of transactions.[12] We cannot speak of one without referring to the other, for they are inextricably connected.

Once we accept that man cannot understand himself outside a social context and cannot achieve anything without support from, or interaction with, other people, our notion of individuality changes. We come to realize that we are not born with our individuality; we achieve our individuality through our associations. "Individuality cannot be opposed to association," said Dewey. "It is through association that man has acquired his individuality and it is through association that he exercises it."[13]

This is why Dewey maintained that the liberal state "must be deeply concerned about the structure of human association. For the latter operates to affect negatively and positively, the development of individuals."[14] This meant that human beings were not inexorably flawed creatures. They were not thrown into this world, ready-made and complete, their characters etched in stone from the outset. To the contrary, they were as wonderful or wicked as their associations allowed them to be. As a result of their ongoing interaction with others, human beings grow and change over time.

Classical liberals acknowledged that society evolved and often made significant advances, but they argued that only individuals who are left alone to make their way in the world can drive progress. Unlike individuals who are forced into cooperative arrangements that offer no incentives to compete, the solitary individual will work assiduously to defeat those who challenge his chances for success. Living in a perpetual state of uncertainty, this lonesome figure will never slacken his resolve lest he suffer the bitter consequences of failure, especially failure of the material kind. This lingering fear unleashes a natural competitive drive and the energy to create new innovations, technological breakthroughs, and other novelties that contribute to social progress. According to conventional wisdom, the virtue of private markets is that they effectively reproduce the natural conditions in which the competitive impulses come alive and drive innovation and social progress. Many liberals came to accept this as an irrefutable economic law.

According to Dewey this was hogwash. Classical liberals, he said, "ascribe all the material benefits of our present civilization to this individualism—as if machines were made by the desire for money profit, not by impersonal science; and as if they were driven by money alone, and not by electricity and steam under the direction of collective technology."[15] In his view, we are mistaken to attribute our capacity for innovation to the quest for "money profit." He instead credited "impersonal science" for the advent of machines, suggesting that social progress stems from the collective efforts of scientists who seek answers to hypotheses for their own sake and only later discover the possible applications of their discoveries. That said, even the profit-minded innovator cannot work alone, unaffected by external influences such as his education and professional relationships. He would never accomplish his goals if he did not interact with the right people, exchange information, learn from them, and receive assistance when needed. The classical liberal would agree that these experiences help the individual achieve his aims, but he would consider them incidental to the power of individual initiative. In Dewey's view, this is an incalculable mistake. If anything, social progress provides more evidence that human relationships are a given, a reality from which we cannot abstract the individual.

The problem with social contract theory was that it did just that: it operated under the specious assumption that man came into, and continues to pass through, the world with his individuality solitary and intact. From this assumption liberals have concluded that man has no innate interest in cultivating social relationships but does so for the sole purpose of protecting his self-contained individuality from harm. A man's life and property represent the "natural" means (or the rights) by which he can preserve his individuality, and he grudgingly enters the social compact in order to safeguard those natural rights. This was an absurd proposition for Dewey who had little use for the concept of natural rights. He said:

> Natural rights and natural liberties exist only in the kingdom of mythological social zoology. Men do not obey laws because they think these laws are in accord with a scheme of natural rights. They obey because they believe, rightly or wrongly, that the consequences of obeying are upon the whole better than the consequences of disobeying. If the consequences of existing rule become too intolerable, they revolt.[16]

The struggle for freedom throughout history has not been a search for some abstract condition we enjoy in our "natural" state. We cannot precisely define freedom in a universal way; we can only experience freedom under certain conditions—meaning, at a certain time, and in a certain place.

Applying the "concept of historic relativity" will show that "liberty is always relative to forces that at a given time and place are increasingly felt to be oppressive. Liberty in the concrete signifies release from the impact of *particular* oppressive forces; emancipation from something once taken as a normal part of human life but now experienced as bondage."[17] Dewey suggested that we must historicize our notion of freedom and remember that oppression and its harmful consequences will forever change and assume different forms. That which once emancipated us from oppression can betray us and become our worst enemy as social conditions change.

We leave ourselves vulnerable to this betrayal when we draw on past experiences with oppression to construct universal truths about liberty and then insist on abiding by these truths for time immemorial.

Dewey liked to cite the example of early liberalism. In the seventeenth, eighteenth, and early nineteenth centuries, people understandably saw the state as the only serious threat to liberty. Indeed, the church had been vanquished, and the large corporation was as yet unknown, while the state was developing a long, distinguished record of oppression, arbitrarily seizing property and torturing and executing its subjects. In the early nineteenth century, people grew to see the state not only as a potential force of oppression but also as a mainstay of economic stagnation and injustice.

Liberals attacked the old feudal economic relationships and political customs, which the state continued to support out of deference to the landed aristocracy, arguing, rightly, that with their unintelligible mass of customs and laws these archaic institutions unfairly erected barriers before those who wanted to invest their capital in manufacturing or banking. This system in general inhibited economic growth and denied people opportunities to prosper economically. It is no surprise that in this historical context many deemed the state an arch-villain, a violator of individual rights, and a roadblock to progress. The solution at the time seemed simple: create a limited government that would enable individuals to flourish and reach their full potential, intellectually, artistically, and economically, and thus open the doors to unprecedented social progress. Unfortunately, what may have been the right solution to particular problems in the past morphed into universal truths about individual and economic rights.[18]

This story took on tragic proportions when the late nineteenth century introduced a slew of problems no one could have foreseen, the most significant of which was the rise of the corporation. Liberals of an earlier age "had no glimpse of the fact that private control of the new forces of production, forces which affect the life of every one, would operate in the same way as private unchecked control of political power."[19] But by the end of the nineteenth century, the power of economic forces was unmistakable. "The forms of associated action characteristic of the present economic order are so massive and extensive that they determine the most significant constituents of the public and the residence of power," said Dewey. "The new forms of combined action due to the modern economic regime control present politics, much as dynastic interests controlled those of two centuries ago."[20] Faced with the consequences of these burgeoning economic forces (urban squalor, abject poverty, growing inequality, dangerous working conditions in factories, exploitation of child labor, uprooting of local communities, and so on), liberals should have reassessed their conceptions of freedom. But many clung stubbornly to outdated notions about individual and economic rights. "The tragedy," lamented Dewey, "is that although these liberals were the sworn foes of political absolutism, they were themselves absolutists in the social creed they formulated."[21]

The good news, according to Dewey, was that liberalism did not have to ignore consequences and exalt universals. He credited the utilitarian liberal Jeremy Bentham for being the first philosopher to declare that "all organized action is to be judged by its consequences, consequences that take effect in the lives of individuals," not by whether it conforms to some abstract political principle. Although Bentham believed the conditions of his time demanded a laissez-faire state, he opened the door for a future liberalism that would endorse positive state action to redress emerging social problems. Once Bentham called into question the "doctrine of inalienable individual natural rights," he removed "the obstacle to positive action by the state whenever it can be shown that the general well-being will be promoted by such action."[22]

Eventually, the term liberalism became disconnected from its laissez-faire origins and associated instead with positive governmental action to assist the poor and other unfortunates, thus giving them the opportunity to realize their full potential. This did not mean that the old liberalism had withered away and died. It was alive and well, merely assuming different names, such as classical liberalism, conservatism, or traditionalism. Much to Dewey's dismay, the old liberalism continued to resonate in the first half of the twentieth century, persuading people that the state should not respond intelligently to specific problems but should instead accord with universal laws about man, society, and economics.

Defeating the old liberalism once and for all required that we embrace a new conception of what it means to be an individual in a world increasingly dominated by big business and industry. Global in its reach, the modern corporation was changing the face of society everywhere. The age of subsistence living was long gone, and so were the days of feudalism. People existed now at the mercy of a technology-driven economy, which was inconceivably vast, byzantine, and relentlessly fast-paced. They had only the faintest knowledge about where they fit in the grand scheme of things. All they knew for sure was that their society had grown far beyond their local communities and now provided them with myriad opportunities and with access to goods, services, and information they could not have imagined in years past.

The irony behind this corporatizing society is that it has increased the number and complexity of associations in society, connecting millions upon millions of people in an unimaginably vast network, but "its animating motives and compensations are so unmitigatedly private." In other words, private individual gain fuels corporatization, but its effects are unmistakably public. Feverishly driven to acquire a stockpile of material goods for his own private enjoyment, the individual becomes ill-equipped to navigate the interconnected and integrated society of which he is a part. He feels lost in the crowd, aware of his own helplessness before the vicissitudes of impenetrable social and economic forces.[23]

People would regain their bearings and feel more secure in a society that discarded the exclusively solitary and profit-minded conception of individualism and replaced it with an individualism that restored the "enduring" but temporarily lost idea that liberty meant giving the individual an opportunity to develop his "inherent capacities."[24] A foe of communism, Dewey never supported providing equal shares of wealth to everyone in society. But he did favor redistributing wealth to the extent that it would promote equality of opportunity, which meant that "each individual would of necessity be provided with whatever is necessary for his realization, for his development, whatever is necessary to develop him to enable him to function adequately. . . . He must have certain opportunities provided for him."[25] While old liberals cautioned that guaranteeing equality must always come at the expense of individual freedom, Dewey dismissed this as a false dichotomy and insisted that equality was actually a necessary precondition for the exercise of liberty.

Merely securing negative liberty, as old liberals proposed, did not suffice, for it failed to provide people with the tools to develop fully their "inherent capacities" and to take charge of their own lives. "The freedom of an agent who is merely released from direct external obstructions is formal and empty. If he is without resources of personal skill, without control of the tools of achievement, he must inevitably lend himself to carrying out the directions and ideas of others."[26] Negative liberty has little meaning for someone without the skills or resources to direct his life as he desires.

In a world where economic forces affect our lives so profoundly, people need more than just empty promises or formal guarantees that hold no more strength than the ancient paper on which they were written. To the contrary, they require "a social organization that will make possible effective liberty and opportunity for personal growth in mind and spirit in all individuals," and that will guarantee everyone sufficient "material security" so that they can "share in the wealth of cultural resources that now exist and may contribute, each in his own way, to their further enrichment." Faced with a bewildering world, people need a helping hand that will assist in their "personal growth in mind and spirit" and, in turn, empower them to partake in existing "cultural resources" that add to the "enrichment" of their lives. This called for a far greater role for the state, a role old liberals were loath to grant it.[27]

Dewey's conception of positive—or what he often called "effective"—liberty becomes apparent here. He betrayed his radical colors most brightly when he equated liberty not with protection or security but with power (anticipating the idea on which postmodern thinkers in the second half of the twentieth century would become fixated). "Freedom" for

Dewey meant "power, the effective power to do specific things." Classical liberals would have us believe that the free person enjoys protection from harm, intrusion, or restraint. Dewey argued that a person is free only when he exercises the power to do what he wants:

> There is no such thing as liberty in general; liberty, so to speak, at large. If one wants to know what the condition of liberty is at a given time, one has to examine what persons *can* do and what they *cannot* do. The moment someone examines the question from the standpoint of effective action, it becomes evident that the demand for liberty is a demand for power, either for possession of powers of action not already possessed or for retention and expansion of powers already possessed.

This suggests that we can understand the hearty defense of negative rights by "the beneficiaries of the existing economic system . . . as a demand for preservation of powers they already possess." In other words, their ostensibly principled stand is a ruse, a veiled attempt to retain the immense power they have enjoyed under the current economic system.[28]

A liberal society, which aims to guarantee freedom for everyone, must find a way to distribute power equitably throughout society and not allow a particular person, class, or clique to monopolize it for themselves or hold a disproportionate share. After all, "the possession of effective power is always a matter of the *distribution* of power that exists at the time," for "there is no such thing as the liberty or effective power of an individual, group, or class, except in relation to the liberties, the effective powers, of other individuals, groups and classes." For Dewey, the relationality of power suggests that one person's power to accomplish certain things relies heavily on the power of others. "No one can *do* anything except in relation to what others can do and cannot do."[29]

Whether we like it or not, we live in a world teeming with associations and interdependencies; other people have powers that affect our lives, and vice versa. We all stand to benefit from cooperating and working together to understand the intricacies of our interconnected lives. In short, this means that the cause of freedom, the power to do things, requires collective effort. Society cannot distribute power equitably if every man embraces the old individualism and decides to go it alone. Dewey summarized his argument succinctly when he said: "Man is free only as he has power, and he can possess power only as he acts in accord with the whole."[30]

## Creating Publics

What remains unclear at this point is the specific role the Deweyan state must play in order to effect this equitable distribution of power and to promote cooperative effort among the people. That the state had to play a far more active role than it did before was a given. But understanding Dewey's position more clearly requires a discussion of perhaps his most important work on political theory, *The Public and Its Problems*, in which he discussed at length the state and its relationship to society.

Dewey maintained that most political theorists in the Western canon have made the mistake of trying to locate the origins of the state in primeval causal forces. Christian theologians believed that God authorized the state to embody his will and direction. Hegelians said that the state manifested the dialectical unfolding of history and the logic of the Absolute. Marxists also subscribed to a dialectical understanding of history, but they argued that changing economic relationships, not some unseen Absolute, determined statehood. Classical liberals called attention to the social contract out of which the state emerged to protect the natural rights of isolated individuals. Although each group identified a different cause, they all attributed the emergence of the state to a single universal cause.[31]

Dewey found it far more useful to understand the state as an institutional response to specific conditions experienced by the public. In his view, as with the attempt to define liberty, the secret to locating the state was not to look backward for universal causes but to look forward to specific consequences of human association. Dewey maintained that there were two kinds of consequences, public and private. When two or more people engage in a private transaction, each of them does so willingly, expecting to experience certain consequences in the process. But, as a result of this transaction, a third party may suffer unintended consequences—or what economists call "externalities." These people constitute the public, and the state emerges to address their problems. "The public," said Dewey, "consists of all those who are affected by the indirect consequences of transactions to such an extent that it is deemed necessary to have those consequences systematically cared for. Officials are those who look out for and take care of the interests thus affected." Theoretically, if private transactions never had indirect consequences of this sort, the public would not exist and there would be no need for a state. But Dewey believed that externalities are inevitable in the modern world. The public will demand that officials look out for their interests and work tirelessly to alleviate their undue pain and prevent it from occurring in the future.[32]

It is important to understand, however, that the government and the state were not the same thing for Dewey. The government comprises various officials, both elected and unelected, who work on the behalf of the public; the state encompasses both these government officials and the public they serve. The role of governmental officials is to give form to the state, to ascertain and articulate the needs of the public, and to ensure these needs are met. According to Dewey:

> The lasting, extensive and serious consequences of associated activity bring
> into existence a public. In itself it is unorganized and formless. By means of
> officials and their special powers it becomes a state. A public articulated and
> operating through representative officers is the state; there is no state with-
> out a government, but also there is none without the public.[33]

The implication here is that the government, consisting of many bureaucrats and officials who serve for a considerable length of time, may enjoy a
certain degree of continuity and stability. Over the years we come to recognize many of the people in government and the buildings they occupy.
By necessity government takes on a familiar form.

We can never say upfront what form the state should take, however, for
it depends on the changing conditions with which the public is confronted.
Society always faces new and unforeseen externalities that demand attention,
so the state is continually transforming itself, assuming responsibilities and
tasks that may have been inconceivable to past generations. In other words,
"the State must always be rediscovered" and "re-made."[34]

In Dewey's view, the great mistake of past political theorists was to cast
the state in a particular mold, as a fixed entity enshrined by timeless institutional forms and august traditions. Ascribing a permanent form to the
state impeded progress and created an environment where only violence
could effect real change. "The belief in political fixity, of the sanctity of
some form of state consecrated by the efforts of our fathers and hallowed
by tradition," he said, "is one of the stumbling-blocks in the way of or-
derly and directed change; it is an invitation to revolt and revolution."[35]
Only a dynamic state, continually redefining its function in society, can
adapt and respond intelligently and vigorously to new challenges.

Dewey was quick to point out that the state would remain dynami-
cally attentive to externalities only if the public kept a close eye on its
officials and made sure they continued to work on its behalf. The public
could not lie dormant or rest assured that government officials would
identify its problems and remedy them. It had to take an active stance
and hold officials accountable when they failed to address emerging social problems. In other words, the state had to be a functional democracy in which an informed and civically engaged citizenry voted in frequent elections.[36]

Although this hardly sounded like an earth-shattering or original solution, Dewey recognized that creating an informed and engaged citizenry was
a tall order, a very tall order. An informed public had to acquire a sophisticated understanding of the externalities affecting it, and this proved more
difficult in the modern age. Indeed, we live in a society where "many consequences are felt rather than perceived; they are suffered, but they cannot be
said to be known, for they are not, by those who experience them, referred
to their origins."[37] Until the public identified the origins of its suffering,

government officials could continue to capitalize on its ignorance and govern without accountability. This was the problem of modernity.

In Dewey's opinion, this problem stemmed from the fact that the origins of externalities were so remote, their workings so complex, and their effects so dispersed, that the public had little chance of acquiring knowledge about them—or of itself. In the modern world of transcontinental connections and complex interdependencies, the public was inchoate, difficult to pinpoint with any degree of certainty.[38] The primary issue was that the machine age had made it possible for a seemingly innocuous private transaction to have a profound effect on the lives of many people who were far removed from the source of their sufferings, and from others with whom they shared common concerns. In other words, the indirect consequences were becoming ever more remote from the initial transaction. Hence, the proverbial example of the businessman in New York City who, by pressing a button or placing a phone call, lays off thousands of workers in Detroit and creates just as many jobs in Indonesia.

In addition, having "expanded" and "complicated the scope of the indirect consequences," modernity had torn society asunder into many "publics" that are "amorphous and unarticulated."[39] To talk of *the* public in monolithic terms was a misnomer, an imprecise linguistic convention we use for the sake of simplicity and elegance. Externalities abounded in modernity, affecting various groups of people, often with vastly different, even conflicting concerns. Finally, these various publics experienced further disintegration at the hands of a radical individualism that had set root in modern society. People did not know their next-door neighbors anymore, let alone the thousands or millions of people across the country with whom they might share a common grievance.

Sadly, the end result of all this was the "eclipse" of the public: we cannot find it, or rather, it cannot find itself. An eclipsed public meant a dysfunctional and undemocratic state, which allowed its governmental officials to wreak havoc with the power vested in them. Until the public awakened from its slumber, democracy would remain but a dream.

Dewey argued that reinvigorating democracy in America demanded the transformation of our Great Society into a Great Community. The Great Society contained a vast network of undefined publics that connected people together in a number of ways but failed to foster community. If anything, the Great Society, fueled "by steam and electricity," was responsible for uprooting communities with "new and relatively impersonal and mechanical modes of combined human behavior."[40]

Although the picture appeared bleak, Dewey believed there was still hope for the Great Community. Even in 1927, when *The Public and Its Problems* was released, Dewey found hope in various means of mass communication, which in his mind could help form coherent publics in American society. If the many "physical tools of communication" could work as Dewey hoped they would, the end result would be a Great Community that remained national in scale and enormous in scope and complexity but which recaptured the intimacy of local communities.[41] The printing press, radio, and film all held great potential for linking together isolated human beings, raising awareness about the many disastrous consequences of private transactions, and stimulating a nationwide conversation about these problems and the various solutions proposed.

It may seem odd that Dewey would envision the creation of a community on so large a scale, but it becomes clear that when he spoke of community, he always had democracy in mind. To put it simply, democracy was the very definition of community. "Regarded as an idea, democracy is not an alternative to other principles of associated life. It is the idea of community itself." For Dewey, neither the size nor the scope of the community was an issue. To merit the name, a community had to foster democracy, a cooperative spirit in which citizens communicate shared concerns, work together to find solutions, and share the burden of their joint actions. "Wherever there is conjoint activity whose consequences are appreciated as good by all singular persons who take part in it," said Dewey, "there is in so far a community. The clear consciousness of a communal life, in all its implications, constitutes the idea of democracy."[42]

In addition, Dewey insisted that democracy could function properly only if its citizens not only shared concerns and worked together but also had access to good information, free from distortion and bias. A democratic society had to promote both "the freedom of social inquiry and of distribution of its conclusions," said Dewey, for the public cannot emerge "without full publicity in respect to all consequences which concern it. Whatever obstructs and restricts publicity, limits and distorts public opinion and checks and distorts thinking on social affairs."[43] With illuminating information at its disposal, the public can develop informed opinions, and it stands in a powerful position to compel government officials to remedy existing problems.

Dewey lamented the fact that American democracy failed to harness its technological capacities and disseminate accurate information on which public opinion could be formed. He considered this the principal reason for our democratic woes. But many democratic realists and elitists—with whom Dewey squabbled throughout his career—maintained that vesting too much responsibility in the public was the problem. In their view, we could not expect intelligent and rational decision-making from the public because most people were irrational, guided by their basest instincts—passions, fears, and emotions—when forming political opinions. The growing complexity of the modern world demanded expanding the authority of experts who have mastered complex issues of public policy and who can be expected to make decisions based on dispassionate reason and acquired knowledge. The public, on the other hand, should be entrusted only with the responsibility of supporting the in-party when it is happy with the current state of affairs and the out-party when things seem to be going badly.[44] In other words, the public should not rule so much as they should function as a check on those who do, preventing government officials from straying too far and egregiously abusing their power.

Dewey maintained that this elitist position was an unfounded conceit of the intellectual class. Although the public may not have the skills to engage in sophisticated social inquiry, they do have the capacity, in Dewey's view, to make intelligent judgments with the knowledge furnished by experts. In reply to those skeptics who doubted the public's capacity for intelligent judgment, Dewey argued that we have no evidence to disparage the public so quickly. We live in a society where "the data for good judgment are lacking," and until that day comes when "secrecy, prejudice, bias, misrepresentation, and propaganda as well as sheer ignorance are replaced by inquiry and publicity, we have no way of telling how apt for judgment of social policies the existing intelligence of the masses may be." For the time being, we must withhold our mistrust of the public and focus our criticism on the media and other purveyors of grossly distorted information upon which the public has based its opinions. While Dewey had to contend with the "yellow journalism" of his day, one can only imagine what he would have thought of today's cable news networks and pundits.[45]

Having defended the public from groundless aspersions cast upon it, Dewey took the offensive against expert rule. He argued that delegating too much authority to experts could have dire consequences. They might have a track record of conducting unbiased research and looking out for the interests of society at large, but experts vested with significant political power could become as corrupt as any other ruling elite. No matter how knowledgeable and well-intended they may be at the outset, experts may remain effective only so long as they pay heed to common concerns and are ultimately answerable to the public. Experts, on their own, cannot identify the public and its needs. The people must find their voice and articulate their experiences, both to each other and to experts, who will then use this information to conduct research and formulate tentative policy solutions, which will undoubtedly have to be revisited at a later date.

In short, expert knowledge relies heavily on constant communication with the public. Dewey argued that the virtue of democracy is that it involves "a consultation and discussion which uncover[s] social needs and troubles." Experts can put their fancy techniques and vast reservoir of knowledge to effective use only if the public talks to them. In perhaps one of his more memorable passages, Dewey employed a vivid metaphor to make his point: "The man who wears the shoe knows best that it pinches and where it pinches, even if the expert shoemaker is the best judge of how the trouble is to be remedied." In other words, the shoemaker cannot improve his product and attract new customers without soliciting input from the wearer and then making the appropriate adjustments.[46]

## "Democracy Must Begin at Home"

To this point, we have seen that the public in a Deweyan democracy must hold government officials accountable for their actions. For this to happen, experts and the media must provide the public accurate, useful information with which to make sensible judgments about the best course of action to solve its problems. But the story does not end here. Dewey argued that the public needed to play a far more active role in politics. Keeping current on the issues and voting every two years in November elections were not sufficient to rouse it from its slumber. Although the Great Community certainly relied on experts and government officials to address common concerns, Dewey believed that the demands of the public can be met fully only in a democracy where all citizens, not just elites, participate directly in the democratic decision-making process.

Participatory democracy presented the best means by which the state could promote the public good and individuals could reach their full potential as human beings. In Dewey's view, democracy was a "way of life" in which "every mature human being" participated in the "formation of the values that regulate the living of men together." The upshot of democratic "participation" was that it promoted "both the general welfare and the full development of human beings as individuals."[47] While society and the individual were forever at odds in the liberal paradigm, participatory democracy demonstrated that rumors about this conflict had been greatly exaggerated.

Dewey believed participatory democracy created a win-win situation. First, the democratic community embodied a social intelligence far greater than any one person or group of people could ever achieve, and this is the kind of intelligence that counts in social and political matters. Each person may contribute a different amount of intelligence, but "the value of each contribution can be assessed only as it enters into the final pooled intelligence constituted by the contributions of all." This "pooled intelligence" (what Dewey also called "embodied intelligence") is "much more important for judgment of public concerns than are differences in intelligence quotients."[48] Participating citizens are far more likely to find solutions that promote the commonweal than a single person or a select group ever could.

Second, each individual participant in the democratic community also has something to gain from this experience. In the process of working cooperatively toward democratic ends, the participant discovers within himself vast reserves of energy and joy, and he begins to associate his own well-being with the good of the whole. The idea is that an individual is far more likely to find happiness from his own active participation, working with others to achieve certain agreed-upon ends. "There is no way," said Dewey, "to escape or evade this law of happiness, that it resides in the exercise of the active capacities of a voluntary agent; and hence no way to escape or evade the law of a common happiness, that it must reside in the congruous exercise of the voluntary activities of all concerned."[49] No matter how well-intended a leader may be, he cannot confer happiness or the good life on another person. Many leaders and philanthropists are often surprised to see that their acts of beneficence stir "resentment"; but Dewey argued that this is an understandable response, given that they failed to engage the "freely cooperative activities" of the very people they wanted to help. "This cooperation must be the root principle of the morals of democracy." People can find happiness and the good life only from their own participation: "the good is the activities in which all men participate so that the powers of each are called out, put to use, and reenforced."[50]

Dewey's emphasis on community and participation demonstrate how far afield he had ventured from orthodox liberalism. Far more concerned about individual alienation from community and the need to create more opportunities for democratic participation, he could not possibly sympathize with liberal wariness of collectivities or with their fear of majority tyranny. Indeed, Dewey famously declared that "the cure for the ailments of democracy is more democracy."[51] To become a way of life for all citizens, democracy has to reach every nook and cranny of our culture, including the family, the school, industry, and religion.[52] Still more, it has to penetrate our souls: "unless democratic habits of thought and action are part of the fiber of the people, political democracy is insecure. It can not stand in isolation. It must be buttressed by the presence of democratic methods in all social relationships."[53] It is important to stress that, for Dewey, democracy was more than a political procedure or type of government; he considered it first a cultural, even a moral, approach to solving problems and interacting with our fellow man. But, of course, the political implications of democracy run deep. The extent to which democratic habits seep into the fiber of our culture determine whether the problems of the public can be identified and resolved.

These "democratic habits" to which Dewey alluded so often resemble the approach found in scientific communities. The virtue of scientific method, he claimed, is that it welcomes diversity of opinion, calls for the free exchange of information, insists that all truth inquiry should draw on observable facts, and demands that all conclusions be subject to further testing under public scrutiny. Although Dewey readily conceded that no democracy has ever "made complete or adequate use of scientific method in deciding upon policies," this was an ideal to which democracy should aspire: the "freedom of inquiry, toleration of diverse views, freedom of communication, the distribution of what is found out to every individual as the ultimate intellectual consumer, are involved in the democratic as in the scientific method."[54]

Dewey wholeheartedly believed that the exercise of scientific method did not have to be confined to experts. Even if citizens do not acquire the specific knowledge and technical expertise of scientists, they can still adopt their general approach—tolerating other viewpoints, exchanging information freely with others, basing truth claims on the available empirical evidence, and accepting the provisionality of any truths they happen to embrace.

> While it would be absurd to believe it desirable or possible for every one to become a scientist when science is defined from the side of subject matter, the future of democracy is allied with the spread of the scientific attitude. It is the sole guarantee against wholesale misleading by propaganda. More important still, it is the only assurance of the possibility of a public opinion intelligent enough to meet present social problems.[55]

The implication here is quite clear: in order for their "embodied intelligence" to meet the challenges of modern life and address the concerns of the public(s), citizens must adopt the scientific attitude in all aspects of their lives. This means that every citizen must resemble the scientist in his approach to life, and society must assume the participatory and deliberative characteristics of a scientific community.

Dewey stressed the importance of extending the scientific attitude to business and industry, because economic relationships and associations have a more profound effect on man than anything else in the modern age. Deeply influenced by G. D. H. Cole, a British political theorist and leading advocate of "guild socialism" (or "industrial democracy"), Dewey argued that democracy would never truly flourish until the worker played a significant role in managing the floors of our factories and shops and in making decisions about the means and ends of production.

Although he supported democratizing the workplace, Dewey opposed hard-line communism or socialism, especially such crude measures as expropriating property and redistributing it equally to the proletariat. Hardly a solution of any kind, the forceful expropriation and radical redistribution of wealth serves only to transfer ownership from one group of people to another and does not address the more important issue of how capital can be put to intelligent use for collective ends.[56] "Without [the] democratization of industry," said Dewey, "socialization of industry will be doomed to arrest at the stage of state capitalism," leaving the "average laborer . . . in the same condition of intellectual and moral passivity and perversion as that in which he now lives."[57]

Dewey favored guild socialism because it placed more emphasis on governance than on ownership, and on socializing intelligence than on capital. Rather than giving workers an equal share of ownership, guild socialism proposed affording them equal opportunity to partake in the decision-making process at work.[58] A democratized workplace fits well with Dewey's conception of the "planning society," in which workers pool their intelligence to make good and creative use of the capital at their disposal, determining on their own to what social ends their efforts should be devoted. While they would certainly keep the interests of owners in mind, workers would also have the power to broaden the concerns of business, paying specific attention to the many externalities for which their corporation should accept responsibility, such as worker alienation, wage inequality, environmental degradation, and the uprooting of local community.

The problem with the hierarchical structure of the capitalist system is that, much like communism, it sustains a "planned society" and only serves the preconceived ends of a particular class—that is, the owners' profits or the Party's Five-Year Plan. A healthy society, according to Dewey, must cultivate a flexible environment in which ends continually change to meet new and unexpected problems. He endorsed guild socialism because he believed it applied the scientific attitude to the world of business and industry.

Dewey lamented the hierarchical structure of capitalism not only because of its inflexibility but also because it prevents workers from reaching their full potential intellectually and creatively. Denied the opportunity to use their minds or imagination, they are subject to the stupefying monotony of routinization favored by profit-minded managers and owners. Because they sell their labor for a wage, workers put themselves at the mercy of owners who exercise sole control over the means and ends of the production process. This means that the "results actually achieved [in the workplace] are not the ends of *their* actions, but only of their employers. They do what they do, not freely and intelligently, but for the sake of the wage earned. . . . The activity is not free because not freely participated in."[59] Although Dewey never had the occasion to read Marx's *Economic and Philosophical Manuscripts,* which had not yet been translated into English, he echoed Marxist alienation theory in suggesting that work should be an end in itself and not just a means to an end.[60] In a world where work and economy represent an ever-growing share of our lives, man can be a free and complete person only if he can participate in the decision-making process at work, if he can share the responsibility of managing the workplace.

The importance of workplace democracy notwithstanding, Dewey argued that the only way to sustain a flourishing participatory democracy was to revive our local communities as sites for civic engagement. Although citizens must always remain mindful of those concerns affecting the Great Community, they can only receive practical democratic experience —engaging in face-to-face interaction with fellow citizens, listening attentively to other points of view, working side by side with neighbors in efforts to address the concerns of the community—in the localities where they spend most of their time.

In its deepest and richest sense community must always remain a matter of face-to-face intercourse. This is why the family and neighborhood, with all their deficiencies, have always been the chief agencies of nurture, the means by which dispositions are stably formed and ideas acquired which laid hold on the roots of character. The Great Community, in the sense of free and full inter-communication, is conceivable. But it can never possess all the qualities which mark a local community. It will do its final work in ordering the relations and enriching the experience of local associations. . . . Vital and thorough attachments are bred only in the intimacy of an intercourse which is of necessity restricted in range.

In his writings on pedagogy, Dewey argued that people learn best by doing and participating: that which remains abstract to us, remote from our palpable experience, can never be completely understood. Reading publicized information to stay informed, voting in elections, and co-managing our places of work with fellow employees—all provide opportunities for action and participation, but in Dewey's view they were not sufficient. There is no substitute for local communal life, for this is where an individual's "dispositions are stably formed and ideas acquired" and where deep "attachments are bred." More than anything else, the local community nurtures and forms the individual, his personality, his ideals, his worldview. Accordingly, it is the best place to cultivate democratic habits. In addition, the local community, of necessity "restricted in range," enjoys the kind of intimate "intercourse" that is required in a participatory democracy. From afar, many larger-than-life figures "may inspire admiration, emulation, servile subjection, fanatical partisanship, hero worship; but not love and understanding, save as they radiate from the attachments of a near-by union. Democracy must begin at home, and its home is the neighborly community."[61]

Dewey often expressed concern that the Great Society threatened to tear human ties and communities asunder, and he believed that the reality of these centrifugal forces made local democratic participation more necessary than ever. He saw local democratic participation as an antidote to the problems of modernity. Increasingly, people "find themselves in the grip of immense forces whose workings and consequences they have no power of affecting. The situation calls emphatic attention," continued Dewey, "to the need for face-to-face associations, whose interactions with one another may offset if not control the dread impersonality of the sweep of present forces."[62]

One of the virtues of local democratic participation is that it fights against the impersonal forces of modernity, providing solid ground on which to lead meaningful lives. Local democracy resists "the dread impersonality of the sweep of present forces." It also, at the same time, discourages withdrawal into a state of narrow provinciality and raises consciousness of the Great Society to which citizens are inextricably connected. Not surprisingly, Dewey expressed his admiration for Jeffersonian democracy, which fosters the "development of local agencies of communication and cooperation, creating stable loyal attachments, to militate against the centrifugal forces of present culture, while at the same time they are of a kind to respond flexibly to the demands of a larger unseen and indefinite public."[63] In other words, local participatory democracy offers the best of both worlds: it enriches our lives by teaching us how to communicate and cooperate with our friends and neighbors and by strengthening our intimate ties within the community, but it also trains us to address those concerns that affect the larger public of which we have become a part in the Great Society.

This last point was especially crucial for Dewey. He strongly believed that a thriving local democracy was necessary to make the larger national public visible and coherent. "Unless local communal life can be restored, the public cannot adequately resolve its most urgent problem: to find and identify itself," said Dewey. "While local, [the public] will not be isolated." Dewey praised local democratic communities because, without sacrificing stability, they are able to cultivate a sophisticated citizenry, "flexible" and "responsive to the complex and world-wide scene in which it is enmeshed."[64]

As he saw it, the public could fully emerge only if citizens came together regularly, face-to-face, to share ideas and experiences, express concerns, and listen to each other regarding matters of local, national, and even international importance. Reading publications to stay informed will always be crucial for the public to become aware of the externalities affecting their lives, but Dewey believed that the many conversations in which we engage within a vibrant local democratic community serve to reinforce and enrich our understanding of these complex issues. No one man can understand fully how some remote transaction affects the public until he has talked to other people and learned from their insights and unique perspectives. Although the social inquiry which makes its way into "print is a precondition of the creation of a true public," Dewey maintained that its "final actuality is accomplished in face-to-face relationships by means of direct give and take. Logic in its fulfillment recurs to the primitive sense of the word: dialogue." As a result, the public remains "partially informed and formed until the meanings it purveys pass from mouth to mouth."[65] After talking with others in our community, sharing experiences and insights, the "embodied intelligence" of our community will know no limits and we will become all the better for it.

The faith in the power of local democratic community to augment social intelligence and transform human nature lies at the heart of Dewey's political thought. He wrote:

> The foundation of democracy is faith in the capacities of human nature; faith in human intelligence, and in the power of pooled and cooperative experience. It is not the belief that these things are complete but that if given a show they will grow and be able to generate progressively the knowledge and wisdom needed to guide collective action.[66]

As this passage indicates, Dewey argued that democracy rests on two foundational truths in which he had unwavering faith: "the capacities of human nature" (the democratic psychology) and "the power of pooled and cooperative experience" to enhance "human intelligence" (the democratic epistemology).[67] Like his pragmatist forebears, Dewey had great contempt for "first principles" upon which a prescribed set of ideas can be built, and he assailed both classical liberalism and Marxism for basing their political systems on specious assumptions about the human condition. Yet Dewey appears guilty of committing the same crime, basing his democratic ethos on contestable ideas derived from the pragmatist tradition. Indeed, fairly late in his career, Dewey argued that "any theory of activity in social and moral matters, liberal or otherwise, which is not grounded in a comprehensive philosophy, seems to me to be only a projection of arbitrary personal preferences."[68] As Dewey would have undoubtedly conceded, pragmatism represented the "comprehensive philosophy" in which his democratic theory was "grounded." It gave him the faith that participatory democracy would flourish "if given a show." We turn now to the origins of that faith, first to Dewey's democratic epistemology, and then to his democratic psychology and metaphysics.

## The Scientific Method Writ Large

Dewey's epistemology began with the pluralistic premise that we live in a "universe" fraught with "real uncertainty and contingency, a world which is not all in, and never will be, a world which in some respect is incomplete and in the making, and in which in these respects may be made this way or that according as men judge, prize, love, and labor."[69] He could never abide the monistic picture of the universe, seamlessly connected and whole. Like James, he welcomed "an open world, an infinitely variegated one, a world which in the old sense can hardly be called a universe at all; so multiplex and far-reaching that it cannot be summed up and grasped in any one formula."[70] Although he saw within this multiverse an opportunity for humanity to make and remake truths in accordance with its ideals, he also understood that throughout history men have had good reason to fear this contingent world, teeming with hazards and pitfalls that, more often than not, produce great suffering.

To defend himself against the caprices of fortune, man has searched for certainty, a set of universal principles on which he could anchor his life. Philosophers have aided this quest for certainty with unabashed enthusiasm, invoking reason and logic to discover absolute truths. But Dewey made it his mission to convince his readers and listeners that this was a quixotic quest. "Upon an empirical view," he said, "uncertainty, doubt, hesitation, contingency and novelty, genuine change, are facts," and no timeless principles or absolute truths can wash these facts away.[71]

Insisting on this quest, Dewey warned, will not help us cope with a contingent world and will in fact heap more unhappiness upon us. The belief in absolute truth makes man susceptible to "the frozen intelligence of some past thinker, sect and party cult: frozen because arrested in dogma."[72] When men hold fast to their dogmas, their disagreements with others turn into violent conflict. Without the means to resolve their differences of opinion peacefully, force becomes the final arbiter of their dispute over truth. "The claim to possession of first and final truths is, in short, an appeal to final arbitrament by force," said Dewey. For when people claim to possess a truth whose origins lie outside the realm of experience, "there is no reasonable, no practicable way of negotiating their differences. . . . The only way out is trial by force, the result of which will give the side having superior force the ability to impose acceptance of its dogmas, at least for as long a time as it has superior forces."[73]

This line of reasoning appears to be a direct response to Bertrand Russell, who declared that pragmatism was culpable of eliminating any objective standard of truth to which we can appeal, of simply equating truth with expedience or with working successfully. "In the absence of any standard of truth other than success," Russell warned, "ironclads and Maxim guns must be the ultimate arbiters of metaphysical truth."[74] Russell believed that reason represented this "standard of truth," which could settle our disputes authoritatively. A proponent of the analytical school of philosophy, he maintained that authoritative settlement of any dispute simply demanded strict adherence to logic, which he understood in algorithmic terms: a complex but fixed system of rules on how one must think to arrive at truth. Dewey maintained, however, that obedience to one set of rules creates the conditions under which "stark and absolute" conflict arises.[75] After all, many people's concrete experiences will belie the "truths" deduced through reason, and, pointing to the empirical evidence at their disposal, these people will quite rightly stand firm in their opposition to the dogma of rational inquiry.

Like Peirce and James, Dewey maintained that reason could not function as the final arbiter of truth in such a formulaic way, because there is not just one method of inquiry. For Dewey, the study of logic was not an exercise in mathematical thinking but rather a descriptive and normative endeavor. Its business was to tell us first how men actually use their minds to solve problems and then identify those methods that prove most successful in their experience. The logician should collect and study methods of inquiry—deduction, induction, and so on—just like the geologist does with rocks and the entomologist does with insects.[76] His aim should be to "analyze and report how and to what effect inquiries actually proceed, genetically and functionally in their experiential context."[77]

The problem with reason is that it remains inflexible and unwilling to alter the method of inquiry when the situation calls for it. Reason works under the assumption that truth is absolute and divorced from concrete reality, and that there is only one formulaic way of accessing that truth. As Dewey put it, "reason designates both an inherent immutable order of nature, superempirical in character, and the organ of mind by which this universal order is grasped. In both respects, reason is with respect to changing things the ultimate fixed standard—the law physical phenomena obey, the norm human action should obey."[78]

For Dewey, truth inquiry was a never-ending process, continually drawing on new empirical evidence as it becomes available. "The attainment of settled beliefs is a progressive matter; there is no belief so settled as not to be exposed to further inquiry."[79] As a result, truth was not an immutable idea waiting to be uncovered by rational means; rather, it was a provisional and eminently malleable means of addressing specific problems.

Dewey was attracted to pragmatist epistemology because it understood knowing not as a grasp of truth or reality but as a method of serving human ends, coping with a hostile universe, and solving concrete problems. Unfortunately, most philosophers mistakenly concerned themselves "with ultimate reality, or with reality as a complete (i.e., completed) whole: with *the* real object." They expended untold energy on trying to solve abstruse philosophical puzzles that had no bearing on the world as men experience it.

Dewey declared it was high time for philosophy to change its ways. Its "recovery," he said, would begin the moment "it ceases to be a device for dealing with the problems of philosophers and becomes a method, cultivated by philosophers, for dealing with the problems of men."[80] Dealing with the problems of men, according to Dewey, required the exercise of intelligence.

In his discussions of inquiry, Dewey offered intelligence as a superior alternative to reason. He saw intelligence as a way of knowing things in a universe without certainty, a method of exercising *"judgment,"* choosing the ends that our actions should serve and determining the best means by which to bring about those ends. "A man is intelligent not in virtue of having reason which grasps first and indemonstrable truths about fixed principles, in order to reason deductively from them to the particulars which they govern," said Dewey. Instead, man is intelligent "in virtue of his capacity to estimate the possibilities of a situation and to act in accordance with his estimate. In the large sense of the term, intelligence is as practical as reason is theoretical."[81]

Judgment is none other than the ability to devise rules for action that are most likely to work in concrete experience, offering solutions to a whole number of problems we may face in our lives. A person does not put his intelligence on display when he deduces absolute truths from a set of fixed principles. Instead, exercising intelligence requires him to draw on his immediate sensory experiences in order to gain practical knowledge with which he can fashion provisional truths—truths that help him cope with this world.

Knowing means putting ourselves in an active relation with this reality, using our intelligence to verify empirically any hypotheses we may have about it. In the process, we *make* truth. Dewey gave a lucid example:

> I hear a noise in the street. It suggests as its meaning a street-car. To test this idea I go to the window and through listening and looking intently—the listening and the looking being modes of behavior—organize into a single situation elements of existence and meaning which were previously disconnected. In this way an idea is made true; that which was a proposal or hypothesis is no longer merely a propounding or a guess. If I had not reacted in a way appropriate to the idea it would have remained a mere idea; at most a candidate for truth that, unless acted upon on the spot, would always have remained a theory.[82]

According to his critics, the fact that the streetcar made the noise remains true, even if Dewey never bothered to look out the window to verify his hypothesis. But Dewey thought that this reply betrayed their misunderstanding of knowledge and truth. He never questioned the reality of the streetcar's making a noise, and he would have readily conceded that this event actually occurred. He only insisted that he would never have known the truth about the source of the noise unless he had taken pains to confirm his hypothesis. Calling on his intelligence to make sense of his immediate sensory experiences, he identified a connection between the noise and the streetcar.

The vital point here is that the sensory data enabled him to solve a specific problem, to answer a question that piqued his interest, but it told him nothing about streetcars in and of themselves (or about the essence of streetcars). His knowledge of the streetcar will always be limited to his relations with it: the noises wafting through his apartment window and disturbing his thoughts, the various routes it may take throughout the city, its arrival and departure times, and anything else that might prove relevant to his life. He will ground any future truths about the streetcar in these kinds of concrete experiences, and he will know the streetcar only to the extent that he interacts with it. As Dewey hoped to show in this example, truth-seeking (truth-making) must serve the more modest function of solving the immediate "problems of men" and no longer indulge the ethereal speculations of philosophers.

Dewey believed that intelligent inquiry occurs in a manner similar to his streetcar example, in which a person turns to empirical evidence and facts to substantiate truth claims. Science adopted this method long ago and put it to effective use for many years, but humanity has failed to apply this method in other aspects of life. Dewey maintained that politics and ethics, still adhering stubbornly to tired dogma, need to embrace scientific method if they want to meet the challenges posed by modernity.

The solution to many of our woes merely requires us to concentrate more on the means of attaining truth. Too often we hold truths as self-evident and then resort to any means necessary to bring about those ends we have blindly accepted.

So as to avoid this kind of Machiavellian approach to politics and ethics, Dewey instructed that we should "place method and means upon the level of importance that has, in the past, been imputed exclusively to ends."[83] As he saw it, the principal mission of pragmatism was to spread the gospel of scientific method, to convince people that its techniques had general applications. "If the pragmatic idea of truth has itself any pragmatic worth, it is because it stands for carrying the experimental notion of truth that reigns among the sciences, technically viewed, over into political and moral practices, humanly viewed."[84] Dewey believed that scientific method was not an arcane technique, useful only to a select few with highly specialized and technical concerns; rather, it was an approach to solving problems and ascertaining truths of any kind, and it required a spirit of cooperation, deliberation, and experimentation. "There is but one sure road of access to truth—the road of patient, cooperative inquiry operating by means of observation, experiment, record, and controlled reflection."[85] No matter the question or problem facing man—whether ethical, political, or social—scientific inquiry has the best chance of finding answers.

Although they certainly made odd bedfellows, both traditionalists and positivists denied that humankind could apply science so broadly. Dewey saw the danger in refusing to allow human beings any intelligent means by which to devise practical solutions to social problems and to make judgments about good and evil. Denying that there are "any natural and human means of determining judgments as to what is good and evil will work to the benefit of those who hold that they have in their possession super-human and super-natural means for infallible ascertainment of ultimate ends."[86]

Most troubling, the stakes become much higher as science continues to make technological advances that are used by the powerful to serve their "ultimate ends." Indeed, the hopes of humankind remain dim if scientific method continues to play an increasingly important role in producing and regulating the "concrete conditions of life," while the social consequences of these technological developments are left "at the mercy of irrational habits, institutions, and a class and sectarian distribution of power between the stronger and the weaker."[87] For Dewey, society can only be saved if it begins to apply scientific method to itself and not just nature. The only cure to the ills of scientific method, and he conceded there are many, is more scientific method.

Dewey's praise of scientific method elicited an onslaught of criticism. The waves of invective crashing against Dewey's pragmatism seemed to become more intense during times of war—when, all of a sudden, these philosophical disputes ceased to be parlor games and seemed to have real-world consequences.

The first wave came when Dewey publicly supported American entry into World War I. His former student and acolyte Randolph Bourne unleashed the most compelling tirade against Dewey's pragmatism in a series of articles originally published in a journal called *The Seven Arts*. Bourne suggested that pragmatism was an adequate peacetime philosophy, a reasonable approach to life when society was not embroiled in crisis. But he declared that Dewey and his fellow pragmatists laid the groundwork for a chillingly amoral instrumentalism, greasing the engines of an unjustified war without a moment's hesitation. Inspiring a new generation of intellectuals who developed impressive technical abilities but no preparation for formulating ends, Dewey unwittingly taught his "disciples" to become "efficient instruments of the war-technique." His disciples embraced a set of progressive values—or "private utopias"—to which they sincerely believed their technical skills would contribute, but their exclusive focus on means led them to support, with immense energy and gusto, an unnecessary war. Dewey wanted pragmatism to be a philosophy that valued life, said Bourne, but "there was always that unhappy ambiguity in his doctrine as to just how values were created, and it became easier and easier to assume that just any growth was justified and almost any activity valuable as long as it achieved ends."[88] Pragmatism had much to say about how to achieve certain ends by applying the scientific method, but it had nothing to say about why we should embrace those ends, the values that guide our actions and give our lives meaning. In short, pragmatism told us much about *how* but nothing about *why*. It produced wonderful technocrats and functionaries but failed to be morally instructive. One cannot help wondering if Dewey felt the sting of betrayal from his former student, for he responded, quite out of character for the normally unflappable philosopher, by using his influence to make sure Bourne would never write another word for the *New Republic* and was removed from the editorial board of *The Dial*.[89] Perhaps Bourne aroused Dewey's anger to such an extent precisely because his words resonated so powerfully.

As World War II loomed, similar attacks came from traditionalists who charged Dewey with extolling a philosophy of means that had nothing to say about the ends we ought to seek. Robert Hutchins, the renowned president of the University of Chicago who instituted its Great Books curriculum, proved an especially animated foe of Dewey's pragmatism in the 1930s and 1940s. In Hutchins's view, Dewey overlooked the fact that we live in a world where people cannot agree on values, the ultimate ends for which humanity should strive. If we could all agree on ends, resorting to the scientific method to achieve those ends would make sense. But the rise of Nazism and Soviet communism showed us all too clearly that humankind had not come close to reaching any kind of consensus about values, and science had no way of resolving these conflicts. "The difference between us and Mr. Dewey," said Hutchins, "is that we can defend Mr. Dewey's goals and Mr. Dewey cannot. All he can do is say he is for them. He cannot say why, because he can only appeal to science, and science cannot tell him why he should be for science or for democracy or for human ends."[90] Although Dewey and Hutchins may have shared many of the same values, Dewey embraced a philosophy that provides only a method by which to reach certain ends, not a justification for those ends. In the end, said Hutchins, only moral philosophy and religion could supply this justification.

Throughout the rest of his career Dewey would have to endure these criticisms in one form or another, often emanating from the most renowned public intellectuals in the country such as Lewis Mumford, Waldo Frank, and Mortimer Adler. The upshot of this barrage of criticism was that it impelled him to clarify his philosophical position in order to prove to his skeptics that pragmatism actually did have something to say about values and moral ends, about why we should do some things and not others. His critics dismissed the notion that science could say anything about moral truth, but Dewey begged to differ. Indeed, scientific method was our only hope of attaining moral truths that addressed the actual problems men were dealing with in their daily experience. But the crucial point to understand was that, for Dewey, the scientific method could only solve the problems of men if applied properly—that is, democratically. In order to create adequate moral values, societies must replicate on a large scale the methods of intelligence and cooperation employed in scientific communities.

A number of scholars have recently pointed to Dewey's democratic epistemology. Contemporary pragmatist philosopher Hilary Putnam argues that Dewey made an explicit "epistemological justification of democracy."[91] He suggests further that Dewey's democratic epistemology rests on three crucial assertions. First, the best way to arrive at provisional truths ("warranted assertions") and fix our beliefs (alleviate our state of doubt) is through scientific inquiry undertaken by a community of competent inquirers. Second, this method of science can be expanded to other areas of inquiry, including ethics and politics. Third, the degree to which ethical and political inquiry is democratic, including in the conversation all members of the community who have relevant experiences to share, determines how effective its provisional truths will be.

Putnam finds this last point a particularly original insight: democracy is "not just one form of social life among other workable forms of social life; it is the precondition for the full application of intelligence to the solution of social problems."[92] The public good can emerge only when everyone in the community contributes their insights and experiences to a larger discussion about the social good. Even the most benevolent despot will never succeed in promoting the social good and public welfare because, no matter how hard he may try to sympathize with the plight of his subjects, he can never truly know of their circumstances, their needs and desires. The implication of this argument, according to Putnam, is that "an ethical community—a community which wants to know what is right and good—should organize itself in accordance with democratic standards and ideals, not only because they are good in themselves (and they are), but *because they are the prerequisites for the application of intelligence to the inquiry.*"[93]

James Kloppenberg reads Dewey in a similar way and suggests that his "democratic community replicates the community of broadly conceived scientific enquiry. . . . Free and creative individuals, in democratic as in scientific communities, collectively test hypotheses to find out what works best. These communities set their own goals, determine their own tests, and evaluate their results in a spirit of constructive cooperation."[94] Kloppenberg argues that Dewey's critics often "misinterpreted" his "enthusiasm for science" as a "narrow concern with technique to the exclusion of ethical considerations," but Dewey actually "valued the scientific method because it embodied an ethical commitment to open-ended inquiry wherein human values shaped the selection of questions, the formulation of hypotheses, and the evaluation of results." Dewey saw the "ideal scientific community as a democratically organized, truth-seeking group of independent thinkers," whose standards for inquiry "reflected moral, rather than narrowly technical, considerations."[95] In Kloppenberg's view of Dewey, scientific method and democracy were nearly indistinguishable. They embraced the same values of "constructive cooperation" and "open-ended inquiry," and they promoted deliberation and discussion among "free and creative individuals" whose standards for inquiry always met "ethical considerations."

In drawing the connection between scientific method and democracy in Dewey's thought, both Putnam and Kloppenberg highlight the fundamental component of his epistemology—the notion that intelligence is a social, not an individual, endowment. Dewey conceded that some people may have superior native intelligence to others, but he also maintained that a handful of brilliant people, even with the highest intelligence quotients imaginable, cannot devise truths that prove most beneficial in social matters. Dewey did not consider intelligence the ability to think logically or solve mathematical puzzles but, rather, the capacity to make judgments based on our experiences. Exercising judgment required an individual to look not only at his own experiences but to the experiences of everyone else in the community, to share ideas and points of view with others.

For this reason, Dewey rejected the rule of experts, whose raw intelligence would undoubtedly exceed most people's, but who would likely make some unwise judgments because of their limited experience. "A class of experts is inevitably so removed from common interests as to become a class with private interests and private knowledge, which in social matters is not knowledge at all."[96] The implication here is that experts, their technical knowledge and pure intelligence notwithstanding, do not have the knowledge necessary to address political and ethical questions, because they are isolated from the experiences of everyone else in society.

On similar grounds, Dewey argued that paternalism of any kind could not work, no matter how well intended. History has shown that "benevolent despots" and "reformers and philanthropists" never can "do good to others in ways which leave passive those to be benefited," Dewey said. "The social welfare can be advanced only by means which elicit the positive interest and active energy of those to be benefited or 'improved' . . . without active cooperation both in forming aims and in carrying them out there is no possibility of a common good."[97] For Dewey, the epistemological lesson here is that a few wise men, drawing on their superior intellects, powers of reason, and technical skills, cannot arrive at moral truths and then confer on others their wisdom about the good life. In order that "social welfare can be advanced," all citizens must become engaged in the process of actively cooperating with their fellow men to formulate and implement their goals, both political and ethical.

Dewey, unlike his critics, did not consider this such a far-fetched idea. He looked "forward to a time when all individuals may share in the discoveries and thoughts of others." Smaller and specialized scientific communities functioned this way, so he saw no reason why larger economic or political communities could not do the same. "No scientific inquirer can keep what he finds to himself or turn it to merely private account without losing his scientific standing," said Dewey. "Everything discovered belongs to the community of workers. Every new idea and theory has to be submitted to this community for confirmation and test. There is an expanding community of cooperative effort and of truth."[98] If this vision were to reach fruition, a participatory democracy would emerge in the form of guild socialism, workers adopting the attitude and methods of science, and creating a community that promotes communication and tolerates dissent. It would be the scientific method writ large, a society wherein "freedom of inquiry, toleration of diverse views, freedom of communication, the distribution of what is found out to every individual as the ultimate intellectual consumer, are involved in the democratic as in the scientific method."[99]

The pragmatism of Peirce and James held that men arrive at provisional truth in their attempts to answer questions and solve problems in a radically contingent world, and that the scientific method represents the best means to attain such truths, not just about nature but also about man and his social and political relations. Dewey was the first, however, to take these ideas a step further and suggest that, for the scientific method to yield truths in ethical and political matters, *everyone* in the community had to adopt the attitude of the scientist, contributing his experiences to the ongoing discussion and testing of hypotheses. It is likely that Dewey stretched the democratic epistemology further than his pragmatist forebears would ever have approved, and clearly, this stretching would lead inexorably toward participatory democracy. Dewey could not make this leap, however, without also addressing the issue of human nature— whether average men and women could in fact improve themselves and learn the skills required of them in an enlarged scientific community.

## Not Every Man "Is Born a Sonofabitch"

Without question, Dewey embraced a democratic psychology. In *Freedom and Culture,* he declared that "democracy needs a new psychology," one that is "allied with humanism, with the faith in the potentialities of human nature."[100] That he believed every man brimmed with potential was evident throughout his career, and he occasionally indulged in hyperbole on that point. In an article he wrote fairly early in his career, for example, Dewey argued that "in every individual there lives an infinite and universal possibility; that of being a king and priest."[101] Putting on display his faith in the promise of human beings, Dewey elicited attacks from critics who maintained that most people were not capable of mastering the skills necessary to think like scientists and participate effectively in self-governance.

In the 1920s a new crop of political scientists, including Charles Merriam and his students Harold Lasswell and Harold Gosnell, believed that most people were inherently irrational. Consequently they argued that we should not encourage the increase of citizen participation in our democracy. If anything, they thought it best to limit citizen participation and reconceive democracy as rule by enlightened and dependable experts.[102] According to Lasswell, the "public has not ruled with benignity and restraint" because their political actions "derive their vitality from the displacement of private affects upon public objects, and political crises are complicated by the concurrent reactivation of specific primitive motives."[103] In other words, citizens participating in a democracy cannot help but express their most base and primal psychological instincts when they engage in civic action.

In *Moral Man and Immoral Society,* Reinhold Niebuhr assailed both religious and secular liberals who believed, quite naively, "that the egoism of individuals is being progressively checked by the development of rationality or the growth of a religiously inspired goodwill and that nothing but the continuance of this progress is necessary to establish social harmony between all the human societies and collectivities." He accused Dewey in particular of not acknowledging the "predatory self-interest" that dictates the behavior of most people, and "the brutal character of the behavior of all human collectives, and the power of self-interest and collective egoism in all intergroup relations."[104] A theologian by training, Niebuhr took seriously the concept of original sin and believed that we denied the wretched nature of man at our peril. He maintained that a naive faith in man's capacity for rational action and benevolence can lead to ill-advised political enterprises with disastrous consequences. To avoid future manifestations of Nazism or Stalinism, human beings should temper any attempts to achieve social perfection with a realistic self-assessment.

Lasswell and Niebuhr would have us believe that by nature we are cruel and irrational creatures, that our instincts define who we are and limit our capacities; Dewey, on the other hand, had difficulty abiding thinkers who could expect only the worst of human beings. According to his former student Sidney Hook, Dewey asked, in a rare moment of exasperation, why he had "to believe that every man is born a sonofabitch even before he acts like one, and regardless of why and how he becomes one?"[105] Dewey would certainly have admitted that humankind has a poor track record, displaying throughout history an uncanny aptitude for cruelty, injustice, and destruction, but he denied that our natures are responsible for our shameful past.

Indeed, he blamed not our instincts but our habits. In his view, we are not inherently irrational; we have been habituated to behave this way. Although men have instincts (or what Dewey often called "impulses") hardwired into them, these alone cannot account for our irrationality, selfishness, or cruelty, because a whole host of conflicting instincts constitute a person. For example, a person may have an instinct for both sympathy and cruelty, but this does not explain why he acts one way or the other: "The instincts, whether named gregariousness, or sympathy, or the sense of mutual dependence, or domination on one side and abasement and subjection on the other, at best account for everything in general and nothing in particular."[106] Like James, Dewey believed that man harbors countless instincts, but a process of habituation must activate those that become manifest. Most of our instincts lie dormant, awaiting a call to action from the conditions of our social environment. In other words, our instincts on their own cannot explain our behavior because they cannot take shape and "produce consequences" until our social environment instills "dispositions" (or habits) within us.[107]

Dewey also agreed with James when he suggested that man had the ability to sublimate his instincts, channeling them in socially productive and psychologically healthy ways. He even went so far as to take issue with Freud on this. He agreed with the famous psychologist that suppression leads to "all kinds of intellectual and moral pathology" but denied Freud's assertion that it represented the natural state of affairs. Instead, Dewey believed that sublimation was the "normal or desirable functioning of impulse."[108]

The role of our social environment in cultivating our habits was crucial for Dewey. We often think of habits as individual patterns of behavior, developed by seemingly endless repetition so we might perform relatively mundane tasks without conscious thought. Although Dewey appreciated the importance of these kinds of habits, he was more interested in those habits that originate from, and have an impact on, our social relationships. He believed that, by and large, human beings are social constructions. "Habit is the mainspring of human action," he said, "and habits are formed for the most part under the influence of the customs of a group."[109] Society shapes men's habits, and in turn their habits define who they are, bringing certain instincts and behaviors to life.

Our habits can become so deeply ingrained within us that we sometimes confuse them with our natural instincts. We often use the terms "nature" or "natural" to describe those dispositions that we have become so "used to, inured to by custom, that imagination can hardly conceive of anything different. Habit is second nature and second nature under ordinary circumstances is as potent and urgent as first nature," said Dewey. "When habits are so ingrained as to be second nature, they seem to have all of the inevitability that belongs to the movement of stars."[110] The power of habit can hardly be overstated. Dewey even went so far as to claim that habits define who we are. "When we are honest with ourselves," he said, "we acknowledge that a habit has this power because it is so intimately a part of ourselves. It has a hold on us because we are the habit."[111] Nevertheless, we should never forget that our habits are acquired characteristics, which we can always change.

All of this implies that man acts selfishly or generously, cruelly or kindly, not because his genes or his soul have impelled him to do so, but rather because his society and culture have habituated him to this kind of behavior—so much so that it appears completely "natural" to him, an intrinsic part of his identity. Although he may not be aware of the fact, he has equal potential for wickedness and virtue. His fate depends on the way society teaches him to relate with others.

Dewey used the example of what economic liberals call the competitive instinct. They often praise capitalism on the grounds that it accommodates our competitive instincts and channels them in such a way as to foster social progress. But Dewey maintained that their argument rests on a false premise—the notion that men are competitive by nature and, except in rare instances, cannot hope to transcend this inborn characteristic. "Neither competition nor cooperation can be judged as traits of human nature," said Dewey. "They are names for certain relations among the actions of individuals as the relations actually obtain in a community."[112]

Economic liberals have also invoked the inherent selfishness of man in their defense of capitalism, and once again Dewey pointed to the social origins of this supposedly immutable attribute. "A very considerable portion of what is regarded as the inherent selfishness of mankind is the product of an inequitable distribution of power."[113] Human beings only behave selfishly, according to Dewey, because of inequitable social conditions perpetuating the idea among both the haves and the have-nots that each person, if he wants to get by in this world, must consider his own needs and desires first. Only then, perhaps as an afterthought, should he extend a helping hand to his fellow man. Dewey insisted this does not have to be the case. More cooperative social arrangements would habituate us to regard the needs of others just as soon as our own and to act accordingly.

Dewey maintained that social relations could shape intellectual as well as behavioral habits. Liberals and democratic realists such as Merriam or Lippmann often spoke about the stupidity of the masses, their inability to think rationally and base their judgments on objective information. The possibility of their developing the capacity for scientific method and democratic participation was out of the question for these thinkers. Dewey thought otherwise, however. "It is said that the average citizen is not endowed with the degree of intelligence that the use of it as a method demands," but such arguments rest "wholly upon the old notion that intelligence is a ready-made possession of individuals." In most cases, a person has the intelligence necessary "to respond to and to use the knowledge and the skill that are embodied in the social conditions in which he lives, moves and has his being." Unfortunately, people have not on the whole exhibited an ability to apply the methods of science to solve social problems because they have not been given the opportunity to learn these skills. Current social arrangements have denied them "the rich store of the accumulated wealth of mankind in knowledge, ideas and purposes. There does not now exist the kind of social organization that even permits the average human beings to share the potentially available social intelligence."[114]

While our society has failed to distribute social intelligence of the political and social kind, it succeeds in many other, usually technical, areas. Dewey believed these successes are a testament to his faith that average people can achieve much more than so-called elites will ever admit. He gave the example of the mechanic whose native intelligence is average but who becomes skilled in his trade because he has the good fortune to live in a social "environment in which the cumulative intelligence of a multitude of cooperating individuals is embodied." Surrounded by experienced mechanics who teach him the trade, including its many methods and procedures, the novice will eventually become a veteran and contribute significantly to the social intelligence of fixing cars. If the average citizen enjoyed a similarly nurturing environment, we can only imagine what he might achieve: "Given a social medium in whose institutions the available knowledge, ideas and art of humanity were incarnate, and the average individual would rise to undreamed heights of social and political intelligence." But until that time comes, it will remain "useless to talk about the failure of democracy." It is hardly surprising that Dewey devoted so much energy to education, for he considered it the only means by which we could assist the average individual to reach those "undreamed heights of social and political intelligence."[115]

Dewey understood education in the broadest terms possible, not just as filling the vacant minds of children with information or providing them the basics in reading, writing, and arithmetic. Education is a life-long process, cultivating habits of mind that enabled people to learn how to think analytically and how to use ideas and information as tools for solving problems in a socially cooperative environment. Its true aim is to instill in students a scientific attitude that prepares them for democratic participation.

Unfortunately, the American educational system came nowhere close to achieving this goal. Schools employed pedagogical methods that encouraged individualism and competitiveness, not sociability or cooperation. Never expected to think critically to gain mastery of a subject, students had only to retain arcane information, which teachers expected them to regurgitate from time to time. The end result was that teachers and students alike saw education as largely a solitary endeavor, a way of serving narrow self-interest, and they learned to regard the information committed to memory as unassailable truth. In other words, the prevailing educational system in America perpetuated individualism and absolutism, both of which were anathema to science and democracy.

Dewey thought the best way to forge scientific and democratic habits in our schools was to require active participation in real-life enterprises—or what he often called "learning by doing." With this approach, learning ceased to be the passive acquisition of knowledge for its own sake and became a goal-oriented and social activity. Along the way, students would acquire information and learn concepts that applied directly, or at least bore some relevance, to the task at hand. At the Dewey School, for example, students spent considerable time in the kitchen, preparing and cooking their own meals, and in the process they learned arithmetic, chemistry, physics, biology, even geography. Dewey described learning at his school as follows: "Absolutely no separation is made between the 'social' side of the work, its concern with people's activities and their mutual dependencies, and the 'science,' regard for physical facts and forces."[116]

Dewey believed this approach of "learning by doing" reconciled both traditional and progressive theories of education. The traditional group, led by advocates such as W. T. Harris, argued that students must expend effort memorizing information in order to learn. Johann Herbart represented the progressive group in his suggestion that learning must always sustain students' interest. Dewey believed that the chief advantage of his method was that it accomplished both: always starting with a problem or a challenge, students engaged actively in long-term projects they considered meaningful and relevant to their lives. All the while, students developed their capacity for intelligent thought and problem-solving.[117] According to Max Eastman, a former teaching assistant for Dewey at Columbia University, Dewey's pedagogical method "saved our children from dying of boredom, as we almost did in school."[118]

While this may have been true, Dewey also had far greater ambitions, which have still not been realized. He meant for schools to function as incubators for democracy, where students would develop the skills and habits conducive to civic engagement. Education, he said, was "the art of giving shape to human powers and adapting them to social service." He believed that schools had to cultivate an "interest in the community welfare, an interest which is intellectual and practical, as well as emotional—an interest, that is to say, in perceiving whatever makes for social order and progress, and for carrying these principles into execution."[119] Dewey placed so much emphasis on education throughout his career because he saw it as a unique opportunity, a process of rehabituating self-absorbed individuals into enlarged-thinking citizens who worked alongside their fellow men to serve the community. But Dewey understood that education did not end in the school. Although we may create schools that "modify the larger and more recalcitrant features of adult society," the educational system will not turn its students into enlarged-thinking citizens unless it is "made general."[120] In other words, we can only hope to bring about a "more equitable and enlightened social order" if a democratic education reaches "all agencies and influences that shape disposition," and if "every place in which men habitually meet—shop, club, factory, saloon, church, political caucus—is perforce a school house, even though not so labeled."[121]

The implication here was that education was a lifelong process, perhaps beginning in the schoolhouse but continuing into adulthood, shaping our habits of mind and conduct. While the school may introduce us to democratic practices, there is no substitute for actual civic participation. The concept of "learning by doing" applies here: participation represents the best way to develop and sustain democratic habits. In other words, the best school of democracy is democracy itself. Dewey maintained a faith throughout his life that democracy could transform its participants both intellectually and morally.

Because Dewey did not subscribe to any first principles or fixed ends, the only moral aim for which the democratically educated person should strive was growth or development itself, the process of learning new perspectives and ideas throughout his life and engaging in creative activities for his own self-realization. We should never rest comfortably at a particular end, as if it were our ultimate goal in life, the Holy Grail of our quest. The process of developing ourselves is the end. "The process of growth, of improvement and progress, rather than the static outcome and result, becomes the significant thing," said Dewey. "The end is no longer a terminus or limit to be reached. It is the active process of transforming the existent situation. Not perfection as a final goal, but the ever-enduring process of perfecting, maturing, refining is the aim in living. . . . Growth itself is the only moral 'end.'"[122]

Critics have often suggested that growth of any kind, no matter how morally repugnant, could meet this standard. A burglar, for instance, could continually improve his skills and add new techniques to his repertoire. But Dewey argued that individual growth demands creative, enriching activity that releases the participant from past problems. His success depends on the degree to which he connects with nature and other people. Burglary could never promote individual growth because it severs connections between the perpetrator and the society in which he operates, making it impossible for him to address fundamental problems in his life.[123]

People could only enjoy true growth if they lived in a community in which people shared a variety of interests with others in their social group and also communicated openly with people who belonged to other groups. The degree to which someone has met this standard of growth depends on his answers to the following questions posed by Dewey: "How numerous and varied are the interests which are consciously shared? How full and free is the interplay with other forms of association?" A criminal band, Dewey argued, does not meet the standard very well, for it has few common interests that tie its members together, and the nature of their work isolates them from other groups. "Hence, the education such a society gives is partial and distorted." Its members will never grow in the true sense of the word.[124]

In comparison to the criminal band, Dewey gave the example of a family that does meet the standard and thus promotes growth among its members. This family shares "material, intellectual, aesthetic interests" to such an extent that "the progress of one member has worth for the experience of other members." In addition, the family "is not an isolated whole, but enters intimately into relationships with business groups, with schools, with all the agencies of culture, as well as other similar groups." The members of this family grow because "there are many interests consciously communicated and shared; and there are varied and free points of contact with other modes of association."[125] As Dewey saw it, this example showed that the standards for growth "point to democracy."[126]

A despotic state fails to foster growth because the official use of terror alienates citizens from each other and their leaders, which means that "there is no extensive number of common interests; there is no free play back and forth among the members of the social group. Stimulation and response are exceedingly one-sided." The members of a group can only share a large number of interests if they all enjoy "an equable opportunity to receive and to take from others. There must be a large variety of shared undertakings and experiences. Otherwise, the influences which educate some into masters, educate others into slaves."[127] A despotic state also isolates itself from other nations, which leads to hardened dispositions—or to the "rigidity and formal institutionalization of life."[128]

Democracy, on the other hand, ensures participation in collective action for all its members and promotes intergroup communication to introduce fresh perspectives in the community. Thus, democracy was the ideal social and political order in which its members could experience growth. "A democracy," said Dewey, "is more than a form of government; it is primarily a mode of associated living, of conjoint communicated experience." This results in a "liberation of powers which remain suppressed as long as the incitations to action are partial."[129]

In the end, Dewey's psychology speaks to the transformative power of democratic participation. A society that makes provisions for widespread civic participation and periodically readjusts its customs and institutions releases energies within its members and develops their moral and intellectual capacities to untold heights. "Democracy has many meanings," Dewey said, "but if it has moral meaning, it is found in resolving that the supreme test of all political institutions and industrial arrangements shall be the contribution they make to the all-around growth of every member of society." Because each of us can achieve selfhood only in a social context, we search for a "mode of associated living" that does not leave us at the mercy of remote economic or political forces but instead empowers us to partake in the making of this world of which we are an inextricable part. This is the very meaning of democracy.

In one of his more memorable passages, Dewey compared associated life to cultivating a garden: "To gain an integrated individuality, each of us needs to cultivate his own garden. But there is no fence about this garden: it is no sharply marked-off enclosure. Our garden is the world, in the angle at which it touches our own manner of being." To achieve individuality and freedom, a person must "cultivate his own garden," even though it cannot be enclosed and completely protected from outside intrusion. He must learn to accept the entire "corporate and industrial world" as a garden that must be shared, and he must contribute, in whatever way he can, to its cultivation. In the process of working collectively to "create an unknown future," he will create himself.[130]

## Free Will

That man will pick up his shovel or hoe and begin working in his garden Dewey almost took for granted. Indeed, his democratic metaphysics was robust. If he devoted little attention to the question of free will or choice, it was because the answer seemed all too obvious to him. He understood intuitively that his faith in democracy would be unthinkable without the belief that human beings could make free choices, drawing on their intelligence to shape their own destiny.

Like James, Dewey found middle ground between the atomism of empiricist philosophy and the monism of various mechanistic and idealist thinkers. Particularistic empiricism rested on the notion that entities in this universe have the capacity to act solely from their own powers and initiative. From this view, the universe appears completely indeterminate and chaotic, teeming with spontaneity but lacking any coherence or meaning. Monism, on the other hand, posited that entities are part of a large interactive system, acting not with self-initiative but in a predetermined way. Whether the system was mechanistic or idealist, this implied a "block universe" in which human freedom was sheer illusion.

Dewey found neither outlook very appealing as a way to describe the human condition. "For no living creature could survive, save by sheer accident, if its experiences had no more reach, scope or content, than the traditional particularistic empiricism provided for. On the other hand, it is impossible to imagine a living creature coping with the universe all at once." As an alternative, he offered "a *via media* between extreme atomistic pluralism and block universe monisms."[131] He saw experience as a transaction, a back-and-forth exchange between human beings who take on certain functions within a larger social organism. Human beings enjoyed freedom to make choices and exercise influence, but always in a social context. The social aspect of free choice notwithstanding, Dewey argued that "all deliberate choices and plans are finally the work of single human beings."[132]

On the subject of free will Peirce and James often invoked Darwinism, suggesting that the doctrine of chance variation could explain spontaneous choice, and although Dewey agreed with this idea in principle, he contributed some original insights to the discussion. In his view, every human being has the capacity to transcend biological and social influences, act with a certain degree of spontaneity, modify his habits, perhaps even have an effect on his social environment. Most thinkers regarded instincts as a set of biological conditions that placed severe constraints on human freedom, but Dewey thought instincts actually liberated us: "Impulses are the pivots upon which the re-organization of activities turn, they are agencies of deviation, for giving new directions to old habits and changing their quality."[133] Once unleashed, instincts obliterate crusty old habits in which we have become mired. Without the liberating energy of instinct, we would remain slaves to our habits. But our "impulses are too chaotic, tumultuous and confused" if left on their own, for they rush "blindly into any opening" they find and show no discrimination in seeking an "outlet."[134] In order to make our instincts work for us, we must harness them with our intelligence, giving them direction and structure. As Dewey said: "Breach in the crust of the cake of custom releases impulses, but it is the work of intelligence to find the ways of using them."[135]

The first step in this process is deliberation, rehearsing in our imagination various ways of acting, either in accordance with "prior habit" or "newly released impulse." We finally make a "choice" when "some habit, or some combination of elements of habits and impulse, finds a way fully open."[136] Rejecting James's belief that we could simply break old habits through the sheer exercise of will, Dewey argued that free choice was a matter of careful reflection, employing intelligence (scientific method) to mediate between our habits and impulses. A person who wants to exercise free choice has to discover why he has acted in certain undesirable ways in the past and then devise means of releasing those latent impulses that can effect change. This involves creating the right social conditions under which he can break his bad habits and forge new and better ones. He relies on his impulses to fuel novelty, but he uses his intelligence to channel them constructively:

> What intelligence has to do in the service of impulse is to act not as its obedient servant but as its clarifier and liberator. And this can be accomplished only by a study of the conditions and causes, the workings and consequences of the greatest possible variety of desires and combinations of desire. Intelligence converts desire into plans, systematic plans based on assembling facts, reporting events as they happen, keeping tab on them and analyzing them.[137]

Dewey's argument is simple: we are free to the extent that we act in the spirit of the scientific method to convert our desires or impulses into plans. This suggests that man liberates himself further in a democracy, which gives him the power to exercise his intelligence and solve problems alongside his fellow citizens. "There is an intrinsic connection between choice as freedom and the power of action as freedom," he said.[138] In other words, a person's free will depends in large measure on the amount of positive freedom—or political power—that he enjoys.

## Conclusion

Dewey emerges in this chapter as the essential link between classical pragmatism and participatory democracy. He said himself that "any theory of activity in social and moral matters, liberal or otherwise, which is not grounded in a comprehensive philosophy, seems to me to be only a projection of arbitrary personal preferences."[139] I have simply taken him at his word and sought to uncover the philosophical foundation of his political theory. My analysis shows that the three tenets found in the thought of Peirce and James—the democratic epistemology, psychology, and metaphysics—were crucial to the formation of his political theory. A striking irony emerges: pragmatists boast of their anti-foundationalism, their belief that human beings can lead more productive and meaningful lives, devoid of intolerance and social injustice, if they reject first principles and fixed truths and focus more on the means to achieving a better life. But the democratic way of life for which Dewey showed so much preference actually rests on three first principles drawn from the pragmatist tradition. This irony suggests (at the risk of abusing Mark Twain's phraseology) that rumors about the anti-foundational bent of pragmatism and participatory democratic thought have been greatly exaggerated.

The irony also points to a tension within participatory democratic thought, whose advocates criticize liberalism for making specious assumptions about the human condition but then cannot avoid doing the same. In their attempt to construct a politics without foundations, they have merely substituted new absolutes for old ones. This raises serious questions about the viability and theoretical coherence of participatory democracy (as we shall see in Chapter 7).

The most ardent proponents of participatory democracy who came in Dewey's wake, including C. Wright Mills and his New Left acolytes, began to see cracks in the foundation. They subscribed to the pragmatist tenets but not without serious reservations, especially for the democratic metaphysics. They feared that bureaucratic systems of organization and control foreclosed opportunities for meaningful political participation. As a result, they often favored confrontational political action in order to invigorate publics and to challenge an increasingly recalcitrant state. Mills became the most renowned spokesperson for this kind of strenuous democratic action outside the state, inspiring a generation of student activists. But as even this more aggressive strategy failed to bear much fruit, the New Left's admiration for participatory democracy began to exceed their hope for its realization.

# C. Wright Mills

*The Oracle of the New Left*

C. Wright Mills (1916–1962) is often regarded as the most prominent luminary—some would say "prophet" or "godfather"—of the academic New Left, for his influence on the student radicals of the 1960s was unrivaled.[1] His attack on the American political establishment for its elitism and exclusionary practices resonated with many young activists who came of age in the late 1950s and early 1960s, including many of the early leaders of Students for a Democratic Society (SDS). One would have been hard-pressed to find a student radical who did not own a dog-eared copy of *The Power Elite* (1956), which SDS leader Paul Booth referred to as "the Bible" of the student movement. Bob Ross recalled the devastating, even revelatory, impact of the book on his worldview: "I remember finishing it late one night and walking out into this cold, snowy dawn, crying. I was already in SDS, already was committed to this notion of participatory democracy, and this Leviathan had been portrayed to me. I walked the streets weeping. What can we do? Is this our fate?"[2]

Sensitive to their own alienation and powerlessness, the student radicals gained a measure of strength, and drew inspiration, from Mills's answer: *this* did not have to be their fate. Toward the end of his career, Mills articulated a faith in students as potential agents of change, in their ability to defeat this Leviathan, to act of their own free will and remake history. They learned from Mills that they could become the masters of fate through collective action, that both the short- and long-term solution to America's woes was the deep and widespread practice of democracy. This message gave rise to their own call for participatory democracy in the *Port Huron Statement* and in many other publications and speeches.

Although Mills never used the term, he made his participatory democratic ethos quite clear by continually stressing the importance of citizen engagement and participation. For Mills, democracy meant far more than periodic elections and the protection of rights by the government. Democracy required ongoing face-to-face discussion, not just among elected representatives but among all citizens, who ultimately shared the responsibility of self-government and, to some extent, played a role in decision-making and policy implementation.

In developing his democratic theory, Mills owed a great intellectual debt to the pragmatists. He earned a bachelor's degree in sociology and a master's in philosophy at the University of Texas, where he studied under three pragmatists, all of whom received their doctorates in philosophy at the University of Chicago. In 1938, the year before he began his doctoral work in sociology at the University of Wisconsin, he conceded the influence of pragmatism on his thinking: "My intellectual godfathers were pragmatists; when I first awoke I discovered myself among them."[3]

Throughout his career Mills continued to operate under many of the pragmatist assumptions about knowledge, human nature, and free will, and he drew heavily on Dewey's concept of the public to formulate his own democratic theory. Mills would later part company with pragmatism on some issues, particularly on their giving priority to method at the expense of ends. He also found pragmatists largely mute on the question of power—who had it and what they did with it. Consequently, he turned to other traditions and thinkers from whom he gained invaluable insights. Without the influence of such figures as Karl Marx, Max Weber, and Thorstein Veblen he would never have developed such penetrating insights into the power structure of American political and economic institutions. Most important, these men informed his critique of the system. But his democratic solution to the problem relied heavily on pragmatism —a philosophical outlook that infused him with the conviction that the search for truth is a never-ending social enterprise, that human beings are educable creatures with almost limitless potential, and that they have the capacity to control their own destinies if given the means to do so.

The influence of pragmatism on Mills was so strong that he would become—as his friend and colleague Irving Horowitz described him—the "embodiment of Jamesian Man." Like William James, Mills had a "heroic definition of self" and a "faith in intellectual activity as a way out of the morass of power." He believed that intellectuals should always eschew "narrow professionalism," by continually asking themselves whether their work has a larger social and political relevance.[4]

Mills also brought the Jamesian ethos of lonely courage and heroism to the way he led his life, cultivating the identity of a rebel, a champion of underdogs and misfits. Adorned in a black leather jacket, the robust and barrel-chested sociologist rode a BMW motorcycle to campus every day, evoking more the image of James Dean from "Rebel without a Cause" than that of a college professor. The craftsman—one who experienced work as an independent and creative process, seeing it through from the point of conception to the final product, and who found joy in his work as an end in itself—represented for Mills the archetype of unalienated man, complete and fulfilled. Hardly an effete intellectual, Mills did not avoid getting his hands dirty to meet his standards of craftsmanship: he built his own house in the suburbs of New York City and routinely repaired his own motorcycle (and once even flew to Germany to get advice from BMW engineers). Mills reached the pinnacle of craftsmanship as an intellectual, however, expressing his ideas with a distinctive voice and muscular prose. Always mindful that ideas should never stray too far from experience, that ideas are guidelines for action, he sought to make an impact with his writing and took pains to reach a broader audience. He regarded his words and ideas as tools that people could use in the attempt to refashion American democracy. Like James, he was the consummate public intellectual.

In many ways, Mills's most striking similarity to James can be seen in his disdain for bigness in all its institutional forms. The recurring theme in his work is unmistakable: opportunities for citizens to control their own destinies, either individually in their private lives or collectively through democratic institutions, have come under attack by the rise of large bureaucratic organizations in both public and private sectors. Mills dedicated his career to raising awareness about the insidious growth of these bureaucratic structures, which operate under the direction of an increasingly centralized and exclusive authority.

Largely invisible to the American people, this authority (or "power elite," as Mills called it) enjoys considerable freedom to implement policies that conform to its own set of narrow interests. Although not a small, unified cabal of conspirators, the power elite—consisting of high-level leaders from corporate, military, and political circles—share a common interest in the perpetuation of a "permanent war economy." America's supposedly democratic system, Mills warned, has no measures of accountability, which means that the power elite faces no real obstacles to its militaristic agenda. Meanwhile, the majority of Americans are at best only vaguely aware of their powerless condition. As Mills put it: "The powers of ordinary men are circumscribed by the everyday worlds in which they live, yet even in these rounds of job, family, and neighborhood they often seem driven by forces they can neither understand nor govern."[5] As Mills was wont to remind his readers, this courts disaster in a nuclear age.

Although many undoubtedly dismissed Mills as a shrill alarmist after the publication of his most famous book, *The Power Elite,* he must have felt vindicated when President Eisenhower delivered his farewell address in 1961, warning Americans of the "conjunction of an immense military establishment and a large arms industry," whose "influence—economic, political, even spiritual—is felt in every city, every State house, every office of the Federal government." While Eisenhower accepted the need for the expansion of our military in the wake of World War II, he stressed that we "must not fail to comprehend its grave implications," and that we must "guard against the acquisition of unwarranted influence, whether sought or unsought, by the military-industrial complex." Eisenhower added ominously: "The potential for the disastrous rise of misplaced power exists and will persist."[6]

The resemblance of the departing president's message to what Mills had been writing for years was uncanny: it was as if one of the most celebrated members of the power elite had had second thoughts and decided to expose his associates and shine a light on their sinister activities. But unlike Eisenhower, Mills did not accept the necessity of American Cold War policy. He maintained that only radical political reconstruction could redirect us from our ill-fated course.

## Reclaiming the American Pastoral

As he began to formulate his radical political project, Mills soon realized he could turn to neither Marxism nor liberalism for guidance. Both ideologies clung to outdated notions bearing little resemblance to the reality of human experience in the twentieth century. Mills would have to draw on other traditions—including pragmatism, republicanism, and Weberian critical theory—in his valiant attempt to create a "New Left" that would challenge the alarming trend toward bigger, more bureaucratized institutions dominated by an increasingly centralized authority. The student radicals who eventually assumed the mantle of the New Left were drawn to Mills because he spoke to their frustration with these outdated traditions, which they believed had been effectively discredited by history. Mills created a new vision of hope, while Marxism and liberalism could only offer platitudes.

Unlike many intellectuals on the left, Mills had a late exposure to Marxist thought, which may have given him the critical distance to discern many of its shortcomings. Just a few years before he died, Mills wrote the following in a letter to a friend: "I've never been emotionally involved with Marxism or communism, never belonged in any sense to it."[7] Perhaps most frustrating about the Old Left was its unwillingness to relinquish tired dogma. Marxists still saw the proletariat as the necessary agent of historical change and waited for the day when labor, having finally become conscious of its exploitation, would rebel against its capitalist oppressors and usher in a classless utopia.

Mills did not find fault with the utopianism of the Marxists, for he believed any worthwhile political philosophy must rest on a radical vision of what could be and ought to be. But he had serious problems with the Marxists' doctrinaire insistence that labor was "The Necessary Lever" of change. The notion that history must unfold in accordance with the inexorable logic of dialectical materialism may have been compelling in the mid-nineteenth century, but in the following century, capitalism proved far more adaptable and resilient than Marx could ever have imagined. Marx dreamed of class revolution, an event that would clear the way for the next and final epoch in human history. It never occurred to him that the rise of the welfare state, which regulated markets, redistributed wealth, and co-opted unions, could effectively satisfy many working-class demands without undermining the capitalist system. Marx never foresaw that the welfare state could postpone class revolution indefinitely.

That capitalism would not inevitably collapse from its own internal contradictions and that labor would not necessarily be the catalyst for this collapse escaped Marxists. All evidence to the contrary, they continued to cling, with surprising obstinacy, to what Mills called the "labor metaphysic." Mills believed that radicals had to think beyond the "labor metaphysic" of the Old Left and embrace a vision that "emphasized the volition of men in the making of history—their history—in contrast to any determinist laws of history and accordingly the lack of individual responsibility."[8] For Mills, the future had not yet been written, and no one person or group was destined to be its principal author.

Mills was particularly critical of those he called "Vulgar Marxists," whose faithful adherence to the labor metaphysic extended to a belief in economic determinism. The Vulgar Marxists believed that economic relationships, the means and modes of production, were the sole determinants of everything in society: political institutions, social arrangements, and both intellectual and cultural achievements. Or, to use Marxist jargon, the economic structure (or base) necessarily preceded the superstructure. Mills agreed that the economic structure played a vital role in shaping society, but he thought Vulgar Marxists mistakenly ignored the fact that non-economic factors influenced social conditions and that the "*interplay* of bases and superstructures" more accurately characterized how history was made.[9]

Escaping the rigid logic of dialectical materialism opened new vistas for radicals and also alerted them to new dangers. First, if the working class failed to awaken from its slumber and challenge the bourgeoisie, and as a result economic relationships remained largely the same, then radicals could find solace in knowing there was more than one way of changing history. Second, having rejected economic determinism, radicals came to realize that changing economic relationships did not necessarily lead to the social utopia envisioned by Marx. The Soviet Union provided an object lesson in the fallacy of economic determinism: the state ownership of capital in Russia ushered in not a golden age but an unprecedented form of totalitarianism. The state could operate independently of economic forces and exercise its power to pursue its own agenda, either benign or malignant.

Despite his many reservations about Marxism, Mills grew to believe that it was an indispensable analytical tool for social scientists and others who hoped to understand the structure of power in modern society and the extent to which moneyed elites shape our world. "No-one who does not come to grips with the ideas of marxism," he wrote, "can be an adequate social scientist."[10] Mills's chief complaint with liberals was that they failed to recognize the power of economic forces. Their complete rejection of Marxism made them blind to the glaring fact that the emergence of large powerful corporations, in whose coffers wealth was increasingly concentrated, not only widened social inequalities but also posed a serious threat to democracy. Liberals naively believed that corporate interests held no more sway over the government than any other groups.

As adherents to the doctrine of pluralism, liberals maintained that the competition for influence among countless groups in the political arena produced a harmonious equilibrium in which policy outcomes reflected public opinion. In other words, pluralism assumed government would comply with the view that prevailed in a fair marketplace of ideas. Mills astutely observed that pluralism is grounded in economic theory:

> The idea parallels the economic idea of the magical market. Here is the market composed of freely competing entrepreneurs; there is the public composed of circles of people in discussion. As price is the result of anonymous, equally weighted, bargaining individuals, so public opinion is the result of each man's having thought things out for himself and then contributing his voice to the great chorus.[11]

Although this model may have accurately described American politics in the eighteenth and early nineteenth centuries, it had long since diverged from any semblance of reality. In the economic realm, monopolies and oligopolies upset the balance of the price-setting mechanism in the free market. Similarly, these same corporations and other powerful elites exercised undue influence in the political arena, effectively muting the weaker segments of the public. Policies, then, end up reflecting not public opinion but elite prerogatives. Despite the harsh realities enacted right before their eyes, liberals continued to believe that the American political system followed the pluralist model.

Mills argued that this was because classical liberal theory rested on a number of outmoded assumptions about the conditions of society. Many liberals assumed that Americans inhabited a "world of small entrepreneurs," where the vast majority of citizens owned property that served as the means to their livelihood. It was as if the liberal imagination were mired in a mythical past, when America was a sparse nation of virtuous self-made men, each of whom enjoyed equal rights and a rough equality of conditions. Liberals envisioned a world in which liberty and equality went hand in hand: set people free to run their own affairs as they please, and wealth and power will spread somewhat evenly throughout the land.

In the eighteenth and early nineteenth centuries, unfettered access to and independent use of property may have been the wellspring of individual freedom, but in the wake of industrialization, "absolute liberty to control property has become tyranny." This means that the very "meaning of freedom, positively put, has to be restated now, not as independence, but as control over that upon which the individual is dependent."[12] The reality of modern life is that most individuals are dependent on large corporations or other institutions for their livelihood. If we do not devise ways to place limits on the property liberties of these corporations, the anxiety-ridden wage earner remains subject to their arbitrary decisions, and the state falls increasingly under their domain.

Liberals also assumed mistakenly that "the individual is the seat of rationality." In accordance with the principles of the Enlightenment, they believed that every man has at his disposal the power of reason to control his own fate, and that the intellectual advances of humankind always reflect back on the individual, elevating both his dignity and his wisdom. But the reality is that "the increase of enlightenment does not necessarily wise up the individual." Instead, the increase of enlightenment may produce the rationalized organization, the "bureaucratic organization of knowledge," which sadly is the case in the postmodern world. A casualty of this trend is the enlightened individual. Weber understood rationalization to be the ability to imagine a better world than the one we inhabit and to devise means by which we can make reality accord with our imagination. The Enlightenment presupposed the individual as the agent of rationalization, but Weber astutely observed that bureaucracy had eclipsed the individual in carrying out this function. As a result, said Mills, the individual no longer represents a "lever for progressive change," and liberal society relies increasingly on rationalized organizations.[13]

In the end, classical liberalism upheld wonderful ideals—a society teeming with free, virtuous, diligent, rational individuals who enjoyed a rough equality of conditions—but functioned poorly as a theory, because it confused ideals with reality. One might think that Mills would have embraced modern liberalism as a necessary corrective—achieving Jeffersonian ends, which are held so dear among classical liberals, by applying

Hamiltonian means. After all, Mills had great disdain for large corporations, and it would seem only a powerful state could bring them under control and curb their excesses. But Mills rejected the very premise that Jeffersonian ends could be achieved by Hamiltonian means. The large, powerful state relies increasingly on a bureaucracy whose experts and technocrats carry out its tasks at a high level of administrative efficiency, but its procedures and routines foreclose opportunities for local, citizen-based democracy. "Post-war liberalism," said Mills, "has been organizationally impoverished: the pre-war years of liberalism-in-power devitalized independent liberal groups, drying up their grass roots, making older leaders dependent upon the federal center and not training new leaders round the country." Mills blamed the New Deal even more for turning "liberalism into a set of administrative routines to defend rather than a program to fight for."[14]

After World War II, liberals came to believe that the chief lesson to be drawn from the examples of Nazi Germany and Stalinist Russia was that any kind of ideological program was dangerous. Daniel Bell, the former City College Trotskyite who became the most ardent defender of liberalism, called ideologues "terrible simplifiers" who found it "unnecessary . . . to confront individual issues on their individual merits." They simply turn on "the ideological vending machine, and out comes prepared formulae. And when these beliefs are suffused by apocalyptic fervor, ideas become weapons, and with dreadful results."[15] Along with many other liberals in his camp, Bell declared the "end of ideology." Because the big questions of political philosophy had been answered, the West could focus its efforts globally on containing the communist scourge and domestically on fine-tuning our liberal democratic institutions and capitalist economy.

The dominant mood of liberalism reflected a wariness of moral passion and a downright fear of utopian thinking. It was far safer to operate within the confines of the modern liberal orthodoxy, in which the welfare state made modest efforts to regulate markets and improve the lot of working Americans but never sought to overreach in the hope of re-creating heaven on earth. As liberalism had become the dominant (if not the *only*) political tradition in the United States, both the left and the right agreed to remain within these narrow parameters. Their differences of opinion were not fundamental but rather matters of emphasis.[16]

The declaration that ideology had simply run its course, no longer bearing relevance in the postwar world, outraged Mills. He believed such a sentiment masked the complacency of liberalism and its lazy acceptance of the status quo and, perhaps most disturbing, reflected a cynical opportunism among liberal intellectuals who had become intoxicated by their proximity to power. Mills claimed that "the end-of-ideology is of course itself an ideology," a mere "slogan of complacency" that reflected "the ideology of an ending: the ending of political reflection itself as a public fact."[17]

Forever fearful of a morally animated public, Bell and others extolled an ideology of political quietude and apathy for the masses and of technocratic engagement for an elite few. They presupposed that the people could not be responsible agents of historical change, that they were easy targets of manipulation for would-be demagogues and tyrants. The final lesson of the end-of-ideology apologists was that the masses should remain fragmented and sluggish so that they would be less prone to getting swept up in the thrill of the political moment. No doubt, images of the infamous Nuremberg rallies were not far from their minds. But according to Mills, their fears betrayed a profoundly anti-democratic ideology that had its own dire consequences.

Much to Mills's dismay, the political system in the United States frustrated democratic majorities at every turn without ever eliciting the discontent of its citizenry. So long as they enjoyed a reasonable level of material well-being, most Americans eschewed political concerns and remained quite content to delegate the responsibilities of governance to their elected officials and the vast administrative bureaucracy. When these institutions did fail them, citizens perked up just enough to demand a housecleaning, perhaps a change in personnel, or the passage of a few laws with more symbolic than substantive value. But they never thought to see the problem as structural, or to effect change at the foundational level.

This general lack of civic engagement enabled a fairly small group of elites to seize the reins of government and—focusing entirely on their own short-term interests—set it on a disastrously militaristic course. It is worth noting that Mills's power elite thesis represented a departure from Marx, who believed that the state acted solely at the behest of the ruling class, the principal owners of capital. Unrestrained by communist doctrine, Mills identified a power elite that comprised leaders from not only economic but also political and military circles.

His repudiation of Marxism notwithstanding, Mills conceded that the economic circle was the most powerful of the triumvirate. Including executives, major stockholders, and corporate lawyers from the two or three hundred largest corporations in the country, this group controlled most of the nation's property and assets. With these immense resources at their disposal, they exercised nearly limitless power over the economy, and over anything or anyone that might affect it. Their chief aim, Mills claimed, was to expand into the global economy in their insatiable quest for more wealth and higher profits.

Second in line were the military officers who held the rank of brigadier general or higher, as well as a few high-ranking civilians in the Department of Defense. Since the outbreak of World War II, the military brass in the United States had overseen a growing bureaucracy, which perpetuated the view that most foreign policy problems demanded military solutions, not artful diplomacy. The upshot of this trend was that a "military metaphysic" permeated American society, in which "all policies and actions fall within the perspective of war" and "all world reality is defined in military terms."[18]

The last and usually least powerful group, according to Mills, included the most influential members of the executive branch: the president, his cabinet, and approximately fifteen hundred of the highest-ranking or most trusted political appointees serving on the White House staff or in the federal bureaucracy. These political elites represented a centralized authority with a vast government bureaucracy under its command. Their raison d'etre was purely Machiavellian—to attain and hold on to power. As a result, they redefined problems of governance as mere issues of administration, or efficiency, and promoted the expansion of the bureaucracy, which would assume more and more responsibility.

Although as the law-making branch of government it was ostensibly the most deliberative and democratic, Mills believed that Congress had declined in stature since its heyday in the nineteenth century. On economic issues it had become increasingly beholden to corporate interests; on ostensibly technical matters it had made a point of delegating its authority to the executive branch; and on military affairs it deferred almost completely to the Department of Defense. Individual members of Congress—perennial seekers of reelection—focused their energies on parochial district- or state-level concerns, not on vital national issues. In the end, the branch of government that was originally designed to raise public consciousness about the most important issues of the day, with spirited discussion and thoughtful deliberation, had abdicated its responsibility—and become effectively mute.[19]

Meanwhile, a small group of powerful elites made history without being held accountable for their actions. Although not in perfect harmony, the interests of these three groups coincided to a large extent, which allowed for a significant measure of cooperation to achieve their common objectives. By the mid-twentieth century the different circles of the power elite came to realize that they each benefited from what Mills called "the permanent war economy," in which the United States would always be at war, on high alert for imminent war, or preparing for a future war.[20] "The American elite does not have any real image of peace—other than as an uneasy interlude existing precariously by virtue of the balance of fright," wrote Mills. "The only seriously accepted plan for 'peace' is the fully loaded pistol. In short, war or a high state of war-preparedness is felt to be the normal and seemingly permanent condition of the United States."[21] This state of affairs allowed each group to realize its objective: the American military elevated its stature, big corporations fattened their profits from government contracts, and politicians received credit for maintaining a healthy and robust economy.

This last point is a particularly important part of Mills's argument, for it explains why the modern liberal state has come to embrace the permanent war economy. Modern liberals shared a common concern about the volatility of the capitalist system, and its tendency to experience boom-bust cycles, which often inflicted great harm on society's most vulnerable. But they soon recognized the permanent war economy as a panacea for this problem. Adopting a conspicuously Keynesian approach, the state spent huge portions of its revenue on the military and thereby infused money back into the economy to keep it strong. Always either preparing for or fighting a war came at a steep cost, however, especially in the nuclear age. It not only militarized American society, cultivating fierce anti-communist hysteria that threatened civil liberties and enforced rigid conformity with social mores, it also aroused disproportionately hawkish views that led humanity down a path, at least potentially, to world annihilation. While an arms race that inflamed tensions between the two great powers may have been patently absurd, liberals had difficulty finding fault with this strategy because it created jobs and raised wages for all Americans, including the labor class. Their scholarly justifications for Cold War foreign policy notwithstanding, liberals had acquiesced to the military metaphysic largely in order to avert economic downturns and their political consequences. Conservatives—or what Mills called the "practical right"—had no need for intellectual rationalizations; their widening profit margin was more than enough justification for nuclear brinkmanship and military adventurism.

According to Mills, the power elite held more in common than just the benefits of the permanent war economy. They also shared "social and psychological affinities" stemming from their common origins, professional milieu, and lifestyles.[22] Whichever power elite circle they belonged to, members generally hailed from the native-born, Protestant upper classes. Their fathers had typically enjoyed success either in the professions or in business, which placed their families in the top third of the income distribution. The vast majority held undergraduate degrees, typically from one of the Ivy League colleges (or, in the case of the military, one of the academies).

Although members of the power elite did not resemble a European-style aristocracy, a small group of nobles sharing hereditary origins and defined by strict codes of honor and chivalry, they were hardly a representative cross section of American society. Sharing a similar social origin and formal education meant that members of the power elite started with the same set of values and modes of communication, which enabled them to build trust and mutual regard more easily. These were people who interacted with familiar tones, getting to know each other quite well in the process:

Their continued association further cements what they feel they have in common. Members of the several higher circles know one another as personal friends and even as neighbors; they mingle with one another on the golf course, in the gentleman's clubs, at resorts, on transcontinental airplanes, and on ocean liners. They meet at the estates of mutual friends, face each other in front of the TV camera, or serve on the same philanthropic committee; and many are sure to cross one another's path in the columns of newspapers.[23]

Hailing from similar backgrounds, the power elite in America became tighter still by mingling in the same circles and enjoying the same activities and pastimes. In the end, these amiable relationships facilitated more effortless coordination among elites.

Mills certainly painted a portrait of familiarity—even intimacy—within the power elite, but he also took pains to stress that its members did not often act in a conspiratorial fashion. Its key figures did not meet clandestinely in any underground lair, smoking cigars and sipping brandy as they hashed out the particulars of the next war. Rather, each circle had its own set of priorities, which often created tension, even downright conflict. Coinciding interests and mutual "social and psychological affinities" could never foster agreement on every issue.

But for Mills, talk about conspiracies was really beside the point. As he saw it, power should not be understood as a monolithic force that moved unwaveringly or with perfect unity toward an intended goal. Indeed, the power elite did not require the benefits of a monolithic unity or a well-organized conspiracy in order to gain a profound influence on government policy and on society generally. The interests of these men coincided enough to form a coherent agenda, their common origins and values made coordination more fluent, and their dominion over the key political and economic institutions made it possible to put their program into effect.

So, how could the power elite successfully accomplish its objectives without any popular backlash? It would seem that, if they were truly ignored by the power elite, the people would make their voices heard at the ballot box. They would elect leaders who listened to them. The answer to this question becomes apparent in Mills's discussion of how publics are formed. To develop this idea, Mills turned to the writings of Dewey, especially *The Public and Its Problems*.

Dewey defined a public as a group of people who suffered from the indirect, usually unintended, consequences of a private transaction. Victim of what economists call externality, the public coalesces in an attempt to address the problem facing it. Residents of a local community form a public, for example, if a nearby factory empties pollutants into a river where they like to fish or swim. Demanding justice, the public will call upon the government to address the problem and will hold the factory owners accountable. Dewey was quick to point out, however, that a response from the government required an ever watchful public infused with democratic habits.

Mills considered the idea of publics invaluable, but unlike Dewey, he focused more of his attention on threats to their existence. In his view, what was once a community of publics was slowly being transformed into a society of masses. Largely indifferent to politics, and unaware of the externalities from which they suffer, the masses were eclipsing knowledgeable and astute publics. The dangers arising from this trend were unmistakable: a society of masses gave the power elite far more latitude to pursue its agenda with impunity. According to Mills, our democratic heritage was under siege.

Not really concerned about historical precision, Mills would often use Weberian "ideal-types" to imaginatively reconstruct America's past.[24] He painted captivating pictures of what America once was and what it might become, of its utopian origins and its dystopian future, of its bygone community of publics and its emerging society of masses. Mills's version of American history revealed a country moving steadily along a continuum, away from its blissful democratic origins and toward a bleak totalitarian future.

In his standard narrative, the America of the eighteenth and early nineteenth centuries beheld vibrant democratic communities in which public matters continually occupied the minds and energies of a virtuous citizenry. Still chiefly rural in character, with a vast frontier awaiting settlers to tame it, America offered everyone the opportunity to earn an honest living, either as farmer or tradesman, through the diligent use of his own property. Not beholden to any other man, the American inhabited a society of rough equals and thus could enter the political arena on a par with his fellow citizens and discuss matters of public import.

A notable characteristic of a society of publics is that "virtually as many people express opinions as receive them," which requires "public communications [to be] so organized that there is a chance immediately and effectively to answer back to any opinion expressed in public." Not just passive recipients of a mass media that bombards them with distorted information and manipulated images, citizens engage in productive discussion and have an equal opportunity to influence the opinions of others. Out of these face-to-face deliberations emerges public opinion, which will then ultimately be reflected in policy outcomes. If not, the public will find "an outlet in effective action against . . . prevailing systems and agents of authority" to bring about a more satisfactory political arrangement.[25] Through all this activity, the public remains autonomous, free of any infiltration by the authoritative institutions of either the state or the corporate world. The picture painted by Mills was none other than the pluralist ideal.

This American pastoral gave way, however, to a stark world of faceless bureaucracies instituting administrative procedures and mechanical routines: a world of alienated people relying on large, labyrinthine organizations to act on their behalf and provide a source of income. As employees, these people become insignificant parts of a large bureaucratic machine of which they can never have more than a superficial understanding and on which they can never make a significant impact. As citizens, they become mere supplicants to a state that usually ignores their appeals and gives preference to a shadowy elite.

Rather than a public, the people in this "opposite extreme" constitute a "mass." In a mass society, "far fewer people express opinions than receive them," for people become mere passive recipients of the opinions conveyed on television and the radio or in newsprint. In effect, the mass media turns opinion-making into a "one-way transmission," in which most people are exposed to the ideas of a small elite but are never given a chance to reply in kind.

If people do become frustrated with the government or their corporate employers, they meet countless obstacles that have been erected by the authorities to obstruct the organizing of any effective political action—or even the expression of alternative points of view. Authorities control most of the key "channels" of communication and organization, including not only the media but also publishers, educational institutions, theaters, meetinghouses, as well as the mail and telephone, all of which prove indispensable in mounting effective political opposition.

Those people who manage to organize a resistance—or perhaps just come together to engage in fruitful discussion—never enjoy complete independence. They remain forever vulnerable to infiltration by "agents of authorized institutions" who short-circuit any "autonomy [they] may have in the formation of opinion by discussion." Although the United States had not yet sunk to these depths, Mills clearly believed it was moving in that direction. Once a democracy, America had now become an oligarchy controlled by a power elite. In his eyes, the "opposite extreme," totalitarianism, was not so very far off.[26]

The political and existential malaise afflicting most Americans presented the most telling evidence of their slide toward totalitarianism. They no longer believed that political action could solve their problems. Thus, they withdrew into their private lives and focused their energies on things they thought they could control—primarily job and family. They deferred increasingly to the "experts" who occupied impressive-sounding positions in the government bureaucracy or who held court in the mass media. Disengaged from public concerns, America was now a nation of "idiots." Indeed, Mills claimed, most people "pay no attention to politics of any kind." Lacking any kind of political affiliation, "[t]hey are not radical, not liberal, not conservative, not reactionary. They are inactionary.

They are out of it. If we accept the Greek's definition of the idiot as an altogether private man, then we must conclude that many American citizens are now idiots."[27] What angered Mills so much was that this idiocy played right into the hands of the power elite, who had no real worries about political resistance. Challenging the status quo or working to bring about fundamental change to the system was inconceivable to the vast majority of Americans. Instead, they continued to work within the current system in the hope of wresting what little they could from it.

The labor class was a case in point. In his most comprehensive treatment of the labor movement, *The New Men of Power* (1948), Mills portrayed a group of leaders who had become too chummy with the power elite to pose any serious challenge to its authority. Much to his chagrin, America's labor leaders had readily entered into an alliance with big business, accepting the permanent war economy as a way to avoid recession or to recover from it, so long as their rank and file received a share of the plunder in the form of higher wages and better benefits. The labor leaders had become crude opportunists who only wanted a larger piece of the American Dream for themselves and their constituents. No longer did they regard the American Dream with a critical eye or imagine a different world that could materialize only through major political and economic reconstruction. Drawing on Thorstein Veblen's theory of pecuniary emulation, Mills described how the labor class had shed its radical stance and begun to imitate the values and lifestyle of the upper classes.

Mills placed much of the blame on the labor leaders: they had failed to educate the rank and file to think more radically. Not surprisingly Mills placed little faith in the labor class as an agent of historical change. At the end of *The New Men of Power* he was cautiously optimistic that a new labor party could reinvigorate the movement. By the mid-1950s, however, his hopes were all but dashed. Despairing over what he considered the co-optation of the labor leadership by business and political elites, Mills saw no reason "to believe that they can or will transcend the strategy of maximum adaptation." The reason for their complacency was that "they react more than they lead and that they do so to retain and to expand their position in the constellation of power and advantage."[28]

Mills did not have high hopes for the growing white-collar class either, for its members suffered from a profound alienation and sense of purposelessness, surpassing even that of the proletariat. The following passage from *White Collar* (1951) captures perfectly their wretched state:

> In the case of the white-collar man, the alienation of the wage worker from the products of his work is carried one step nearer to its Kafka-like completion. The salaried employee does not make anything, although he may handle much that he greatly desires but cannot have. No product of craftsmanship

can be his to contemplate with pleasure as it is being created and after it is made. Being alienated from any product of his labor, and going year after year through the same paper routine, he turns his leisure all the more frenziedly to the ersatz diversion that is sold him, and partakes of the synthetic excitement that neither eases [n]or releases. He is bored at work and restless at play, and this terrible alternative wears him out.[29]

Like the hourly worker, the white-collar worker must sell his labor to an employer. But he is even more impoverished spiritually—more alienated—because he pushes paper and presses buttons for a living and has no opportunity even to partake in the process of production. Lost in the bureaucratic maze of the corporate world, he is completely disconnected from the tangible means and ends of his work.

In the idyllic era of eighteenth- and early nineteenth-century America, most men could work their way into the entrepreneurial middle class, using their own property and ingenuity to earn a living. Composed primarily of small farmers, small businessmen, and professionals, members of the middle class enjoyed considerable autonomy and had an intimate familiarity with both the process and the results of their work. But the independent middle-class worker was going the way of the dinosaur. Even the original white-collar worker, the independent professional or small businessman who used his mind and not his hands for a living, could not escape the trend toward centralization of power and wealth in American society. In his place emerged workers who worked for—and were beholden to—large and bureaucratic organizations.

White-collar workers held particular interest for Mills because their dramatic increase in numbers meant they would soon constitute the predominant class in America, and also because their plight was representative of the modern human condition. Indeed, "the troubles that confront white collar people are troubles of all men and women living in the twentieth century." To make matters worse, the prospects for making white-collar workers aware of their state and organizing them for political action were highly unlikely. "Among white-collar people, the malaise is deep-rooted," said Mills; "for the absence of any order or belief has left them morally defenseless as individuals and politically impotent as a group."[30]

Although neither the labor nor the white-collar classes seemed likely agents of historical change, Mills still did not lose heart completely. He believed that the recipe for a "democratic order" was quite simple: "articulate and knowledgeable publics, and political leaders who if not men of reason are at least reasonably responsible to such knowledgeable publics as exist."[31] He believed that his mission in life—as he thought it should be for all social scientists—was to fight the political apathy and inaction that characterized mass society and thereby create the conditions for such a democratic order.

Mills sought to raise awareness about the prevailing power structures in society and, in the process, create knowledgeable publics that would seek meaningful change, and he hoped to do this by shedding light on those larger social and historical forces that shape the biographies of individual lives. He hoped that, with the help of intellectuals and artists endowed with what Mills called the "sociological imagination," people might some day come to see clearly the distinction between their personal troubles and the larger social issues affecting their lives. Troubles, according to Mills, are "private" matters that "occur within the character of the individual and within the range of his immediate relations with others." Issues, on the other hand, are inherently "public" in nature and "transcend these local environments of the individual." They involve "the larger structure of social and historical life." In many cases, an issue can be described as a "crisis in institutional arrangements," in which "some value cherished by publics is felt to be threatened."[32]

Broadly speaking, individuals must accept responsibility for their troubles, but society as a whole must address issues that concern a public and challenge its values. When a person loses his job because he did not get along with his boss, for example, this is a trouble with which society has no business interfering. But if he is the victim of a layoff, along with thousands of others, there may be a larger issue at stake, involving broader structural and institutional arrangements, which threaten the belief that all hard-working Americans deserve a good job and a decent wage.

As Mills saw it, the job of the intellectual is to help the American people make these distinctions and identify the structural and institutional origins of social issues. "What [the social scientist] ought to do for the individual is turn personal troubles and concerns into social issues and problems open to reason—his aim is to help the individual become a self-educating man, who only then would be reasonable and free."[33] The creation of a "self-educating man" is a crucial first step in the formation of a public.

Although intellectuals play such a vital galvanizing role, what sustains publics more than anything else, according to Mills, is face-to-face discussion among their members. From the intense conversation taking place within and among the many publics in American society emerges not only a coherent public opinion but the "general will" of the people—people who turn ideas into effective action. "The key feature of public opinion which the rise of the democratic middle classes initiates is the free ebb and flow of discussion. In this community of publics anyone who would speak, can and anyone who is interested, does." Mills saw "parliament or Congress" as the model for the many "scattered little circles of face-to-face citizens discussing their public business."[34]

Like legislative bodies, publics must comprise active participants who make themselves heard and take pains to turn their ideas into reality. Like legislators, citizens must devote themselves to civic life. It is true, as Mills pointed out, that intellectuals can use the classroom and liberal education to raise awareness about issues and form "self-cultivating publics." But unless citizens engage in continual discussion about the issues that affect their lives, and unless they participate in organized action to address these issues, publics will quickly disintegrate.[35]

Political conversation and action—not just among elites but among *all* citizens—form the glue that prevents publics from fragmenting into a mass society of atomized individuals. For Mills, political conversation and action represented the only means of fostering publics that would assume the mantle of self-governance and hold both government officials and corporate entities accountable. Restoring the vibrant democratic communities of yore required, quite simply, widespread talk and action.

Unfortunately, Mills did not clearly specify how talk and action should be promoted. In his less radical moments, he said that nurturing moribund publics back to life required—in addition to an active intelligentsia —a competent and knowledgeable civil service, responsible national parties, and robust free associations.[36] Innumerable mainstream political thinkers, then and now, have made similar proposals, finding democratic hope in stronger parties or in a renewal of civil society. But in many other instances Mills suggested that these measures were perhaps necessary but hardly sufficient means of forming publics. So he offered more radically democratic proposals as well, calling for a "society in which everyone affected by a social decision, regardless of its sphere, would have a voice in the decision and a hand in its administration." Temporary victories won "by election, revolution, or deals at the top will not be enough," said Mills. "In the day-by-day process of accumulating strength as well as in times of social upset, the power of democratic initiation must be allowed and fostered in the rank and file."[37]

Like Dewey, he became an advocate of Cole's guild socialism, a program that would institutionalize face-to-face discussion and democratic decision-making in the workplace. The workers themselves—not the owners or a central planning committee—would decide by what means and to what ends capital would be used.[38] Mills believed that guild socialism represented a vital part of the plan to derail the permanent war economy and get a "permanent peace economy" on track. Despite his enthusiasm for guild socialism, Mills never offered any details about how a postmodern industrial society might implement workplace democracy. This is probably because he did not want to commit himself to a particular democratic form. He readily conceded that the New Left had "less a program than a collective dream."[39]

In calling for "more direct democracy of daily life," however, Mills clearly endorsed a radical strengthening of political participation, involving as many citizens and workers in the process as possible.[40] Although an ardent advocate of participatory democracy, he suggested that direct citizen engagement in political affairs would not replace representative institutions but rather supplement them. To be sure, when Mills argued that the main purpose of a public was to hold authorities accountable for their actions, he implied that even a radically democratic America would still have a need for leaders and elected officials.

## The Pragmatist Within

Despite his misgivings about pragmatism, Mills's faith in participatory democracy is deeply rooted in the American philosophy. Unlike many of his pragmatist predecessors, Mills was not a philosopher, so he did not write extensively about the epistemological, psychological, and metaphysical assumptions undergirding his political thought. But what he did say about them proves quite revealing, for the pragmatist tenets shine forth in his work.

At times he seemed to overstate his disavowal of the pragmatists, perhaps in order to assert his own intellectual independence, but in truth, he parted company with them only on the last tenet, the democratic metaphysics, and even here the disagreement was a matter of emphasis. Given his belief that modern systems of organization and control restrict free will, he did not believe education and mild-mannered talk alone could galvanize dormant publics to engage in civic life and hold government and private sector leaders accountable for their actions. Accordingly, he endorsed a more confrontational form of political action than Dewey and the other pragmatists ever thought necessary. While man had the capacity for sustained civic engagement, he needed to join a movement that operated outside the system if he wanted to transform himself and the world around him in a fundamental way.

Mills's democratic epistemology becomes apparent in his writings on the sociology of knowledge. In his essay entitled "Methodological Consequences of the Sociology of Knowledge," Mills pointed out that the way people acquire knowledge and make truth claims is historically conditioned. The many systems of empirical verification devised by men are socially formed and are dependent on the social and linguistic context out of which they arise. There is no way to identify the one truly best system. "Criteria, or observational and verificatory models, are not transcendental. They are not drawn theoretically pure from a Greek heaven. . . . Nor are they part of an *a priori,* or innate, equipment of 'the mind' conceived to be intrinsically logical."[41]

Like the pragmatists before him, Mills believed that "empirical verification cannot be a simple and positivistic mirror-like operation." Any verificatory model is the product of "the selective language of its users," and that language leaves behind a "social-historical imprint."[42] Because verificatory models vary according to social-historical conditions, truths derived from these models are also conditional and relative, not universal or absolute. For Mills, truths are not reflections of reality. Language and social norms shape our conceptions of reality—or, in other words, they govern in large part how we actually perceive and evaluate it.

But Mills was not a nominalist. Our "social-historical imprint" may always color our view of reality, but this does not rule out the existence of a reality independent of human consciousness. Our understanding of reality can never be direct or pure; we must draw on the socially conditioned interpretations of our experiences to make sense of it. We rely especially on intellectuals to make sense of the many "ideas, beliefs, images—symbols in short—that stand between men and the wider realities of their time." Indeed, the "intellectual ought to be the moral conscience of his society, at least with reference to the value of truth . . . he ought also to be a man absorbed in the attempt to know what is real and what is unreal."[43] For Mills, truth and the methods of acquiring truth are indeed relative, but the underlying reality of which our truths try to make coherent sense is not. That which is real exists whether we believe in it or not.

That said, no one can ever know for certain whether he has a complete and accurate apprehension of reality. Making truth claims about reality is always a probabilistic affair. Like the pragmatists, Mills argued that all assertions "refer to a degree of truth" and "include the *conditions* under which they are true." In Peircean fashion, he added: "Assertions can properly be stated as probabilities, as more or less true."[44] We can never be completely certain about our truth claims, so we always have to accept their provisional status. As a probabilistic affair, truth acquisition can never work as a solitary enterprise, according to Mills; it requires a community of inquirers collaborating to increase their chances of success. Echoes of Peirce are evident here. Mills admired Peirce largely because he endorsed a method that made "the conditions of successful scientific inquiry exclude selfishness."[45] Acquiring truths is a community activity and cannot be restricted to a few elites, no matter how brilliant. He wrote, "Only through the social confirmation of others whom we believe adequately equipped do we earn the right of feeling secure in our knowledge."[46]

Mills's rejection of the fact-value distinction plays an important role here. Positivists favor the sharp distinction between facts and values and argue that we can never derive how one ought to act (i.e., values) from what we believe is real (i.e., facts). In *Sociology and Pragmatism,* Mills approvingly cited the following line from Dewey to suggest that we should seek praxis, a unity between values and facts through action: "The 'ought' is itself an 'is'—the 'is' of action." Mills wrote:

Around that sentence a great deal of the thought of John Dewey pivots. For the understanding of his total thought it is one of the most important sentences he has ever written: (a) The category of the act, linked with theory, is an answer to the separation of the *is* and the *ought*. And this separation operates elsewhere as science and morals, as science and art or value, etc. It is "action" with which he gets them together. (b) In so using the category of *action*, it becomes the repository of morals. It replaces ought.[47]

This passage suggests that Mills agreed with Dewey and the other pragmatists that we find our values through our actions, from the consequences of our interaction with the factual world. If, for example, a particular activity produces objectionable results, we will label it "bad" in some way. Values do not exist prior to, or independent of, the factual world; they are in fact constitutive of it. But the positivist contends that the fact-value distinction becomes evident when there are two or more parties with competing value systems whose disagreement persists despite exhaustive investigation of the facts. Each party may interpret the facts differently, and there is no higher or objective authority to which the parties can appeal to resolve their conflict.

Even Mills conceded that the final arbiter of truth in such disputes over values is sometimes coercion. "In the end, if the end comes," he said, "we just have to beat those who disagree with us over the head; let us hope the end comes seldom." Fortunately, Mills saw an alternative to violence. "In the meantime," he said, "being as reasonable as we are able to be, we ought all to argue."[48] Reasonable discussion represents the best way to settle differences of opinion and reach a mutually agreeable compromise. As with the pragmatists, Mills's conception of truth is an agreement, however tentative, among members of a community.

This is why he decries truth claims—and, worse yet, policies—that emanate from a powerful elite working within a closed system. A state that delegates authority to divinities, sages, experts, or men of power often traffics in distorted and manipulated information and forecloses intelligent democratic debate:

> The absence of publicly relevant minds has come to mean that powerful decisions and important policies are not made in such a way as to be justified and attacked, in short, debated in any intellectual form. Moreover, the attempt to so justify them is often not even made. Public relations displace reasoned argument; manipulation and undebated decisions of power replace democratic authority. More and more, as administration has replaced politics, decisions of importance do not carry even the panoply of reasonable discussion in public, but are made by God, by experts, and by men like Mr. Wilson [Secretary of Defense].

The consequences of deferring to one person or a small group who operate in secrecy—and withhold "classified" information to protect national security—is bad policy. Mills cited the example of American nuclear arms policy, where there has not been "any genuine public debate" and "the facts . . . have been officially hidden, distorted, and lied about." The result was a foreign policy dominated by "crackpot realists, who, in the name of realism have constructed a paranoid reality all their own and in the name of practicality have projected a utopian image of capitalism."[49] This paranoid view of reality gave way to McCarthyism, the doctrine of Mutual Assured Destruction (MAD, an eerily apt acronym), and the predominance of the "military metaphysic" in American life. The utopian image of capitalism fostered a blind faith in classical economic theory and an undue wariness of state intervention to promote equity and the commonweal.

Mills's kinship to the pragmatists became manifest as he revealed an ardent democratic epistemology—a belief that opening discussion to the light of day, with widespread public debate, was the only way to create a reasonably accurate interpretation of reality and intellectually honest policies. Much to his dismay, American political culture seemed to be moving further away from this democratic ideal. There's little wonder why, in his darkest moments, Mills foresaw a grim future. That said, he never lost hope in the possibility of reinvigorating public debate and putting an end to the power elite's monopolistic control over information and political discourse.

Because he was a sociologist by training, Mills's democratic psychology, his belief in the malleability of human nature, should come as no surprise. If sociology has a prime directive, it is to reject biological or instinctualist explanations of human behavior and to understand human beings as works in progress, unfinished products of historical conditions. Making his case that "the limits of 'human nature' are frighteningly broad," Mills approvingly cited the following passage from a review of the Kinsey Report: "the book is not about human males, but about men in the United States in the mid-twentieth century. . . . The very idea of human nature is an assumption of social science." In the end, the reviewers concluded that there "may be nothing but 'human culture,' a highly mutable affair."[50]

Mills thought it best to conceive of human beings as historical creatures. He had little use for "psychological theories," which "rest upon the assumption that society is nothing but a great scatter of individuals and that, accordingly, if we know all about these 'atoms' we can in some way add up the information and thus know about society." Indeed, the atomized and psychologically static individual "is not a fruitful assumption," for all we can say with certainty about the nature of man is that he enjoys "wide biological limits and potentialities," which explains "the enormous human variety of types and individuals."[51]

To truly understand human beings, we should not look within them in search of fundamental truths about their psychology or instincts. It would be far more productive, said Mills, to start from the outside and investigate the social and historical conditions that shape them. This means we can best understand man by first examining the organization of the society in which we find him; but we will learn nothing about society if we search for the immutable traits of the individuals who constitute it.

In developing his view of human nature as social and mutable, Mills drew heavily on the work of George Herbert Mead. The famous sociologist who belonged to the pragmatist school spent many years working with his friend and colleague John Dewey, first at Michigan and then at Chicago, before Dewey left for Columbia in 1904. The relationship bore fruit for both men and left an unmistakably pragmatist imprint on Mead. He was not merely derivative of Dewey, however. Mead was a remarkably original thinker who made canonical contributions to the field of sociology.

Most significant for Mills were Mead's concepts of the generalized other and the significant other. The generalized other resembles the Freudian idea of the superego—the internalization of an external authority that defines a set of social norms and taboos. This internalized authority forms what many of us call a person's "conscience"—his moral compass. In other words, the generalized other represents a person's mental conception of what instituted leaders in society condemn as unacceptable behavior. "Externally," our leaders issue "sanctions against those who fail to meet instituted expectations," ranging anywhere "from the lifted eyebrow of the club leader to the death penalty imposed by the state." But instituted leaders do not always have to express their disapproval, for we internalize their expectations of us and act accordingly. "Internally, the members [of a society] incorporate the institutional head's expectations as a more or less crucial component of their particular or generalized other, and then punish themselves when they are out of line."[52] As Mills saw it, we continually engage in conversation with the generalized other, which reminds us how we ought to behave.[53]

While the generalized other forms our conscience, our significant others give us a picture of ourselves. "Significant others . . . are those to whom the person pays attention and whose appraisals are reflected in his self-appraisals."[54] In short, significant others function as mirrors, reflecting what others see in us. A mother, for example, may serve as a significant other for a child; his view of himself may in large part reflect how his mother views him. An individual typically has a select number of significant others, and they will likely change over a lifetime.

These two concepts—the generalized and significant others—come together for Mills in an interesting way, shaping his democratic metaphysics. A person's generalized other, which shapes his attitudes about morality and appropriate modes of behavior, gets filtered through his particular significant others. This is why people in a given society will hold a range of views about what constitutes morally acceptable behavior. Those people who play a significant role in our lives give us a glimpse of ourselves through their constant appraisals of our behavior, and their appraisals convey, in incomplete form, the expectations of the generalized other.

Our significant others function as unreliable intermediaries—in other words, as a collective transmitter through which we can hear the garbled voice of the generalized other. Sometimes, Mills contended, our significant others may not be aware of the generalized other and thus fail to communicate its views altogether. As a person accumulates more significant others, he becomes exposed to a more diverse array of opinions about what is expected of him.

This will require him to make choices about how to act, which will in turn allow him to achieve a self-defined identity. But this free will is available only "in a society where there are inconsistent expectations exacted of the person, and hence alternatives offered." Societies that offer "few choices" do not allow a person to "take it upon himself to achieve an individual integration of self."[55] In other words, social conditions determine the possibility of free will. One can enjoy free will only if he is exposed to a plurality of significant others. For Mills, the self is a social creation, arising out of a particular sociohistorical setting in which people enjoy the opportunity to choose from a number of alternatives placed before them. This means that man is not always the individualistic creature—at worst both selfish and acquisitive—that economists and liberal theorists have assumed. Indeed, the individual self could only emerge in a particular set of historical circumstances, when society began to offer alternative (and often inconsistent) expectations of its members.

Mills drew another crucial lesson from this Meadian analysis: although a social construction, man still has a considerable amount of freedom to define himself and control his own destiny. The creation of alternative roles from which people could choose opened the door to at least a limited form of free will. But it is important to acknowledge the persistence of an unresolved tension in Mills's thought between larger social forces and the individual. In his view, the open society that extended myriad options to the individual gave way increasingly to a system of social control.

The unresolved tension in Mills's work reveals what can be described as a lukewarm democratic metaphysics, a belief that human beings may have only a limited capacity to master their own fate. There may have been times in history when man enjoyed free will, especially in the seventeenth and early eighteenth centuries. But Mills believed that inherent to modernity was a creeping totalitarianism, which placed severe restrictions on what most people thought and did with their lives. Only aggressive democratic action—stalwart resistance to bureaucratic organizations controlled by the power elite—could hope to reverse this trend and awaken people to their predicament. For meaningful change to occur, power had to be met with power.

In his less sanguine moments, Mills expressed a fear that the modern liberal system had lulled people into a complacency that stripped them forever of the will to exercise this power. Quite content with the economic security provided by the permanent war economy, most people were more than willing to abdicate their civic responsibilities. Like the Grand Inquisitor's flock in *The Brothers Karamazov,* they preferred security to freedom.[56]

According to Mills, we are always vulnerable to manipulation because of our reliance on language to communicate. We must all operate within the framework of a shared language, beset by rules and conventions, and this assists the generalized other in defining parameters that circumscribe our thoughts and actions. "We can view language," said Mills, "as a system of social control." Embodied in the structure, grammar, and vocabulary of any language is a set of "implicit exhortations," from which anyone would be hard-pressed to deviate. As social creatures, we depend on language to facilitate communication. But as it pervades every facet of our lives, language leaves an indelible imprint, becoming far more than just an instrument of communication as it compels obedience to "social norms and values" and lays out the "institutional and political coordinates" that shape "collective action."[57] It would seem that the price of civilization, which could never emerge without language, is at least a modicum of freedom. The only consolation is that, in a truly pluralistic society, people still enjoy plenty of choice, and they can make their voices heard in a democratic forum.

We witness real threats to freedom when cultural workmen commandeer language to misinform and manipulate the public on behalf of the power elite. In these instances, we become subject not to an ambiguous generalized other but to a baleful significant other. At one time, the generalized other offered some, if somewhat circumscribed, alternatives from which we could freely choose. But modernity has seen the rise of a significant other of which most of us have little knowledge but which reflects how we see ourselves—first and foremost, as consumers.

Having constructed what Mills called a "cultural apparatus," an elaborate method of producing and distributing information, our cultural workmen—including writers, artists, and scientists—devote their various forms of expertise to manufacturing demand for goods and services we do not need and delivering these goods and services as satisfactorily as possible. In essence, our cultural workmen have devised ways to tell us what we should like and how we should experience it. "The cultural apparatus," Mills warned, "not only guides experience; often as well it expropriates the very chance to have experience that can rightly be called 'our own.'" Indeed, we cannot see and experience reality—or even ourselves—independently of the cultural apparatus. "Taken as a whole, the cultural apparatus is the lens of mankind through which men see; the medium by which they interpret and report what they see. It is the semiorganized source of their very identities and of their aspirations."[58]

There was a time when intellectuals and artists enjoyed autonomous control of the cultural apparatus, but like the small and independent businessman, autonomous cultural workmen have become scarce. Long gone is the "world of pamphleteering offered to a Tom Paine," which enabled him to reach large and well-informed publics. The means of distributing knowledge and information has become increasingly dominated by elite-controlled bureaucracies. "Between the intellectual and his potential public," Mills lamented, stand "technical, economic and social structures which are owned and operated by others."[59] Rather than galvanizing publics as Paine once did, the intellectual has become a sandman for the power elite, helping put publics to sleep. In their slumber, the people experience pleasant dreams of conspicuous consumption.

Mills called this age of sleeping publics the Fourth Epoch. The hallmark of the Fourth Epoch, setting it apart from the Modern Age, is "that the ideas of freedom and of reason have become moot; that increased rationality may not be assumed to make for increased freedom."[60] Although our society has adopted "rationally organized social arrangements," the individual does not enjoy more freedom as a result. Mills believed that these arrangements, mainly coming in the form of large bureaucracies, are "a means of tyranny of manipulation, a means of expropriating the very chance to reason, the very capacity to act as a free man."[61] These arrangements serve to alienate man from his fellow man and create the conditions under which he can commit the great atrocities of the twentieth century with businesslike efficiency.

In place of the free moral agent has emerged the "Cheerful Robot," a man who will perform, without question or complaint, those functions assigned to him. He is often quite unaware of the ends his actions serve, and even if he cares to know, he would find it nearly impossible to find out. For the ever-increasing division of labor in bureaucratic organizations prevents most men from reasoning about the vast structures of which they constitute insignificant parts. The Cheerful Robot is content to eschew such questions, finding solace in the security and regularity afforded to him in the Fourth Epoch. He inhabits a rigid society, neither free nor democratic, but he sees no reason to challenge it.

The example of the Cheerful Robot teaches us that it "will no longer do merely to assume, as a metaphysic of human nature, that down deep in man-as-man there is an urge for freedom and a will to reason." Indeed, Mills made it abundantly clear that "*all* men do *not* naturally *want* to be free; that all men are not willing or not able, as the case may be, to exert themselves to acquire the reason that freedom requires." Free will is not an irrevocable trait of humankind. Like all things mortal, it is eminently fragile, requiring constant care and maintenance. Sadly, for Mills, many of us will readily renounce our freedom for material or spiritual security. But he believed that many people, if an ever-shrinking minority, stand firm in their desire to exercise free will. Rejecting determinism outright, he thought his role as an intellectual was to identify those conditions under which men are able to act freely and become "willing and able to bear the burdens freedom does impose and to see them less as burdens than as gladly undertaken self-transformations."[62]

But, according to Mills, human beings can never enjoy a radical freedom and simply do whatever pleases them. At best they can experience a limited form of freedom in which they have "the chance to formulate the available choices, to argue over them—and then, the opportunity to choose. That is why freedom cannot exist without an enlarged role of human reason in human affairs."[63] Man is free when he applies reason directly to his affairs by identifying the options available to him and deliberating with his peers until they reach an agreement. It is important to stress here that, unlike other critics of modernity, Mills did not believe reason was necessarily subject to the bureaucratic organization. Although appropriated in the twentieth century for the most nefarious purposes, reason could once again become the domain of men who seek an accurate understanding of reality and who engage in thoughtful discussion with others in their community to arrive at provisional truths. Men could use reason in their quest to control their own destinies—to make history.

Mills did not understand history solely as the study of structural forces and trends that determine human behavior. Such historical explanations are often responsible for bringing about "conservative ideologies," which suggest that institutions "have taken a long time to evolve, and accordingly they are not to be tampered with hastily." He believed a better approach to history was to consider the impermanence of institutions, which were created by men but which do not in any way reflect traits inherent to their nature. In other words, Mills preferred to consider the study of history as biography: those choices available to human beings over the course of time and the consequences of the choices they have made. The study of history should focus not on the factors that limit human behavior but on the opportunities open to human beings, enabling them to move in new and unprecedented directions. Lamenting the lack of imagination among most social scientists who refuse to envision a utopian view of the future, Mills demanded that we all embrace a new "theory of history-making" in which men are free to "influence the course of history."[64]

We must no longer see the future as something we can predict with a set of variables. "The future is what is to be decided—within the limits, to be sure, of historical possibility. But this possibility is not fixed; in our time the limits seem very broad indeed." In the end, said Mills, "we must often study history in order to get rid of it."[65] Of course, most social scientists operate under the assumption that we can never "get rid" of history, and Mills would agree that we must operate with the "limits of historical possibility." But he considered these limits to be so "broad" that history had little power over us. It is we who make history; history does not make us.

Mills's biographical understanding of history may seem to contradict his discussion of the Cheerful Robot and the dawn of the Fourth Epoch, in which men have succumbed to a fate beyond their control. Although he often claimed that opportunities to act freely have been foreclosed in the Fourth Epoch, at other times he also said that men can be the authors of their own biographies and histories. Which is it? To sort out this apparent inconsistency, it is useful to explore further Mills's concept of fate. He wrote:

> Fate has to do with events in history that are the summary and unintended results of innumerable decisions of innumerable men. Each of their decisions is minute in consequence and subject to cancellation or reinforcement by other such decisions. There is no link between any one man's intention and the summary result of the innumerable decisions. Events are beyond human decisions: history is made behind men's backs.[66]

There may have been a time when history was the mere aggregation of separate individual actions, which resulted in a kind of drift, a casting about unpredictably in unintended directions. But, for Mills this understanding of fate is not absolute.

In recent times, humankind has indeed developed a capacity for history-making, using the advances of science and technology to pave the way toward a planned future. The hitch is that these means of history-making have become increasingly centralized, concentrated in the hands of a small and powerful elite. Thus, there is no contradiction in Mills's thought, for "history may indeed be made—but by narrow elite circles without effective responsibility."[67] Human beings have finally become masters of their fate, but at the moment only a small number of them actually exercise this power. The vast majority of men feel ineffectual and alienated—and rightly so. They have to submit to a reckless course of events they had no hand in shaping, and they feel obliged to conform to the expectations of an especially exacting significant other, the power elite itself.

The good news is that we can indeed make history, and the number of people involved in this process can always grow. Although a frightfully compliant and unquestioning creature, the Cheerful Robot always has the potential to reclaim his humanity by exercising his free will. To do so, he must use reason "to formulate choices, to enlarge the scope of human decisions in the making of history."[68] Freedom requires the use of reason, and reason can only be practiced by widening the scope of perspectives

C. WRIGHT MILLS ::: 155

through democratic deliberation. In other words, democracy is the anti-dote to the epidemic of complacency afflicting the many Cheerful Robots who inhabit postmodern society. Only democracy can take history-making away from the power elite and turn it over to the public.

Notwithstanding the manipulative forces that subvert the use of reason and the formation of vigilant publics, Mills believed that the power of face-to-face discussion should not be underestimated. Many factors sway public opinion, he said, but "the most effective and immediate context of changing opinion is people talking informally with other people."[69] Mills based this assertion on findings from a study of public opinion in Decatur, Illinois. He and his fellow researchers sampled eight hundred women and asked them questions concerning their opinions and attitudes on a variety of issues. Then a few months later, the researchers returned to these women and asked them the same questions to see if any of them held different opinions. Of those who did, the researchers asked follow-up questions to determine what had made them change their minds. Much to their surprise, they found that face-to-face discussion was much more likely to change a person's opinion than any other factor, including the mass media. Their findings suggested that people tend to choose media outlets with which they already agree. This means that "the chief influence of the mass media is not really to *form* or to *change* opinion but to *reinforce* a line of opinion already held."[70] Nevertheless, as a reinforcer of public opinion serving at the behest of the power elite, the mass media proved highly effective, leaving one to wonder how anyone can escape its influence and form alternative points of view.

Mills contended that resistance to the overarching influence of the media remains possible so long as it is not controlled by a monopoly. Even if there are only a few media outlets, a person "can play one off against another; he can compare them." One can also compare what the media says to his own experiences and understanding of reality, though Mills conceded that this approach may not work so well, because we can only perceive the world through the lens of the cultural apparatus.[71]

By far the most effective method of resistance, according to Mills, is to compare what the mass media says to the experiences of many other people with whom we engage in conversation. "Individuals may gain points of resistance against the mass media by the comparison of experience and of opinions among themselves," said Mills. "These discussions of the primary public are at once the spearhead and the master context against which resistances may develop."[72]

According to Mills, opinion leaders in these discussions play a crucial role as the "radiant points, the foci of the primary public."[73] They serve to facilitate the communication of knowledge and opinion by organizing informal discussion groups. Never shy about sharing their views, opinion leaders introduce people to alternative ideas. And because they are drawn to vigorous debate, opinion leaders encourage others to share their experiences and express their opinions.

That said, it may not be obvious why face-to-face discussions, inspired by these leaders, exercise greater influence on opinion formation. After all, as Mills pointed out, opinion leaders select the media that reinforce their opinions just like everyone else does. This suggests they would function as stooges of the media, not as foci of resistance. It would also stand to reason that people would listen to opinion leaders with whom they agree and spurn all the others.

But in "two very crucial respects" talking differs from simply consuming what the media delivers to us. First, the people with whom we engage in discussion cannot be turned off or ignored as easily as the many forms of media in today's world, such as television, radio, newspapers, and so on. In the midst of a conversation, "very often you have to listen, at least for a while, even if you don't agree." Second, one cannot easily reply to what the mass media says and receive an immediate answer back. There are no opportunities to ask for clarification or further evidence, or to offer a strong retort to what appears to be an incorrect assertion. In face-to-face discussion, people can enjoy a "give and take" that "just can't exist in mass media communication."[74]

This all means that talking creates a dynamic that is far more conducive to opinion change, for it provides a real opportunity for participants to hear different, even clashing, points of view with which they must come to terms. In face-to-face conversation, propriety bars them from simply ignoring what others say. They will not just listen passively to people with whom they disagree vehemently—or even those of whom they are skeptical. Whereas a self-selected mass media projects an aura of incontestable authority, our interlocutors in a lively discussion are our equals whose opinions must hold up to strict scrutiny. If their opinions appear valid, even after our most valiant attempts to refute them, we are often persuaded to change our minds.

Mills believed that the implications of this study were profound: man can engage in reasoned discussion to resist the manipulative influence of the cultural apparatus and then work alongside his fellow men to bring about change that conforms with his socially formed opinions. Once people escape the influence of the mass media—which projects a distorted, even imaginary, view of reality—they are free to choose, after careful consideration and fruitful discussion, among a number of alternative ideas upon which they will ultimately act. Face-to-face discussion is the hallmark of any participatory democracy in which publics hold their leaders accountable and even have a hand in political decision-making.

Although he always found hope in participatory democracy, by the late 1950s Mills came to believe that only confrontational action would prove effective in resisting entrenched power structures. Conscious of the power elite's grapple hold on political institutions, Mills suggested that only an aggressive form of democratic politics, including social movements and public demonstrations, could defy the current system and wake up dormant publics. Because mild-mannered discussion was not enough to break through the web of power, people needed to confront the system directly if they wanted to make history.

Mills made reference to a "movement" that could be "powerful enough to put into practice the policies required to stop the main drift, and, at the same time, implant into the very mechanisms of society the democratic impulses which it instills and releases in its members."[75] He envisioned democratically engaged citizens operating outside the state to effect change, devoting their energies to causes about which they feel strongly. Such dedication would "make, in the union drive, all the workers militants; in the electoral campaign, all the electorate precinct workers."[76] In Mills's view, only this kind of tireless activity and militant confrontation could sustain publics and serve as a vital check on the state.

In *The Causes of World War III*, Mills declared it was "imperative to make demands upon men of power and to hold them responsible for specific courses of events."[77] With the prospect of world war between the superpowers looming over all of humankind, Mills believed peace and disarmament were the most important issues facing intellectuals and activists, and he saw much to praise in the methods of social protest adopted by many of them.

In his renowned "Letter to the New Left," Mills approvingly cited examples of student activism and outrage over American foreign policy, as well as rumblings of discontent among intellectuals in the Soviet bloc. He was happy to report that the many examples of "messy unrest" and "moral upsurge" throughout the world, usually coming in the form of "direct non-violent action" appear "to be working, here and there. Now we must learn from their practice and work out with them new forms of action."[78] It is not surprising, then, that Mills also found hope in the student movements of the late 1950s and early 1960s. He applauded the marches, sit-ins, and demonstrations staged by southern students. He regarded the young intelligentsia as the most likely "radical agency of change," the focal point of a New Left that embraced utopian thinking and posed serious challenges to the "*structure* of institutions, the *foundation* of policies."[79]

To the surprise of many, Mills even praised the revolution in Cuba in his provocative and entertaining book, *Listen, Yankee!* "Revolution is construction," said Mills, who saw Castro as the personification of praxis, the confluence of dreams and reality. "The revolution is a way of changing reality—and so of changing the definition of it."[80] In the last few years of his life, Mills began to romanticize revolutionary action as a way of creating truth through willful practice, of aggressively imposing a particular view of justice onto the world. He came to believe that only heroic action could usher in a better future for humankind. Civil, deliberative democracy would get us nowhere.

Mills's emergent radicalism represented a significant departure from his call, earlier in his career, for a competent civil service, responsible political parties, the revival of free associations, and the creation of a publicly engaged intelligentsia. It was even a far cry from his hopeful vision of "a society in which everyone vitally affected by a social decision, regardless of its sphere, would have a voice in that decision and a hand in its administration."[81] He began to view democracy as an action performed from the outside-in, protesting against prevailing power structures from a position of intellectual honesty and political purity, and bringing about change through the exertion of political pressure. Mills seemed to have lost hope in the possibility of practicing democracy from within the system, because its democratic institutions had become irrevocably corrupted. All that remained was the mere form or shell of democracy, serving only to keep up appearances and mask the activities of the power elite. Only confrontational politics, involving protests against a farcical democracy and its reckless policies, could spur a democratic renewal.

A major reason for Mills's break with pragmatism was its apparent unwillingness to embrace confrontation as a necessary strategy for democratic actors. Seeing social and political problems as the failure to apply intelligence in the right way, Dewey believed that creating self-aware publics was an educational process. As a result, Dewey had very little use for conflict as a legitimate democratic strategy. For Mills, on the other hand, conflict was not only justifiable; it was necessary. He called attention to the obstacles created by prevailing power structures and believed that publics only emerge in the wake of direct confrontation with the power elite. In advocating incrementalism and a reformist agenda, argued Mills, pragmatism had revealed itself to be a philosophy of acquiescence before the dominant liberal paradigm. Having adopted wholesale its individualist ethos, pragmatists had given way to extreme caution lest property rights or civil liberties become in any way compromised. The result was a failure to address the deep structural and foundational issues confronting the American people.

Critical of what he saw as their preoccupation with means, at the expense of ends, Mills accused pragmatists of being "too technological and not deeply enough political."[82] As he saw it, the pragmatists informed the end-of-ideology position taken by Daniel Bell, Seymour Martin Lipset, and others, who declared that there was no longer any reason to debate the great political questions about the ends of a just society that only questions about means—method and technique—remained to be answered. A philosophical movement founded by middle-class intellectuals whose "political experience . . . has been limited to the university," pragmatism taught the virtue of patiently solving problems through trial and error.[83] The problem with this approach, according to Mills, was that it worked under the assumption that America is still a "Jeffersonian rural democracy," in which citizens can competently apply the method of intelligence and let ends take care of themselves.

Mills took Dewey to task especially. "In insisting upon treading its way through many particular problems, Dewey's pragmatism has relaxed its hold on men unwillingly lost in the interstices of gigantic trends," he wrote. "Dewey has said that patience is something he has learned to treasure. But patience may mean defeat and this must be faced." Pragmatism continued to teach patience and undying faith in applying intelligence to social problems incrementally, but this approach offered little hope to those who saw no end in sight. Indeed, Mills accused Dewey of being "tied to a continual reconstruction of the world in which he moves slowly and has no 'final end.'"[84] For Dewey, a comfortable middle-class intellectual, patience may have been a virtue, but others in more desperate circumstances may have seen it as "defeat." From their perspective, the pragmatists' reforms seemed more aimless or futile than conducive to achieving a certain end.

Cast adrift by strong historical currents over which he has no control, man cannot turn to pragmatism to reorient himself and find direction. Lacking any vision of where he should end up, he can do nothing but tread water to avoid drowning and allow the tides of history to tug and push him in various directions. He merely reacts to the immediate problems posed by the swift currents of history; he does not alter his predicament by swimming to terra firma or prevent future occurrences by considering what put him in this oceanic tumult in the first place. This does not mean that the pragmatist is unintelligent, said Mills, but he is guilty of eschewing ends to the point that he will only apply short-term fixes to specific problems and never address (or even perceive) the larger issues at stake.

Mills cited Progressive Era reforms as an example. Although thoughtful and well-intended experiments to which many publics responded quite favorably, the progressive reforms of the early twentieth century, such as civil service reform and trust-busting, could do nothing to block "the big structural shifts of high capitalism," which, in the long run, served to undermine those very reform efforts and to "wipe out" civically engaged publics.[85] The progressives, who, according to Mills, adopted a pragmatist approach to solving social problems, failed to combat the social and economic trends that threatened not only their specific reforms but democracy itself.

It is important to note, however, that Mills's criticism of pragmatism stems, at least in part, from what appears to be a willful misreading of Dewey. Dewey offered a radical critique of liberalism and pluralism and was an early and ardent supporter of participatory democracy. Mills seemed to overlook these crucial elements of Dewey's thought.

Furthermore, Dewey was far more aware of the dominant power structures in society than Mills gave him credit for. It is true that Dewey stressed the importance of education in a well-functioning democracy to inculcate its citizens with the scientific method, but he recognized the many obstacles to the full application of social intelligence. "Vested interests," Dewey warned, "are powerfully on the side of the status quo, and therefore they are especially powerful in hindering the growth and application of the method of natural intelligence in action."[86] Accordingly, Dewey showed a preference for radical change, not incrementalism and piecemeal reform: "liberalism must now become radical, meaning by 'radical' perception of the necessity of thoroughgoing changes in the set-up of the institutions and corresponding activity to bring the changes to pass," said Dewey. "For the gulf between what the actual situation makes possible and the actual state itself is so great that it cannot be bridged by piecemeal policies undertaken *ad hoc*."[87] Nevertheless, despite his awareness of the "vested interests" that resisted intelligent political action and his call for radical politics to bring about "thoroughgoing changes" in our institutions, Dewey never advocated a confrontational strategy to challenge the status quo.

This gets at the main difference between Dewey and Mills. Dewey's vision of participatory democracy always evoked civilized deliberation and thoughtful discussion among members of a harmonious community. Acutely conscious of the power elite's hold on political institutions and the American people, Mills believed only a confrontational form of democracy could defy the current system and rouse dormant publics. For Mills, education and mild-mannered debate were not enough to break through the web of social and political domination. The power elite would hear only the voices of an angry mass, committed to using its strength in numbers as leverage to gain control of vital political institutions and to effect social change.[88]

Dewey may never have imagined this kind of confrontational politics, but it was a logical outgrowth of his call for deepening democracy. Mills saw confrontational politics as the only way for marginalized groups to have their voices heard and to contribute substantively to civic life. Confrontation served as a crucial check on the inevitable concentration of power in the postmodern world, allowing the wisdom of publics to prevail over the selfish designs of the elite. In short, only through confrontation could people become masters of their own fate; only through confrontation could they make history. Although he ostensibly forsook pragmatism, Mills actually built on its philosophical tradition, adding what he saw as a necessary correction to Dewey's political timidity—and to his naive democratic metaphysics.

## The Legacy of an Oracle

It soon becomes evident to the reader of Mills that his work contains an unresolved tension. At times he seems optimistic about the efficacy of face-to-face discussion (or talk) in forming engaged publics who can hold their elected officials accountable for their actions. But he gave way increasingly to pessimism about the resilience of the Cheerful Robot in a mass society that conditions him to remain apathetic and complacent.

This ambivalence paralleled another tension in his work. While Mills often expressed a deep faith in the emergence of a vibrant participatory democracy that supplements and buttresses our representative institutions, he became more convinced that only confrontational politics, hopefully nonviolent but sometimes necessarily revolutionary, could effectively awaken dormant publics and put pressure on the power elite. In his darker moments, Mills saw man as a profoundly alienated creature whose "narrowed routines and environments" separate him from the experiences of others—a creature who merely drifts through life and, bereft of any independence, behaves in accordance with "the confused standards and uncriticized expectations" of people he neither knows nor trusts.[89] Mills turned to heroic revolutionary action as man's only way out of this malaise and internment to fate. This tension was the legacy that his New Left acolytes would inherit.

Arguably, the most important figure of the New Left is Tom Hayden (1939– ). Both an intellectual and an activist, Hayden embodies the spirit of the student movement. Displaying an unparalleled charisma and intensity, he assumed a vital leadership role in SDS. Almost anything he said or did would make a deep impression on its growing membership. Hayden's status as a luminary in the movement came not only from his words but also from his actions. Indeed, his involvement in the civil rights movement earned him battle scars. As a field organizer for SDS he traveled to Mississippi in the summer of 1961 to assist in organizing the Freedom Schools started by Bob Moses and Charles McDew, activists for the Student Nonviolent Coordinating Committee (SNCC). Not long after his arrival, a group of Klansmen attacked Hayden and another activist, Paul Potter. A photographer surreptitiously took a snapshot of Hayden, curled in the fetal position, withstanding the kicks and punches of an angry mob. Circulated in newspapers throughout the country, the photograph would serve as testament not only to the brutality of racial segregation in the South but also to Hayden's unwavering commitment to democracy and social justice.

It was as a reporter and editor for the *Michigan Daily* that Hayden learned the craft of writing, enabling him to become the chief spokesperson for SDS—and a generation of student radicals. And he could hardly express an opinion without echoing the words of his intellectual hero, C. Wright Mills. Like the hero he never met, Hayden took to wearing a leather jacket and riding a motorcycle, projecting the image of a brooding rebel as he cruised the streets of Ann Arbor. In his memoirs, Hayden admits to falling "under the powerful influence" of Mills, who "quickly became the oracle of the New Left."[90] When Mills died in March 1962, at the age of forty-five, Hayden "experienced chest pain" and, decades later, would "still relive the depression that began that moment." He feared that Mills's early demise "was an omen of things to come," a sign that the man who had devoted his life to fighting a system that bred complacency in the face of madness finally fell in defeat. The power elite, it seemed, had gotten the better of his hero. Could anyone expect SDS, whose historic meeting in Port Huron, Michigan, was only three months away, to succeed where this great man had failed? Hayden had just completed a draft of the *Port Huron Statement,* a document that "was strongly influenced by C. Wright Mills's independent radicalism." Understandably, the tragic news of his death gave him pause.[91]

Never one to give up, however, Hayden continued to work tirelessly as both a thinker and an activist, and Mills's ideas would always resonate with him. In a 1985 interview with James Miller, Hayden admitted: "I was completely absorbed in his writing. He was the inspiration for what I was trying to do." Hayden and other student activists drew inspiration especially from "Letter to the New Left." Mills showed his faith in "students as an agency of change," said Hayden, and the letter made them feel as if they had been "anointed" by the great man. They were instilled with "enormous confidence."[92] It is hardly a surprise, then, that as a graduate student in philosophy at the University of Michigan, Hayden wrote his thesis on Mills.[93] Although many thinkers shaped Hayden's political philosophy, Mills reigns as the most important and thus represents a central link between pragmatism and the New Left.

Following Mills, Hayden often lamented the eclipse of coherent publics in American society. In a memo addressed to the SDS executive committee, for example, Hayden invoked his hero by stressing his concern "about *the complete absence of an active and creative set of publics, people working in union to conform the structures and direction of events to their interests.*" Social and economic injustices would persist, he added later in the memo, "as long as an active public is absent, as long as those interested in the democracy without a public are in power."[94] When publics remain inactive, said Hayden, people are unable to make the connection between their private troubles and larger social issues.

In one of his more famous speeches, "Student Social Action," Hayden used vivid examples to bring Mills's ideas to life. He cited the man who complains about "the commercials on television" but does not understand they are a product of "a capitalist system that created pseudo-needs in people—a prerequisite of mass society—so as to continue profit in times of over-production." Hayden also invoked the student who gets "upset about the idiosyncrasies of the Negro cleaning lady in his corridor," but who would be far more sympathetic if he realized that "one-third of all Negro women in America are forced to be domestics" for paltry wages. Incapable of seeing any of their personal troubles from a broader perspective, people fail to hold leaders accountable for their actions, and the power elite is free to do as it likes. In the end, these people are subject to "a mixture of drift and manipulation by an unseen 'them,' the modern equivalent of 'fate.'"[95] Mills's imprint here is unmistakable.

Also like Mills and the pragmatists before him, Hayden subscribed to the three pragmatist tenets. Embracing a democratic epistemology, he believed truth is socially constructed and always provisional. He made his views about the provisionality of truth evident in the *Port Huron Statement* by rejecting the truth claims of liberalism and communism and then declaring "we have no sure formulas, no closed theories—but that does not mean values are beyond discussion and tentative determination." Even the *Port Huron Statement* itself, the founding manifesto of SDS, would be considered a "living document" that did not contain a single inalienable assertion or truth.

In "Student Social Action" Hayden made the case that truth acquisition is a social enterprise. Describing his ideal university, in which faculty and students would work in a cooperative rather than an authoritarian or adversarial learning environment, Hayden painted a colorful landscape of a vibrant community of truth seekers. The people of this community welcome people of all backgrounds, treat each other as equals, share knowledge, and ultimately reach agreements on what is always an amendable truth. "These two communities," said Hayden, referring to faculty and students, "share the real enterprise of learning, and as there can be no final unamendable Truth in a community of free inquiry, there can be no arbitrary authority structure for the relation of teacher and student. A company of scholars is a company of equals in the crucial sense that none has a premium on the truth." The community of this ideal university "will be culturally, racially, religiously, and internationally integrated," so that it represents the views and perspectives of all people. Of equal importance, this community will "promote student exercise of democratic prerogatives," with participants tolerating and entertaining all ideas, even the most unpopular. In the pragmatist spirit, people "will appreciate the educational benefits of testing ideas through real action," understanding that "ideological fantasy" is a dangerous artifact of an isolated existence that will always lead man astray.[96] In the pragmatist spirit, Hayden admonishes his listeners to develop truths in a democratic community and then continually test those truths in their experience.

Hayden was keenly aware that an advocate for participatory democracy had to have a firm belief in the corrigibility not only of truth but also of man himself. Although, in the past, man has not always proved his capacity for sound moral judgment and social cooperation and in fact has usually fallen far short of the ideals he has set for himself, this does not mean that his nature precludes him from rising to the challenge in the future. In Hayden's estimation at the time, humankind's potential for growth was nearly unbounded. Instead of setting limits on his spiritual, intellectual, and moral development, man's nature endowed him with the great promise to transcend history and instinct. "'Human nature' is not an evil or corrosive substance to be feared or contained," Hayden wrote a few months before the meeting in Port Huron; "rather, it represents a potential for material and spiritual development which, no matter how lengthily or rapidly unfolded, can never be dissipated."[97]

In the original draft of the *Port Huron Statement,* Hayden included a line that perfectly captures the democratic psychology: "We regard *Man* as infinitely precious and infinitely perfectible." Only when a number of participants at Port Huron took issue with this clause—reminding people of the doctrine of original sin and, in the fashion of Niebuhr, arguing that hubristic claims about the perfectibility of man has led humankind down the path to totalitarianism—was the sentence reworded. It now read: "We regard *men* as infinitely precious and possessed of unfulfilled capacities for reason, freedom, and love."[98]

Still, this attenuation of the message did not challenge the basic idea expressed in the *Port Huron Statement,* that man was brimming with "unrealized potential for self-cultivation, self-direction, self-understanding, and creativity." Like Mills, Hayden and his cohorts believed that our abilities—though perhaps not limitless—far surpassed what we have accomplished up to now. That we have not lived up to our potential and have been responsible for the horrors of the twentieth century does not bespeak the limits of human nature. Indeed, Hayden wrote that SDS rejected "the doctrine of human incompetence," believing instead that "men have been 'competently' manipulated into incompetence." If society were organized differently, "not for minority, but for majority, participation in decision-making," there would be "little reason why men [could] not meet with increasing skill the complexities and responsibilities of their situation."[99] The transformation of man into something better—a being who cultivates "his capacities for reason, freedom, and love" to untold heights—was just beyond the horizon. But this transformation required the right social environment, where people had ample opportunity to participate in the affairs of their communities. Democratic participation was what allowed us to grow as human beings. Indeed, "government and politics represent a desirable, necessary (though not sufficient) part of the experience through which man discovers and develops himself; they are among the instruments by which man becomes the measure and maker of all things."[100]

Whether people will choose to participate in a democratic community, with all its reputed epistemological and psychological benefits, is a question of free will—as in the third pragmatist tenet, democratic metaphysics. Hayden, like Mills, believed that the power elite manipulated people into a state of apathy and contentment, stripping them of their political will. Nevertheless, he had faith that people do indeed have the freedom to overcome these dominating power structures, to become independent agents. If given the opportunity and made to understand the advantages of political participation, people could enjoy a "genuine independence," an ability to transcend petty concerns about "image or popularity," which are foisted upon them by unseen, manipulative forces, and to devote their energies "to finding a moral meaning in life that is direct and authentic for the self." Intrepid in the face of difficult problems, the free or independent person, whenever he sees fit, will think on his own, shirk convention, question the "values of the Top People," and renounce old ways of doing things. Although many have argued that "only a privileged few can be independent" in this way, Hayden maintained that "independence can be a fact about ordinary people."[101]

Our refusal up to this point to accept the mantle of freedom and embrace our civic responsibilities does not mean we are doomed to be slaves of the system. Every person can assert his independence—and impose his will on the world. Up to this point, however, people seemed to prefer security to freedom; they had no interest in taking unnecessary risks by either challenging "the Top People" or their own habits. But, to Hayden, the imminence of World War III and the plight of Southern blacks raised the stakes to an unbearable level, making democratic action absolutely necessary. Exercising our free will through democratic participation, taking charge of our collective destiny, was the only way to avert disaster. "We must have a try at bringing society under human control," Hayden declared. To do this, we "must wrest control from the endless machines that grind up men's jobs, the few hundred corporations that exercise greater power over the economy and the country than in feudal societies, the vast military profession [and] the irresponsible politicians."[102]

It is clear from Hayden's writings that he had a faith in man's capacity to shape his own destiny. But how was man supposed to "wrest control" from the power elite and bring "society under human control"? On this question Hayden conveyed an ambivalence about the meaning of democracy that recalls Mills: sometimes it seems he favored prudent democratic discussion and deliberation; at other times he grew impatient with caution and civility and revealed a penchant for heroic, even dramatic, democratic action—for direct confrontation with the power elite.[103]

In his more pragmatic moments, Hayden echoed the political philosophy of John Dewey and suggested that human beings must submit to a deliberate and scientific approach to solving problems. Eschewing an unrestrained impetuosity, they should endorse incremental reforms and always make sure their ideas accord with social reality before committing themselves to a particular course of action. In addition, they should remain fully aware of the assumptions on which their truth claims rest and, in the spirit of intellectual honesty and humility, acknowledge openly the weaknesses in their own arguments. "Life is too complex," he once said in a speech, "for anything but a commitment to experimental procedure, built on a deep understanding of our presuppositions and the alternative presuppositions which we are rejecting. We must be continually willing to reconstruct our ideas as they prove inadequate in social conditions."[104]

Not content with "visionary statements alone," Hayden also advised his readers to "develop both intermediate ideals and consistent programmatic goals." To illustrate his point, he gave the example of holding socialized medicine as an ideal but seeing elderly medical care as a realistic short-term goal that accords with and represents a progressive step toward that ideal.[105] When in this pragmatist mode, Hayden portrayed participatory democracy as a way of addressing issues and solving problems communally—a deliberative process that "depends on trust, friendship, a stable set of rules for arriving at decisions."[106]

But Hayden could never relinquish his more romantic view of democratic action. Because he believed that face-to-face discussion among level-headed citizens alone would not awaken publics and bring about fundamental change, Hayden embraced a more confrontational brand of politics. Like Mills, he praised the mass unrest and revolutionary fervor that swept across much of the developing world in the 1950s and 1960s. "The revolutions in the new nations," said Hayden, "are important because they are trying to defy the tendencies toward stultification by the hard assertion of individual personality." We must not quibble over the "intellectual faults" of these revolutionary leaders but should instead praise their "personally-willed participation, intervention in the movement of human affairs."[107]

In these moments, it seems, Hayden shed his circumspect demeanor completely and embraced political heroism, however ill-conceived, for its own sake. The results of heroic action were less important than that it showed a commitment to substantive change and a willingness to take a moral stand against the social injustices perpetuated by the existing organization of power. Decisive action against injustice was *the* antidote to apathy, a way of becoming an authentic human being, fully alive. In a 1985 interview with Miller, Hayden said that democratic participation "meant number one, *action*; we believed in action." He continued:

> We had behind us the so-called decade of apathy; we were emerging from apathy. What's the opposite of apathy? Active participation. Citizenship. Making history. Secondly, we were very directly influenced by the civil rights movement in its student phase, which believed that by personally committing yourself and taking risks, you could enter history and try to change it after a hundred years of segregation. And it was this element of participation in democracy that was important. . . . And we believed, as an end in itself, to make the human being whole by becoming an actor in history instead of just a passive object. Not only as end in itself, but as a means to change, the idea of participatory democracy was our central focus.[108]

Direct action of this kind would not only awaken people, especially the participants, to the issues facing their society; it would also foment change.

Confrontation was the most effective means of making history. After all, as Hayden wrote in the *Port Huron Statement,* powerful elites in this country "respond not to dialogue, but to pressure." The segregated South was a prime example: the white establishment would respond only to acts of civil disobedience—the sit-ins, stand-ins, marches, and demonstrations. For this reason, the civil rights movement was a major inspiration for Hayden and others in SDS, showing Americans how democratic action could harness the power of the powerless and bring down the forces of oppression.

For inspiration Hayden often turned to the writings of Albert Camus— the French existentialist who saw decisive action as a safeguard against nihilism in the modern age, the most effective way of building moral commitments and hope in a world devoid of universal truth or values. That these commitments may be misguided hardly mattered to Hayden. The dangers of this heroic existentialism are all too obvious: by exalting heroic democratic action through "the hard assertion of personality," Hayden seemed to court radical change—by any means necessary and for those ends consistent with the designs of a revolutionary vanguard. This raises an important question: how does this view of democracy differ from Leninist or Maoist revolution? Perhaps not much. "In its style," Hayden conceded, "SDS was a group like the Jesuits or Bolsheviks. It was a small band of true believers taking action to catalyze and convert."[109]

These kinds of confession might suggest that Hayden jettisoned all pragmatist influences, and one must wonder whether confrontational politics runs contrary to the spirit of democratic deliberation. At the point where politics involves intense conflict, talking tends to stop and spirited action takes the forefront. Hayden never bothered to square his penchant for rebellion and confrontation with his more Deweyan rhetoric. Mills's work exhibits a similar tension. Toward the end of his life, he began to see revolutionary action as the only way to topple—or even weaken—the securely entrenched power elite. Even before he began praising Castro and anticolonial revolution throughout the world, he renounced the pragmatists and dismissed them as naively ignorant of how power really works in modernity. Mills's message was quite clear: the democratic community of competent inquirers had become a luxury for which we no longer had either time or use.

Both Mills and Hayden believed that when civil forms of democracy fail to work, a more confrontational approach becomes the only option. But heroic confrontation requires a leap of faith. Never certain of the consequences of such action, the hero plunges into the unknown. He acts and hopes for the best. Although impetuous action of this kind can be interpreted as an existentialist solution to our despair in the modern world, the very opposite of a pragmatist solution, it is wrong to create a dichotomy between pragmatism and existentialism.

In espousing revolutionary action, both Mills and Hayden took pragmatism to its natural limits. In the hope of constructing a better future for himself and his community, which has not emerged after more prudent approaches have been tried exhaustively, the true pragmatist will not shy away from experimenting with revolution. Some kinds of revolution would be beyond the pale, proving too violent or exclusive for pragmatist tastes. But the pragmatist would never rule out the chaos of unorthodox political approaches, for he remains open to all ideas and solutions to problems. Dewey did not live long enough to witness the civil rights and student movements, but his call for a more radical politics suggests he would have lauded these efforts to bring about social justice. Indeed, if sit-ins involving a large number of willing participants bring about the desired effects, if they successfully put a chink in the armor of segregation or perhaps serve as an enlarging experience for those involved, the pragmatist would endorse them wholeheartedly.

Furthermore, confrontational politics does not necessarily preclude peacefulness, inclusiveness, broad participation, and consensus building. For instance, SNCC adopted confrontational methods in its struggle against segregation and racial injustice, yet it still operated internally under strict democratic principles. Before any action was taken, participants had to reach a consensus, and most leadership roles were rotated periodically to avoid the consolidation of power in the hands of a few. Proud of SNCC's democratic practices and decentralized power, members liked to see themselves as part of a "movement" instead of an organization.[110] SNCC's example suggests that we can view the confrontationalism of Mills and Hayden within the traditions of both pragmatism and participatory democracy.

In its early years, the New Left envisioned participatory democracy as a way to transform individuals and society at large for the better, and SDS activists in the early 1960s put this ethos into practice. Indeed, the Port Huron conference, with its caucuses and plenary assemblies running throughout the night, was an example of participatory democracy in action. Later on, participants in the Economic Research and Action Project (ERAP), most of them members of SDS, descended on poor neighborhoods in cities throughout the country, organizing residents to fight for much needed change in their ailing communities. At the outset, members of ERAP lived communally and made all decisions, even the most mundane, on a consensual basis, and they imparted participatory democratic values to the people in their communities. In one of their pamphlets, they declared without a hint of irony that "freedom is an endless meeting"—a decidedly bizarre mantra but one that reflects a serious, even fanatic, commitment to democratic principles. Instructed and inspired by the civil rights movement, they also understood that confrontational politics was sometimes necessary in resisting dominant power structures, but they held to a firm belief in both nonviolence and collective decision-making.

As the movement seemed to lose ground in the face of an escalating war in Vietnam and intractable racism and poverty at home, their democratic politics increasingly gave way to a petulant lashing out, born of frustration and a sense that all hope had been lost. This peevishness culminated in the splintering of SDS and SNCC in the late 1960s and the formation of far more radical groups such as the Weathermen and the Black Panthers, who abandoned the democratic ideals of the *Port Huron Statement* and endorsed the use of violence to achieve their ends. This petulance, mixed with melancholy, can be seen in the writings of Sheldon Wolin, the renowned political theorist whose experience at Berkeley in the mid 1960s heightened his sympathies for radical politics. For him, democracy in its purest form must maintain a fugitive and rebellious spirit, a notion he undoubtedly derived, at least in part, from Mills and his followers in the New Left.

# Sheldon Wolin and Melancholic Democracy

Sheldon Wolin (1922– ), an emeritus professor at Princeton University and one of the most influential political theorists in the American academy, has taken to heart the lessons of Mills and the New Left. In his view, the American political system offers no opportunities for meaningful citizen participation and, as a result, remains unresponsive to the needs of the people. Doubtful that political institutions of any kind can accommodate widespread civic engagement, Wolin favors formless and confrontational democratic action that operates outside the system and periodically reaches a crescendo in times of crisis. Outraged with the current state of affairs, the people can effect change by making noise, staging protests, issuing public demands, and holding elites accountable for their actions.

For Wolin, participatory democracy is a fleeting affair, to be experienced only in a social movement or a protest of some kind. It can never be institutionalized on a permanent basis, for the demos must feed on an ample supply of spontaneity and energy if its genius is to be fully realized. Although not an obvious heir to the pragmatist tradition, Wolin actually takes its tenets to a logical extreme. In his view, democracy can yield political truth and transform its participants only if it remains pure (that is, truly inclusive, open, and deliberative), uncorrupted by institutional procedure and routine.

## Searching for the Political

Wolin has devoted his career to gaining a fuller understanding of "the political," an ideal, perhaps illusive condition of political engagement in which the participants act toward common ends. For him, the political stands in opposition to politics, or what most would call politics-as-usual, in which participants grapple for power to serve private goals:

> I shall take the *political* to be an expression of the idea that a free society composed of diversities can nonetheless enjoy moments of commonality when, through public deliberations, collective power is used to promote or protect the well-being of the collectivity. *Politics* refers to the legitimized and public contestation, primarily by organized and unequal social powers, over access to the resources available to the public authorities of the collectivity.

Perhaps most important for Wolin, the political requires deliberative participation on the part of not only elected politicians or other elites but of the "public" as well.[1]

Politics, on the other hand, is something with which we are all quite familiar, involving competition among "organized and unequal social powers" for positions of authority. Only an elite few, those selected to represent a particular social power, are able to become "public authorities of the collectivity" and thus make decisions that affect its well-being. Attaining power is often an end in itself for the contestants, and although their decisions affect the well-being of the collectivity, they do not promote the common good so much as they carry out the agenda of the social power(s) they represent. Because these social powers are "unequal," some contestants have more resources at their disposal than others do to realize their objectives. By its very nature, politics excludes certain groups from political decision-making and distributes power unequally. Inherently exclusive, politics fails to work toward common ends, according to Wolin.[2]

Only an inclusive political process, which allows all citizens to participate, can successfully promote the common good. It is no surprise that later in his career Wolin made it clear that the political can really only manifest itself democratically. He *does* suggest that democracy "is one among many versions of the political," probably because he hesitates to deny the possibility of other manifestations he has not envisioned. Nevertheless, democracy represents the political par excellence for Wolin: "Democracy is a political moment, perhaps *the* political moment, when the political is remembered and re-created." Pure democracy for Wolin is far different from any of the variants that have emerged in the last two thousand years.[3] To deserve the name, a democracy must be inclusive, participatory, and deliberative. In Wolin's conception of what he sometimes calls radical democracy, all citizens share in political decision-making and work collectively and painstakingly to find solutions to social problems. Power is decentralized and diffuse, resting in the hands of the many, who, though diverse and heterogeneous, seek to understand other points of view and to reach mutual agreements on disputed matters. Anything short of this vision compromises the power of the people and threatens to consolidate power in the hands of a few who ultimately work toward private, not common, ends. Our politics—with its periodic elections, endless campaigns, and political parties—amounts to nothing more than a sham or a mockery of democracy because it fails to accommodate deeply participatory modes of political experience.

Wolin's vision of democracy is so uncompromising that he believes any formalization or institutionalization brings about its death. Once institutionalized, democracy becomes co-opted, a domesticated servant of the state, and it quickly loses its participatory characteristics. This explains why Wolin hesitates to provide a clear picture of what democracy might look like in practice. Blueprints and plans are anathema to democracy because they immediately place limits on the possible and necessarily guide politics in particular directions. "Institutionalization brings about not only settled practices regarding such matters as authority, jurisdiction, accountability, procedures, and processes but routinization, professionalization, and the loss of spontaneity," says Wolin.

> Institutionalization depends on the ritualization of the behavior of both rulers and ruled to enable the formal functions of state—coercion, revenue collection, policy, mobilization of the population for war, law making, punishment, and enforcement of the laws—to be conducted on a continuing basis. It tends to produce internal hierarchies, to restrict experience, to associate political experience with institutional experience, and to inject an esoteric element into politics.[4]

Contrary to the democratic spirit, institutionalization introduces structure and routine to politics, which in turn creates hierarchies and restricts access to power. Formless, spontaneous, even anarchic, Wolinian democracy has no "settled practices" and thus can manifest itself in a variety of ways. Although democracy may temporarily occupy institutions, those institutions should never take hold of it and impose a particular form or structure.[5]

Undoubtedly frustrating for some readers, Wolinian democracy remains a somewhat nebulous concept. Perhaps it is best understood as a process of political renewal in which citizens are "creating new cultural patterns of commonality" and "contesting the forms of unequal power." Wolin even provides examples: "Individuals who concert their powers for low-income housing, worker ownership of factories, better schools, better health care, safer water, controls over toxic waste disposals, and a thousand other common concerns of ordinary lives are experiencing a democratic moment."[6] In other words, democracy emerges in the form of a social movement or protest against the state, a rationally disorganized reaction against formal institutions and power structures. Wolin even suggests that we disconnect democracy from various mechanisms of control and embrace its anarchic qualities. "Instead of a conception of democracy as indistinguishable from its constitution," he says, "I propose accepting the familiar charges that democracy is inherently unstable, inclined toward anarchy, and identified with revolution and using these traits as the basis for a different, *a*constitutional conception of democracy." In its pure state, democracy must remain "resistant to rationalizing conceptions of power" and "might be summed up as the idea and practice of rational disorganization."[7] Accepting the accusation that democracy has anarchic and revolutionary tendencies, Wolin is free to examine and illuminate it without the familiar qualifiers (constitutional, liberal, and so on) clouding our vision. He seeks to understand democracy unadulterated, and unlike most political theorists, both old and new, he argues that its domestication (or constitutionalization) is unnecessary, based on unwarranted fears.

According to Wolin, though democracy may be disorganized and anarchic, it finds coherence and commonality in a shared place, history, and culture. Every person is located in a place in this world where his experiences with nature and other people shape his identity. We must situate a person in his cultural and historical context to understand him.[8] Like many critics of liberalism, including communitarians, Wolin has little use for a politics that reduces the citizen to an unencumbered self—to an individual whose identity is completely independent of the culture and history that produced him. He regards the unencumbered self as an ahistorical fiction that uproots the individual from the histories, traditions, mores, and customs that constitute him and connect him to his fellow men. "A political being" is not "an abstract, disconnected bearer of rights, privileges, and immunities" but, rather, a "person whose existence is located in a particular place and draws its sustenance from circumscribed relationships: family, friends, church, neighborhood, workplace, community, town, city."[9] The identity of a political being is contextual, inseparable from the experiences he shares with others in his community. Shared experience—past, present, and future—is an important element of Wolinian democracy, but one must not assume he endorses homogeneity or uniformity.

In eschewing institutionalization and formalization, Wolinian democracy remains (to use his terms) both "localized" and "feudal," comprising a complex web of relationships and a diversity of interests and traditions that resist such forces of centralization and uniformity as the modern state or corporation. When people of various interests and experiences come together for a common purpose, when they engage collectively in political action to resist the current organization of power, and when each individual participates fully, they become a demos. Wolinian democracy, then, is complex and diverse, spontaneous, loosely organized, but geography and history create a common identity around which the demos can organize and become animated.

Like individuals, the demos is capable of heroic political action and strives to enhance its power. In fact, the demos has a considerable advantage over political individuals: it is far more powerful and fearsome. The demos has an immense capacity to challenge existing laws and political institutions, even to transgress or subvert them. In a clever inversion of Nietzsche's master and slave moralities, Wolin argues that the transgressive tendencies of the demos resemble those of the superman, whose will to power is insatiable yet never grounded in resentment or malice.[10]

Wolin concedes, however, that unchecked demotic power can exceed mere transgression. It can become destructive, annihilating not only all political, social, and economic institutions but also, in the end, itself. For this reason, political theorists have long disparaged the demos as a grave threat to the political order and the rule of law, and they have defended other political forms—aristocracy, monarchy, republicanism, liberal democracy—on the grounds that they can contain demotic power.

Liberals have been especially worried about threats to individual rights. Time and again liberals have invoked the familiar Tocquevillian phrase, "tyranny of the majority," to justify institutional obstacles to citizen participation. Of course, what Wolin would call obstacles, liberals would regard as safeguards—the idea being that institutional checks and balances serve to fragment power and thus prevent a majority faction from trampling on the rights of an unfortunate minority.

But liberalism, Wolin argues, represents more than just an attempt to attenuate the excesses of majority factions through institutional safeguards. It constitutes a concerted effort to derail any kind of meaningful political action and to redirect human energies toward private economic pursuits:

> The task, as Madison and later liberals saw it, was to encourage institutional devices that would control the effects of politics, not to reconstitute politics. Citizens would be engrossed in private actions, for when men and women are given freedom they use it to promote their self-interests, and it would be unjust and oppressive to limit that pursuit in the name of encouraging common action for common ends.[11]

Liberals seek to disassemble the demos, because they consider any kind of "common action for common ends" to be "oppressive," a threat to individual rights. They encourage citizens to withdraw into their own private lives and pursue solely what is in their self-interest. In Wolin's estimation, liberalism has been especially complicit in encouraging the growth of the administrative state, whose chief purpose is to assuage our anxieties about the many sources of pain and suffering in the world.

Primarily concerned with threats to its right to life, the unencumbered self voluntarily contracts with equally worried people. This imaginary contract, according to Wolin, provides justification for the hyper-rationalized, bureaucratized, and centralized liberal state whose ostensible function is to protect individual rights but whose actual objective is to centralize and augment its own power and to nurture and support capitalism at home and abroad. This leaves little room for political action and puts individuals at the mercy of a labyrinthine bureaucratic state, enormous faceless corporations, and the ebb and flow of the economy.

The result is the withering of freedom and power for individuals and their communities. Preoccupied with profit margins and the acquisition of worldly goods, liberal man is acutely sensitive to the pain caused by the loss of wealth. Feeling vulnerable to whimsical shifts in the market economy, he turns weakly to the state for protection. Plagued by anxiety, liberal man does not care about sharing the exercise of political power; he measures the legitimacy of a regime by the extent to which the state can successfully apply what J. S. Mill called the pleasure principle—maximize pleasure and minimize pain.[12]

The political, then, gives way to increasing reliance on the state to improve our lives, to guarantee our safety and provide services, and liberal man loses a portion of his humanity as a result. The modern state has made almost any kind of democratic action nearly impossible by turning citizens into consumers, active political participants into passive political spectators, socially connected beings into atomized individuals. It is not surprising that Wolin shows little concern for demotic destructiveness: it is highly unlikely to occur in modernity. The dangers of unfettered democracy pale in comparison to the palpable evils of political passivity and disaffection.

Assisted by bureaucracy and centralized administration, and nurtured by social and economic elites, the modern state effectively depoliticizes what were once considered political matters, transforming them into administrative or technical issues. The assumption becomes that the large political questions have all been answered, that a bit of fine-tuning or a few slight adjustments to our current economic policies can make everything right again. Most of us can just abandon politics and leave it to the experts to fix any glitches in the system. Our political engagement need not extend beyond periodic evaluations of these experts, reelecting them if we like the material results of their actions or replacing them if we do not. So long as the economy grows apace, providing a plethora of goods and services to which we have become accustomed and feel increasingly entitled, we accept the status quo. Should the economy slump or should the state fail to provide services to our satisfaction, we elect new people who espouse a few alternative policies but never entertain more radical solutions—such as fundamental changes to the system. In today's political economy, says Wolin, we cease to be citizens—to be fully human—and become docile recipients of the technocrat's expertise.

In recent years, Wolin has ascribed far more sinister designs to the state. The postmodern capitalist state that lays claim to "superpower" status (that is, the United States) bears resemblance to the Nazi regime in that it too "aspires to totality." Wolin suggests that the totalitarianism against which we always thought the "free world" had achieved a series of stunning and decisive victories has merely assumed a new and inverted form—a form that appears far more benign than earlier incarnations, such as Stalinism or Nazism, but that has similarly terrifying features. This latest threat to human freedom is what Wolin calls "inverted totalitarianism."[13]

Wolin is quite aware of the obvious differences between the Nazis and the postmodern capitalist regime. Whereas racial hatred inspired the Nazis, the "ideology of the cost-effective" and economic efficiency motivates the postmodern state. Whereas the Nazis sought to mobilize the citizenry to support their initiatives, the postmodern state "works to depoliticize its citizenry" and "promote a sense of weakness, collective futility that culminates in the erosion of the democratic faith." Whereas "big business" in Nazi Germany ultimately served the interests of the state, "corporate power has become predominant" in the postmodern state. These differences only go to show that inverted totalitarianism can achieve the same nefarious aims as its earlier incarnations. Although their means may differ, totalitarian regimes of all stripes are fiercely ideological and aggressive on the world stage, and perhaps most disturbingly, they create a "general climate of fear and suspicion" that reduces "the citizen" to a "nervous subject."[14]

The recent war on terror in the wake of September 11 lends credence to Wolin's alarmism. One only has to consider the Patriot Acts, which sanction intensified domestic surveillance, or the torture and indefinite detention of "enemy combatants," which exemplify the Bush administration's brazen defiance of the Geneva Convention, or the invocation of a new doctrine of preemptive war in order to justify the invasion of Iraq. Things could not be much gloomier for Wolin.

On the surface, he is an unlikely candidate to advocate radical democracy. A World War II veteran born into what has been popularly referred to as the "greatest generation," Wolin was nevertheless radicalized later in life by his involvement with the Free Speech Movement at Berkeley. He then adopted a decidedly anti-institutional, almost anarchic, understanding of democracy. But in the years following this experience, especially after the Reagan Revolution reached its high point, he has struck an increasingly melancholy note in his writing. He seems to be almost eulogizing those deeply participatory moments he believes modernity has taken away from us for good. This melancholy may not seem consistent with the optimism of his pragmatist forebears, but if anything, Wolin has remained too faithful to the first two pragmatist tenets—the democratic epistemology and the democratic psychology—and has taken them to their logical extreme. The result is an uncompromising view of democracy that ultimately undermines his democratic metaphysics, the faith that people face no serious obstacles to engaging in civic action. While Wolin believes that democracy is a transformative activity, promoting the general welfare and the moral and political development of its participants, he claims these experiences are fleeting, for postmodern forms of power foreclose opportunities for meaningful political participation.

## Bringing Power to Truth

Like the classical pragmatists, Wolin adopts a democratic epistemology. He believes that people learn socially and experientially, that the truth is an agreement reached after painstaking discussion and deliberation among those people whose experiences are relevant to the question at hand. In support of this idea, Wolin accepts and employs the postmodern notion that power precedes knowledge (or truth). He does not believe that truth corresponds to some fixed or a priori reality but, instead, embraces the idea that truth is a social construct, grounded in our experience with power relationships. Deference to an elite group of experts, for instance, serves only to give them a monopoly on the truth. It thereby disempowers the majority of people, whose experiences could contribute considerably to the discussion and to the creation of knowledge and truth. An inclusive and participatory politics will reconstitute power so as to promote the common good—and a radically different conception of truth. Empowering the entire citizenry, not just a fraction of it, will yield political knowledge and practices—truths, if you must—from which the collectivity as a whole benefits.

All societies face the dilemma, says Wolin, of "creating a common rule in a context of differences." Yet a society cannot "overcome" the dilemma so much as it can "lessen the crudities of the judgment" and find a "political comprehensiveness" that attends to the "dominant values held by the major groups in society." The best way to achieve such comprehensiveness, claims Wolin, is to promote widespread political engagement:

> The numerous acts whereby the citizen takes part in the political processes of the society help contribute to the comprehensiveness, and generality, of decisions; they are the methods of expressing the differences resident in society and thus make it possible for better informed judgments to emerge. . . . Participation is the basic method for establishing areas of agreement or political consensus.

For this reason, says Wolin, it was "fatuous" for Leo Strauss to claim that "agreement may produce peace but it cannot produce truth." Political agreement can produce truth, but a certain kind of truth—one that is held together by citizens who decide on public matters "by consensus." Wolin concludes: "A political judgment, in other words, is 'true' when it is public, not public when it accords to some standard external to politics." Only a deeply participatory democracy can bring about "true" political judgments that can bring about a better and more just society. There are no standards of justice and truth that come prior to public discussion in a democratic forum.[15]

This last point becomes clear in Wolin's criticism of the French philosopher Michel Foucault, whose career was devoted to illuminating the configuration and deployment of power in modernity. In Foucault's writings, says Wolin, "the emphasis is upon the repressive, dominating quality of power." He "gives us a vision of the world in which humans are caught within imprisoning structures of knowledge and practice, but he offers no hope of escape. Every discourse embodies a power drive and every arrangement is repressive. There is no exit."[16] Any attempts to transcend the structures of power are ultimately futile in the Foucauldian universe, and this futility is the "consequence of having accepted an unqualified Nietzschean conception of knowledge as generated by power drives that leaves no room for conceptions of theoretic vocation and civic commitment." Wolin accepts the Foucauldian notion that power is ubiquitous but rejects the pessimistic view that power is always deployed to oppress and dominate.

Wolin suggests that power directed toward common ends can actually be liberating. In Wolin's view, Foucault came to the conclusion that neither political theory nor civic action offers an escape from the structures of power because he "confused politics with the political." Foucault failed to understand that the political can "constitute the terms of politics so that struggles for power can be contained" and directed toward "common ends, such as justice, equality, and cultural values. Commonality is what the political is about." This is possible because people who engage in the political develop a "critical vantage point," a perspective that transcends both narrow self-interest and dominating systems of power.[17]

Because Foucault believed all truth claims are really just attempts to dominate, he rejected the possibility of such a critical vantage point. Truth, he claimed, can never be "validated by procedures and conventions recognized by some appropriate community of inquirers." Thus there is no truth in this world, only "truth" with scare quotes, assertions of which we must forever remain wary because they are necessarily contaminated by some discourse of power. Of course, this assertion—that all truth claims are attempts to dominate or repress—is a truth claim in itself, which suggests that Foucault "repeated the same error of totalistic thinking with which he taxed classic theory."[18]

Wolin, on the other hand, avoids this pitfall by maintaining that a "community of inquirers" can often validate truths and make judgments through consensus-building. People are not imprisoned within Foucaldian "discursive formations," which prevents them from ever sharing experiences with other people in their community to arrive at truths. To the contrary, our shared experiences with power shape our identities more than anything else and thus serve as a basis for socially constructed truths. Change the organization of power, which affects our lives in a direct and tangible way, and you will reshape the prevailing discourse and create new truths. According to Wolin, real truths (without scare quotes) are not objective or independent of power relationships, but they do stem from a critical vantage point that only political theorizing or demotic action can provide. People have the capacity to imagine a better world for their communities (political theory) and to act collectively to realize their dreams (civic action). Never privileging the desires of a particular individual or group, theorizing and civic action can together promote a "participatory, community-oriented politics" that ultimately redirects power—and hence truth—toward common ends. For Wolin, truth emerges when, drawing upon their experiences, all citizens in a political community deliberate and then decide what is best for the whole. Truth is the judgment—and the sole jurisdiction—of the demos.[19]

That Wolin has an unfailing faith in the demos becomes even more apparent when he scoffs at the liberal fear of majority tyranny. Even Aristotle, an anti-democrat to the core, conceded that "the demos was better at deliberating public policies than were the few." Despite the familiar warnings from the liberal camp that the demos poses a grave threat to individual property rights, there is really nothing to fear. Wolin points to Athenian democracy, which "was guilty of few, if any, excesses against the wealthy. The importance of this point is that the demos was not so much concerned with gaining forms of social recognition as [with] creating a distinct political place where power was equally shared. In short, the ideal was political, not social."[20] The Wolinian demos does not wish to engage in class warfare and butcher the bourgeoisie; it wants merely to broaden political participation and diffuse power. Moreover, the democratic impulse tends to be restorative, not destructive or tyrannical, according to Wolin. It restores the political and can heal a society ravaged by human or ecological degradation:

> The possibility of renewal draws on a simple fact: that ordinary individuals are capable of creating new cultural patterns of commonality at any moment. Individuals who concert their powers for low income housing, worker ownership of factories, better schools, better health care, safer water, controls over toxic waste disposals, and a thousand other common concerns of ordinary lives are experiencing a democratic moment and contributing to the discovery, care, and tending of a commonality of shared concerns.[21]

Wolin is far more sanguine about what collectivities can accomplish than liberals or other detractors of democracy. He suggests here that their capacity to address "shared concerns"—of which there are thousands of examples, however modest—belies liberal warnings about majority tyranny.

Democracy's tyrannical tendencies may be greatly exaggerated, says Wolin, but in his recently published tome, *Tocqueville between Two Worlds,* he concedes that democracy may have two opposing propensities: one toward diversity, particularity, and decentralized power; the other toward uniformity, homogeneity, and totalizing statism. According to Wolin, Tocqueville believed that only participatory democracy, something akin to the fifth-century Athenian political experience, could offset the latter propensity. Wolin could not agree more: the only cure to the ills of "democracy" is real (or deepened) democracy. "[I]f democracy failed to cultivate participatory forms that engaged politically the energies of the ordinary citizen," Tocqueville suggested, "political populism would be displaced by a cultural populism of sameness, resentment, and mindless patriotism, and by an anti-political form he labeled 'democratic despotism.'"[22]

Despite paying considerable lip service to the idea, Tocqueville did not fear majority tyranny so much as this "democratic despotism"—an "anti-political form" of democracy where citizens do not play a decisive role in decision making, where a culture of apathy, passivity, and social alienation prevail instead. Democratic despotism leaves individuals isolated and powerless, resentfully withdrawing into private life, and mindlessly conforming to the dictates of state and economy. Participatory democracy, on the other hand, brings people closer to the implications of political decision-making, instilling in them a respect for the exercise of power, and cultivating a wariness of simple, impetuous solutions.

This was why Tocqueville praised the New England town meeting. "The township was not so much the faithful reproduction of democracy as its crucial qualification," serving to redirect its conformist and socially leveling tendencies. As Tocqueville saw it, the township represented an arena for petty politics (politics on a small scale). It was accordingly able to connect citizens directly to social concerns, awakening their moral sympathies and showing them that their "political involvements made a difference." Moreover, the "immediacy of [a township's] politics has not the inconsiderable virtue of restraining the democratic appetite for generalization [uniformity and statism]" and participants have "a natural respect for limits because the implications of a law are more readily grasped."[23]

In its consideration of immediate concerns, the demos—the counterpoint to majority tyranny—understands readily that its decisions affect the lives of other people, and as a result, it exercises power far more judiciously than liberal alarmists would ever give them credit for. Judicious and deliberate, the Wolinian demos demonstrates a self-consciousness usually characteristic of individuals. He sees the demos as a political actor that, like an individual, can form a coherent and critical perspective. Hardly an unthinking mob that merely reacts against oppression, the demos has the capacity to wield power responsibly and make astute decisions on important political questions.

There have been few true democracies in history, according to Wolin, so his portrait of the demos relies heavily on one shining example—fifth-century Athens. If we are to believe his historical account of Athenian democracy, the demos certainly sounds impressive:

> Athenian democracy of the fifth century was shaped by class conflicts, rivalries between the rich and the well-born, the ambitions of politicians, and the struggle for empire. It developed as the demos became a self-conscious actor. Democracy began as a demand for a "share" of power in the institutions for making and interpreting the laws and deciding questions of diplomacy and warfare. It culminated in popular control over most of the main political institutions at Athens.

The portrayal of the demos as a "self-conscious actor" that took "control over most of the main political institutions" is essential to Wolin's political understanding, for, as we saw earlier, truth emerges from the judgment of the demos.[24]

If we are to take this epistemology seriously, we must accept a radically different conception of the demos. Drawn from a diversity of individuals with "scattered experiences," the demos develops into a coherent whole with a "self-consciousness about common powerlessness and its causes. The demos is created from a shared realization that powerlessness comes from being shut out of the councils where power's authority is located." Now aware of its exclusion from the corridors of power, the demos finds unity from common experience and demands. From this struggle, the demos "becomes political, not simply when it seeks to make a system of governance more responsive to its needs, but when it attempts to shape the political system in order to enable itself to emerge, to make possible a new actor, collective in nature."[25] The ragtag collectivity, whose political struggles contribute to its maturation and development, turns into a self-conscious and unified political actor with an unprecedented capacity for governance.

The Wolinian demos displays not only self-consciousness but also the heroic or agonistic qualities usually attributed to individuals. "Because the heroic has been claimed as an individualistic category, the idea of an agonistic demos seems not only unfamiliar but oxymoronic," says Wolin. Most people would consider it "intuitively absurd that an agonistic demos, like an agonistic Alcibiades, might be driven by the needs of its nature to strain at constitutional restraints." Perhaps the "anonymity" of the demos prevents observers from seeing its "heroic" qualities. But like Alcibiades or other political heroes throughout history, the demos strives for power, sometimes transgressing established rules or "constitutional restraints" in the process. The heroic action of the demos often manifests itself in the form of "revolution or popular uprising, collective disobedience, and mass protest." As a result, the demos is "typically regarded as destructive or disruptive of established order and as anticonstitutional or threatening to become as such."[26]

Wolin suggests it is unfair to interpret the agonistic behavior of an Alcibiades as heroic and to view similar behavior from the demos as destructive and threatening. Both individual and demotic agonism stem from the same primal urge to acquire power. If anything, demotic agonism is far more heroic, suggests Wolin, for the individual seeks to achieve private ends while the demos attempts to redress power inequalities, which Wolin believes are the primary source of injustice in the world. Thirsting for power, the demos can certainly be destructive in the short term, but it seeks to redistribute power more equitably—a far more heroic aim than individual glory.[27]

Wolin prefers demotic power also because he sees it as an expression of Nietzsche's master morality. The demos exerts its will to power not out of resentment but out of a relentless, even joyful, drive to expand, to create new opportunities for participation, to transgress boundaries. Elite power, on the other hand, manifests a slave morality, its exertions stemming from fear and resentment of the demos.[28] As a result, elites have long conspired to persuade us that democracy threatens the common good.

Wolin does concede that there is a darker, self-destructive side to demotic agonism. After the demos has consolidated its power domestically, it may channel its surplus energy outwardly, beyond the borders of its homeland. "The demos exists as striving, but that drive may be directed not at assuring duration to its existence but at challenging its own finitude. The tangible expression of that problematic would be the leap from polis to empire."[29] Wolin does not believe that a few demagogues convinced the Athenian assembly to carry out their imperial designs. To the contrary, the "empire was a testimony to both the transgressive and aggressive impulses of the Many and to an epical hero whose agon goes mostly uncelebrated by poets and philosophers and only ambivalently by ancient historians." As with an Alcibiades or an Alexander, this desire can become all-consuming, leading to imperial designs that literally uproot the demos from its polis. When Alcibiades left his beloved Athens to fight for its archenemies, the Spartans, he considered his act not so much a betrayal of his city but rather an attempt to recover what had been lost. Although he no longer inhabited the city, he was still an Athenian in spirit. Similarly, after having suffered its second invasion, the Athenian demos uprooted itself from the city and took to the high seas. The polis might have been lost, said Pericles, but the Athenian demos could sustain itself at sea, as a naval power. The demos, like Alcibiades, abandoned its polis to further its imperial designs but still retained its Athenian identity.[30] What becomes apparent here is that while the demos will undoubtedly redistribute power more equitably at home, it may display the characteristics of a tyrant in its contact with the outside world. And in its attempt to repress strangers abroad, the demos might overextend itself, leaving itself vulnerable to military defeat, social disarray, and ultimately the loss of identity.

The dangers of democratic excess and surplus energy are even more serious in modernity. Should the demos ever harness the power of the state, says Wolin, there is no telling what the damage might be. Democracy is "incompatible with the modern choice of the state as the fixed center of political life," which means that it would be both an unlikely and an undesirable occurrence. "Democracy in the late modern world cannot be a complete political system, and given the awesome potentialities of modern forms of power and what they exact of the social and natural world, it ought not to be hoped or striven for."[31]

Wolin does not pursue the matter further, but once one considers his discussion about democratic imperialism, it seems obvious that he fears the demos could perhaps misuse modern forms of technologically enhanced military power currently at the state's disposal. To put it bluntly, the demos may not restrain itself from using nuclear, chemical, or biological weapons to destroy its adversaries abroad. Wolin suggests that there are limits to the epistemological authority of the demos, whose knowledge of the truth cannot extend beyond the polis, the center of common history and experience. This implies that even Wolin thinks democracy requires some constraints, though hardly the constitutional limits currently imposed on it in the United States. If the Wolinian demos can somehow remain localized and contain its energy to domestic concerns, its epistemological authority would remain unassailable.

The issue of democratic imperialism aside, Wolin's epistemology must be squared with that of his professional nemesis—the behavioral social scientist, whom he calls "the methodist." There are some obvious similarities between Wolin and the methodist, for they both accept implicitly the idea that truth is probabilistic and socially and inductively constructed. It would hardly be a stretch to describe Wolinian truth as a generalization drawn from a large sample of democratic participants. After all, the truth emerges, according to Wolin, when all citizens share power and deliberate collectively—the more inclusive the process, the better. But Wolin bitterly rejects methodism for its conservative and anti-democratic tendencies. Methodism, he argues, is a "proposal for shaping the mind" in such a way that "reinforces an uncritical view of existing political structures."[32] Having little use for creativity, imagination, or spontaneity, methodism applies fixed techniques and procedures to test hypotheses.

Since Descartes, those with a methodological disposition have eschewed anything that smacks of disorder, doubt, or diversity. They have instead embraced whatever bears the mark of regularity, uniformity, and homogeneity. They gravitate toward the familiar and summarily dismiss any alternative approaches or creative solutions to problems. Furthermore, Descartes argued that the methodical person had to erase all "acquired habits, beliefs, and values" until he "stood divested of [his] cultural heritage in an ahistorical silence." In theory, this ahistorical being, uncorrupted by received beliefs and values, is an impartial observer of politics and approaches the subject with a scientific detachment, but Wolin argues that this is not so. In rejecting tradition and the past and always searching for regularities in political behavior, the methodist can only draw on current practices as his reference point for what is normal. Accordingly, he betrays a conservative bias against fundamental change and an unreflective penchant for the current system of power.[33]

Wolin believes that an insightful political science—any insightful science, for that matter—relies on careful consideration of the past and our traditions. Erasing the past putatively serves the requirements of objectivity but actually destroys any possibility of gaining a critical perspective. Students of politics and political actors alike must reflect on—and come to terms with—the myriad of experiences and ideas that have shaped who we are, no matter how shameful, contradictory, or muddled they may be. In so doing, we draw on what Wolin calls our "tacit political knowledge," which is far more "suggestive and illuminative" than "explicit or determinate."[34]

Not surprisingly, Wolin is not optimistic about the application of science to the political. In the expanded edition of *Politics and Vision,* he comments specifically on the link between the scientific method and democracy in a chapter partially devoted to John Dewey. Wolin's treatment of Dewey reveals a qualified sympathy for his overall project. Unlike theorists in the Baconian tradition, who believed it was incumbent on the state to harness the power of science and technology to serve the interests of progress, Dewey was suspicious of this marriage. Like Wolin he understood that the state and the agents of advanced capitalism could deploy science and technology to augment their own power. So, instead, Dewey proposed a marriage between science and democracy: "[He] proposed a conception of science that not only placed it at the disposal of democracy but emphasized the intellectual affinities, even the continuities, between scientific method and everyday practices."[35]

Dewey understood democracy as nothing other than the scientific method writ large. Science represented the paragon after which true democracy must pattern itself: "Science, Dewey insisted, was a moral undertaking. Scientists not only practiced cooperation but presumed a community to which they could present their findings and count on unfettered discussion. . . . Dewey's ultimate ideal was a society in which scientific values permeated the culture and shaped human desires towards more cooperative and egalitarian ends."[36] Dewey believed that every human being is capable of learning from the laboratory of life, formulating hypotheses, testing them with empirical data, and sharing the results with others in the "scientific" community. This democratic laboratory is the classroom in which participants (or students) receive an education, learning collectively how to redress problems through experimentation. Dewey also stressed that only face-to-face participatory democracy, local in character, could adequately replicate the scientific method so as to promote the general social welfare.

Although Wolin seems to agree with the tenor of Deweyan democratic theory, he finds fault with Dewey for "evading questions about power." Dewey was so "fixated on the findings of method, the conduct of experiments, and the communication of result" that he largely ignored "[q]uestions of how problems become identified, who controls the communications of results, and who evaluates the consequences."[37] Dewey assumed that every democratic participant would be the equivalent of a scientist who is familiar with the methods of experimentation, and he never explored the possible asymmetries of power and knowledge intrinsic to scientific culture.

Accordingly, Wolin challenges the democracy-as-method metaphor, suggesting that science employs esoteric "concepts and language" that so exceed "the common understanding as to be incomprehensible to the vast majority of citizens."[38] Wolin does not haughtily suggest here that some people are too stupid to understand science. Rather, he maintains that the cult(ure) of science is inherently elitist and fails to promote the equal exchange of information in the ideal way described by Dewey. Grafting this scientific way of life onto the greater populace would not bring about democracy but would instead only maintain the inequalities already in place. Dewey held naive, romantic notions about science and, as a result, failed to recognize that it was susceptible to interest politics and that it could even perpetuate hierarchies of knowledge and power. Now heavily financed by the modern state and big business, science has been properly exposed as impure and corruptible, vulnerable to co-optation. For Wolin, this only reinforces what was true all along: science and democracy do not mix.[39]

Thus, while Wolin may subscribe to a democratic epistemology, he does not believe that the demos simulates the scientific community in any way. Democracy is far too fluid and anarchic, resisting any form or procedure one might impose on it. This formlessness is what allows democracy to remain egalitarian, inclusive, and deeply participatory.

It is also important to remember that the Wolinian demos is a peculiar community, taking on the characteristics of an individual, including self-consciousness and willfulness, in its struggle. The demos coheres around this nascent political identity, and marshaling immense power to achieve its aims, will not hesitate to transgress boundaries, sometimes leaving a path of destruction in its wake. The scientific community, on the other hand, has embraced institutionalization and all the hierarchies, routines, and procedures that come with it. As a result, it has a far more conservative disposition and will rarely defy protocol, let alone follow a revolutionary course of action.

His sharp criticisms notwithstanding, Wolin does not disparage scientific methods without qualification. His major beef is with current methodological practices. He acknowledges that "the invention of methods, like the invention of theories, demands a higher order of creativity and is entitled to the highest praise." Problems arise "when that discovery is institutionalized in a training program," for it impoverishes education and "poses a threat not only to so-called normative or traditional political theory, but to the scientific imagination as well." It endangers those creative qualities that are crucial to both theorizing and understanding the factual world, such as "playfulness, concern, the juxtaposition of contraries, and astonishment at the variety and subtle interconnection of things."[40]

Wolin suggests here that behavioral social science—that is, methodism—is not even good science, for it institutionalizes and routinizes the search for knowledge, spurning all creativity and imagination in the process. Good scientists employ method when appropriate, but they do not limit themselves to this approach. They always remain mindful of historical context and the messy confluence of traditions, and they must playfully acknowledge contradictions and nuances in their analyses of the empirical world.

Like the pragmatists before him, Wolin believes in the intersubjectivity of truth—that any community, even a scientific community, constructs a truth after painstaking discussion and deliberation, sharing all relevant knowledge and experiences with one another. And this is not always a neat process; it often requires participants to break the rules, to improvise unique solutions to social problems, and to abide patiently the not always fruitful contributions of others (or themselves, for that matter). As William James admonished, the search for truth must remain open and never foreclose imaginative approaches or intrepid forays into the unknown. Celebrating the regimens of training and technique, the professional methodist shuns both the past and the imagination and has no patience for what he considers to be unproductive digression. Perhaps we can understand him better as a technician, not a scientist, for he practices method stolidly and predictably.

What most separates Wolin from his pragmatist forebears epistemologically is his treatment and understanding of power. The demos has the inside track on political truth because it reorganizes power so as to serve common ends, not because it adopts superior methods of inquiry. Although Wolin's formulation draws on postmodern notions of power to which the classical pragmatists were not privy, the metaphor of statistics still resonates in his epistemology. After all, statisticians praise larger sample sizes for enhancing statistical power. One might rephrase Wolin's democratic epistemology as follows: Increasing the sample size of participants changes the dynamics of power which in turn generates truths that serve the common good. In the end, Wolin's epistemology resembles closely that of the pragmatists: both argue that truth is consensual, the product of painstaking discussion and deliberation among people who draw on their relevant experiences.

## The Transformative Power of Democracy

Like the pragmatists, Wolin also subscribes to a democratic psychology, the notion that man is an educable and mutable creature, capable of moral development. The idea of an unwaveringly flawed "human nature" is really just a defeatist myth, justifying political apathy and compliance with the status quo. Man will remain stagnant if he continues to embrace political passivity and the predominance of the modern state, but should he become a political animal, share power equitably, and engage with his fellow men to make a better world, he will improve not only society, as we saw in the previous section, but also himself.

Because democracy is the fountainhead of truth, the democratic experience is the school in which one receives a proper education. For Wolin, democracy affords its participants a transformative experience, teaching them to think beyond narrow self-interest, to have empathy for people unlike themselves, and to work with others toward common ends. He says, "In my understanding, democracy is a project concerned with the political potentialities of ordinary citizens, that is, with their possibilities of becoming political beings through the self-discovery of common concerns and modes of action for realizing them."[41]

To make sense of Wolin's democratic psychology, we must first turn to his view of human nature. Briefly stated, man is not bound by his nature; he is a collection of ingrained habits. The political constitution—or the way in which society organizes power—disposes people toward certain patterns of behavior and demands of them an obedience to the status quo. Over time this organization of power circumscribes what man thinks he is capable of accomplishing in this world; it "determines" his "political identity." As Wolin put it: "The historical project of most societies, including our own, is to shape its members so that they do more than obey or submit: they become *disposed,* inclined in such a way that political authorities can count on their active support most of the time." These "dispositions," which constitute every person, are far more than just "learned behavior"; indeed, they are "inscribed demands" or "exactions" whose effects strengthen "over time and become cumulative." What we believe are unassailable truths about politics and humanity are really just demands we have internalized unwittingly and embraced as our own. Our acquiescence to these demands reinforces our own dispositions and se-cures the power of political authorities. In turn, these authorities can count on our support because over the years we have become so accus-tomed to the way power is organized in society that we blindly accept its inequities. We assume the organization of power reflects inexorable reali-ties about human nature and life itself, but Wolin reminds us that "power and identity are never fixed once and for all: they are historical projects being worked out over time and in a claimed space."[42]

Man is a mutable creature whose character is not circumscribed by the laws of nature but rather habituated over time by power relationships. Power, not nature, places limits on the possible; power, not nature, deter-mines who we are. Changing our political constitution, then, will trans-form who we are. The current political constitution, says Wolin, gives us "an essentially anticivic education," for it teaches that "the first duty is to support the self-interest of the group because politics is nothing but a struggle for advantage." This kind of interest-group politics works on the assumption that life is necessarily a zero-sum game with winners and los-ers. It "dissolves the idea of the citizen as one for whom it is natural to join together with other citizens to act for purposes related to a general community" and replaces it with "the idea of individuals who are grouped according to conflicting interests." In other words, the system adopts a divide-and-conquer strategy. It conditions us to believe that we are not "civic creature[s] bound by preexisting ties to those who share the same history, the same general association, and the same fate." Instead, each of us defines himself by a group or vocational identity—"a business execu-tive, a teamster, a feminist, office worker, farmer or homosexual"—that "naturally divides [us] from others." As a result, each group competes for a finite share of resources, serving only its own interests and never enter-taining the possibility of a broader perspective.[43]

In addition to dividing us, the system also teaches us to identify our own well-being with the growth of state power, both domestically and in-ternationally. We may surrender our own political power in the process, but many (not all) of us find it worthwhile after receiving unprecedented economic and material benefits in return.[44] The American experience is espe-cially instructive, as most of us have profited from both the welfare state and aggressive imperialism. The former has provided social security benefits and corporate subsidies, for instance, while the latter has afforded us cheaper con-sumer goods and low oil prices. As far as we are concerned, things are fine so long as the state and the political economy can deliver the goods and im-prove our lives in these very materialistic ways.

But despite what we are led to believe, human nature does not require us to be this way, suggests Wolin. The modern state has habituated people to this way of thinking, which means there is always the possibility that a new organization of power can reeducate them and broaden their perspective. Wolin calls for revolution to challenge existing power structures and thus change our dispositions, our habits of mind and action: "Nothing short of a long revolution" will subvert "the current structure of power" and change the way people think; it "is illusory to believe . . . that the same human dispositions toward power—passivity by the many, control by the few—will serve as well for a new social order as for the current one."[45]

Under the right conditions we can all become "new beings"—citizens in the true sense of the word. Unlike the "groupie," says Wolin, the citizen transcends this "stage of unreflective self-interest" and, learning to "think integrally and comprehensively rather than exclusively," develops a "perspective of commonality."[46] Participatory democracy is the school in which groupies acquire this education and transform themselves into citizens who think beyond narrow self-interest to consider common concerns.

In Wolin's view, Tocqueville was instructive on this point. The French aristocrat maintained that modernity has increasingly conditioned man to withdraw inwardly into the private sphere and to lead a life of crass self-interest and materialism. Tocqueville argued that participatory democracy was the best antidote to reverse this trend, to defeat social alienation and rampant individualism. The New England townships show by example that participation can rehabituate or reeducate people, teach them that their own interests actually coincide with the common interest, that they enrich their own lives by cooperating with others.[47] Wolin readily concedes that the citizen of the New England township never undergoes a complete moral transformation in which private interests unequivocally give way to the common good. After all, the township is the stage for petty or "circumscribed" politics. But he thinks this form of participation, undoubtedly an imperfect model of democracy, is a step in the right direction.

Pure democracy may exist only in the realm of theory, but this does not detract from its value as a model. Indeed, fifth-century Athens provides us an example of participatory politics on a grand scale. In this case, the demos did not limit itself to questions of local governance or emerge on the margins of society to rebel against the existing system. While it still resisted boundaries and transgressed convention, it engaged in mainstream and large-scale politics, taking control of the city's most important political institutions and addressing the most pressing issues of the time, including even foreign policy. The result was "the self-transformation of the demos into the citizen body, of the subject into citizen."[48] Wolin argues that this transformation was confirmed by decidedly anti-democratic observers who described how the Athenian demos became a "politically committed class." It "evolved into a different being whose essence is civic: a full-fledged citizenry whose being is validated through the numerous institutions in which it takes an active part," says Wolin. "The beast has somehow become a deliberating citizen."[49]

Although political theorists have often waxed lyrical about the importance of civic education for the general health of the polis, they have usually argued that a group of elites or even god should be responsible for this task. People could not change on their own, in other words. Even Rousseau, whom Wolin considers a pseudo-democrat, could not "conceive of a self-fashioning people," so he devised "a deus ex machina, a Great Legislator who is to transform human nature."[50]

Wolin maintains that people can transform themselves by participating in the democratic process. Democracy is the school in which its participants learn how to deliberate and wield power collectively. As the Athenian experience testifies, citizens undergo a profound transformation when they engage in democratic politics:

> Deliberative politics was the crucial element in the experience by which a demos constructed itself as a political actor. Deliberative politics was for the demos a mode of political development, and by the same token certain other types of politics—bureaucratic, charismatic, or even representative government—arrest that development. A participatory and egalitarian politics that is deliberative serves the political education of the demos.[51]

From their engagement in "deliberative politics," citizens learn to transcend narrow self-interest, empathize with their fellow men, and focus on the long-term implications of their actions. They develop "a mode of thinking that deals in considerations and categories different from those used in one's own affairs," and they deliberate "for the future more than for the present," which at the very least "requires repressing immediate gratifications."[52] Interacting with others in his community, the democratic citizen becomes a different kind of human being, future-minded and selfless.

So, why does democracy transform its participants in this way? Wolin maintains that "transgression was crucial to the making of a democratic actor."[53] As they resist conventional norms and boundaries in their struggle for power, participants open new vistas, new possibilities not only for the distribution of power but also for self-understanding. Democratic citizens come to realize that it is within their power to alter themselves and society as a whole, that their own development feeds back into the society they seek to remake. Wielding power to resist what we often consider to be natural or normal—about both ourselves and society—is the key to demotic transformation. "Democracy," says Wolin, "is committed to the claim that experience with, and access to, power is essential to the development of the capacities of ordinary persons."[54]

To make his case, Wolin once again points to fifth-century Athens. Defying "the norms of nature to set up their own standards," the Athenian demos became a "new political presence that had succeeded in developing its own political culture." The effect of democracy on its participants can be so powerful that there is little wonder why Plato, an Athenian citizen, believed it to be "an invasion of the psyche, contesting for nothing less than the 'soul' of all citizens."[55]

Wolin's democratic psychology does not rest on his readings of the New England township and fifth-century Athens alone. Wolin also draws from personal experience. As a professor at Berkeley in the 1960s, Wolin became involved in the Free Speech Movement, a radicalizing experience that changed him and many of his colleagues forever. "The intensity of the experience . . . changed everyone involved. For many of us it was the experience of moving from an apolitical to a deeply political existence, from a protected status with known boundaries to a condition that was risky and unfamiliar."[56] In resisting the university's draconian speech laws, Wolin was introduced to a new kind of existence, fraught with risk and variability but enriched by deep political engagement. His experience taught him that in order to be fully and authentically human one must act collaboratively in defiance of political norms and forms.

## Episodic Democracy

Wolin's theory seems to lack a robust democratic metaphysics, a faith that people, if given the opportunity, will awake from their slumber of passivity and act to make the world a better place. Although he claims that real change demands meaningful political action, Wolin is hardly sanguine about the prospects of this ever happening. Occurrences of the political or of democracy, according to Wolin, are "episodic, rare," while politics as usual "is continuous, ceaseless, and endless." He says:

> The political has become specialized, regularized, and administrative in char-
> acter and quality. Institutionalization marks the attenuation of democracy:
> leaders begin to appear; hierarchies develop; experts of one kind or another
> cluster around the centers of decision; order, procedure, and precedent dis-
> place a more spontaneous politics: in retrospect the latter appears as disor-
> ganized, inefficient. Democracy thus seems destined to be a moment rather
> than a form.

The modern state has so effectively foreclosed opportunities for political action that only in momentary democratic uprisings does Wolin find any kind of hope. Democracy has become "fugitive," surfacing episodically in reaction to crises, rocking the boat a bit until the state makes the neces-sary adjustments to domesticate political action and suppress any serious critical opposition.[57]

The hope for a marriage between the modern state and democracy rests on a profound misunderstanding: that people can engage in meaningful political action within the modern state apparatus. This is impossible because the state by its very definition seeks to bureaucratize and mechanize, to establish a set of procedures and protocols. In the process, it serves to contain spontaneity and promote passivity. As the state and our reliance on it grow, the opportunities for democratic moments diminish. No wonder Wolin believes "the idea of a democratic state is a contradiction in terms."[58]

Although the emergence of the modern state has foreclosed opportunities for democratic action, Wolin argues that democracy has always been a fragile enterprise. And he offers a possible explanation for this: democracy is an inherently unsettling experience for its participants, who will eventually betray a "conservative temper" and make attempts to impose a form on it. He points to the demise of true democracy toward the end of the fifth-century B.C. in Athens. After the revolution against the Thirty Tyrants, "the restored democracy" made a series of decisions about citizenship eligibility, "indicating that democracy had 'settled down' and found its constitutional form, its ne plus ultra."[59] Wolin argues that before this settling moment, Athenian democracy could be described as "a succession of popular uprisings that succeeded in transforming the so-called ancestral constitution and its various boundaries."[60] It was a "culture not only of participation but of frequent rebellion," in which boundaries were challenged and never clearly delineated.[61] But this rebellious spirit came to an end when the Athenian assembly clearly drew these lines, distinguishing between those who could and those who could not participate. Athenian democracy adopted a "constitutional form," which marked the beginning of its domestication and institutionalization—its death.

At times, Wolin waxes lyrical about the prospect for revolutionary action in which "citizens withdraw and direct their energies and civic commitment to finding new life forms" and their "whole mode of thinking [is] turned upside-down" such that they "renounce the state paradigm."[62] These glimmers of optimism may seem inappropriate given what he has said about the "fugitive" character of democracy. But it is important to understand that Wolin's democratic metaphysics rests ultimately on his democratic psychology. Most of us may be disposed toward political passivity, making the prospects for democratic action quite dim, but a series of democratic moments could always change our dispositions. In other words, these democratic moments—if enough of them erupted—could have a cumulative effect and eventually reverse the way we think and act. One gets the sense that Wolin is not holding his breath here, but he does maintain hope that citizens can subvert the "state paradigm" and in a profound way reclaim their humanity.

His cautious optimism notwithstanding, Wolin never fully convinces his readers that there is much hope for democracy, for he is never able to resolve tensions inherent within it. He insists that democracy must remain localized, grounded in a place and a people's history. At the same time he argues that, in order for it to take hold, democracy today has to transcend parochial concerns and address the larger issues at stake in the modern world. That is to say, democracy will never manage to subvert the state—which not only perpetuates an antidemocratic organization of power but also influences all of our dispositions—if it refuses to look beyond local concerns. "While it is of the utmost importance that democrats support and encourage political activity at the grassroots level, it is equally necessary that the political limitations of such activity be recognized," says Wolin; "the localism that is the strength of grassroots organizations is also their limitation. There are major problems in our society that are general in nature and necessitate modes of vision and action that are comprehensive rather than parochial."[63]

The problem is, how can democracy be both local and national in character? Wolin perceives the conundrum here. He understands that local democratic movements can be "bigoted, provincial, myopic, and anti-intellectual"—that their "exclusive concern with backyard politics" may only exacerbate "historical legacies of wrong and unfairness" for which the modern state is largely responsible.[64] The current problems besetting society today are "general in nature" and thus demand a "comprehensive" response, a large scale democratic movement that uproots the source of all that is wrong. In the early 1980s, he detected "hopeful signs of discontent . . . at this more general level in the antinuclear movement, the opposition to an imperialistic foreign policy, and the defense of human rights." But he has been unable to maintain this optimism in our current age of complacency. As he despairs over the emergence of "inverted totalitarianism," Wolin never explains how a comprehensive response to general problems can be accomplished, leaving this problem for future thinkers who may develop "modes of vision and action" currently beyond our scope.[65]

While Wolin admits that a tension between the particular and the general exists, he seems to underestimate the severity of the issue. Many political thinkers have suggested that the size and scope of modern society make participatory democracy impracticable, but Wolin dismisses this claim outright. He argues that democracy is only incompatible with the modern state, not with the size and scope of modern society.[66]

He overlooks an obvious question: does not the vastness and complexity of modern society invite state intervention and regulation of society and economy—not only for sinister reasons, like imposing order and perpetuating social hierarchies, but also for more legitimate reasons, such as to improve the quality of life for millions of people living in close proximity to each other? As Stephen Holmes argues in his review of *Tocqueville between Two Worlds*, democratic majorities often call on the state to offer its expertise in accomplishing honorable social goals. As women entered the workforce in larger numbers, for example, voters asked the state to play a more significant role in caring for the elderly. Holmes cites this example to suggest that democracy and the modern state are not "inherently at odds."[67]

Even if we accept Wolin's argument that our growing reliance on the state erodes true democracy, he is unable to explain why we would ever turn to participatory democratic movements to improve our lives. Indeed, even professional legislatures, whose members enjoy far more time to devote to politics than do ordinary citizens, have increasingly delegated authority to the executive branch and the bureaucracy to address complex issues extending beyond their expertise. Eschewing the delegation of authority to experts, participatory democracy may turn back the clock—maybe even work against social progress for women, for example—and reintroduce social and economic conditions that most people would consider far too primitive and reactionary to embrace. Wolin would respond that we have been conditioned to think this way, to believe that only the state can marshal the expertise to solve complex social problems. It is difficult, however, to imagine the demos addressing problems that affect hundreds of millions of people inhabiting a land that stretches from the Atlantic to the Pacific.

Given this unresolved tension between the particular and the general, the local and the national, Wolin's democratic metaphysics appears weak. If pressed on this issue, Wolin would probably agree. He has written about the founding period in American history and has lamented the failure of the anti-Federalists and other proponents of local participatory democracy to defeat the ratification of the Constitution. For Wolin the Constitution represents a radical departure from the democratic heritage of the colonial experience in America, expressed most succinctly in the Declaration of Independence.[68] The Constitution marks the beginning of a new America, "primarily economic and intentionally antidemocratic."[69] Although vestiges of the democratic tradition in America remained after the ratification, the Civil War drove the final nail in democracy's coffin. It may have put an end to slavery, but in so doing it resolved the tension between local democracy and the centralized state. The latter won decisively, "reducing the power of the states, and working a revolution in the *moeurs* of the American citizen: instead of a participating member of the polis, he would be a voter."[70] Wolin's narrative of early American history suggests that certain key events undermined our democratic heritage and set us on a perilous course toward increasing centralization, bureaucratization, and imperialism. In this light, recapturing what we lost so long ago seems a nearly impossible task.

One wonders why Wolin has devoted his career to a way of life he believes is nearly unattainable—and when it is attainable, only momentarily. Indeed, his Weberian pessimism precedes him, and he has only just stopped short of declaring outright that democracy is dead. He even suggests that the vocation of the political theorist resembles that of the eulogist, devoted to preserving the memory of democracy and articulating the significance of its loss for humanity.[71]

But, for Wolin, democracy is not exactly dead; it lies dormant, waiting to reawaken in moments of crisis and to emit occasional shocks to the state. This suggests that he does not lack a democratic metaphysics so much as he has embraced a soberer version of it. Quite realistically, he accepts that the modern state will never disappear. It is here to stay. But he does hope for more democratic moments that can, first of all, keep the state in check and, perhaps more important, give people an opportunity to experience, however briefly, their humanity to the fullest.

In the end, his democratic metaphysics strikes a melancholic, even tragic, chord. He describes democracy as "a mode of being that is conditioned by bitter experience, doomed to succeed only temporarily, but . . . a recurrent possibility as long as the memory of the political survives."[72] And those participants fortunate enough to taste the bitterness of democracy enjoy a strange kind of power, which Wolin describes as "experience, sensibility, wisdom, even melancholy distilled from the diverse relations and circles we move within."[73] He seems to suggest that in modernity democratic power endows its participants with a critical perspective, one that drives them to act but continually reminds them of the futility of it all, evoking what humanity once had but can never have again. Accordingly, Wolin's radical democracy assumes the tenor of a "melancholic democracy"—more a sad remembrance of what has been lost than an upbeat theory of what can be.

## The Sandlot

Wading through the oeuvre of Sheldon Wolin is a formidable enterprise, to say the least, and one can become quickly entangled in a jungle of apparent tensions and contradictions. Examining his work through the lens of the three pragmatist tenets, however, reveals an overall coherence to his democratic theory. He believes that deliberative collectivities, unrestrained and unbounded, have a grapple hold on the truth (democratic epistemology); that man is mutable and thus has the capacity to direct his habits of mind and action toward common concerns (democratic psychology); and that men will on occasion, and in defiance of the state, seize the opportunity to act collectively (democratic metaphysics). In some ways, Wolin has taken the pragmatist tenets to their logical extreme in his democratic theory. His rabid anti-institutionalism invokes the Jamesian admonition that the search for truth must always remain open, forever eschewing attempts to foreclose new approaches.

It is no wonder that his democratic theory, in the context of modernity, ends on a melancholy note. The open universe seems but a dream in a world increasingly dominated by technology, in a world where everything would come to an abrupt halt without our established routines, procedures, and processes. Ephemeral and elusive, democracy is a precious experience that can never be sustained long enough to yield its purported epistemological or psychological benefits.

To give these rather abstract concepts some life, it may be helpful to consider the game of baseball as a metaphor for democracy. Wolinian democracy evokes images of the sandlot, a place where neighborhood kids gather to play the game they love. Imagine a rickety wooden fence in the outfield, sweatshirts used as bases, unmowed grass with brown and yellow patches, and countless bumps and divots in the ground that make for tricky bounces in the infield.

The children do not care. They play for neither money nor fame; they play for the sheer thrill of the game. There is no need for umpires, for the players regulate the game and settle disputes themselves. While there is general agreement on the rules of the game, they are hardly fixed. For instance, if more or fewer than eighteen players arrive on a particular day, the rules will be altered to ensure fair play and equal playing time. One team may be short a player, for which they will receive just compensation by giving the other team only two outs per inning instead of three. Both teams may have more than nine players, which will require either rotating substitutions or allowing more than nine players on the field. Or perhaps an older, more powerful player may agree to bat left-handed so as not to give his team an unfair advantage. A late arrival may change the entire dynamic of a game, requiring some ad hoc adjustments, maybe even switching a player from one team to another. It hardly matters in the end, for they may choose not to keep score today. Winning is hardly as important as an evenly matched, well-played game.

Finally, there are no spectators or fans. Whoever arrives at the sandlot, no matter how late, receives a warm invitation to play or, if he prefers, to be directly involved in another way—perhaps as a scorekeeper or a base coach. Everyone is a participant, contributing to the game in his own way, sharpening his skills, and enjoying an authentic baseball experience. Collectively these participants represent the demos.

Constitutional (or liberal) democracy, on the other hand, evokes images of professional baseball and all the associated glamour. Adorned in their freshly washed and pressed uniforms, muscle-bound athletes play on an impeccably manicured field in a forty-five-thousand-seat stadium. They observe set rules, strictly enforced by umpires. Without these impartial judges there would be chaos on the field, for the owners and the fans issue a clear mandate: winning is everything. With billions of dollars on the line for owners, players, and merchandisers, what was a gentleman's game in the nineteenth century becomes a mass spectacle, drawing millions of fans to the ballpark or their televisions.

The most important feature of the professionalized game is its exclusiveness, drawing a clear line between players and spectators. Passively watching the trials and triumphs of their heroes on the field, spectators can only find meaning in their own lives from the comfortable confines of their luxury box seats or living room. They can experience baseball only vicariously. Representing the fans of their fair city, players constitute a meritocratic elite who enjoy not only the rare opportunity to play but also the bargaining position to negotiate multi-million-dollar contracts. In the end, all the money and fanfare corrupt the players, whose celebrity turns them into commodities for product endorsement and makes them forget why they loved the game in the first place. As is the case in politics today, Wolin would suggest, both players (i.e., politicians) and spectators (i.e., citizens) are unable to have an authentic experience of baseball (i.e., democracy).

In keeping with the momentary and melancholic nature of Wolinian democracy, the sandlot will not last forever. The better players will go on to play organized ball, some kids will move away, and others will develop different interests. Maybe a local Little League organization will turn the sandlot into an enclosed, unblemished field complete with bleachers and a concession stand. Other potential sites for spontaneous play will be harder to come by, as parents and property owners place more restrictions on where children can play.

Lest their lives be beset with tragedy or disaster, we plan every aspect of our children's lives, even their recreation. With good intentions we try to manage their activity, to make sure things do not get out of hand and no one gets hurt. Ultimately, the fear of broken windows and legs and the ensuing lawsuits inspires managed recreation. Wolin would suggest that such attempts to eliminate risk take the fun and spontaneity out of life, create merit-based hierarchies, and set limits on inclusion. Recall that talented kids play more than others in Little League, and that overly involved parents often take these organized games far too seriously and put undue pressure on their ten-year-olds, even in ostensibly supportive environments. It goes without saying that the intrusive adults in this metaphor represent the paternalistic state.

It becomes apparent as we play out this metaphor that, sadly, democracy is a fragile enterprise. A myriad of factors can undermine the unity of its participants—that is, the demos—and send them in different directions. As opportunities for participation become more scarce in this world, it is almost as if the stars and planets have to be perfectly aligned for an authentic democratic experience to occur. As baseball has become increasingly professionalized and institutionalized through media technology (television, video games, and so on), it becomes far easier and more pleasant for us to be spectators. We would rather experience the game vicariously, not authentically, as this provides many of the game's thrills without its discomforts, both mental and physical. Wolin recognizes there is a certain inevitability to all this, but he holds on to the dream that, whenever possible, people will choose to take part in those spontaneous, natural experiences in life, like sandlot baseball or pure democracy, and when reflecting on those days, will remember with sorrow what has been lost and dimly hope to recapture it.

# Benjamin Barber and Quixotic Democracy

Political theorist Benjamin Barber (1939– ), the Gershon and Carrol Kekst Professor of Civil Society at the University of Maryland, is a renowned advocate of participatory democracy whose sharp critique of liberal democracy proves far more convincing and illuminating than his democratic remedies. Unlike Wolin, however, Barber does not consider the "democratic state" an oxymoron. He has been far more sanguine about the possibility of creating permanent institutions that spur citizen participation in the political process.

A self-acknowledged heir to the pragmatist tradition, Barber has dedicated his career to the proposition that an open community of inquirers can devise and implement policies that promote the commonweal and transform all participants into enlarged-thinking citizens. Although he has acknowledged the many social and cultural obstacles blocking the way to the realization of this dream, he maintains an ardent faith that people would choose to participate in time-consuming neighborhood assemblies if given the opportunity. In the Deweyan spirit, Barber claims that participatory democracy can become a mainstay in political life, a vital supplement to existing representative institutions. More than just a momentary response to a crisis, participatory democracy can become a way of living.

## Setting Free the Animals

In his landmark work, *Strong Democracy,* Barber argues that liberal democracy—what he calls "thin democracy"—rests on a set of metaphysical assumptions that perpetuate the "belief in the fundamental inability of the human beast to live at close quarters with members of its own species."[1] To liberals, the idea that communities, working collectively for the greater good, can reflect the better angels of our nature is inconceivable, even perniciously idealistic. In their view, collectives quickly become unruly hordes posing a threat to the rights of individuals. As a result, liberal politics amounts to little more than "zookeeping," devising the right institutional mechanisms and barriers to ensure that these human beasts can co-exist peacefully within a finite amount of space.

Liberal man is not innately social or political so much as he is a solitary figure whose greatest wish is to be left alone and guaranteed protection from would-be intruders. His engagement in politics extends no further than the voting booth, where he periodically chooses elites to govern on his behalf. So long as these elites successfully limit the amount of conflict in the zoo, liberal man feels content and will happily reelect them. Perhaps it goes without saying that, for Barber, liberalism lacks imagination and vision; it embraces a far too pessimistic and simplistic understanding of man.

At the heart of liberal reductionism, says Barber, are three often conflicting dispositions—anarchism, realism, and minimalism. Valuing the negative rights of the individual and the relentless pursuit of property above all, liberalism is disposed toward anarchism. It endorses a radical individualism that rests on the belief that the state only stands to get in the way of the individual and become an unwanted authoritarian presence. Understanding that individual rights will never be secure in a stateless society, liberals also embrace realism and allow for the state's use of power to mitigate conflict and instill order. Hobbes, probably the first liberal political philosopher, was a realist par excellence, believing that only an absolute sovereign could protect man from the ferocity of his peers. Later, liberals such as Locke and Madison argued that such a formidable state might successfully restrain the actions of tyrannical men but would never be able to restrain itself.

So, in an attempt to find a happy medium between anarchism and realism, liberals have tended toward minimalism, the notion that the state is a necessary evil whose authoritarian tendencies can only be avoided if it maintains strict neutrality on the common good, endorses pluralism and tolerance, and creates institutional safeguards to limit its own authority. While we might see minimalism as a reasonable balance between our desire for liberty and our need for political power, according to Barber, it never resolves the tension so neatly. Our natural condition requires the creation of the state to protect our liberties, but the state itself poses a threat to those very liberties it is meant to protect. The point at which the state satisfies the demands of realism without compromising the concerns of anarchism may in the end be impossible to pin down, thus exposing the incoherence of liberal thought.

Barber finds liberalism frustrating largely because it rests on a number of faulty assumptions about humanity. Liberals presume, sometimes without realizing it, that "humans are material beings in all they are and in all they do—that their social and political time and space are literally material or physical time and space." Thus they believe that humans are "governed by laws that correspond to the laws of physical mechanics."[2]

As physical entities first and foremost, liberal human beings assume the characteristics of a Newtonian atomic particle. Each human is a distinct and self-contained unit, an atom whose motives and actions are always whole and indivisible. No two people can occupy the same space at the same time physically, politically, socially, or psychologically. Finally, only that which excites our senses can affect us either physically, emotionally, or intellectually, and each one of us responds to these external stimuli in exactly the same way.

This mechanistic conception of man leads liberals to believe that man is by nature a solitary, hedonistic, and politically apathetic being who seeks only to maximize his own sensual pleasure and to remove any impediments toward that goal. Free to the extent that nothing impedes his motion, liberal man believes other human beings, no matter who they are, represent a potential threat to his freedom. People interact with other human beings only when it is mutually beneficial, serving each person's private and hedonistic interests. Otherwise, they prefer to be alone, free from any intrusions on their personal space and any obstacles in their way. Both the anarchist and realist tendencies of liberalism view every human being in exactly the same way, as a "radically individuated particle."[3]

At the same time, liberals hold disparate views about the role of the state, mainly because each tendency rests on a distinct understanding of political space. The liberal-anarchist sees political space as infinite and imagines there is enough space in the world for individual atoms to roam freely without any danger of conflict. Only the state threatens the free movement of each atom; other atoms never present such a menace. On the other hand, the liberal-realist sees political space in finite terms: it is a "densely populated" universe wherein freely roaming atoms are apt to collide with one another. Tension and conflict among atoms is the norm, requiring the state to intervene, to create boundaries so that individuals are protected from encroachments by others. The liberal-minimalist, whose search for middle ground leads him to value tolerance and mutual respect, flirts with the idea that "conflict does not exhaust the potential of human concourse," that human beings have the capacity to work together toward greater ends, but ultimately he too, says Barber, can never relinquish an atomistic conception of humanity.[4] Liberals may disagree about how much entropy animates the particles in the political world, but they all agree that the fundamental objective of politics is to keep these atoms away from each other. Collective attempts at promoting the common good will only increase the level of entropy, almost certainly putting these atoms on a collision course.

Forever fearful of the authoritarian tendencies of collectives, liberals always detect something sinister beneath the surface of their ostensibly good intentions. This wariness breeds conservatism, an outright fear that any democratic action, no matter how well reasoned and popular, may trample the "natural" rights of individuals. Better that we erect institutional barriers to collective energies than risk their potentially dire consequences. Better that we do nothing at all, even if circumstances demand action, than proceed impetuously and regret it later. For, in the liberal universe, there are only a few oases of certainty in a vast empty desert, and our lives are in peril any time we wander too far from these wondrous gifts of nature. Desperately clinging to these natural oases, liberals refuse to accept that communities can build their own oases, even towns and cities, in the arid desert. It is never wise to build a city on a foundation of sand, they warn.

Liberals call this political paralysis by a variety of euphemisms—prudence, circumspection, caution—which, they claim, uncertainty makes necessary. But, oddly, liberals are selective with their skepticism. The political convictions of majorities may arouse their incredulity, but liberals are quite certain of their atomistic assumptions about humankind. They never bother to question these assumptions from which they deduce certain political "truths" (namely, that government exists solely to safeguard the free movement of autonomous atoms), and they assuredly espouse political quiescence among the citizenry.

As Barber understands it, liberals fear political conviction and change because they skitter back and forth between radical absolutism and radical skepticism and cannot find a reasonable middle ground. Either in an absolutist or a skeptical frame of mind, liberals come to the same conclusion— that collective action of any kind can only cause trouble. The problem with this emphasis on "keeping men apart rather than . . . bringing them together" is that it comes at the "price of undermining activity."[5]

Uncertain that concerted action will yield beneficial results, and afraid that it may even invite disaster, liberals prefer inaction to all else. But the lack of certainty, says Barber, should not necessarily preclude concerted action. Minimalist timidity introduces its own dangers:

> Afraid of overstepping the prudent boundaries set by skeptical reason, the liberal is politically paralyzed. Because he is uncertain of his beliefs, he hesitates to act. But in a world of necessary actions and ineluctable consequences, the liberal's diffidence cannot mean that nothing happens, only that *he* causes nothing to happen. He may modestly abstain from acting on

behalf of public goods that he does not think can be legitimated, but his reticence only means that private and clearly illegitimate forces will control his destiny unopposed. Refusing to impose himself or a public will on others, he willy-nilly permits market forces, which are neither public nor just, to ride roughshod over his fellow citizens.[6]

Understanding liberty merely as "freedom from" intrusions on our personal space and property encourages a dangerous passivity that leaves many people vulnerable to an increasingly boorish private sector. Vigilantly adhering to constitutional limits, the liberal state agonizes over the extent to which it can lawfully intervene on the behalf of the majority will, while economic elites consolidate their power and play an increasingly dominant role in our lives. We may not be certain about the consequences of any given civic action, but Barber maintains that political paralysis invites a certain end: the "random coercion and arbitrary force" of faceless corporations that will "seize hold of our common destinies."[7] Merely protecting negative freedoms succors the economically powerful, and it does nothing to aid the less fortunate or to promote a broader sense of the social good. After all, elites have far more resources at their disposal, not only to assert their authority in the private sector but to buy influence in the public sphere.

The minimalist attempt to reconcile liberty with power, anarchism with realism, discounts the prospect of citizenship, the idea that human beings are more than just autonomous particles, that in fact they often define themselves in the context of their political community. According to Barber, the citizen cares about far more than his own sensual pleasure and maintains strong political convictions and loyalties. Barber's citizen does not recoil from imagining a better and more just society than the one he currently inhabits, or from taking action to make his dreams a reality. "With some pluck and creativity we can too build a city on a foundation of sand!" says the citizen. Perhaps most important to Barber is the idea that liberty and power are connected, that freedom depends on taking control of our destiny and not simply acquiescing to the world we face. Only nominally free, most liberal men remain vulnerable to the caprices of market forces, and invisible to the helpful hand of the state, while a politically engaged citizenry can alter the balance of power in society, curbing the cruel excesses of the market, and making the state responsive to common needs. Without power to go along with it, freedom exists in name only; it is merely an abstraction that has no real meaning based on experience. Like Rousseau, Barber believes that man is born not free but in chains, and that he achieves freedom not by eluding his fellow man but by cooperating with him.

For Barber, man is an inherently social creature. Embracing an atomistic conception of man, liberals fail to take into account the fact that human beings are profoundly conflicted creatures whose selves are often split between competing loyalties or impulses, that our identities are the products of our relations with others, and that we often respond willfully (and not mechanistically) to the world around us. As Barber reminds his readers, no man possesses an undivided and unencumbered self that completely precedes social relations, and his actions are not merely predetermined responses to external stimuli. Each of us is ambivalent and complex, socially constructed and interdependent, idiosyncratic and willful. Identity is not monolithic or clearly defined. Every one of us resembles a community quilt, whose intricate patterns, the product of many hands and influences, reveal myriad inconsistencies and contradictions.

Man's freedom, then, is not tantamount to the unimpeded atom, for in large part he is the product of his community. Each of us is a "complex entity made up of different and conflicting parts. We can no longer speak of the entity being coerced or being free as a whole; we must specify which parts and which objects are in question."[8] My body, for example, may be free and uninhibited but my mind may not be. It may be under the spell of a powerfully persuasive influence or of unseen habits of mind formed by years of education, socialization, and subliminal messages. As such, man is free only to the extent that he is aware of all the outside influences and internal contradictions that constitute him and can then consider his options before acting. Reflexive or instinctive actions—mechanistic responses to external stimuli—indicate that he is in chains. As long as man is a conscious and deliberative actor, keeping in mind the opportunity costs of any decision and the regret he may feel later, he is free.

If we are to understand human beings in this more sophisticated way, as inherently social and conflicted creatures who are free to the degree that they are aware of their condition of interdependence, we will not conclude—as liberals do—that humanity is a lost cause, worthy only of a political system based on our worst, most pessimistic expectations of it. We will not assume that people are primarily hedonistic and selfish and then devise a political system that offers no hope other than protecting each individual particle from intrusion on its personal space. Nor will we understand politics in crudely pluralist terms, as an arena wherein private interests compete for influence over the state and fight over its finite amount of goods and services. Instead, suggests Barber, we will see man's capacity to view issues from someone else's perspective, to cooperate with others in the community, and to sacrifice personal gain for the sake of another. We will understand human freedom in social terms, as an awareness of the world around us and our complex relationship to it. Accordingly, we may imagine a far different political landscape, one in which people transcend their individual interests and become politically engaged citizens, directing their energies toward the commonweal.

Through his relationships with others, man can—quite unlike an atomic particle—transform himself. Unbound by preconceptions of what it means to be a human being, he can define himself by the manner in which he interacts with others. He can liberate himself from unconscious influences and the dogma of hedonism through democratic action. When reminded of Rousseau's admonition that men must be "forced to be free," liberals shudder with fear, recalling the bloody excesses of the French Revolution. But Barber finds this phrase far more innocuous than it sounds, for it simply suggests that, to be free, citizens must be made acutely aware of the civic duties for which they are responsible in their community. Democracy, with all its institutional mechanisms for deliberation and careful consideration of alternatives, creates the conditions under which citizens can exercise this kind of freedom. Unfortunately, liberal democracy provides opportunities for democratic participation only to a handful of elites—those fortunate enough to become our elected representatives.

A champion of participatory democracy, Barber offers a version that he calls "strong democracy." While "strong democracy has a good deal in common with the classical democratic theory of the ancient Greek polis," says Barber, it "does not quite envision politics in the ancient sense of a 'way of life,' and is explicitly hostile to the still more extravagant claim that politics is *the* way of life." Like liberals, Barber is sensitive to the dangers of totalizing politics and resistant to communitarian notions that the political should subsume every facet of our lives. Yet he is also frustrated with the citizen passivity and market dominance inherent in liberal politics. Strong democracy represents an attempt to find a middle ground. It "envisions politics not as a way of life but as a way of living—as, namely, the way that human beings with variable but malleable natures and with competing but overlapping interests can contrive to live together communally not only to their mutual advantage but also to the advantage of their mutuality."[9]

In a strong democracy, citizens engage more actively in politics but do so voluntarily, understanding that their participation will benefit themselves and the community as a whole. Strong democrats do not relinquish their private lives as citizens of the ancient polis do. At the same time their participation strengthens their attachment to their community and thereby transforms them in a profound way. To make this happen, citizens in a strong democracy participate directly in all three phases of politics—deliberation, policy-making, and implementation. Strong democracy, unlike Wolinian democracy, does not represent a wholesale rejection of liberalism and its institutions or uphold a radical vision of the political. Instead, Barber intends strong democracy to be an achievable goal that will modify rather than undermine existing liberal institutions.

Barber considers the liberal fear of majority tyranny to be overstated. In fact, he often quotes Louis Hartz who quipped that the "American majority has been an amiable shepherd dog kept forever on a lion's leash."[10] But he also recognizes the need for liberal institutions to protect minorities from potentially repressive collective action. By grafting strong democratic institutions onto existing institutions, Barber wants merely to change the emphasis of American politics—to remove many, but not all, limits on majority action. If this were to happen, the "amiable shepherd dog" would have the opportunity to roam on his own once in a while or, at the very least, enjoy the freedom that comes with a longer leash. We are animals that do not thrive in captivity and, in fact, can only reach our potential if set free from the "zoos" constructed and maintained by liberals.

Liberals maintain that citizens could never govern themselves well because they do not have the expertise to address complex policy issues and would rather succumb to the persuasive rhetoric of demagogues than engage in politics with any degree of seriousness. Barber respectfully disagrees, asserting that participation itself provides the education any citizen needs to contribute intelligently. We can expect a deliberative citizenry to govern itself well—far better, in fact, than a group of elites ever will. So long as strong democratic institutions are put in place, citizens will rise to the occasion.

Perhaps the most important phase of strong democracy is the first, in which citizens engage in public deliberation—or what Barber calls "political talk." In his view, political talk "protects the political process from rigidity, orthodoxy, and the yoke of the dead past" and also "enlarge[s] perspective and expand[s] consciousness [among the citizenry] in a fashion that not so much accommodates as transcends private interests and the antagonisms they breed."[11] To institutionalize political talk, Barber calls for the creation of neighborhood assemblies throughout the country, which would provide a forum in each community for citizens to deliberate with fellow citizens on important political matters, especially those of local interest. Citizens would not only voice their opinions but also listen to the perspectives of others in their community. Barber suggests that the art of listening may be the linchpin to strong democracy, for only through listening are we able to see beyond our private interests and consider ideas that challenge the dogma to which we have become blindly attached. With such a broadened perspective, we become citizens who can arrive at a mutual understanding and reach a consensus about the appropriate mode of action.

This leads us to the next phase of strong democracy. Once citizens have carefully considered an issue from various perspectives, they can move on to the decision-making process. Although Barber seems to extol the virtues of political talk more than anything else, he understands that people will only avail themselves of opportunities for deliberation if they can ultimately exercise political power. Talk means nothing if it does not lead to action.

So it comes as no surprise that Barber proposes institutionalizing a national initiative and referendum process to empower the citizenry. It is important to note, however, that he attempts to remedy the problems plaguing direct democracy in many states right now. He is aware that direct democracy is vulnerable to manipulation by elites, and that in its current form the referendum does little to encourage deliberation before citizens issue an up-or-down vote. This is why he endorses a process that resembles the one once used in the Republic of Raetia, where the referendum did not so much settle a matter as spark further debate.[12]

Barber proposes that neighborhood assemblies host meetings in which citizens may discuss the issues relevant to an impending referendum vote. To encourage further deliberation he recommends that referenda be voted on twice before they become law. He also favors a multi-choice referendum ballot that offers a "more varied and searching set of choices capable of eliciting more nuanced and thoughtful responses" from the citizenry. Rather than just yes or no, citizens will have five voting options: (1) unequivocal yes; (2) yes in principle, but with some reservations about the particulars of this proposal; (3) unequivocal no; (4) no with respect to the particulars of this proposal, but not opposed in principle (suggest "reformulation and resubmission"); (5) no for the moment, but not necessarily opposed in principle (postpone further action at this time).[13] Barber claims that this multi-choice format would inform the second round of deliberation. For example, if a majority votes "yes" on a referendum, but a large portion of that majority lends its support "with some reservations," citizens will have the opportunity to explore these reservations in the neighborhood assemblies. The idea here is that two-stage voting and a multi-choice format will encourage thoughtful decision-making and will also ensure that the shepherd dog remains amiable—and, perhaps more important, regretful.

In Barber's view, free political actors should experience regret about the lost opportunities that come from making any important decision. Infused with a feeling of "perpetual regret" for what could have been done or not done, participants in a strong democracy understand politics as an ongoing and endless process in which we always correct the mistakes, or build on the incomplete successes, of the past. Citizens should feel compelled to revisit an issue ad nauseam lest any better options (or even subtle modifications for improvement) are overlooked. (One wonders at what point regret turns into political paralysis—the kind with which liberals are often infected. Barber poses this question himself but, unfortunately, does not venture to answer it.)

Where regional or national issues are concerned, Barber has exhibited in the past a fairly naive belief that the use of telecommunications technology could establish links among numerous assemblies and facilitate nationwide discussion. While critics of participatory democracy have often focused on the problem of scale, the sheer size and scope of modern nation-states, Barber has asserted that it "is susceptible to technological and institutional melioration." Once we see the potential political benefits of modern technology, he has suggested, "scale becomes a tractable challenge rather than an insuperable barrier."[14]

But, to be fair, Barber's mid-1980s confidence in technological melioration has matured quite a bit. In more recent writings, he presents a more sober and nuanced analysis of democratic hopes in a world increasingly dominated by technology. He sees how technology, harnessed by the state or big corporations, can erect just as many barriers as it can create avenues to strong democracy.[15]

This may explain in part why in his recent writings, especially in *A Place for Us,* he has concentrated less on institutionalizing strong democracy and more on fostering a strong democratic brand of civil society. Barber defines strong democratic civil society as the realm that mediates conflicts between the private and the public. We are conditioned to think that the tension between the state and the private sector, or between the community and the individual, is a "zero-sum game"—that a more active state means diminished liberty and more dependency; that a more robust private sector (and diminished state) leads to rampant inequality and destruction of the commonweal. But Barber maintains that this third sector, democratic civil society, can foster a spirit of cooperation between these two spheres. Democratic civil society

> can place limits on government without ceding public goods to the private sphere, and at the same time it can dissipate the atmosphere of solitariness and greed that surrounds markets without suffocating in big government's exhaust fumes or in the stifling air of would-be communities. Both government and the private sector can and should be humbled by the growth of civil society, for it absorbs some of the public aspirations (its commitment to public work) without being coercive, and it maintains liberty without yielding to the jungle anarchy of commercial markets.[16]

Lying at the threshold between the public and private spheres of life, democratic civil society can appropriate the best elements of each in its quest for common ends: it is participatory and communal (like the public sector) yet voluntary and uncoercive (like the private sector).

Barber has recently situated strong democratic practices outside (or at the very edge of) traditional state institutions because, like Wolin, he has begun to see that big government has eclipsed opportunities for meaningful political participation just as much as big business has. Caught in the cross fire, civil society has been a casualty of an ongoing war between the private and public sectors over the course of American history. While the private sector crushed civil society in its mad rush to turn profits, the public sector heroically came to the people's defense but undermined their chance to participate in the process by not involving them in any fundamental way.[17]

As the state and private corporations played a larger role in our lives, all we could do was watch passively and leave public concerns to these entities in which we had no active role to play. Barber has always understood "the tendency of all institutions to ossify and become distanced from their constituents (the so-called iron law of oligarchy)."[18] His later works suggest that even strong democratic institutions, if controlled by state, can have this same tendency. As a result, strong democracy can better avoid ossification if it remains somewhat independent of the state—and of business.

Instead of drawing a blueprint of potential strong democratic institutions, he now calls for fuzzier measures that encourage the growth of more spontaneous and less formally institutionalized democratic participation. For instance, he advocates the creation of public spaces in which citizens can meet ad hoc to redress public problems; he no longer stresses the importance of institutionalizing a nationwide network of neighborhood assemblies. He also calls on consumers to organize boycotts against corporations that engage in unscrupulous business practices such as outsourcing production to offshore sweatshops or squashing union drives, which suggests he holds little hope for democratic state action to curb corporate excesses.[19]

Nevertheless, we should not mistake his growing wariness of the state for any kind of retrenchment, for he still believes participatory democracy is the solution to our current political woes. Having dedicated most of his career to deepening democracy, Barber has consistently shown a deep respect for Hartz's shepherd dog, believing that it can always learn new tricks, no matter how old it grows. In "the absence of independent ground" or foundational truth, citizens in a strong democracy can join together and learn from their experiences to address problems in their communities. It should come as no surprise, then, that Barber often draws explicitly on the pragmatist tradition and understands his theory and his work as a vital part of it.[20]

The big three classical pragmatists—Peirce, James, and Dewey—feature prominently in his writings and deeply influence his political thought. As he sees it, strong democracy goes a long way toward completing the pragmatist project, which forsakes philosophical hubris, the ill-advised quest for certainty, and any reliance on foundational truth, and which instead sees both knowledge and man himself as social constructions. "Strong democracy," Barber says, "is pragmatism translated into politics in the participatory mode."[21] Like the pragmatists, he embraces uncertainty and sees it as an opportunity for people to resolve conflict and decide their own destiny collectively rather than defer to metaphysical assumptions that bear the fraudulent stamp of truth (democratic epistemology). And like the pragmatists, he believes man's nature is not fixed but educable, forever shaped by his interaction with others in his community (democratic psychology). Quite manifestly Barber embraces a democratic epistemology and psychology, but his democratic metaphysics is somewhat shaky. Although not as defeatist as Wolin, whose uncompromising epistemology and psychology completely undermine his democratic metaphysics, Barber has also shown a frustration with modernity's tendency to limit the exercise of free will and foreclose democratic opportunities.

## Conceiving Politics Itself as Epistemology

Barber's democratic epistemology is quite evident in his work. He admonishes us to accept our epistemological limits as human beings and find truth only in what works experientially, not in the metaphysical dogma of religion or rationalism. The point at which this experience-based truth becomes contestable, where people with varying experiences come to different conclusions, strong democratic politics emerges as the arena in which citizens can engage in discussion with others in their community and, after bringing their experiences to bear on the issues at hand, reach a tentative settlement about the right course of action.

These settlements serve as provisional truths, which for the moment are the best answers to the questions before the community, but forever remain open to reexamination and further scrutiny. As Barber puts it: "Politics concerns itself only with those realms where truth is not—or is not yet—known. . . . Where consensus stops, politics starts." Because the business of democracy is to work toward a consensus not yet reached, to generate provisional truths, it actually serves as "its own epistemology."[22] Politics as epistemology suggests that power determines truth. Indeed, Barber would agree with this formulation but with the vital caveat that this truth must be an expression of communal will.

Liberals, on the other hand, believe that their metaphysical assumptions about humanity should be the basis of politics. Each man is a "radically individuated particle" whose only aim in life is to be free of all encumbrances, and this "truth" informs our political knowledge. Or, more specifically, when we frame the human experience in these atomistic terms, we conclude that people do not have the capacity for meaningful collective action and thus should live in a polity that does more to protect their negative rights than to offer them opportunities for political participation. Liberal epistemology, then, is deductive, beginning with a set of general principles from which we logically derive specific political knowledge, such as the proper role of government and its institutions. Barber maintains that this reliance on syllogistic thinking stifles our political imagination. Under the liberal regime (in both senses of the word), we cannot deviate from this chain of logic, which determines from the outset what is political truth. Unconstrained by this logic, strong democrats see no limits to what man can learn and accomplish politically. Instead of ceding politics to a rigid epistemology, we should "depict epistemology in political terms," which means "conceiving politics [itself] as epistemology and thereby inverting the classical liberal priority of epistemology over politics."[23]

Although Barber does not say it in so many words, the strong democratic epistemology shows itself to be inductive, resting not on unsubstantiated assumptions but on empirical facts, which members of a community interpret collectively and deliberatively and from which they then infer useful political guidelines. The community can then continually reconsider and modify these guidelines as new data come to the surface. The effectiveness of these guidelines is limited only by the degree to which the democratic process is inclusive. Says Barber:

> Knowledge understood as socially constructed . . . has a genuine validity, but it is a validity that is conditioned and thus conditional. It will be more or less persuasive to the degree the community from which it arises can be shown to be more or less democratic, more or less self-reflective, more or less inclusive. The only truth the modern school can have is produced by democracy: consensus arising out of an undominated discourse to which all have equal access.[24]

As the level of participation increases, with more people contributing their experiential knowledge and political imagination to the discussion, the emerging guidelines will have more general appeal—they will be "persuasive" (or effectively "true") for a larger number of people. Indeed, Barber embraces the Peircean "metaphor of truth as a cable woven together from many slender strands," which he believes is redolent of a strong democratic polity. "Many citizens are bound together intimately through their common citizenship, and they interact guided by opinions that in themselves are slender and provisional but that when woven together into a communal will and a public purpose inspire powerful conviction."[25]

Individual citizens may never know anything with absolute certainty, but when they form a deliberative collective, they represent a formidable force of common conviction. Together, they become convinced that a certain approach or course of action is the best political solution, and they exert their power to make it happen. We may find much more comfort and satisfaction in certainty, but it is not available to us, especially in the realm of politics, where truths and principles will forever be strenuously contested. With certainty out of the equation, the trick, then, is for people to reach an agreement on what works for them. "Since the objective is to find working maxims rather than fixed truths and shared consciousness rather than immutable principles, what is needed is a common language and a mode of seeing that will facilitate legitimate political judgments."[26]

Politics does not involve the search for truth—we have philosophers engaging daily in that fruitless activity. Instead, it entails making judgments, seeing the problem before us, communicating our various perspectives to each other, developing a shared vision of our goals, and ultimately finding "working maxims" that achieve these aims. Only a democratic community can make political judgments, for

> political judgment is defined by activity in common rather than thinking alone and is hence what democratic politics produces rather than (as with foundations) what produces democratic politics. Democratic political judgment can be exercised only by citizens interacting with one another in the context of mutual deliberation and decision-making on the way to willing common actions.[27]

In a world devoid of intrinsic meaning or truth, communities bear the responsibility of making these judgments, figuring out together what works best for them.

Liberals decry this as politics without foundations, and they assert that a healthy polity must have first principles to which it can always return in times of crisis. Without these foundational truths supporting our political institutions, they will necessarily collapse. But Barber remains undaunted by these cries of alarm, for he agrees with Dewey that political knowledge requires not foundations but the application of method—and "the method turns out to be democracy itself."[28] Democratic regimes certainly inherit foundations, but Barber claims that they flourish "both in spite of the foundations that have supported their birth and in the absence of all foundations. Like every political system, democracy too has a birth mother, and thus rests on foundations." But democracy differs from other systems because it "is necessarily self-orphaned, the child who slays its parents so that it may grow and flourish autonomously."[29]

Democracy as a form of parricide is a chilling image, indeed, but Barber asserts that "hacking up its aged parents" is a "melancholy necessity."[30] Citizens of a democratic polity must be prepared to rebel against the traditions they inherit. They must come to realize that our common experience informs our political knowledge more than received wisdoms. If democracy has any foundations other than those it so enthusiastically renounces, the foundations can be found only within the democratic process itself. For democratic methods or procedures provide the means by which communities can bring conflicts into the open and resolve them.

Barber has no doubt that citizens applying the democratic method are capable of making sensible judgments. While strong democracy "does not place endless faith in the capacity of individuals to govern themselves," it does maintain "that the multitude will on the whole be as wise or even wiser than princes." And, says Barber, strong democracy accords with these words spoken by Theodore Roosevelt (incidentally, a former student of William James): "The majority of the plain people will day in and day out make fewer mistakes in governing themselves than any smaller body of men will make in trying to govern them."[31] While most political theorists have doubted the wisdom of "plain people" and have instead placed their faith in the wisdom of aristocrats or philosophers or in the mitigating effects of institutions, Barber believes that people applying the democratic method, deliberating with their fellow citizens to address common concerns, will govern themselves perfectly well.

The Republic of Raetia is a telling example. In the published version of his dissertation, *The Death of Communal Liberty,* Barber recounts the history of this once thriving and idyllic participatory republic nestled in the Swiss Alps. At the heart of freedom in the Republic of Raetia, which achieved independence in 1524 but lost it at the hands of Napoleon in 1799, was the commune. Later to become a Swiss canton by the name of Graubuenden in the early nineteenth century, Raetia was a loose confederation of communes, each about the size of a neighborhood, in which citizens participated directly in every aspect of political life. Men in each commune deliberated for long hours on issues of importance to them, reached consensus before making final decisions, and even worked together to implement their proposed solution.[32] The central government in the republic had surprisingly little authority, and even though this radical decentralization of power created many organizational inefficiencies (even chaos) and thus slowed the pace of economic and technological progress, citizens experienced the exhilarating freedom of deciding their own destinies with others in their community.

Despite what liberal critics would expect, Raetian citizens did not experience majority tyranny. "As a creative participant in the formation of the communal will, the [Raetian] individual needed no guarantees for the containment of communal power." Nor did he need "sacred rights" to protect him from "the encroachments of an ambitious bureaucracy." The reason is that in "the most fundamental sense, the citizen *was* the communal authority: its will was his will, its needs were his needs, its instrumentalities were his very limbs, and its power was his sweat and blood."[33]

The Raetian citizen did not require protection from communal authority because he saw the community as an extension of himself, of his own needs and desires expressed in his willful democratic participation. Having devoted countless hours to deliberating with his fellow citizens and reaching consensus with them, the Raetian identified with those very communal decisions in which he had played a vital part. Although difficult for modern liberals to conceive, the Raetian did not understand liberty as individual freedom from intrusion or obstacles but, rather, in communal terms, "as collaborative self-reliance and community autonomy."[34]

Given his enthusiasm for communal expressions of liberty, Barber does not understand why liberals fear an unrestrained demos, and why they think that "parchment barriers" (as Madison referred to the Bill of Rights in his initial criticism of it) will effectively protect individuals from majority tyranny. In the United States, the Constitution secures a number of rights to which every person is entitled, and because they are supposedly grounded in reason and perhaps god, they precede political discussion. They are pristine political truths that real-world politics should never sully. The problem, says Barber, is that these rights, abstract and untouchable, would never constrain a potentially tyrannical majority whose members had no involvement in the construction of those rights and hence no real attachment to them. The majority would either ignore those rights outright or, if need be, find clever ways around them. One hundred years of Jim Crow, for example, speaks to the crafty circumvention of the Civil War amendments (as well as a few of the original ten) by an oppressive white majority.

More effective, according to Barber, would be an appeal to public discourse: "an appeal to the citizenship of its members, reminding them that they are embarked on a public course of action that cannot meet the objections of reasonable public discourse. Lynchings are carried out but they are not often defended." Putting an end to lynchings and other forms of racial oppression requires not liberal institutions that ostensibly protect rights but rather "an appeal to the civic and human ties that connect the participants under normal circumstances." Indeed, says Barber, the "most powerful constraints on irrationalism and mob behavior" can be found in "reasonableness, commonality, participation, and citizenship." Engaging people in public discourse, giving them the chance to articulate and defend their intended actions, is apt to produce second thoughts and can, perhaps, moderate their behavior. In cultivating "ongoing public talk and participation in public action," strong democracy places internal checks on the "extremes of popular passion" and creates among the people "a spirit of reasonableness."[35]

Liberal democracy, on the other hand, can only introduce external limits, delivered to us from on high, to prevent mob rule. As the contemporary political landscape teaches us, a mindless invocation of rights will not spark useful dialogue. Those accused of violating rights will only call forth a similarly abstract political principle in their defense, thus hardening their resolve to act inhumanely. As Barber sees it, appeals to abstract rights or first principles sever our ties with others in the community; they discourage the hard yet rewarding work of political talk and striving for a reasonable middle ground.

Although political talk is hard work, it affords participants the opportunity to define rights democratically. In the liberal framework, we must rely on the wisdom of philosophers and founders who decide which rights are indeed "natural," and we must refrain from challenging the truth of their judgments. But Barber says, "Rights are not like triangles or the Second Law of Thermodynamics: the issue is not truth and error but at best right opinion, intersubjective agreement, and common ground."[36]

Rights do not precede political discussion but are rather its end product. Only after exhaustive deliberation can citizens come to an agreement on those rights to which all human beings are entitled, and even then, they remain contestable, open to further challenge and debate. "What is required is not foundational mandates or individual mental acumen in rigidly applying fixed standards to a changing world, but such political skills as are necessary to discovering or forging common ground," says Barber. "Rights themselves are constantly being redefined and reinterpreted, dependent for their normative force on the engagement and commitment of an active citizen body."[37]

No political truths, not even those "inalienable" rights celebrated in the liberal tradition, exist prior to civic engagement. If we merely adhere to "fixed standards" or absolutes, we risk the danger of embracing antiquated ideas, so-called rights that no longer have any relevance in today's world. We face this problem in the United States, where large corporations have received the status of "legal persons" and thus enjoy the rights of private individuals. The reality is that corporations are public entities whose impact on society can hardly be overestimated and whose very existence depends on those "states they now assail."[38] Nevertheless, the unassailable wisdom of the liberal tradition insists that corporations are entitled to these "natural" rights, which precede political discussion, even when history teaches us that the legal status of corporations is mere artifice, and even when our experience demonstrates quite clearly that corporations exert an unimaginable amount of power and influence in our society today. In a strong democracy, civically engaged citizens could revisit this question and perhaps agree to curb those rights currently enjoyed by corporations.

In Barber's view, political truths of any kind are agreements reached by a group of civically engaged and deliberating citizens. We should never blindly accept received wisdoms about the nature of human beings or about the "natural" rights to which they (or their organizations) are entitled. For "truth is no longer to be mined from extraterrestrial bodies labeled God or nature or reason or metaphysics." Like the pragmatist thinkers to whom he continually pays tribute, Barber believes all received wisdoms are contestable and open to debate, and even those truths arrived at consensually and deliberatively are provisional, inviting reexamination and refinement. But the truth—even provisionally useful truth—will never emerge unless we conform "to communicative processes that are genuinely democratic and that occur only in free communities." No one should be excluded from the discussion, for the emergence of truth requires input from everyone concerned with the issue at hand:

> The conditions of truth (such as "truth" is in this residual post-modernist form) and the conditions of democracy are one and the same: As there is freedom, as the community is open and inclusive and the exchange of ideas thorough and

spirited, so there is both more democracy and more learning, more freedom and more knowledge. Knowledge is always provisional: ideas conditionally agreed upon. And just as no argument will be accorded merit because of its source alone, so no individual will be privileged over others simply because of who he is (white or male or straight) or where he comes from (old money, the wrong side of the tracks, the United States of America).[39]

In short, uncompromising openness and the vigorous exchange of ideas are the key to devising provisionally useful truths. Barber claims his strong democracy, which remains open to all and involves continuing and never-ending deliberation, provides the forum wherein citizens can create such truths—and in the process re-create themselves.

## Democratic Transformation

In arguing that strong democracy transforms its participants, turning them into citizens who engage in politics not merely to satisfy private objectives but to work toward common ends, Barber makes evident his democratic psychology. Barber is quite explicit about the pedagogic value of political participation, arguing that the democratic process serves as a school where participants receive a civic education and begin to think beyond themselves (and their private interests) and more in public terms. "Community grows out of participation and at the same time makes participation possible; civic activity educates individuals how to think publicly as citizens even as citizenship informs civic activity with the required sense of publicness and justice. Politics becomes its own university, citizenship its own training ground, and participation its own tutor."[40] While we may learn some valuable information about our rights and the law in the classroom, people do not receive a real civic education until they are politically engaged. If given the opportunity to wield "some significant power," people "will quickly appreciate the need for knowledge, but foist knowledge on them without giving them responsibility and they will display only indifference."[41] The knowledge gained from political engagement turns private individuals into public-minded citizens. Says Barber: "In a strong democratic community . . . the individual members are transformed, through their participation in common seeing and common work, into citizens. Citizens are autonomous persons whom participation endows with a capacity for a common vision."[42]

Talking with and working alongside others to solve problems common to us all enables us to see ourselves and our relationships with others in a radically different way. From our political participation we learn to sympathize, to imagine what it is like to walk in another man's shoes, and this experience changes us profoundly. Barber often invokes Rousseau to make his point clear: "What is crucial about democratic community is that, as Rousseau understood, it 'produces a remarkable change in man'; that is to say, through participation in it, man's 'faculties are exercised and developed, his ideas broadened, his feelings ennobled, and his whole soul elevated.'"[43]

This belief in the transformative power of democracy is grounded in the idea that human nature is malleable. As a social creature, man's nature is determined by the way he interacts with others. Man is a reflection of his sociopolitical relationships; he is as base or noble as the community in which he is embedded. "Strong democratic theory posits the social nature of human beings in the world and the dialectical interdependence of man and his government," says Barber. "Like the social reality it refracts, human nature is compound; it is potentially both benign and malevolent, both cooperative and antagonistic." But we should also understand that "these qualities can be transformed by legitimate and illegitimate social and political forces. For man is a developmental animal—a creature with a compound and evolving telos whose ultimate destiny depends on how he interacts with those who share the same destiny."[44]

Human beings are not fatally flawed, their sins indelibly etched into their very souls. Each one of us is a blank slate with the potential either to sink into the abyss of depravity or to rise to the heights of righteousness. Accordingly, we should devise a political system that provides its citizens with a civic education that elevates us. Setting people in an environment where ruthless competition and crass materialism are the norm runs the risk of turning them into those depraved creatures liberals assume we are by nature.

Liberal theorists have long assumed (or have, at least, argued) that human beings have certain immutable traits, traits sown into their very nature. We must accept men as they really are—solitary and independent, selfish and acquisitive, hedonistic and pain-avoiding, base and corrupt, power-seeking and aggressive—and not rest our hopes on their moral betterment. Consistent with Judeo-Christian theology, liberal man has fallen from grace and has little chance of redemption, and thus we should never expect too much of him. We should instead assume the worst and devise a political system based on those assumptions. But while most men are untrustworthy, liberals of a more anarchist disposition remind us that we should exalt and leave unfettered those few individuals who can transcend the human condition and, exceeding all expectations, become something better than the rest us—something akin to the Nietzschean superman. The end result is a political system that frustrates concerted civic action, lest men do too much damage, but yields to those unique individuals—those Rockefellers, Carnegies, Edisons, or Picassos—whose creativity, entrepreneurship, ingenuity, greed, or fame (or some combination thereof) makes them exemplary and admirable beyond all measure. These men do not rely on help from others; they stand alone and firm, enduring without complaint the stark reality of life and imposing their creative will onto the world.

In a world with many base men and a few extraordinary ones, the political solution is to discourage the collective action of the former and to facilitate the individual heroism of the latter. Either way, the result serves to keep people away from each other. And while society and collectivities are inevitable in a world with a finite amount of space, liberal man chooses to view these social relationships as mere contracts. In his universe, there can be "no fraternal feeling, no general will, no selfless act, love or belief or commitment that is not wholly private," because human relationships—what appear to be fraternal bonds or moral commitments—are really just the result of rational calculation to serve the hedonistic aims of individuals.[45] The problem with "the liberal theory of human nature," says Barber, is that it "define[s] man in ways that deprive him of the potential strength of mutuality, cooperation, and common being."[46] The liberal conception of human nature completely ignores the possibility that politically cooperative experiences can be formative and contribute to our moral education and development.[47]

This is not to suggest that liberals reject civic education altogether. They have often praised the virtues of a liberal education, which can prepare our schoolchildren for citizenship and instill those values friendly to liberal democracy such as tolerance, diversity, and mutual respect, among others. Although Barber believes democratic participation is the true school wherein citizens receive their civic education, he does not ignore the importance of liberal education in our schools. He claims, however, that merely instilling values in our future citizens, as if they were empty vessels awaiting the elixir of knowledge, falls short of a true liberal education. As he sees it, liberal education is not a matter of merely receiving dogma delivered to us from the teacher's lectern, of passively accepting as true whatever emanates from his mouth.

Instead, liberal education must be an adequate preparation for democratic participation, compelling students to challenge conventional wisdom, think critically, and deliberate over the options presented to them. According to Barber, education is "training in the middle way between the dogmatic belief in absolutes and the cynical negation of all belief," and "well-taught students" learn there is a harmonious balance "between Absolute Certainty and Permanent Doubt."[48] In promoting this kind of middle ground, liberal education becomes a training ground for democracy. Like citizens in a strong democracy, students learn to challenge truth claims and—through a slow, communal, and deliberative process—to forge provisional truths that can withstand these challenges.[49]

Barber acknowledges the danger of postmodern excess, in which students and intellectuals find joy in deconstructing truths until there are none left. Truths may be illusory, as postmodernists contend, but they are necessary nonetheless, says Barber. "Civilization, Yeats reminded us, is tied together by a hoop of illusion. It would be dangerous to pretend that the illusion is real, but it is fatal to dispense with it altogether." Barber continues: "Justice and democracy are the illusions that permit us to live in comity. Truth and knowledge are the illusions that permit us to live commodiously. Art and literature are the illusions that make commodious living worthwhile. Deconstruction may rid us of all our illusions and thus seem a clever way to think, but it is no way at all to live."[50]

These "illusions" may not be true in the Platonic sense, as they are not concepts that correspond to any a priori reality (such as the Forms or Divine Law), but if they help us "live commodiously" and make our lives "worthwhile," if they actually prove rewarding and enriching in our common experience, they are true in the pragmatic sense. Once students understand this, they will not wallow in a malaise of existential despair but will instead see the value of citizenship, pursuing the truth in a democratic fashion, holding up all truth claims to the test of common experience. Some conservatives such as Alan Bloom have claimed that democratizing education in this way has already proved disastrous, promoting a dangerous relativism that has all but sent us down the precipice toward nihilism. Accordingly, these conservatives agree with Plato that only a gifted elite should receive the full breadth of a liberal education, which involves challenging received wisdoms and flirting with relativism. The rest of us, meanwhile, should obediently accept the absolute truth given to us.[51]

Liberals have not been immune to this line of thought. Because they hold that there are a few men more gifted than the rest of us, liberals exalt expertise and leadership in politics. With regard to expertise, Barber argues that deference to specialists and professional politicians, whose "only distinctive qualification . . . turns out to be simply that they engage in politics," is completely unnecessary. So-called experts have more political knowledge than the rest of us simply because they enjoy the privilege of participating in politics. Any of us could attain this expertise if given the opportunity to engage in politics. "Strong democracy," says Barber, "is the politics of amateurs, where every man is compelled to encounter every other man without the intermediary of expertise."[52]

Barber acknowledges that leadership is a trickier issue. Not all people are born leaders, and this poses a serious problem for strong democracy. Those more naturally gifted leaders could rise before their fellow men and provide them the guidance and comfort for which so many of them are desperately searching. This leader-follower dynamic encourages passivity in the vast majority and thus threatens to undermine strong democracy. As leaders assume more power and authority, followers soon relinquish their demanding duties as citizens and show deference to those they believe more capable of governing. But Barber maintains that natural leaders, though potentially inimical to strong democracy, could also facilitate the democratic process.

To begin with, leaders could prove very helpful in the transition to strong democracy. An ideal transitional leadership would "guide people toward self-government" and, when their job is finished, withdraw to the role of citizen. These leaders would inspire citizens to assume the awesome responsibility of self-governance and help them understand that leaders like themselves are no longer necessary. Although Barber does not concede this point, the transitional leadership would be "founders" of the strong democratic regime, but their success would depend largely on our forgetting their crucial role. We could not memorialize them as we do our founders in the United States today.

After the establishment of strong democracy, natural leaders may also provide an ongoing facilitating function, playing the role of "teacher" or "judge" to ensure that the process runs smoothly without directing it toward specific outcomes. Barber likens the facilitating leader to a psychologist or group therapist who helps his "patients" find answers to their questions and problems on their own.[53] In a strong democracy these leaders would always encourage participation and never assume an authority that would encourage deference and passivity in the citizenry. It seems that natural leadership poses the greatest challenges for strong democracy at its early stages, when citizens have yet to assume their civic responsibilities with relish. But as average citizens grow more confident in their capacity to govern, they would likely resist and squelch the demagogic tendencies of natural leaders.

Nevertheless, Barber does not satisfactorily resolve the tension between leader and follower, between expert and amateur. Although he maintains that strong democracy rejects the "intermediary of expertise," the natural leader in a strong democracy will always assume roles, such as the facilitator, that require a certain expertise most of us do not possess. How these leaders or experts will learn to restrain themselves from disrupting the strong democratic process remains unanswered.

Despite the challenges presented by leadership, Barber's democratic psychology never wavers. He takes on faith that men are educable and that political participation provides the proper education: "Faith in democracy requires a belief neither in the benevolence of abstract human character nor in the historical altruism of democratic man. Altruists do not need government. What is required is nothing more than a faith in the democratizing effects that political participation has on men, a faith not in what men are but in what democracy makes them."[54]

Some would argue that this is a giant leap of faith. Although Barber asks of his reader "nothing more" than a belief in the transformative effects of democracy, many critics maintain a natural incredulity. After all, human beings have had limited experience with participatory democracy, and those few historical examples do not accord entirely with theory. There is no clear evidence that participating citizens in the Athenian assembly or in the New England town meeting during its heyday ever underwent the kind of radical transformation described by Barber. And even if they did—or could—experience this transformation, we are still left with another question. With all the temptations and distractions plaguing the postmodern world, will people today actually take the time to engage extensively in democratic politics?

## The Death of Political Will

Despite an overall optimism that pervades most of his work, Barber has on occasion betrayed an almost Wolinian melancholy, even at the earliest stage of his career. The title of his dissertation, *The Death of Communal Liberty,* speaks volumes about his democratic metaphysics, his faith that people possess the will to govern themselves. The story he tells is a rueful one. A confederation of autonomous communes, each of which was a model of participatory democracy, the Republic of Raetia stubbornly preserved its communal liberty even in the face of persistent colonization and subjugation by foreign aggressors, only to succumb, finally, to the forces of modernity. Even Napoleon, who indeed took away Raetian independence, could not destroy the people's communal liberty, but advances in centralized administration, technology, and commerce eroded their sense of citizenship and alienated them from their local communities. Now a Swiss canton called Graubuenden, the former Raetia is a ghost of what it once was, containing 220 communes that have relinquished a good deal of their power to the central government and, as a result, have experienced a precipitous decline in direct political participation. While the central government has managed to turn a confederation of relatively backward villages into an economically robust nation state, it has come at an incalculable expense. Barber suggests that this sad ending, the death of communal liberty in Graubuenden, was inevitable. In the final sentence of the penultimate chapter, he poses the problem in the form of a question: "Is life in small, self-governing relatively autonomous rural communes possible in the Western industrial world in the 1970's?"[55]

His answer is plainly no. He considers it "improbable that the communes will survive in anything like their traditional, face-to-face democratic form" and claims that the "failures of communalism and direct democracy reveal the inevitability and potency of pluralistic centralism in an industrializing society."[56] And while he hopes "that these dying forms contain the promise of an alternative mode of political life," Barber sees no escape from the politically devastating effects of modernity. Communes in modern-day Graubuenden face a difficult dilemma, "the product of a century-long collision between indisputably vital communal norms and the apparent requisites of national survival in an industrializing world. Progress in this context may mean the surrender of both meaningful personal autonomy and real self-government."[57]

As Barber ruefully relates, modernization has forever transformed life in the Swiss communes. One of the more distressing trends is that young people, who alone can ensure the survival of the communal ideal, are drawn away from their home villages, often compelled to move elsewhere for educational and economic opportunities, but just as often lured by an outside world teeming with activity and temptation. Modern transportation systems—including the automobile, which Barber considers the instrument of liberal individualism—have uprooted people from more traditional communities, allowing them to travel greater distances for work and recreation. Multinational corporations have moved into these communities, providing jobs for those people who can no longer subsist on those sheep-herding or fishing practices that might have strengthened communal bonds but certainly frustrated economic progress.[58]

Neo-Luddite attempts to preserve or recapture the pastoral purity of these traditional communities have failed time and again, says Barber, because it is impossible to "impede the inroads of cosmopolitanism; any more than silence can impede noise; or placidity, ambition."[59] Barber suggests that the many trappings of modern life—such as economic efficiency, intractable consumerism, centralized administration, professional expertise, mass mobilization, and immediate access to information—are incompatible with the kind of rustic simplicity that democratic life seems to demand. And though he has maintained a spirited optimism throughout his career, an undercurrent of despair and hopelessness runs beneath the surface, only to emerge in those few moments of what may be theoretical candor.

Barber does not simply wax nostalgic for a bygone era of democratic authenticity, as Wolin seems to do; he refuses to relinquish his democratic hopes. He has hitched his wagon to strong democracy, which he believes is the "alternative mode of political life" that can reconcile modernity with communal liberty.[60] At first, this may not seem feasible largely because of problems of scale. After all, millions of people cannot fit into an assembly hall and discuss an issue that affects us all, such as the national defense budget. Modernity has deracinated people from their small, tight-knit communities and thrown them willy-nilly into a global world, vast and alienating yet inconceivably interconnected. Citizens in a small participatory democracy can get to know each other and develop a strong mutual understanding, but the modern world does not afford such opportunities. Suspicion of the unknown Other is the norm, and unseen suffering (or just grumbling) half-a-world away, or even in a nearby town, hardly elicits sympathy.

As Barber sees it, because we live in a world where many of our actions have significant implications for those very people from whom we are alienated, we must recapture in some way what traditional democratic communities once had—but on a larger scale. We may not be able to meet face-to-face with people in our community as we once did, but sophisticated communications technology could approximate this experience. If we allow ourselves to dream big, communications technology has the potential to turn this enormous planet riddled with war and mutual distrust into a global village. While the dream of a global village may seem far-fetched at this point, technology could at the very least connect people to their fellow countrymen and their government, promoting an ongoing dialogue on issues of national importance, and empowering people throughout the country to gain crucial political knowledge and to work collectively to address these issues.

Barber understands, however, that there is nothing inevitable or teleological about the democratic use of communications technology. He sharply criticizes those democratic futurists who believe technology will one day lead us to a glorious promised land of widespread political participation. Technology can be as democratic or fascistic as those who harness its power. Nobody would claim that the radio was a democratizing force in Nazi Germany, where the mass media was under the control of a repressive state. In the summer of 1994, the genocidal regime in Rwanda seized control of the radio stations, from which it waged a deadly campaign of misinformation and propaganda, inciting Hutus to slay their Tutsi neighbors with the machetes they had been given a few months earlier. Fully aware of these sobering examples, Barber says: "Ends condition means, and technology is just a fancy word for means. The new telecommunications are less likely to alter and improve than to reflect and augment our current socioeconomic institutions and political attitudes."[61]

Although technology does not serve genocidal ends in this country, it hardly serves the public interest either. In our liberal democracy, technology has been used primarily for commercial purposes—to serve private interests and to further the ends of capitalism. This does not have to be the case, of course. Technology could be used to "assist political change . . . but unless there is a political will directed at greater participation, the potential remains only that: a potential."[62] Technology could be used for democratic purposes if we had the "political will." Why do we lack this will? Certainly, liberal attitudes have become deeply entrenched in our society, and so long as they prevail, technology will continue to be the servant of private interests.

Barber also sees a problem with technology itself, noting its "vulnerability to undemocratic forces." This is especially troubling because Barber has often argued that technology represents the only solution to democracy's woes in the modern world. If technology proves susceptible to undemocratic forces, there would seem to be very little hope for strong democracy. Nevertheless, Barber cannot ignore the warning signs. Large corporations have seized control of our communications and media technology to instill and reinforce the values of passive individualism and consumerism—to undermine our democratic will. Evoking an Orwellian nightmare, Barber argues that, at its worst, technology in the postmodern world has become an agent of soft totalitarianism, a means by which "subtle tyrants possess their subjects' hearts and minds through the control of education, information, and communication and, thereby, turn subjects into allies in the enterprise of servitude." While technology "need not inevitably corrupt democracy," its "potential for benign enslavement cannot be ignored."[63]

Like many critics on the left, Barber believes the problem in the United States begins with the deregulation of the media and communications, which has led to the concentration of ownership. Advocates of deregulation often claim that it has loosened government control over the media and given consumers more choice and access to a wider range of information. But Barber argues that the proliferation of television channels has merely created the illusion of greater choice, since they are all owned by a mere handful of media conglomerates. These companies, which "exercise an effective monopoly," produce a narrower range of programming than ever before and, as a result, provide fewer sources of alternative news or entertainment.[64] The hundreds of channels to which we have access merely give us more of the same, perpetuating an overwhelming cultural homogeneity that is inimical to democracy.

A true diversity of media outlets and information sources is essential to democracy, because it "thrives on dissent, deviance, political heterogeneity, and individuality."[65] Even the internet, a purportedly democratic technology that gives every browser immediate access to literally billions of Web sites, has become increasingly dominated by large media corporations that limit the real choice of content. It is only a matter of time, according to Barber, before big corporations close this vast and open frontier.[66]

While corporate control of media technology has imposed a rigid uniformity of media content, it has also had an atomistic effect on society, promoting reclusion and a withdrawal into private life. That corporate-controlled technology shapes us to be the same but also divides us from each other may sound contradictory, but it is not. Under the sway of this market-driven technology, we all come to believe in, and readily conform to, capitalist ideals that encourage people to spurn community and pursue their private interests with vigor.

In short, we conform to the ethos of solipsism when democracy demands the opposite—that each of us choose to work toward common ends and become citizens. Technological advances like television and the internet, both hailed as purveyors of democracy, do little to connect us to a larger community. Instead they keep us at home more than ever. In fact, they do more to support our consumerist habits, telling us what to buy and providing us the convenient means to do so, than they do to teach us the values of citizenship. Without our necessarily realizing it, these technologies turn us into passive recipients and adherents of capitalist dogma.

Many futurists assert that, because it is both interactive and inclusive, the internet in particular provides opportunities for democratic action and community-building. Barber is not so sanguine. "How can there be 'common ground' [on the internet] when ground itself vanishes and women and men inhabit abstractions?" he asks. While it is conceivable that "some new form of community" could emerge "among the myriad solitaries perched in front of their [computer] screens," it is not likely to happen. "It has yet to be shown," says Barber, "that anonymous screen-to-screen interaction can do for us what face-to-face interaction has done." Technologies like the internet, which give us access to information and connect us electronically to other people, have not proved to be adequate substitutes for face-to-face interaction. No matter how much internet enthusiasts "prattle on about 'community,'" it is doubtful that "an anonymous exchange with strangers whose identity is a matter of invention and artifice [can] replicate the kind of conversations that occur spontaneously among fellow PTA members about a school board election."[67] Indeed, Barber's exploration of the internet has revealed very few traces of community or democratic activity. If anything, the internet has afforded users new ways to exclude others and cultivate their prejudices.[68]

Finally, Barber maintains that the technological focus on expediting tasks with speed and efficiency does not agree with the deliberate pace and tedium of democracy. We live in an impatient world, where people expect instant gratification and demand entertainment and stimulation every second of the day. Indeed, we bore quite easily. But strong democracy demands that we slow down and revel in the "cumbersome" and "certifiably unentertaining" process of deliberation. The age of computers cannot abide this measured pace, the "prudence, slow-footed interaction" of democracy.[69]

We also have become increasingly accustomed to the binary logic of computers, making a choice "between on and off, *A* and *B,* yes and no," and then moving to the next decision without ever looking back. Democratic politics, on the other hand, eschews simple dichotomies and requires "complex and nuanced" reasoning from its participants.[70] It obliges them to entertain the possibility that both A and B are correct, or that neither is correct, to challenge the very premise of the question, to feel "perpetual regret" about decisions of the past, and to engage those past decisions in an endless dialectic of revision.

Technology is often hailed as a great convenience, allowing us to complete life's tasks in a short amount of time and thus giving us many hours for leisure. Barber hopes that one day we will reach a point where technology affords us plenty of time to engage in politics.[71] But he understands that technology, guided and controlled by capitalist forces, has conditioned us to make speed an imperative in our lives. Changing our expectations of what one can reasonably accomplish in a day, technology has made us busier and more frantic than ever. Unfortunately, this frenetic pace is anathema to democracy. Our technological "tools are in a certain sense out of synch with democracy, out of control," says Barber, and it becomes increasingly clear why Thoreau "worried about how easily we can become the tools of our tools."[72]

We may want to use technology for democratic purposes, but this proves impossible if technology has taken hold of us. For example, he warns his readers that cyber-democracy, which lets citizens vote for or against policy proposals with a simple click of a computer mouse, is susceptible to majority tyranny. In allowing people to make decisions instantaneously, without taking the time to deliberate with their fellow citizens or to consider carefully all the relevant positions and facts, this unmediated form of participatory democracy "would do more to undermine democracy than to reinforce it."[73]

The vulnerabilities of technology to undemocratic forces speak to the larger issue of democracy's fragility. "About the future role of democracy in society we cannot be certain," says Barber. "Because it is a fragile form of social organization, its prospects are clouded." Despite its uncertain future, Barber maintains his faith in democracy. But he also continues to fear that these hopes will be dashed for good if technology fails us now: "This may be our *last opportunity* to turn the technology of the new age into a servant of an old political idea: democracy. Democracy has a difficult time surviving under the best of circumstances" (my emphasis).[74]

Although Barber is always quick to remind the reader that the political consequences of technology are not preordained in any way, that technology can be either the savior or the death-knell of democracy, he seems to suggest here that our window of opportunity will not remain open forever. Once market forces co-opt our technologies for their own purposes and then those technologies plant their stamp of corruption upon us, all is lost. Before we are conditioned to use technology from the confines of our homes solely for the purposes of solipsistic activity, we must summon the political will to develop state-of-the-art technologies that can really enhance civic communication, that can draw people out of their homes and into neighborhood assembly halls where they can engage in serious political deliberation, not only with others in their local community but with participants in other assemblies across the country—or the world— via a vast and sophisticated telecommunications network.

In recent years, Barber has rested his democratic hopes on civil society and not on the state alone, lest the state eclipse opportunities for democratic participation. But it is quite obvious that strong democracy, depending on these technological enhancements, will require massive state support. A largely unorganized civil society could never get such a complex and large-scale operation off the ground; only the state could muster the requisite resources for this kind of radical change. Barber must be aware of this necessity, but he never concedes this point. After all, the likelihood that the national government would invest in such a costly program—which would take power away from political elites and which currently enjoys little popular support—is quite slim. And, even if this were to happen, a state-run participatory democracy may become hopelessly bureaucratic and fail to replicate the conditions of community experienced in ancient Athens or Raetia. Meanwhile, time is running out. It may not be so long before we become the "tools of our tools," a phrase that evokes a dystopian future often depicted in science-fiction films.

## Organized Ball

Barber may not exhibit the melancholy and defeatism of Wolin, but his democratic theory does betray what I would call a thin optimism. He goes to great lengths to criticize liberal democracy for being too thin, but his faith that people will summon the will to engage in politics is a bit thin as well. Participatory democratic theories, as I have argued, rest on three tenets. Barber's strong democracy has a robust democratic epistemology and psychology, but his weakening democratic metaphysics threatens his entire enterprise, even if he is unwilling to admit it. Wolin knowingly betrays a feeble democratic metaphysics, and as a result I characterized his theory as "melancholic democracy," a sad remembrance of what democracy once was and will never be again, except for brief moments.

I would suggest that Barber's theory strikes the tone of a "quixotic democracy." As if tilting at windmills, he insists that it is possible to create permanent institutions in which citizens can participate meaningfully in the political process and thereby take direct control of their own fates. He clings to what he acknowledges, in his more intellectually honest moments, is a remote possibility at best.

To shed some light on Barber's political theory, it may be useful to revisit briefly the baseball metaphor explored in the previous chapter. We can liken strong democracy to an organized baseball league that remains inclusive and amateur. Anyone can participate in the league, either as a player or in another capacity, and these participants decide collectively on the rules of the game. Voluntary umpires will preside over games to ensure fair play. While participants certainly enjoy the sheer thrill of the game, their objectives extend far beyond the desire for an authentic experience. They believe the game will have realizable community benefits—such as health and fitness or good sportsmanship—for which they all strive.

With all this in mind, participants do all they can to make sure the league is not a short-lived enterprise. They want it to endure and take root in the community—or, rather, they want the game itself to nurture the community that is planted in its soil. They will build fields, order uniforms, make schedules, and organize practices. Although structured, the game will not abide exclusionary practices or hierarchies of any sort, for the ultimate goal is not to field the best players and win games but to partake in the game and its communal benefits. More talented players will not feel impeded because they will find a useful role in teaching the fundamentals and raising the overall quality of the game.

I would suggest that the image evoked here is—in many ways—far less convincing than the sandlot. Many of us have experienced something that approximates sandlot baseball, a brief moment in one's life when the stars seem to align in such a way that everything is perfect, with players coming together spontaneously to play the game they love in the way they see fit. But the baseball league analogous to strong democracy resembles nothing this author has ever seen. Indeed, it challenges the imagination: participants expend time and energy building an organized league that will last for future generations to enjoy, that will become a vital part of community life, yet somehow over the long term they will manage to suppress their competitive impulses and preserve both inclusion and equality in the league. This seems highly unlikely. I already described in the previous chapter the competitive nature of even Little League baseball and its many hierarchies and exclusionary practices. While this is not to say that strong democracy is unfeasible, it should give us pause. In the end, Wolin may be right in suggesting that an irreconcilable tension exists between participatory democracy and institutionalization, between participatory democracy and politics-as-usual.

# Participatory Democracy

*An Impoverished Theory and Its Legacy*

Although Wolin may prove more convincing than Barber, vital questions remain unanswered: during those long stretches of time when deep citizen participation does not occur, what viable form of democracy will respond best to the demands of the people and at the same time safeguard individual freedom? In a world where people continue to suffer from injustice and the inequitable distribution of wealth and opportunity, do we not owe it to ourselves to theorize about politics as well as the political? Are we supposed to place all our hope in the emergence of pure democracy, which will serve as a periodic check on the state, and then surrender to the "reality" that the state will necessarily co-opt any systematic efforts to hold it accountable and make it responsive to the people's needs? It would be a grave indulgence if one were to insist, as the melancholy Wolin seems to do, that democracy and politics are inherently at odds, that there is no hope for man to achieve justice or a meaningful life under ordinary circumstances in the postmodern world. But this is where participatory democracy leaves us: either to suffer fools who dream of institutionalizing widespread civic engagement or to weep over the disappearance of this beloved way of life without searching for an alternative.

## Participatory Democracy as a Theoretical Ideal

Once situated within the pragmatist tradition, participatory democracy reveals itself to be impracticable, largely a theoretical concept with little hope for real-world application. The impracticability of participatory democracy first becomes evident when its contemporary enthusiasts, such as Wolin and Barber, raise serious doubts about man's free will in the modern world. Betraying weak democratic metaphysics, both Wolin and Barber themselves concede that postmodern systems of organization and control have made it increasingly difficult for citizens to become truly engaged in civic affairs.

Holding a more pessimistic view of power in the modern world, participatory democrats do not share with classical pragmatists an optimism about man's freedom to make choices. In their understanding, we are all constrained by social, economic, and political forces that have rearranged our priorities in a fundamental way and lulled us into a dangerous state of complacency. Few would deny the allure of the myriad entertainments available to the consumer, who must then spend more time at work to satisfy this demand. Even fewer would deny that technology continues to accelerate the hectic pace of society and that we have less time for—and, quite frankly, have become unaccustomed to—the ponderous reflection and thoughtful deliberation that democratic participation requires.

Participatory democracy places far too many demands on the postmodern citizen, whose political will has become systematically enervated by a megastate that fosters longer workdays, insatiable consumerism, the apotheosis of the moving image over the written word, and a growing dependence on interactive technologies that both captivate us and make our lives easier. It is not surprising that psychologists diagnose more and more people, including adults, with Attention Deficit Hyperactivity Disorder (ADHD), a condition that seems to have become endemic in American society. Always demanding immediate gratification, American citizens cannot abide the slow pace, the halting resolutions, and unsatisfying compromises of the democratic process. As a result, they are willing to delegate political authority to the professionals, whose job is to endure the arduousness of politics and the inevitable accusations of impropriety by a scandal-seeking press and public.

The withering democratic metaphysics to which both Wolin and Barber concede threatens the entire participatory democratic project. Even if we were to accept the democratic epistemology and psychology, these two tenets require conditions that are unattainable in today's world. Democracy can improve our political knowledge and educate us to be upright citizens only if we hear the call for widespread, authentic civic engagement and if we live in an environment conducive to the kind of sustained and deliberative democratic activity championed by John Dewey and his New Left heirs. If we no longer have the will to attend all those meetings and devote a significant portion of our time to civic life, we will never enjoy the reputed epistemological and psychological benefits of participation. Participatory democrats know this intuitively, which is why to varying degrees they express a measure of pessimism in their work and rarely venture outside the realm of theory—and seem a bit foolish or awkward when they do.

Participationists such as Wolin and Barber may admit that modernity constrains man's free will and thus makes their theory impracticable, but they both suggest that the first two tenets—the democratic epistemology and psychology—are alive and well. This means that participatory democracy may remain useful as a coherent political theory, an ideal for which humanity should still strive in hopes of somehow approximating it in practice, even if only for brief moments. This clearly seems to be Wolin's view.

But viewing participatory democracy through the lens of pragmatism also enables the critic to evaluate the merits of the first two tenets and subject them to careful scrutiny. Quite conceivably, human beings may not attain truth in the inductive and deliberative manner pragmatists claim, and they may not enjoy malleable natures that await only a proper education for improvement. If either of these tenets fails to withstand such careful scrutiny and proves to be untenable, participatory democracy fails to stand up even as a theory—and, of course, proves even more impracticable than initially suggested.

## The Blank Slate Reconsidered

Recent empirical research has posed serious challenges to the democratic psychology. In his recent book, *The Blank Slate: The Modern Denial of Human Nature,* Harvard psychologist Steven Pinker argues that nature places limits on what human beings can reasonably accomplish. He contends that a number of recent discoveries "make it unlikely" that "human nature might radically change in some imagined society of the remote future."[1]

Synthesizing a large body of research, Pinker finds plenty of evidence to support his claim that human nature has limits. He points to studies showing that the practices of nepotism and inheritance stem from the prime status of family ties in all human societies; that, generally, human beings have shown an innate preference for reciprocating favors and exchanging goods to sharing with others in their community; that there are genetic and neurological explanations for the preponderance of violence in all human societies; that human beings from all societies exhibit ethnocentrism and other forms of group-against-group hostility; that personality traits and individual ability are, to some extent, influenced by genetics, which suggests that social inequality will emerge in even the most fair economic systems; that people are prone to deceive themselves about their own independence, wisdom, and integrity as a way of coping with life; and that the moral sensibilities of human beings reveal innate biases, such as associating "the good" with our family and friends, and with conformity, social stature, cleanliness, and beauty.[2] According to Pinker, this research implies that the intellectual and moral capacities of human beings are not limitless, and some people operate within narrower bounds than others. Although this is not the proper forum in which to assess the validity of these studies, the surfeit of evidence in support of Pinker's thesis should at the very least give us pause—and make us think twice before we endorse a political ethos that relies so heavily on the education of its citizens.

Science and theology rarely have an opportunity to form alliances, but they have been able to do so on the issue of human nature. The renowned theologian Reinhold Niebuhr was perhaps the most eloquent and forceful detractor of those optimists who overestimated the moral and political capacities of human beings. Drawing on the scriptural doctrine of original sin, Niebuhr maintained that political wisdom can be found only in accepting the limitations of human beings, acknowledging that they are sinful creatures, often motivated by egoism, self-interest, and the will-to-power. In his view, the horrors of the twentieth century could largely be attributed to the "children of light," the optimists who maintained a naive belief in "progress" and "the perfectibility of man."[3]

Although well-intended, the children of light were guilty of pride in averring that man could reach untold heights, both morally and politically, if only given the chance. They held that any wrongdoing is a matter of ignorance that can be easily remedied with the proper education and application of reason. It never occurred to them that faith in the malleability of man could, in the hands of darker forces, lead to the kind of pernicious social experimentation witnessed in the twentieth century. And it was inconceivable to them that reason could serve—instead of master—sinful impulses. The Stalinists, for example, thought they could cure the Soviet citizen of bourgeois false consciousness, an idea they used to justify forcing famine on millions of kulaks while collectivizing agriculture in the Ukraine. Similarly, the Nazis were bent on creating a master race of human beings, and they saw the Final Solution as a necessary and logical step toward realizing their dreams. With the assistance of reason, twentieth-century humankind hardly progressed. If anything, it fell further into the abyss than ever before.

Most optimists never have the far-flung ambitions of the Nazis or Stalinists, but they remain guilty of championing an unchecked freedom that allowed "the children of darkness"—those who believed that self-interest and the will-to-power were the only guiding principles in the world—to carry out their designs with few impediments. Unwilling to see the darker side of human nature, optimists refused to recognize the tension between freedom and order, and they underestimated the extent to which freedom could unleash the selfish and vainglorious motives of men.

Niebuhr was especially critical of democratic optimists such as John Dewey who insisted that more and deeper democracy represented the panacea to all social ailments, reconciling the tensions between freedom and order, liberty and equality, and the individual and the community. As he praised the virtues of his Great Community, Dewey failed to understand that groups of men (or factions) are even more susceptible to unrestrained self-interest and egoism than individuals. A great admirer of James Madison, Niebuhr regarded factions as an unmitigated, yet inevitable, evil that afflicts all free democratic societies. The problem with factions is that they magnify the darker impulses already residing in the heart of man.

> Individual men may be moral in the sense that they are able to consider interests other than their own in determining problems of conduct, and are capable, on occasion, of preferring the advantages of others to their own. . . . In every human group there is less reason to guide and to check impulse, less capacity for self-transcendence, less ability to comprehend the needs of others and therefore more unrestrained egoism than the individuals, who compose the group, reveal in their personal relationships.[4]

On their own, individuals will occasionally exhibit the capacity for selflessness, justice, and love. But as part of a group, these individuals are subsumed by the herd instinct. In the name of the commonweal or national unity, they fight doggedly for the partial interests and ambitions of the group, rarely hesitating to trample on even the most basic liberties of those who get in their way.

Although an artifact of the children of light, democracy can quickly become the instrument of the children of darkness. Not surprisingly, Niebuhr had only contempt for Deweyan democracy, which he considered just another fantasy conjured by the children of light—another fantasy with potentially devastating consequences. For unfettered democracy created too many opportunities for the darker side of human nature to unveil itself.

Walter Lippmann, journalist and former student of William James, also raised questions about the civic capacities of ordinary citizens in his two influential books, *Public Opinion* and *The Phantom Public*. What made Lippmann's criticisms especially damaging was the fact that they rested on similar psychological grounds. He agreed with the pragmatists that man was largely a bundle of habits. But he did not conclude, like Dewey, that the average citizen could develop a scientific habit of mind and, in the spirit of open-mindedness, remain committed to collaborating with his fellow citizens to learn from the collectivity of their experiences. Most people, he said, operate under the heavy influence of their culture and heritage. "In the great blooming, buzzing confusion of the outer world we pick out what our culture has already defined for us, and we tend to perceive that which we have picked out in the form stereotyped for us by our culture." Each man perceives the world "through a class, darkly," and he reinforces his stereotypes within his social set and passes them along to the next generation.[5] These stereotypes are habits that no one can easily break.

If he had the time and energy, man could theoretically counteract these stereotypes by subjecting them to scientific scrutiny—by treating them as tentative hypotheses that must be tested and evaluated. But reality places limits on the possible. Most men will not avail themselves of opportunities to deliberate with their fellow citizens and will not constantly question their own preconceptions about the world. Most of us cannot achieve this scientific disposition and instead "believe in the absolutism of our own vision, and consequently in the treacherous character of all opposition."[6] As creatures of habit, said Lippmann, human beings are far more constrained than Dewey and other optimists are willing to admit. Although not bound by instinct or biological necessity, humanity may still be trapped within prisons of its own making —a cultural heritage that places limits on what we can know, achieve, and become.

John Dewey complained to Sidney Hook that critics of democracy assumed every man was an incorrigible "sonofabitch." But democratic enthusiasts might acknowledge that most people cannot be expected to become purveyors of the common good. It may be unfair to characterize every man as a would-be Kenneth Lay, the former CEO of Enron; it is equally unfair to expect every man to exhibit the lifelong public and moral commitments of an Abraham Lincoln. Denying this obvious fact can lead to disastrous consequences politically.

To assume that man is a soft piece of clay that can be molded into any conceivable shape or form, a blank slate on which any teaching can be written, invites the kind of political hubris or overreaching of which we should remain forever wary, especially in the wake of twentieth-century totalitarianism. Prudent politics requires a sober acceptance of our psychological limits, recognizing that not even the best education will turn men into angels. To some degree, we will always harbor a lust for power and material gain, and in our darker moments we will demonstrate an alarming capacity for evil and an uncanny ability to witness the misery of our fellow men with little or no sympathy.

If we accept that human nature has limits, we must reevaluate the democratic psychology, which presupposes the infinite malleability (the near perfectibility) of humankind. And we must not dismiss so casually as elitist those political institutions that are mindful of human frailties and designed to fragment power and channel human energies toward moderation. Niebuhr expressed this sentiment with enviable elegance:

> The preservation of a democratic civilization requires the wisdom of the serpent and the harmlessness of the dove. The children of light must be armed with the wisdom of the children of darkness but remain free from their malice. They must know the power of self-interest in human society without giving

it moral justification. They must have this wisdom in order that they may be-guile, deflect, harness and restrain self-interest, individual and collective, for the sake of the community.[7]

## The Wisdom of the Multitude?

Developments in the philosophy of science over the last eighty years or so present serious challenges to the epistemological assumptions underlying participatory democracy. The pragmatists viewed science as a process of verification by a community of competent inquirers who experimentally test their hypotheses against the empirical world. They maintained that induction, proceeding from specific facts to general conclusions, was the best way to obtain reliable knowledge. That induction invited statistical analysis, taking a representative sample of empirical observations to arrive at more reliable conclusions, did not escape the pragmatists. This meant that truth inquiry was a probabilistic affair: as more and more scientists confirm a particular hypothesis, the likelihood of its being true increases.

First to challenge the pragmatist understanding of the scientific enterprise was Karl Popper. As early as 1919, a young Popper began to see the flaws in this line of thinking when he became interested in what he called "the problem of demarcation"—making the distinction between science and pseudoscience (or nonscience). As he pondered this issue, Popper noticed that many ostensibly scientific theories were impossible to refute. The examples of Sigmund Freud's psychoanalysis and Alfred Adler's individual psychology showed that empirical facts could always be selected or interpreted to verify a theory. Proving Freud or Adler wrong was downright impossible: "I could not think of any conceivable instance of human behaviour which could not be interpreted in terms of either theory." In this way, each "resembled astrology rather than astronomy."[8] Popper observed that Albert Einstein's theory of relativity could not be so easily accommodated by a biased selection of the evidence. Unlike psychoanalysis and individual psychology, this theory was fraught with risk, vulnerable to tests that could instantly invalidate it.

Based on these observations, Popper argued that the guiding principle of scientific inquiry was not verification, as was traditionally understood, but falsification. Real scientists construct falsifiable or refutable theories and then devise rigorous methods of testing them. Only after passing these tests can theories claim to be verified or confirmed—indeed, to be true, if only provisionally. Adopting what Popper called a "critical attitude," the scientific community never ceases in its efforts to falsify and debunk existing theories. All the while, scientists remain disinterested, forever uncertain about the truth of their theories and indifferent to the outcome of their tests.

Popper's views about the provisionality of scientific truth echo Peirce and James, but his emphasis on falsification represents a radical departure from pragmatism. In rejecting verification as the operating principle of scientific inquiry, Popper came to the conclusion that theory construction in science is not an inductive process. In accordance with David Hume, the eighteenth-century Scottish empiricist, Popper argued that induction cannot be logically justified for two chief reasons.

First, the frequent conjunction of events—for example, the sun rises in the morning and then the rooster crows—does not mean that it will necessarily continue in the future. It does not follow logically that the rooster will crow tomorrow morning just because people have heard him do so thousands of times in the past. Based on this past information alone, one cannot make any logical conclusions about what the rooster will do tomorrow. Popper pointed out:

> It is far from obvious, from a logical point of view, that we are justified in inferring universal statements from singular ones, no matter how numerous; for any conclusion drawn in this way may always turn out to be false: no matter how many instances of white swans may have been observed, this does not justify the conclusion that *all* swans are white.[9]

Past experiences can never tell us with certainty what is universally true.

Second, and even more damaging, according to Popper, was that induction failed to escape its own internal contradictions. Because the principle of induction is itself a universal statement, its veracity must be justified inductively, drawn from empirical evidence. Justifying these inductions would require support from another round of empirical evidence—and so on. Thus, the attempt to defend the principle of induction using its own logic leads to an infinite regress. Induction cannot logically justify itself, a problem the pragmatists seemed to overlook.

Hume believed that, out of verbal habit, people make inductive inferences about future events, even though they are not logically justifiable. In other words, people observe many times that Y follows from X, and eventually they begin to say, "X *causes* Y." This verbal habit leads people to believe that this apparent causal connection must be true. With unshakable confidence, they predict that once X occurs, Y will surely follow. Drawing on Hume's psychology, the pragmatists argued that these habits or theories become rules for action under which people operate in their daily lives. Born of frequent repetition, these verbal habits become fairly reliable theories. Induction may have been indefensible on logical grounds, but what mattered most was that it worked in practice.

Dissatisfied with both psychological and utilitarian justifications of induction, Popper parted company with both Hume and the pragmatists on the subject of habit. He did not consider habit formation an adequate explanation of how scientists—or anyone, for that matter—devise theories or laws. Indeed, the typical result of repetition is not a verbal formulation, such as a law or theory, but rather an automatic or reflexive action of which one ceases to be conscious.

As a result, Popper took issue with the idea that habitual behavior is analogous to belief in a theory or law. Habit formation involves repeating the same behavior until it is second nature, performed flawlessly without giving it the least thought. But theories and laws try to identify regularities among experiences that are similar but not precisely the same. Every morning when the rooster crows, for example, the experience varies slightly. The exact color of the sky, configuration of the clouds, and sound of the crow can never be repeated. The observer interprets these distinct yet similar events as a regularity that can be explained by a particular law or theory—that is, the sunrise prompts roosters to crow. Theory, then, explains the repetition of similar events; repetition of the same events does not produce theory.

But even assuming, for the sake of argument, that theories were merely verbal habits, Popper believed that Hume and the pragmatists still stood on shaky ground. For the fact remains that habits, just like theories, do not originate in repetition. The actions that eventually become habitual are discovered first in that awkward phase of trial and error.

People often experiment with actions or modes of behavior on a hunch, hoping they will yield the expected results. After one or two successes, people identify this course as the best available and, over time, will develop a habit through repetitive action. Likewise, they tend to devise theories hastily, in a spontaneous burst of inspiration, long before they have collected much supporting evidence. Indeed, "we actively try to impose regularities upon the world; we try to discover similarities in it, and to interpret it in terms of laws invented by us. Without waiting for premises, we jump to conclusions. These may have to be discarded later, should observation show that they were erroneous."[10] Even scientists are eager to formulate half-baked theories about the conjunction of events, which they can then test, only settling on a tentative belief after many failed attempts at falsification.

Like Peirce and James, Popper believed that people could only make sense of their experiences if they actively and willfully engaged the world. The problem with induction was that it implied the opposite, that we are all passive agents, waiting for the empirical world to make its regularities known before we dare to formulate a theory or hypothesis. As any pragmatist would readily admit, that is not how any person, scientist or not, operates.

The implication here is that, in addition to overlooking the logical deficiencies of induction, the pragmatists also overstated its practical value. Indeed, according to Popper, theory construction was a two-step process in which induction never played a role. To begin with, scientists make wild guesses based on little information and influenced primarily by a "horizon of expectations" that frames their view of the world. Then they test these guesses or hypotheses deductively, following the simple syllogism: *if the hypothesis fails the test, it has been proved false; if not, the hypothesis has been provisionally corroborated.* Popper believed that the scientific enterprise formed a productive dialectic between guessing and deducing, between imagination and logic. Formulating theories "opens up the way to new knowledge" about the world, but scientific experiments and tests "save us from following a track that leads nowhere: which helps us out of the rut, and which challenges us to find a new way."[11] Theories propelled us forward into uncharted terrain; tests told us whether this terrain was hostile to our wanderings.

Despite its logical and practical shortcomings, induction held an appeal for pragmatists because it comported quite nicely with their probabilistic understanding of truth. Although absolute certainty about the truth escaped the grasp of humankind, they believed that degrees of certainty did not. Largely due to Charles Peirce's influence, probability theory became the very basis of pragmatist epistemology. Enthralled with the power of statistical inference, Peirce argued that we could become more confident about our truth claims as more corroborative evidence came our way.

Popper contended that this runs contrary to logic on a number of levels. First, determining the probability of a hypothesis is nearly impossible. The whole endeavor presupposes that hypotheses or theories are the same as events, the results of which can be counted and then tabulated. With hypotheses this is easier said than done. It requires counting "the number of experimentally testable statements belonging to the theory," and then determining "the relative frequency of those which turn out to be true." The "relative frequency can then be taken as a measure of the probability of a theory."[12] But anyone would be hard-pressed to create an exhaustive list of "experimentally testable statements" that constitute a particular theory.

Second, even if compiling such a list were feasible, calculating the relative frequency of a hypothesis—or its logical probability—says nothing about its degree of corroboration (or of truth). Indeed, there is a significant difference between logical probability and the degree of corroboration. While calculating probability involves simply counting the number of tests a hypothesis has passed, the degree of corroboration is determined by assessing the "severity of the various tests" to which the hypothesis is subjected.[13] According to Popper, scientists are not interested in highly probable hypotheses because they do not have much explanatory power. Cautious and vague, highly probable hypotheses border on the tautological, providing very little new information about the world.

Far more interesting and richer in explanatory power are the riskier, and thus less probable, hypotheses that can be subjected to strenuous testing. Less probable hypotheses tend to be more precise statements from which many other statements can be deduced.

> The *degree of corroboration* of a theory can surely not be established simply by counting the number of the corroborating instances. . . . For it may happen that one theory appears to be far less well corroborated than another one, even though we have derived very many basic statements with its help, and only a few with the help of the second. As an example we might compare the hypothesis "All crows are black" with the hypothesis . . . "the electronic charge has the value determined by Millikan". Although in the case of a hypothesis of the former kind, we have presumably encountered many more corroborative statements, we shall nevertheless judge Millikan's hypothesis to be the better corroborated of the two.[14]

In other words, in determining the degree of corroboration, the quality of the tests matters far more than the quantity. A risky hypothesis that is corroborated a handful of times will enjoy a higher degree of corroboration than a highly probable hypothesis corroborated countless times.

Popper's example is illustrative: the statement "all crows are black" is highly probable but ultimately just definitional, leading to no additional knowledge about crows or the larger avian population. The degree of corroboration can never be high when a hypothesis has little to say. Although far less probable (and eventually falsified), Robert Millikan's hypothesis, that every electron has a constant and measurable charge, introduced a wealth of knowledge to the world of physics and had countless applications. Just a few instances of corroboration made this hypothesis far more informative and insightful than hundreds of empirical observations that support the tautological statement about crows. If scientists only sought highly probable hypotheses, they would never make any advances in our knowledge. For this reason, said Popper, it is wrong to associate the probability of a hypothesis with its degree of truth. Only the severity of the tests, not the number or percentage of them successfully performed, can tell a community of inquirers whether they should accept a hypothesis as provisionally true.

Popper shattered centuries of conventional wisdom about the scientific enterprise, and he called into question pragmatist assumptions about the primacy of inductive logic and the probabilistic nature of truth. As a result, his ideas challenge the epistemological assumptions underlying participatory democratic theory. Based on inductive logic, participatory democracy rests on the notion that adding more participants to the political process will increase the probability that their policy choices are the right ones.

Popper's philosophy of science shows that this is decidedly not true, for there is nothing logical about induction. A bounty of evidence supporting a theory does not increase its likelihood of being true, now or in the future. Each bit of evidence represents an isolated test that has failed to falsify a theory. These tests cannot be assembled, like stones or bricks, to build an increasingly solid theory. At most, these tests constitute a house of cards that at any moment can collapse. For Popper, a theory that has been tested and corroborated countless times is no more likely to be true than one that has been corroborated only two or three times:

> I think we shall have to get accustomed to the idea that we must not look upon science as a "body of knowledge," but rather as a system of hypotheses; that is to say, as a system of guesses or anticipations which in principle cannot be justified, but with which we work as long as they stand up to tests, and of which we are never justified in saying that we know that they are "true" or "more or less certain" or even "probable."[15]

This suggests that we can never be more certain about the validity or utility of a democratically constructed law than one issued by an autocrat. That countless citizens offer their knowledge and experience to test a hypothesis, coming together in thoughtful deliberation to make policy, cannot make us more certain of its wisdom. In other words, participatory democracy does not necessarily mean better outcomes.

The onslaught against the pragmatist epistemology did not end with Karl Popper. In his ground-breaking work, *The Structure of Scientific Revolutions* (1962), Thomas S. Kuhn introduced to the world startling insights into the process of scientific inquiry. He showed that, far from being open and deliberative, the pursuit of scientific knowledge is just as bound to its historical context as other institutions and thus not necessarily an agent of progress. The belief that science marches us steadily toward the ultimate truth is naive, based on an idealistic view of how scientists operate.

Drawing on historical examples, Kuhn debunked the notion that scientists belong to an open community of competent and disinterested inquirers who use their expertise to invent creative ways of enhancing our knowledge and discovering truths. In reality, he said, most scientists are nothing more than highly educated technicians working within the narrow confines of a dominant paradigm, which begins with a canonical piece of research that lays out a set of plans and procedures for future research. Not taught to be intellectually flexible and innovative, scientists gladly use all the tools, practices, and methods prescribed by their paradigm for solving puzzles in their field.

Only when an existing paradigm fails to solve a number of puzzles do scientists feel a crisis is upon them, compelling them to think more broadly about their discipline and to entertain alternative approaches. A revolution occurs when scientists shift their allegiance to a new paradigm that can resolve this crisis, whereupon they lock themselves into a new set of plans and procedures. The history of science, then, can be characterized as long stretches of tedium and conformity, punctuated by brief revolutionary moments.

Kuhn's work dropped a bomb on the world of science and philosophy, for he showed that science was not immune to ossification and corruption. Like any other institution, science could become trapped in its own web of practices and specious assumptions, and only a crisis could bring about significant change. Kuhn argued that the scientific community was not an open society wherein members freely exchange information and ideas and make piecemeal reforms to standard practices as needed. On the contrary, his study of the history of science revealed its authoritarian tendencies.

Scientists defer to those few intellectual authorities whose exemplary research has become regarded as canonical and unassailable. The most devout followers of this canon enforce obedience to the given paradigm and quickly ostracize heretics. Kuhn even went so far as to suggest that "the member of a mature scientific community is, like the typical character of Orwell's *1984*, the victim of a history rewritten by the powers that be."[16] Hyperbolic comparisons to an Orwellian universe notwithstanding, Kuhn withheld any judgment of scientific practices and, in fact, considered their authoritarian tendencies a useful source of stability.

But many critics of science used Kuhn for their own purposes. Postmodernists were especially eager to invoke Kuhn's work, which in their view corroborated their claim that discourse can never escape relationships of power. Critics of America's Cold War policy believed that Kuhn offered a plausible explanation for why the scientific community had proved so vulnerable to co-optation by an ominous military-industrial complex. Although Kuhn did not endorse such critical applications of his work, he did believe that power arrangements affect how scientists seek knowledge and severely limit their range of activity.

As a result, Kuhn also called into question the notion of scientific progress. The many historical examples he cited in his landmark work "indicate that scientific progress is not quite what we had taken it to be. . . . We may, to be more precise, have to relinquish the notion, explicit or implicit, that changes of paradigm carry scientists and those who learn from them closer and closer to the truth."[17] A new paradigm may resolve the latest crisis, but there is no guarantee that overall it represents a step forward epistemologically. It may be just another framework within which scientists are forced to operate.

If Kuhn is to be taken seriously, one must reconsider whether participatory democracy—understood, in Deweyan terms, as the scientific method writ large—is always the best way to attain political knowledge. Even under the most ideal conditions, when participating citizens successfully employ the methods of science, democratic communities may not always produce the best policies, for they too will work within a closed system, a particular paradigm that limits their thinking and modes of operation. In a worst case scenario, they may yield to an Orwellian authority whose demagoguery and "doublespeak" may prove irresistible. At best, they will operate within the narrow parameters of a dominant political ethos and become susceptible to what social scientists call "groupthink."[18] In their attempt to acquire knowledge and devise policies that solve social problems, democratic communities may not draw openly on all relevant experiences. Instead, they may gather information too selectively and thus fail to entertain alternative ideas—ideas that might have proved extremely beneficial to the community.

Kuhn's notion of paradigm shifts may give credence to Wolin's concept of "fugitive democracy." Kuhn suggested that science in its ideal form—described by both the pragmatists and Popper as an open process in which every scientist constantly devises and tests hypotheses with the utmost rigor—occurs episodically. Only during those occasional revolutionary moments in history do scientists reach this ideal. But not long after the revolution they settle into a new routine, conforming to a set of practices and procedures that constitute the dominant paradigm in their field.

Similarly, Wolin argues that true and authentic democracy will erupt for brief moments and perhaps emit forceful shocks to the political system until the state tames and co-opts it. The state may make some accommodations to the demands of the short-lived demos, and thereby alter its own paradigm, but the democratic moment will quickly vanish and then ossify into a set of bureaucratic procedures and protocols. In both the worlds of science and democracy, groupthink and bureaucratic regimen represent the normal state of affairs. Deliberation among participants in a free and open forum will emerge only in times of crisis, when the need for alternative points of view becomes that much more pressing.

Despite the devastating critiques offered by Popper and Kuhn, there is reason to think that the democratic epistemology is the one pragmatist tenet that holds some water. In his endlessly insightful *The Wisdom of Crowds*, James Surowiecki suggests that large and diverse groups are quite adept at solving problems of both cognition and cooperation and far less prone to groupthink than smaller and more homogeneous groups. He cites a large body of research from a variety of fields to support the Peircean claim that truth-making is a social and probabilistic endeavor: as a group gets larger (i.e., the sample size increases) and more diverse (i.e., the sample becomes more representative of the wide variety of perspectives within the greater population), it can approximate with more precision the true answer (i.e., more accurately estimate the population parameter).

One of his more illustrative examples of a group's ability to solve cognitive problems is the story of Francis Galton, an old and curmudgeonly British scientist who, while attending a country fair in the town of Plymouth in 1906, made a discovery that challenged his long-held opinion that the mass of people was irretrievably obtuse. He happened to come across a competition in which attendees of the fair could place bets on the weight of a fattened ox ready for slaughter. In hopes of receiving a prize, eight hundred people paid sixpence to give their best guesses. Expecting to confirm his opinion of the mass, Galton calculated the mean of all the guesses and compared it to the actual weight of the ox. To his amazement, the collective wisdom of the gamblers that day was right on the mark: the average guess was 1,197 pounds, just one pound shy of the ox's actual weight of 1,198 pounds. Hardly an advocate of democracy throughout his long life, Galton was not unaware of the political implications of his finding. Indeed, he grudgingly conceded that the "result seems more creditable to the trustworthiness of a democratic judgement than might have been expected."[19] While this anecdote may be dismissed by some as mere coincidence, Surowiecki demonstrates quite persuasively that crowds display this kind of intelligence all the time, often in the most unlikely places. If he is right, there is good reason to take more seriously the democratic epistemology.

The internet's own Wikipedia represents a fascinating case study of the democratic epistemology. In the last couple of years, there has been considerable interest in the popular media about the success of this free on-line encyclopedia, to which anyone with internet access can contribute content. Founded in 2001, Wikipedia has nearly 4 million articles in two hundred languages (with over a million articles in English alone). Receiving about fourteen thousand hits per second, it is now ranked by many sources as the seventeenth most popular site on the internet.[20]

Skeptics have expressed doubts about the accuracy and reliability of a democratic information source that welcomes contributions from experts and amateurs alike. But Wikipedia enthusiasts point to evidence that suggests the masses may give the experts a run for their money. Alexander Halavais, assistant professor of communications at Quinnipiac University, tested the self-correcting capacity of Wikipedia's collective intelligence by slipping thirteen factual errors, some of them quite obscure, into several articles. Expecting many of these errors to remain undetected for a considerable length of time, Halavais was surprised to discover that all his falsehoods had been deleted within three hours after he posted them.[21]

In 2005 *Nature* published the results of its study in which researchers compared the factual accuracy of a random sample of science-related entries in Wikipedia and in Encyclopaedia Brittanica. They found that the average science entry in Wikipedia had four mistakes; Brittanica had about three.[22] Although Brittanica proved more accurate, Wikipedians interpreted these findings as a victory for the open-source encyclopedia, which at five years old is far younger than its two-hundred-year-old rival. As they see it, the nascent Wikipedia can only improve as its community of contributors and editors expands, adding more knowledge and intelligence to its collective brain. Meanwhile, with each entry written, edited, and reviewed by a handful of experts, the decrepit Brittanica will languish with outdated, possibly biased, material. Many people, not surprisingly, see Wikipedia as the triumph of the free marketplace of information and ideas over the closed system reserved for experts.

That said, Wikipedia is neither an unqualified success story nor a model of participatory democracy. In 2005 a thirty-eight-year-old man from Nashville, Tennessee, decided to play a joke and posted an entry full of falsehoods on John Seigenthaler, a distinguished journalist and former editor of the *Tennessean*, who briefly worked for Robert Kennedy in 1961. The entry claimed erroneously that Seigenthaler lived in the Soviet Union for a short period, and more egregiously, that he had been implicated in the assassinations of John and Robert Kennedy. This was a classic case of what Wikipedians call "vandalism"—intentionally posting false information on the site, which meticulous volunteer editors typically find and remove within hours, sometimes minutes. Somehow these particularly libellous falsehoods on Wikipedia remained undetected for 132 days. This story received considerable attention in the media, bringing public attention to the fact that Wikipedia is vulnerable to abuse of this sort. By no means was this an isolated incident, for as the number of users has continued to grow, so have the instances of vandalism, as well as unintentional errors and unresolved disputes over content.

Aware of these problems, Wikipedia administrators have established over the last few years a number of procedures and policies that try to bring order to the democratic process. The founder of Wikipedia, Jimmy Wales, appointed volunteer administrators who—with help from software "robots" that run routine scans—police the site for abuse. He also assembled a mediation committee that tries to resolve content disputes (or "editing wars") amicably. For those occasions when this process does not work, he created an arbitration committee that makes a final ruling. Until a resolution is reached, administrators will sometimes temporarily "protect" the disputed entry, prohibiting anyone from making edits or adding new content.[23] The result of all these procedures and policies is that "Wikipedia has become a regulatory thicket, complete with an elaborate hierarchy of users and policies about policies."[24]

According to a study conducted by two researchers at IBM, the amount of text on the site devoted to issues of coordination, administration, and governance has grown from 15 to 30 percent in less than a year. Meanwhile, only about thirty-three hundred people, representing fewer than 2 percent of Wikipedia's registered users, do 70 percent of the work on the site.[25] This would suggest that the vast majority of Wikipedians are consumers of the site or, at best, only occasional contributors. A select few, those with the time and inclination, do the bulk of the work, both editorial and administrative. In place, then, are an increasingly complex set of institutional mechanisms—devised to improve accuracy and resolve disputes—and a relatively small cadre of elites who keep the whole operation running. It would seem that Wikipedia's democratic moment, if there ever was one, has become subject to creeping institutionalization and de facto exclusivity.

Paradoxically, despite these decidedly anti-democratic measures, Wikipedia is not always successful at curbing the excesses of democracy. The site's more controversial entries have become the terrain of ideological warfare. In these instances, when rival camps wage feverish editing wars without any hope of reaching a compromise, majority tyranny sometimes prevails over truth.

William Connolley, a climate modeler at the British Antarctic Survey and an expert on the issue of global warming, learned the hard way that expertise cannot always contend with a determined opposition. An avid contributor to Wikipedia in his areas of expertise, Connolley found himself in the midst of a fierce editing war. For over two years he fought with skeptics who doubted that human activity was behind global warming, and one of the skeptics even stooped to insulting Connolley directly. The case eventually went to arbitration, and after three months, the committee punished Connolley for his active role in the editing war by placing him on a six-month parole that limited him to one edit per day. While two of his opponents received stiffer sentences (they were banned from making any edits at all for six months), he felt unnecessarily abused for having fought so earnestly on behalf of the truth. His sentence was later revoked, and he has since become a site administrator, but Connolley believes his story speaks to what is most troubling about Wikipedia: it "gives no privilege to those who know what they're talking about."[26]

This shortcoming led Larry Sanger, who was present at the founding of Wikipedia, to jump ship and help develop a new Web-based encyclopedia that is far less democratic. "Wikipedia has gone from a nearly perfect anarchy to an anarchy with gang rule," he observed.[27] To be sure, Sanger's sharp criticism appears overstated, for stories like Connolley's remain the exception, not the rule. Most of the content on Wikipedia is not captured by intellectual thugs who make matters difficult for those with useful and accurate knowledge to contribute. But these exceptions do illustrate how the open marketplace of information and ideas can potentially degenerate into mob rule and thereby undermine the entire enterprise of truth inquiry.

The example of Wikipedia points to another important caveat emphasized by Surowiecki. Not only must a group be large and diverse, says Surowiecki, it must also comprise people who contribute private knowledge that is largely independent of what everyone else in the group thinks. This way, each person in the group adds piecemeal to the collective wisdom. But this principle of independence presents considerable problems, requiring an element of decentralization that does not always exist.

Because human beings have been so adept at developing powerful networks of communication that bring them more closely together in both a literal and a virtual sense, groups are vulnerable to "information cascades," in which people blindly adopt the ideas and opinions of trailblazers—those who set trends that everyone else follows. Information cascades prevent people from drawing on their private knowledge and, instead, induce them to follow the herd and its latest fashions. The end result is a collective intelligence that reflects the knowledge and opinions of a select few, not of everyone in the group. Information cascades resemble the phenomenon of groupthink, though they can affect much larger and more heterogeneous groups. Defying conventional wisdom within participatory democratic theory, this insight suggests that groups are actually smarter when they deliberate less.

Surowiecki does not quite come out and say it, but the political implications are clear: too much democratic deliberation violates the principle of independence because it can cultivate an environment where most people will feel reluctant to contribute the modest amount of private knowledge they do have to offer. The trick is to devise mechanisms that safeguard the sanctity of independent thought and, at the same time, aggregate the private knowledge of all the individuals in the group. The weight-betting scheme at the country fair in Plymouth is exemplary.

If we apply this notion to democratic practices, the initiative or referendum should, in theory, do a far better job of aggregating the wisdom of the demos than a Wolinian social movement or a Barberian network of neighborhood assemblies ever would. The initiative allows citizens to make decisions in the privacy of the voting booth, but both social movements and neighborhood assemblies are susceptible to capture, either by charismatic leaders who exercise immense influence over their followers or by a cabal of narrow interests that shapes group opinion with more subtle—but no less effective—means.

Yet we all know from experience that the initiative has often produced wretched policies. One reason for this is that initiatives are not immune to "information cascades." Recent research has shown that the initiative is vulnerable to capture by elites. Because state campaign finance laws do not currently apply to initiatives, interest groups can spend enormous sums of money on lawyers to influence the wording of ballot questions in their favor and on slick advertising to manipulate public opinion. These well-funded campaigns tend to dominate public discourse and drown out alternative voices and sources of information.[28]

In the brief chapter entitled "Democracy: Dreams of the Common Good," Surowiecki offers another plausible explanation for the disappointing policy performance of initiatives: many political problems are not epistemological in nature, for there is no objective truth about what constitutes the common good. Large, diverse, and decentralized groups have proved adept at uncovering—or at least approximating—objective truths, such as the weight of an ox or the location of a submarine lost in the ocean, but they have no simple method of arriving at a "true" policy solution that satisfies everyone. Politics involves compromise, making difficult choices after a series of bargaining sessions wherein some people win and others lose. One would be hard-pressed to convince the losers that this compromise was in any way "true."[29]

Surowiecki suggests that politics is more a problem of cooperation than one of cognition. Groups have an aptitude for solving such problems, but only in a far less immediate and definitive way. Solutions to cooperation problems "tend to emerge over time, rather than being the product of a single collective decision," and they always remain "fragile or vulnerable to exploitation by others." The virtue of democracy may be that it develops the cooperative capacities of its participants, convincing them that losing on occasion is not only acceptable but necessary:

> [Democracy] is not a way of solving cognition problems or a mechanism for revealing the public interest. But it is a way of dealing with (if not solving once and for all) the most fundamental problems of cooperation and coordination: How do we live together? How can living together work to our mutual benefit? Democracy helps people answer those questions because the democratic experience is an experience of not getting everything you want. It's an experience of seeing your opponents win and get what you hoped to have, and of accepting it, because you believe that they will not destroy the things you value and because you know you will have another chance to get what you want.[30]

In those instances when we have no means of accessing the true "public interest," a polity could greatly benefit from the graciousness of losers. Only those people conditioned to the democratic way of life, it might be said, could accept political defeat with equanimity and, knowing in their hearts that one day they too will prevail, remain on friendly terms with the victor.

Democracy, then, demands a faith in the overall fairness of the system and a willingness to accept, however grudgingly, undesired outcomes. In other words, democracy does not produce truth or transform us into other-regarding creatures, but it does teach us—à la Mick Jagger—that you can't always get what you want.[31] It is not clear that one must engage deeply in politics in order to come to terms with this proverbial wisdom.

## The Institutional Legacy

As the previous section indicates, there is good reason to doubt the belief that large and diverse groups have a higher political IQ and thus a keener knowledge of the public interest. Nevertheless, the democratic epistemology has left an institutional legacy—a legacy that fails to meet the expectations of both the New Left and today's participatory democrats. In the wake of the student and civil rights movements, many political (and corporate) institutions in the United States have undergone reforms that rest on the notion that our democracy can only function properly if we rely increasingly on the wisdom of the multitude. These institutional reforms, many of which emerged in the 1960s and 1970s, tried to accomplish at least one of three objectives: *transparency and openness* to make information widely accessible, *diversity and inclusion* in the decision-making process, and *empowerment* of the historically disadvantaged and excluded.

The idea behind transparency is that as much information as possible should be made available to the public so that its members can become aware of the many activities of government and business and then make informed decisions as both voters and consumers. Institutional reforms with this aim include the Freedom of Information Act (first passed in 1966 and amended many times since), which requires government agencies to make all unclassified government documents available to the public; sunshine laws that open congressional committee work and debate to public scrutiny; open meetings legislation, which grants public access to various government meetings; the elimination of "teller voting" on the House floor (1970) to ensure that the record will reflect the vote of each member on proposed amendments to bills; the Federal Election Campaign Act (1971), which requires the public disclosure of campaign finance records; whistle-blower laws that protect both public and private employees from reprisal for reporting corruption, malfeasance, and fraud; the creation of congressional oversight agencies such as the General Accounting Office; and consumer protection laws that require companies to place warning labels on their products, to disclose the ingredients of processed foods, and to issue recall notifications when their products have safety flaws or do not function properly. The demand for transparency works under the premise that the public can only make wise decisions in what Oliver Wendell Holmes called a free marketplace of ideas. Easy access to information is the first step toward deriving truth democratically.

The next step requires devising inclusive institutions in which a wide array of perspectives are able to contribute to the decision-making process. The introduction of primary elections during the Progressive era exemplified this impulse to promote institutional inclusion by taking the nominating power away from party bosses and professionals and transferring it to the rank-and-file members of the party. The demand for inclusion and diversity really began to gain momentum in the late 1960s and has continued to this day. Protestors outside the 1968 Democratic national convention in Chicago expressed, among many other grievances, their frustration with the dominance of elites at the national party convention and what they saw as the systematic exclusion of certain issues from the party platform. Formed partly in response to the unrest and rioting outside the convention, the McGovern-Frasier Commission made recommendations that led to a number of party reforms, including the creation of presidential primaries in nearly every state (thus requiring potential nominees to campaign nationwide in an attempt to garner the support of rank-and-file party members) and a revised delegate selection process that guaranteed proportional representation of women and minority groups.[32]

Along the same lines, the government has enacted affirmative action policies that require government agencies and contractors to hire more women and minorities. These programs were designed to redress past injustices and to safeguard against racial and gender discrimination, but researchers have recently begun to learn that promoting diversity benefits the corporate bottom line. According to Taylor Cox and Carol Smolinski, authors of a Glass Ceiling Commission report entitled *Managing Diversity and Glass Ceiling Initiatives as National Economic Imperatives* (1994), empirical research has shown that diversity in the workplace, especially within the decision-making ranks, helps companies market their products more effectively to an increasingly pluralistic American society and around the world. Diversity creates an environment where innovation and creativity thrive and enhances the collective capacity for problem solving. As a result, companies that make greater efforts to hire and promote women and non-whites and to comply with Equal Employment Opportunity Commission (EEOC) and other regulatory requirements financially outperform their less inclusive competitors. Cox and Smolinski cite a study that rated the diversity performance of the Standard and Poors 500 companies and found that the one hundred most diverse of them averaged an annualized rate of return of 18.3 percent while the one hundred least diverse averaged only 7.9 percent.[33] As companies and investors learn that diversity makes good business sense, actually increasing their profits and stock valuations, the EEOC may not have to enforce compliance with its regulations.

Such attempts to ensure the proportional representation of groups in both our political and corporate institutions notwithstanding, the idea of diversity and inclusion culminated in the rise of direct democracy—that is, the initiative and referendum—in state politics. Although many states implemented direct democracy mechanisms during the Progressive era, it was not until the late 1970s that they came into vogue. With the passage of California's Proposition 13, which dramatically reduced property tax rates, people began to see the initiative and referendum as means to circumvent unresponsive state legislatures and governors and to take direct action on issues about which they were concerned. The last two decades of the twentieth century saw the radical expansion of direct democracy. From 1981 to 2000, citizens placed 660 initiatives on state ballots, of which 303 passed.[34]

The idea that citizen lawmaking leads to better outcomes has driven this growth. Ardent supporters of direct democracy believe that citizens know far better what is in their interest than a handful of representatives ever would. Although recent research suggests that the initiative process is vulnerable to capture by moneyed elites and special interests, these sobering findings have done little to curb widespread enthusiasm for direct democracy as a viable—even necessary—alternative to representative democracy. To borrow Surowiecki's language, the initiative and referendum represent, in the eyes of its advocates, the ideal means of aggregating the private knowledge of citizens and bringing to the fore their collective wisdom. Whether this is true is beside the point. That so many people think it is true speaks to the growing legitimacy of the democratic epistemology, the idea that truth, more often than not, emerges from the crowd rather than a small roomful of experts.

There has been considerable talk in the last few decades about empowering historically disenfranchised groups, including blacks and women. This has relevance to the democratic epistemology because, in many cases, the concept of empowerment has drawn on the rather postmodern notion that power precedes knowledge (the reverse of the enlightenment idea that knowledge gives one power). In other words, people need power to make their voices heard and to put their knowledge into practical effect; knowledge that does not receive the backing of power will remain forever obscure and never achieve the status of "truth."

Multiculturalism and identity politics have played a significant role in giving historically disadvantaged groups the opportunity to add their often ignored trials and triumphs to the story of America, reshaping the canons of art, literature, and history. The strategy of these groups has been to find strength in collective action, making their alternative narratives known to the world. This enterprise has not only been an immense source of pride for these groups; it has also given them the power to redraw the boundaries of worthwhile knowledge, to reconsider what is "true" about America, and to dispel old myths while creating new ones.

Conservatives have accused multiculturalists of promoting historical revisionism and relativism, of suggesting that all knowledge is, first and foremost, political terrain on which combatants seek to exercise power arbitrarily, without guidance from an objective authority. Dismissing the suggestion that there may be standards with which one can make intellectual and aesthetic judgments, multiculturalists view all such claims through the lens of power and regard them with suspicion. They view the canon not as a fountain of enlightenment but as a reflection of race, class, and gender inequities. For this reason, conservatives believe that multiculturalists represent what Harold Bloom calls the "school of resentment."[35] While these debates continue to rage, receiving serious attention in the academy and intellectual circles, their broader social impact has largely been made in the arena of public education. Not surprisingly, the local school committee has been the site of intense debates over what our children should be taught.

Perhaps the idea of empowerment reached its institutional apex during the War on Poverty. In 1964 Congress passed the Economic Opportunity Act, which included language about "community action" in the implementation of federal antipoverty programs. Created as part of this act, the Office of Economic Opportunity (OEO) oversaw a number of antipoverty programs designed to foster community development and to empower the residents of poor neighborhoods to wage the war on their own terms. Most famously, the act included a provision that said the poor were to have "maximum feasible participation." At the time it was unclear to many people what this meant exactly, but in retrospect the fingerprints of the New Left are impossible to miss. Here was an ideal opportunity for participatory democracy in action. These community action programs (CAPs), as they came to be known, represented a new twist on the welfare state, an unprecedented effort to give people the resources to rebuild their communities as they saw fit.[36]

As the War on Poverty got underway, "maximum feasible participation" became a battle cry for activists and neighborhood leaders who wanted to strip local officials and bureaucrats of their power and take it for themselves. Unfortunately, the CAPs never functioned as democratically as the idealistic drafters of the 1964 act had hoped. In many communities there ensued an ongoing struggle for control over federal government funds, leaving the people themselves largely outside the process. Quite often charismatic local leaders and activists exercised undue influence within their communities. Surowiecki might suggest that the CAPs suffered from too much deliberation, creating elite-driven information cascades that overpowered the trickling voices of the multitude. That the CAPs failed to empower local communities democratically probably explains why few government programs since then have used this model.

More economically focused attempts at empowering the disadvantaged and excluded have met with more success. For example, the federal government has created urban empowerment zones, typically poor and economically isolated neighborhoods in which investors receive tax incentives to open new businesses or build housing. Many of these designated areas have experienced revitalization, providing more economic opportunities to residents, as both entrepreneurs and workers, and improving quality of life in once blighted neighborhoods.

In a similar vein, many urban educational and service programs—such as Job Corps, Head Start, and Legal Aid—continue to provide poor people with the means of taking control of their lives and bettering themselves. Affirmative action programs can also be seen as a means of economic empowerment. The emphasis now is not to turn the poor into active citizens but rather to make them more attractive candidates for employment and to provide them with exciting economic opportunities. In other words, the empowerment strategy shifted from giving the poor a voice in the political arena to teaching them a skill set to sell in the labor market.

While the New Left ethos has undoubtedly left an institutional legacy in a variety of forms, it hardly resembles the ideal vision of participatory democracy evoked in the *Port Huron Statement*. This is because, of the three pragmatist tenets, only one (the democratic epistemology) made any kind of lasting impression. Right or wrong, we have grown to accept in the United States that a well-functioning democracy requires input from a wide array of people, and many of our institutions reflect this ethos.

It is important to note, however, that while the democratic epistemology emphasizes the importance of painstaking deliberation, our institutions have not demanded such a commitment from our citizens. Perhaps because our democratic metaphysics, our faith that citizens are poised for willful civic action, is so weak, we have turned to far simpler and less time-consuming methods that help us access the wisdom of the masses. First, we have made sure that information is widely available and transparent. The Freedom of Information Act and whistle-blower laws exemplify these efforts. Second, we have gone to great lengths to promote diversity and inclusion. The initiative and referendum are prime examples of an attempt to maximize the sample size—to aggregate the private knowledge of as many people as possible. Affirmative action policies do not follow the large sample approach; instead, by promoting diversity and proportional representation within the ranks of decision-makers, they create a small but highly representative cross section of the multitude. Either way, both the large sample approach and proportional representation introduce a diversity of perspectives. Finally, we have made attempts to empower the historically disadvantaged, typically by providing them various means to economic success. Although not all that the New Left might have dreamt of, these attempts to create openness, diversity, and prosperity are their institutional legacy. Dreams of transformation and endless plenary assemblies have fallen by the wayside. Participatory democracy, as such, was never to be.

# Epilogue

So what are we to make of the committed, ever faithful participatory democrats? In June 1962 Tom Hayden and fellow members of SDS displayed a profound democratic faith. Although most of the participants at Port Huron did not subscribe to any orthodox religious teachings, many of them felt as if their experience there portended a wondrous future for humanity. It was hard for participants not to feel this sense of destiny when, after many hours of discussion in plenary assemblies while hammering out the finer points of their manifesto, they walked into the evening and beheld the aurora borealis. The almost mystical atmosphere described by some Port Huron participants reflected their near religious zeal, an undying faith in humankind, in what it could achieve collectively and democratically. Without a shadow of doubt, they believed that human beings could arrive at provisional truths in a deliberative fashion, that they were educable and not chained to an immutable nature, and that they were free of any obstacles to civic engagement. The origins of this faith can be found in pragmatism.

Ironically, participatory democracy has turned to a reputedly anti-foundational philosophy for its foundations. The early pragmatists prided themselves on their anti-foundationalism, insisting that human beings can only promote tolerance and social justice if they reject first principles and fixed truths and focus their attention on the means to achieving a better life. But the democratic faith of John Dewey, and then the New Left, rests ever so precariously on a set of first principles—what I have called the pragmatist tenets. The problem is that all three tenets are questionable.

This criticism of participatory democracy notwithstanding, we must remember the issues that animated intellectuals and activists in the 1960s. The Students for a Democratic Society, for example, gave voice to legitimate concerns—racial segregation in the South, the growth of social and economic inequality in America, the alarming policy of nuclear brinkmanship in our relations with the Soviet Union, and the government's apparent disregard for the demands and needs of the American people. Undoubtedly, SDS saw the last problem as the root cause of all the others. They believed that existing political institutions would never represent the interests of the people.

So why did they become fixated on participatory democracy as the solution to what others have seen as a problem of representation?[1] They turned to participatory democracy because they believed it was the only way in which citizens could be given a fair hearing and a voice in directing government policy, the only way to ensure that the common good would prevail over elite or special interests. In an epistemological sense, representation could not substitute for self-determination. It is easy to see why, at the time, they embraced this misguided sentiment.

Throughout the 1960s, however, student radicals became increasingly enamored with the idea that democracy was a transformative experience for the participant. Arnold Kaufman, who coined the phrase "participatory democracy" and stressed its transformative benefits in his earlier writings, grew to regret that this idea would give rise to the cult of authenticity. In his only book, *The Radical Liberal,* which was first released in 1968, Kaufman complained that the issues at hand—racial segregation, poverty, the Cold War, Vietnam—began to play second fiddle to the self-realization of the participant:

> Many members of "the Movement" have grown impatient with the calculations and compromises that effective participation in that process imposes. They are, as I have said, too often concerned with the state of their souls than with the preferences and welfare of those they aim to help. They are too often unwilling to act in ways they regard as inauthentic for the sake of a greater prospect of definite results.[2]

Kaufman found this fixation with authenticity especially "self-indulgent" because the "children of middle-class parents have somewhere else to go if they fail," often "beating their perilous way back to lucrative professional careers," while the people for whom they ostensibly work so hard do not enjoy such a luxury. True radicals, said Kaufman, had to consider the "welfare of those they aim to help," not their own purity. As a result, defining authenticity as a principled refusal to engage in political calculation and compromise was "perverse," "insincere," and "ineffectual."[3]

At best, we can see this as the youthful cry for authentic experience in a world laden with superficialities and phoniness; at worst, the petulant demand for an indefinite extension of adolescence. Neither provided adequate justification for participatory democracy. Nevertheless, the damage was done: the emphasis shifted from truth to transformation.

After the student radicalism of the 1960s and early 1970s, participatory democracy made a swift retreat behind the ivy-covered walls of academia. Recalling the glorious, if short-lived, days of 1960s radicalism, its adherents continue to praise the political as the highest and most rewarding way of life. Participatory democrats make the presumptuous claim that to be political is to be fully human and alive, that he who eschews the political life deprives himself of his humanity. Other activities that can make life meaningful—whether creative, intellectual, social, familial, fraternal, or spiritual—do not compare.

This belief in the unrivaled transformative power of political engagement has made it difficult—if not impossible—for participationists to relinquish the uncompromising view of democracy to which they have clung since their first protest or teach-in forty years ago. No doubt, they have never forgotten their first "freedom high"—the intense feeling of individual purpose and fulfillment described by many participants in the civil rights and antiwar movements.[4] Radical democrats, such as Wolin, appear especially fixated with achieving authenticity and purity. Others seem to follow Kaufman's lead in suggesting that our political system must create opportunities for civic participation while it also continues to function as a liberal state that secures rights, both negative and positive, for its citizens. This institution-friendly approach reflects the ideas of Barber and his fellow deliberative democrats. The former group (the radical democrats such as Wolin) remains ill-tempered and cranky; the latter (the deliberative democrats such as Barber) seems to have grown up. Nevertheless, participationists from both camps are enamored with the notion that, more than just a means to common ends, the political is an end in itself for the participant. This might explain why Wolin and Barber remain deeply committed to participatory democracy when all evidence and logic suggest it is nothing but a chimera.

Indeed, they both acknowledge that a sustainable form of participatory democracy, which demands a surplus of political will, is not an achievable goal. While Wolin is well aware of this sad reality, Barber can only admit as much in moments of intellectual honesty, for he is not quite ready to relinquish his hope of institutionalizing participatory democracy. Wolin's theory assumes the tenor of a "melancholic democracy"—a mournful remembrance of what has been lost and can only be recaptured in brief moments, if at all. Barber's ostensibly more mature theory takes on the tone of a "quixotic democracy"—an upbeat message about what could be, even though it remains at best a remote possibility. The participatory democrat, then, must be either sullen or foolish, a Hamlet or a Quixote.

Neither choice seems terribly appealing in a world that demands real political solutions. But participatory democrats can rest assured that they make fine literary companions, eloquently calling our attention to an ideal way of life, however incoherent or fantastic it may be. It is the height of irony that pragmatism, a philosophy stressing the practical and prosaic, should lay the foundation for such a romantic and poetic political tradition.

Because participationists claim to care about concrete matters of social justice, it would behoove them to come to terms with certain realities. We live in a world full of options, a world in which there are countless paths leading toward self-fulfillment. Politics presents just one of these. Once participationists understand this, they can let go of the presumption that an apolitical life is a tragic waste, and they can acknowledge that the commonweal does not necessarily hinge on widespread civic participation. A political system that promotes the common good only requires the proper institutional framework in which accountability and integrity are the hallmarks of leadership.

Perhaps a final return to the baseball metaphor will shed some light here. Despite the participationist's lament, it is perfectly acceptable that we are a nation of spectators. One does not have to play the game or find some other form of direct involvement in order to have a rewarding life. Indeed, for most people, there is more to life than baseball. Accordingly, we should accept that we live in a world of players and spectators. The problem is that, figuratively speaking, many people today go to the game but have insufficient interest in what the players are doing on the field and thus cannot hold them accountable for their actions. They either spend too much time in the concessions line or allow other amusements, such as the wave or errant beach balls, to distract them. Even worse, many people never go to the ballpark at all—or even watch the games on television.

Our goal, then, should not be to make everyone a participant in the game, but to turn each person into a reasonably attentive spectator, a fan who follows the game with some regularity. Attentive spectators keep the players honest and make certain that they try their hardest and follow the rules. They preserve the integrity of the game—ensure that it is not a mere charade or spectacle put on by the players in collusion with the coaches and umpires. So long as major league baseball is structured and organized in the right way, its players, coaches, and other direct participants will have an incentive to satisfy the fans and maintain the quality of the game. In other words, good fans help save the game from degenerating into a pseudo-sport like professional wrestling, but they do not have to devote endless hours to all things baseball. They need only be attentive, not deeply engaged—aware, not involved.

The game of politics is largely the same: we spectators are in charge of maintaining its integrity. This requires us to pay attention to politics, to be aware enough that we will vote intelligently and hold public officials accountable for their actions. We do not have to participate in neighborhood assemblies or social movements.

Of course, there are exceptions to this rule. African Americans, for example, would not have won their civil rights without a mass movement driven by thousands of dedicated participants. There will always be moments of crisis when civil society must play a crucial role in challenging the state. There is always a need, even during normal times, for some citizens to engage in civil society to raise awareness about important issues ignored by the state. But, in most cases, when political leaders fail to heed our wants and desires, or when we spectators fail to pay adequate attention to what our leaders are doing, it should be understood as an institutional problem.

Institutions guide the behavior of political actors with incentives and deterrents, carrots and sticks. Leaders will respond to the wishes of us spectators if the institutions in which they operate reward and punish them accordingly. Likewise, spectators will only become a part of this incentive structure if institutions can guarantee that there are benefits for doing so, that their watchfulness will make a significant difference in their lives. This all suggests that, if the political system fails to promote the commonweal, the focus should be on reforming institutions, not on converting all spectators into deeply committed citizens. For this reason, theorists who write about political parties, legislatures, and institutions generally may be able to teach us far more about democracy than either the foolish or sullen participationists ever could.

# Notes

## Introduction

1. *Port Huron Statement.* Note: Until the late twentieth century, political theorists used the term "man" instead of the more compassing term preferred today, "human." For the sake of consistency—and with apologies to female readers—I too use "man."

2. *Port Huron Statement.*

3. Interviews are from the film "Rebels with a Cause."

4. Max cited from ibid.

5. See Hayden, *Reunion,* 42, 75–81; Hayden and Flacks, "The *Port Huron Statement* at 40." In his memoirs Hayden also mentions that Albert Camus exerted an important influence on the SDS and the *Port Huron Statement,* not so much on their democratic thought but, rather, on their view of the "absurdity" of the human condition. Inspired especially by Camus's *The Plague,* the SDS activists perceived a sense of despair and alienation infecting humankind, but they turned to Mills, Kaufman, and Dewey for democratic solutions to this "plague."

6. Hayden and Flacks, "The *Port Huron Statement* at 40"; Arnowitz, "A Mills Revival?"; "Letter to the New Left," in Mills, *Power, Politics, and People.*

7. Hayden, *Reunion,* 78.

8. Mills, *New Men of Power,* 252–53.

9. Hayden and Flacks, "The *Port Huron Statement* at 40"; Hayden, *Reunion,* 42; Mattson, *Intellectuals in Action,* 197.

10. Kaufman, "Human Nature and Participatory Democracy," 198.

11. Kaufman, *Radical Liberal,* 58–59 (see also "Human Nature and Participatory Democracy," 191–93); Kaufman, "Two Cheers for American Education," 23; Kaufman, "Affluent Underdog," 350.

12. Mattson, *Intellectuals in Action,* 197–207, 210, 218–19. See also Kaufman, "Teach-Ins: New Force for the Times."

13. See the Epilogue for a discussion of Kaufman's criticism of the student movement.

14. See Mattson, *Intellectuals in Action,* 72–74, 191–96.

15. Richard Rorty is a notable example. Rorty sympathizes with attempts to expand citizen participation, but he believes that participation has limits: "Even someone like myself, whose admiration for John Dewey is almost unlimited, cannot take seriously his defense of participatory democracy." See Rorty, *Achieving Our Country,* 104.

16. See R. Putnam, *Bowling Alone;* T. Patterson, *Vanishing Voter.* The 2004 presidential election is a notable exception, when voter turnout approached 60 percent, largely because of the war in Iraq.

17. R. Putnam, *Bowling Alone,* 42–43. Putnam cites the *Roper Social and Political*

*Trends* surveys, which indicate that the number of Americans who had attended at least one public meeting on town or school affairs in the previous year declined by 40 percent between 1973 and 1994.

18. Hayden and Flacks, "The *Port Huron Statement* at 40."

19. See Diggins, *Promise of Pragmatism.*

20. Menand, *Metaphysical Club,* xi–xii.

21. Ibid., 364.

22. James, *Pragmatism,* in *Writings 1902–1910,* 573–74.

23. Chesterton, in Menand, *Metaphysical Club,* 362.

24. Dostoevsky, *The Brothers Karamazov;* Nietzsche, *The Gay Science,* Aphorism 354.

25. Russell, *Philosophical Essays,* 106–9 (109).

26. Russell himself does not suggest this is a reversal of the Machiavellian motto (this is my suggestion), but he does criticize pragmatism for focusing exclusively on method (the means) instead of values or principles (the ends).

27. James, *Writings 1902–1910,* 583. James was quite comfortable with this formulation (truth as expediency), but it made Russell shudder.

28. Russell, *Philosophical Essays,* 109.

29. James, *Writings 1902–1910,* 510.

30. Peirce, *Collected Papers,* 5:402n2.

31. Peirce, "The Fixation of Belief," in *Collected Papers,* 5:384.

32. Peirce, "How to Make Our Ideas Clear," in ibid., 5:407.

33. James, *Psychology: Briefer Course,* in *Writings 1878–1899,* 145, 150.

34. Peirce, "A Guess at the Riddle," in *Collected Papers,* 1:407. To learn more about the influence of Darwinism on pragmatist thought, see Wiener, *Evolution and the Founders of Pragmatism;* Menand, *Metaphysical Club.*

35. Dewey, *Public and Its Problems,* in *Later Works,* 2:327.

36. Dewey, "Creative Democracy: The Task before Us," in *Later Works,* 14:227.

37. Kloppenberg, in Westbrook, "Pragmatism and Democracy," 130.

38. See Posner, *Law, Pragmatism, and Democracy,* 99–111. In his discussion of Deweyan democracy, Posner uses the term "epistemic democracy"—"the idea that the best forms of inquiry and of decisionmaking in general, not just political inquiry and decisionmaking, are democratic in character." He argues that the pragmatist idea that truth acquisition was a public enterprise opened the doors for a more deliberative or participatory conception of democracy in Dewey's work.

39. I use the term "metaphysics" because this is the subfield of philosophy that deals most directly with the issue of free will.

40. For a classic statement on the pluralist school, see Schumpeter, *Capitalism, Socialism, and Democracy;* Truman, *Governmental Process.*

41. See, for example, Macpherson, *Political Theory of Possessive Individualism.*

42. Pateman, *Problem of Political Obligation,* 173ff.

43. Berlin, *Four Essays on Liberty,* 130.

44. Other scholars who support deliberative democracy include Joshua Cohen, Jon Elster, Amy Gutmann, Jane Mansbridge, and Carole Pateman. On the issue of scope and impact, see especially Pateman, *Participation and Democratic Theory.*

45. Barber, *Passion for Democracy,* 10.

46. Other scholars who sympathize with radical democracy include Seyla Benhabib, Wendy Brown, Ernesto Laclau, and Cornell West.

47. Wolin, *Presence of the Past,* 154.

48. Consider, for example, Rousseau's insistence that the general will is "always right." Should one decide stubbornly to exercise his private will, he must be "forced to be free." See Rousseau, *Basic Political Writings,* 206.

# 1—Charles Peirce

1. Philosopher Richard J. Bernstein has argued that Peirce's thought, especially his idea of community, has "important consequences for democratic theory," even though he did not necessarily conceive of community in democratic terms. See Bernstein's chapter entitled "Community in the Pragmatic Tradition" in Dickstein, *Revival of Pragmatism,* 144.

2. Kant, *Critique of Pure Reason,* 647–48.

3. Peirce, *Collected Papers,* 5:397.

4. See Menand, *Metaphysical Club;* Diggins, *Promise of Pragmatism;* Moore, *American Pragmatism;* Dickstein, *Revival of Pragmatism.*

5. Peirce, "Uniformity," in *Collected Papers,* 6:99.

6. Peirce, "The Architecture of Theories," in ibid., 6:12.

7. Peirce, *Collected Papers,* 5:402.

8. Ibid., 5:196.

9. T. Knight, *Charles Peirce,* 54.

10. Peirce, *Collected Papers,* 1:325.

11. Ibid., 5:5.

12. Ibid., 8:256.

13. Ibid., 5:44.

14. Ibid., 1:303.

15. Ibid., 8:267.

16. Ibid., 1:175.

17. Ibid., 8:266.

18. See T. Knight, *Charles Peirce,* 80–81.

19. More complex relationships can certainly involve four or more objects, but Peirce proved logically that such experiences are always reducible to a series of triadic relationships.

20. Peirce, *Collected Papers,* 5:212.

21. Ibid., 5:96.

22. Ibid., 1:171.

23. Ibid., 1:55.

24. Ibid., 1:635.

25. Ibid., 1:135.

26. Ibid., 6:334.

27. Menand, *Metaphysical Club,* 177–80, 228.

28. Peirce, *Collected Papers,* 5:171.

29. Peirce, "Some Consequences of Four Incapacities," in ibid., 5:275.

30. Peirce, "Deduction, Induction, and Hypothesis," in ibid., 2:623.

31. Peirce, *Collected Papers,* 5:407.

32. Peirce, "Prolegomena to an Apology for Pragmatism," in ibid., 4:547n1.

33. Peirce, *Collected Papers,* 5:311.

34. Ibid., 5:408.

35. Moore, *American Pragmatism,* 65.

36. Peirce, "Review of Fraser's Edition of *The Works of George Berkeley*," in *Collected Papers,* 8:12.

37. Peirce, *Collected Papers,* 5:407.

38. Ibid., 7:51.

39. Moore, *American Pragmatism,* 64.

40. Peirce, "Reply to the Necessitarians," in *Collected Papers,* 6:610.

41. Peirce, "The Doctrine of Chances," in *Collected Papers,* 2:654.

42. Ibid., 7:571.

43. Peirce, "Evolutionary Love," in *Collected Papers*, 6:294.
44. Peirce, *Collected Papers*, 6:294.
45. Ibid., 1:175.
46. Ibid., 1:407.
47. Peirce, "The Doctrine of Necessity Examined," in ibid., 6:44.
48. Peirce, *Collected Papers*, 5:65.
49. Peirce, "Man's Glassy Essence," in ibid., 6:267.
50. Peirce, *Collected Papers*, 6:59.
51. Ibid., 6:260.
52. Peirce, "The Law of Mind," in ibid., 6:148.
53. Peirce, *Collected Papers*, 1:673.
54. Ibid., 8:320.
55. Ibid., 8:311.
56. T. Knight, *Charles Peirce*, 94.
57. Peirce, *Collected Papers*, 5:130.
58. Ibid.
59. Ibid., 1:611.
60. Ibid., 8:38.

# 2—The Lonely Courage of William James

1. Peirce was a notorious womanizer. It is believed that he lost his teaching position at Johns Hopkins University—and subsequently was blackballed from receiving any other academic posts—in large part because of extramarital affairs. Just two days after the divorce from his first wife was finalized, the coup de grace occurred when he married Juliette Pourtaliai, a French "woman of uncertain origins," with whom he had been romantically involved (and cohabiting) for some time. His erratic behavior stemming from drug use did not help, either. Suffering from facial neuralgia, Peirce used cocaine, morphine, and ether to alleviate the pain. See Menand, *The Metaphysical Club*, 158–60, 280–83.

2. Peirce, *Collected Papers*, 5:414.

3. See James, *Writings 1902–1910*, 487–504.

4. Lippmann, "An Open Mind," 801.

5. James to H. G. Wells, *Letters of William James*, 259–60.

6. James, *Writings 1902–1910*, 333–34, (1289).

7. For detailed accounts of James's private life and its relation to his thought, see Simon, *Genuine Reality*, and Allen, *William James*. For determinism and materialism, see Cotkin, *William James, Public Philosopher*, and Myers, *Life and Thought*.

8. James, *Writings 1878–1899*, 569–70.

9. James to Tom Ward, *Letters*, 152–53.

10. James, *Writings 1878–1899*, 487.

11. James's diary, cited in Perry, *Thought and Character*, 1:322.

12. James's unwillingness to accept such a god is reminiscent of the character of Ivan in *The Brothers Karamazov* by Dostoevsky. Ivan refuses to love and worship a god that created a world in which innocent children are tortured to death. This god may indeed exist, but on principle Ivan rejects him and his promise of eternal harmony and salvation. As Ivan sees it, a future perfect harmony cannot vindicate the tears and suffering of even one child, and if given an invitation to partake in this harmony, Ivan would "most respectfully return him the ticket" (245).

13. James, *Writings 1878–1899*, 581, 590.

14. James, *Writings 1902–1910*, 499.

15. Ibid., 537.

16. See Cotkin, *William James.*

17. James, *Writings 1902–1910,* 533–34, 531.

18. Balfour, *Foundations of Belief.* James cites this passage many times, for example in his essay "Philosophical Conceptions and Practical Results" and in *Pragmatism.* See *Writings 1878–1899,* 1086, and *Writings 1902–1910,* 531–32.

19. Cotkin, *William James,* 79.

20. Renouvier, in Menand, *Metaphysical Club,* 219.

21. James's diary, cited in Perry, *Thought and Character,* 1:323.

22. James, *Principles of Psychology,* in *Writings 1878–1899,* 573–74.

23. James, *Writings 1878–1899,* 566–67.

24. Clifford cited in ibid., 462.

25. James makes this argument more than once, but see especially "The Will to Believe" in *Writings 1878–1899,* 457–79.

26. James, *Writings 1878–1899,* 464–65.

27. Ibid., 502.

28. James, *Writings 1902–1910,* 612.

29. James, *Writings 1878–1899,* 570.

30. James to Maxwell Savage, in Scott, *Selected Unpublished Correspondence,* 534.

31. James to Mrs. Glendower Evans, in Moore, *William James,* 21.

32. James, *Writings 1902–1910,* 771–72.

33. Ibid., 891–92.

34. James to Mrs. Glendower Evans, in Moore, *William James,* 21.

35. James, in Perry, *Thought and Character,* 2:443.

36. James, *Writings 1902–1910,* 687.

37. James, *Writings 1878–1899,* 1079–80.

38. Ibid., 1081.

39. James, *Psychology: Briefer Course,* in ibid., 352. James said here "Our natural way of thinking about these coarser emotions is that the mental perception of some fact excites the mental affection called the emotion, and that this latter state of mind gives rise to the bodily expression. My theory, on the contrary, is that *the bodily changes follow directly the perception of the exciting fact, and that our feeling of the same changes as they occur* IS *the emotion.* Common-sense says, we lose our fortune, are sorry and weep; we meet a bear, are frightened and run; we are insulted by a rival, are angry and strike. The hypothesis here to be defended says that this order of sequence is incorrect, that the one mental state is not immediately induced by the other, that the bodily manifestations must first be interposed between, and that the more rational statement is that we feel sorry because we cry, angry because we strike, afraid because we tremble, and not that we cry, strike, or tremble because we are sorry, angry, or fearful, as the case may be."

40. James, *Writings 1878–1899,* 1087–91.

41. James, *Writings 1902–1910,* 905.

42. Ibid., 518–19. James wrote: "*If theological ideas prove to have a value for concrete life, they will be true, for pragmatism, in the sense of being good for so much.*"

43. Ibid., 618.

44. Ibid., 521.

45. Ibid., 512.

46. Ibid., 513.

47. Ibid., 573.

48. Ibid., 508–9.

49. Ibid., 574.

50. Ibid., 581–83.

51. James, in Perry, *Thought and Character,* 2:450.

52. James, *Writings 1878–1899,* 528–29.

53. See especially the chapters entitled "Pragmatism" and "William James's Conception of Truth," in Russell, *Philosophical Essays*.

54. James, *Writings 1902–1910*, 509.

55. Ibid., 583.

56. For example, he says in *The Meaning of Truth*, "This is why as a pragmatist I have so carefully posited 'reality' *ab initio* and why, throughout my whole discussion, I remain an epistemological realist." *Writings 1902–1910*, 925.

57. Ibid.

58. Ibid., 593.

59. Ibid., 376.

60. Ibid., 580.

61. Rationalists usually claimed that the soul—or perhaps god or the absolute—assembled one's discrete experiences into an uninterrupted train of thought. James was not comfortable with this solution to the problem because it led to monism, the "block universe" to which he was so averse.

62. James, *Writings 1902–1910*, 782.

63. Ibid., 1008.

64. Ibid.

65. Ibid., 599.

66. Ibid., 860.

67. Kloppenberg, *Uncertain Victory*, is particularly insightful on the social aspect of James's epistemology. I must credit him for opening my eyes to this reading, with which I became increasingly sympathetic as I read more of James's work.

68. James, *Writings 1878–1899*, 536.

69. James, *Writings 1902–1910*, 576–77.

70. James, *Writings 1878–1899*, 595.

71. Ibid., 610.

72. Ibid.

73. Ibid., 610–11.

74. Ibid., 851.

75. Ibid.

76. Ibid., 862.

77. Ibid., 860.

78. Ibid., 948, 751.

79. Ibid., 146.

80. Ibid., 750.

81. Ibid.

82. Ibid., 756–57.

83. Ibid., 145, 750.

84. Ibid., 369–73.

85. Ibid., 375–77.

86. James, in Cotkin, *William James*, 147; James to François Pillon, *Letters*, 2:74; James (to another friend), in Perry, *Thought and Character*, 2:199.

87. James, *Writings 1902–1910*, 1283, 1290.

88. Ibid., 1290.

89. Ibid., 1292.

90. Ibid., 1291.

91. See Cotkin, *William James*.

92. James, *Writings 1878–1899*, 638.

93. Ibid., 625 (quotes), 630.

94. Ibid., 394.

95. James, *Principles of Psychology*, in ibid., 417–18, 416–17.

96. Ibid., 419.

97. Ibid., 826.

98. James, in Perry, *Thought and Character*, 2:90.

99. James, *Writings 1878–1899*, 146, 150.

100. Cotkin, *William James*, 69.

101. James, *Writings 1878–1899*, 863–64; James to Mrs. James, *Letters*, 2:43.

102. James, *Writings 1878–1899*, 864.

103. Ibid., 865.

104. Ibid., 866.

105. Ibid., 877, 875.

106. James, "Robert Gould Shaw," in Burkhardt, *Works of William James*, 72–73.

107. Ibid., 66–67.

108. James to Mrs. Henry Whitman, *Letters*, 2:90.

109. James to Ernest Howard Crosby, in Scott, *Selected Unpublished Correspondence*, 266.

110. "Individualistic communitarianism" is my term, though it is a slight variation on George Cotkin's misleading characterization of James's political philosophy as "anarchist communalism" (*Public Philosopher*, 174). James welcomed diversity and favored smaller social systems, but he never advocated the abolition of all forms of institutional organization, only those large faceless bureaucracies that stunted individual action.

111. James, *Writings 1902–1910*, 1289.

112. James, *Writings 1878–1899*, 611–12, 611.

113. James, *Writings 1902–1910*, 1246.

114. Ibid., 1246–48, (1247).

115. James, *Writings 1878–1899*, 610.

116. James, *Writings 1902–1910*, 1245–46.

# 3—The John Dewey School of Democracy

1. Dewey's complete works comprise thirty-seven volumes, which do not include his unpublished writings and letters.

2. Dewey never used the term "participatory democracy" (if the reader recalls, it was coined by Arnold Kaufman), but I use the term frequently in discussing Dewey because (as I will argue in considerable detail) it accurately and succinctly reflects his conception of democracy.

3. Commager, *American Mind*, 19.

4. See Menand, *Metaphysical Club;* Martin, *Education of John Dewey*.

5. Most notably, Dewey volunteered to deliver lectures at Hull House, founded in Chicago's West Side by Jane Addams to help poor immigrants acclimate to American society, to provide them with the skills necessary for life and work, and to introduce them to the refinements of education and high culture. Dewey's relationship with Addams and volunteer work at her famed settlement house deeply influenced his thinking on social issues.

6. Dewey, "No Matter What Happens—Stay Out," in *Later Works*, 14:364.

7. Dewey, *Later Works*, 2:328.

8. See Dewey, "Science as Subject-Matter and as Method," in *Middle Works*, 6:78; and *How We Think*, in *Middle Works*, 6:232–37.

9. Dewey, *Individualism, Old and New*, in *Later Works*, 5:80–81.

10. Dewey, *Later Works*, 2:353.

11. Dewey, *Freedom and Culture*, in *Later Works*, 13:117.

12. For more on this, see Bernstein, *John Dewey*, 71, 81–84.

13. Dewey, "Lecture Notes: Political Philosophy, 1892" (38), in Westbrook, *John Dewey*, 44.

14. Dewey, *Liberalism and Social Action,* in *Later Works,* 11:31.

15. Dewey, *Later Works,* 5:78.

16. Dewey, *Later Works,* 11:15.

17. Ibid. 35.

18. Ibid. This paragraph draws heavily on Dewey's first chapter, ibid., 5–22.

19. Ibid., 28.

20. Dewey, *Later Works,* 2:302.

21. Dewey, *Later Works,* 11:26.

22. Ibid., 14, 17.

23. Ibid., 66–76, 69 (quote).

24. Ibid., 25.

25. Dewey, *Lectures on Psychological and Political Ethics: 1898,* in Westbrook, *John Dewey,* 93.

26. Dewey (with Tufts), *Ethics,* in *Middle Works,* 5:392.

27. Dewey, *Later Works,* 11:41.

28. Dewey, "Liberty and Social Control," in *Later Works,* 11:360–61.

29. Ibid., 361.

30. Dewey, "Philosophies of Freedom," in *Later Works,* 3:102.

31. Dewey, *Later Works,* 2:247–49.

32. Ibid., 243–44, 245–46 (quote).

33. Ibid., 277.

34. Ibid., 255, 256.

35. Ibid., 257.

36. Ibid., 278, 334.

37. Ibid., 317.

38. Ibid., 314.

39. Ibid., 317.

40. Ibid., 296.

41. Ibid., 323–24.

42. Ibid., 328.

43. Ibid., 339.

44. Walter Lippmann is probably the most famous democratic realist to make this argument. See especially *The Phantom Public.*

45. Dewey, *Later Works,* 2:365, 366 (quotes).

46. Ibid., 364. Dewey's shoemaker metaphor seems to have been a response to Max Weber, who expressed his wariness of popular sovereignty in a letter to a friend in 1908: "As if one were to speak of the will of shoe consumers which should determine the technology of shoemaking! Of course the shoe consumers know where the shoe pinches, but they never know it can be improved." Weber, in Kloppenberg, *Uncertain Victory,* 390.

47. Dewey, "Democracy and Educational Administration," in *Later Works,* 11:217–18.

48. Dewey, *Later Works,* 2:366–67.

49. Dewey, *Middle Works,* 5:277.

50. Ibid., 276, 286.

51. Dewey, *Later Works,* 2:327.

52. Ibid., 325.

53. Ibid., 11:225.

54. Ibid., 13:135.

55. Ibid., 168.

56. Ryan, *High Tide,* 112, 180.

57. Dewey, "Creative Industry," in *Middle Works,* 11:335.

58. Ryan, *High Tide,* 180.

59. Dewey, *Democracy and Education,* in *Middle Works,* 9:269.

60. Ryan, *High Tide,* 317.

61. Dewey, *Later Works,* 2:367, 368.

62. Ibid., 13:176.

63. Ibid., 177.

64. Ibid., 2:370.

65. Ibid., 371.

66. Ibid., 11:219.

67. Although Dewey does not mention freedom of choice (democratic meta-physics) in this passage, we will see that he most certainly assumed this was an essential element of the human condition.

68. Dewey, "Nature in Experience," in *Later Works,* 14:150.

69. Dewey, "Philosophy and Democracy," in *Middle Works,* 11:50–51.

70. Dewey, *Reconstruction in Philosophy,* in *Middle Works,* 12:114.

71. Dewey, *Human Nature and Conduct,* in *Middle Works,* 14:213.

72. Dewey, "The Economic Basis of the New Society," in Ratner, *John Dewey's Philosophy,* 431. This essay was written specifically for Ratner's edited volume, which comprises excerpts from Dewey's published works.

73. Dewey, "Lessons from the War—in Philosophy," in *Later Works,* 14:321–22.

74. Russell, *Philosophical Essays,* 109. See Introduction for a more detailed discussion of Russell's criticism of pragmatism.

75. Dewey, *Later Works,* 14:322.

76. Moore, *American Pragmatism,* 201.

77. Dewey, "Experience, Knowledge and Value: A Rejoinder" in Schilpp, *Philosophy of John Dewey,* 533. Dewey wrote this essay to respond to the various commentaries included in Schilpp's edited volume.

78. Dewey, *The Quest for Certainty,* in *Later Works,* 4:170.

79. Dewey, *Logic: The Theory of Inquiry,* in *Later Works,* 12:16.

80. Dewey, "The Need for a Recovery of Philosophy," in *Middle Works,* 10:46.

81. Dewey, *Later Works,* 4:170.

82. Dewey, "The Intellectualist Criterion for Truth," in *Middle Works,* 4:67.

83. Dewey, *Later Works,* 4:222.

84. Dewey, "The Problems of Truth," in *Middle Works,* 6:31.

85. Dewey, *Middle Works,* 6:78; Dewey, *A Common Faith,* in *Later Works,* 9:23 (quote).

86. Dewey, "Some Questions about Value," in *Later Works,* 15:107.

87. Dewey, "The Problems of Men and the Present State of Philosophy," in *Later Works,* 15:160.

88. Bourne, "The Twilight of Idols," in *The Radical Will,* 343.

89. See Westbrook, *John Dewey,* 203–12; Menand, *Metaphysical Club,* 401–7.

90. Hutchins, "Education for Freedom," 1315.

91. H. Putnam, *Renewing Philosophy,* 180.

92. Ibid.

93. H. Putnam, *Words and Life,* 175.

94. Kloppenberg, in Westbrook, "Pragmatism and Democracy," 130.

95. Kloppenberg, "Pragmatism: An Old Name for Some New Ways of Thinking?" in Dickstein, *Revival of Pragmatism,* 101.

96. Dewey, *Later Works,* 2:364.

97. Dewey (with Tufts), *Ethics,* in *Later Works,* 7:347.

98. Dewey, *Later Works,* 5:115.

99. Ibid., 13:135.

100. Ibid., 150–51.

101. Dewey, "The Ethics of Democracy," in *Early Works,* 1:246.

102. Westbrook, *John Dewey*, 281–82.

103. Lasswell, *Propaganda Technique*, 4–5.

104. Niebuhr, *Moral Man and Immoral Society*, xii–xxiii.

105. Dewey, in Hook, *Out of Step*, 66.

106. Dewey, *Later Works*, 2:242.

107. Ibid., 13:140.

108. Dewey, *Middle Works*, 14:108–9. See also Westbrook, *John Dewey*, 291–93.

109. Dewey, *Later Works*, 2:334–35.

110. Ibid., 13:108, 96.

111. Dewey, *Middle Works*, 14:21.

112. Dewey, *Later Works*, 13:142.

113. Ibid., 7:347.

114. Ibid., 11:38.

115. Ibid., 50, 39.

116. Menand, *Metaphysical Club*, 323; Dewey, *School and Society*, in *Middle Works*, 1:98.

117. Ryan, *High Tide*, 141–45.

118. Eastman, *Great Companions*, 250 (quoted in Diggins, *Promise of Pragmatism*, 305).

119. Dewey, "My Pedagogic Creed," in *Early Works*, 5:86; Dewey, "Ethical Principles underlying Education," in *Early Works*, 5:64–65.

120. Dewey, *Middle Works*, 9:326, 328–29.

121. Ibid., 5:426.

122. Ibid., 12:181.

123. Moore, *American Pragmatism*, 232–33.

124. Dewey, *Middle Works*, 9:89.

125. Ibid.

126. Ibid., 92.

127. Ibid., 90.

128. Ibid., 92.

129. Ibid., 93.

130. Dewey, *Later Works*, 5:122–23.

131. Dewey, "Experience, Knowledge, and Value: A Rejoinder" in Schilpp, *Philosophy of John Dewey*, 544.

132. Dewey, *Later Works*, 2:249.

133. Dewey, *Middle Works*, 14:67.

134. Ibid., 124, 175.

135. Ibid., 118.

136. Ibid., 132, 134.

137. Ibid., 175.

138. Dewey, *Later Works*, 3:104.

139. Ibid., 14:150.

# 4—C. Wright Mills

1. See especially Miller, *Democracy Is in the Streets;* Mattson, *Intellectuals in Action;* Hayden, *Reunion.* Hayden calls Mills a "prophet" and Mattson refers to him as the "godfather" of the New Left.

2. Quoted in Miller, *Democracy Is in the Streets*, 87.

3. Mills, "The Value Situation and the Vocabulary of Morals" (unpublished), quoted in Tilman, *C. Wright Mills*, 107. I am especially indebted to Tilman for his discussion of the pragmatist influence on Mills's thought.

4. Horowitz, *C. Wright Mills,* 117.

5. Mills, *Power Elite,* 3.

6.<http://www.americanrhetoric.com/speeches/dwightdeisenhowerfarewell.html>.

7. Mills, letter to Hallock Hoffman, October 7, 1959, C. Wright Mills Papers, box 4B398, quoted in Mattson, *Intellectuals in Action,* 44.

8. Mills, *The Marxists,* quoted in Eldridge, *C. Wright Mills,* 35.

9. Ibid., 34.

10. Ibid., 33.

11. Mills, *Power, Politics, and People,* 36.

12. Ibid., 191.

13. Ibid., 193.

14. Ibid., 601.

15. Bell, *End of Ideology,* 405.

16. If Ralph Nader had been around to compare the Democratic and Republican parties to Tweedledum and Tweedledee, as he did quite famously in his bid for the presidency in 2000, liberals like Daniel Bell and Seymour Martin Lipset would most certainly have taken it as a compliment to our political system.

17. Mills, "The New Left," in *Power, Politics, and People,* 249. When it was originally published in the *New Left Review* (1960), this essay was called "Letter to the New Left," and it had a profound effect on a generation of radical students, such as Tom Hayden and other members of SDS.

18. Mills, *Power, Politics, and People,* 239.

19. Ibid., 32.

20. Daniel Bell was the first to develop the concept of the "permanent war economy" (he even coined the term), when editor of the *New Leader* in the early 1940s, but he moved increasingly to the right, as the Cold War began to heat up, and later abandoned the idea. Mills would run with it for the rest of his career. For more on the influence of Bell's early thinking on Mills, see Mattson, *Intellectuals in Action,* 47–48.

21. Mills, *Power Elite,* 184.

22. Ibid., 278.

23. Ibid., 281.

24. For more on Mills's use of ideal-types and his indebtedness to Max Weber, see Miller, *Democracy Is in the Streets,* 88–89.

25. Mills, *Power, Politics, and People,* 355.

26. Ibid. For more on the transformation of an American community of publics into a society of masses, see this whole passage (ibid., 353–65), and Mills, *Power Elite,* 298–324.

27. Mills, *Power, Politics, and People,* 24.

28. Ibid., 104–5.

29. Mills, *White Collar,* xvi–xvii.

30. Ibid., xv, xvi.

31. Mills, *Power, Politics, and People,* 613.

32. Mills, *Sociological Imagination,* 8–9.

33. Ibid., 186.

34. Mills, *Power, Politics, and People,* 356.

35. Ibid., 366 (for more on liberal education, 367–73).

36. Ibid., 37–38.

37. Mills, *New Men of Power,* 252.

38. Ibid., 253–59.

39. Ibid., 250.

40. Ibid., 260.

41. Mills, *Power, Politics, and People,* 455–56.

42. Ibid., 459–60.

43. Ibid., 611.

44. Ibid., 461.

45. Mills, *Sociology and Pragmatism*, 210.

46. Mills, *Power, Politics, and People*, 300.

47. Mills, *Sociology and Pragmatism*, 368–69. For more on Mills's theory of praxis and the influence of pragmatism, see Tilman, *C. Wright Mills*, 130–35.

48. Mills, *Sociological Imagination*, 77.

49. Mills, *Power, Politics, and People*, 609–10.

50. Mills, *Sociological Imagination*, 6, 164.

51. Ibid., 163–64.

52. Gerth and Mills, *Character and Social Structure*, xvi.

53. Mills, *Power, Politics, and People*, 426.

54. Gerth and Mills, *Character and Social Structure*, 96.

55. Ibid., 101.

56. Dostoevsky, *The Brothers Karamazov*.

57. Mills, *Power, Politics, and People*, 433.

58. Ibid., 407, 406–7.

59. Ibid., 296.

60. Mills, *Sociological Imagination*, 167.

61. Mills, *Power, Politics, and People*, 238.

62. Mills, *Sociological Imagination*, 175.

63. Ibid., 174.

64. Ibid., 179.

65. Ibid., 154.

66. Mills, *Power, Politics, and People*, 243.

67. Ibid., 245.

68. Mills, *Sociological Imagination*, 174.

69. Mills, *Power, Politics, and People*, 586.

70. Ibid., 589.

71. Ibid., 591–92.

72. Ibid., 593.

73. Ibid.

74. Ibid., 595.

75. Mills, *New Men of Power*, 252–53.

76. Mills, in Mattson, *Intellectuals in Action*, 75.

77. Mills, *Causes of World War Three*, 95.

78. Mills, "The New Left," in *Power, Politics, and People*, 258–59.

79. Ibid., 254–59, (256, 254).

80. Mills, *Listen, Yankee!* 114–15.

81. Mills, *New Men of Power*, 252.

82. Mills, *Power, Politics, and People*, 166.

83. Ibid., 167.

84. Ibid., 168.

85. Mills, *Sociology and Pragmatism*, 331.

86. Dewey, *Later Works*, 9:51.

87. Ibid., 11:45. See Tilman, *C. Wright Mills*, 150–59 for more on Mills's misreading of Dewey.

88. See Tilman, *C. Wright Mills*, 160.

89. Mills, *Power Elite*, 320, 322.

90. Hayden, *Reunion*, 77–78.

91. See Hayden, *Radical Nomad*, 55–56.

92. Miller, *Democracy Is in the Streets*, 79, 87.

93. Hayden's thesis, entitled "Radical Nomad: Essays on C. Wright Mills and His Times," was completed in 1964 but was not published until later, under a slightly altered title, *Radical Nomad: C. Wright Mills and His Times.*

94. Hayden, "Memo to SDS Executive Committee, Others." Italicized words were originally underlined, presumably for emphasis, in Hayden's memo.

95. Hayden, "Student Social Action."

96. Ibid.

97. Hayden, "Manifesto Notes."

98. See Miller, *Democracy Is in the Streets,* 121–22; Hayden, *Reunion,* 95–96; and the *Port Huron Statement* itself.

99. *Port Huron Statement.*

100. Hayden, "Manifesto Notes."

101. Hayden, "Student Social Action."

102. Ibid.

103. In my following discussion of this tension within Hayden's thought, I rely heavily on James Miller's insights. See his *Democracy Is in the Streets,* esp. 98–100, 144–47.

104. Hayden, "Freedom of the Student Press" (speech delivered in 1961), quoted in Miller, *Democracy Is in the Streets,* 99.

105. Hayden, "Politics, the Intellectual, and SDS."

106. Miller, *Democracy Is in the Streets,* 147.

107. Hayden, "Memo to SDS Executive Committee, Others."

108. Hayden, in Miller, *Democracy Is in the Streets,* 144.

109. Ibid., 51, 98, 150. For more on Miller's take on the influence of existentialism on Hayden's confrontational approach, see ibid., 145–48.

110. For an excellent account of SNCC's activities and internal operations, see Lewis, *Walking with the Wind.*

# 5—Sheldon Wolin and Melancholic Democracy

1. Wolin, "Fugitive Democracy," 31.

2. Ibid.

3. Ibid., 31, 43.

4. Wolin, "Norm and Form," 36.

5. Wolin, "Transgression, Equality, and Voice," 63.

6. Wolin, "Norm and Form," 58.

7. Ibid., 37.

8. Wolin, "On the Theory and Practice of Power," 198.

9. Wolin, "What Revolutionary Action Means Today," 27.

10. Wolin, "Transgression, Equality, and Voice," 75.

11. Wolin, "What Revolutionary Action Means Today," 20.

12. See *Politics and Vision,* ch. 9, especially the section on J. S. Mill's pleasure principle.

13. Wolin, *Politics and Vision,* 591.

14. Ibid., 591–93.

15. Ibid., 56–58. The Strauss quotation is from *Natural Right and History,* 11.

16. Wolin, "On the Theory and Practice of Power," 198, 186.

17. Ibid., 198, 199.

18. Ibid., 191, 186.

19. Ibid., 199.

20. Wolin, "Transgression, Equality, and Voice," 66, 83.

21. Wolin, "Fugitive Democracy," 43.

22. Wolin, *Politics and Vision*, 595.

23. Wolin, *Tocqueville between Two Worlds*, 220, 215, 213–14.

24. Wolin, "Norm and Form," 36.

25. Wolin, "Transgression, Equality, and Voice," 64.

26. Ibid.

27. Ibid., 65

28. Ibid., 75.

29. Ibid., 74.

30. Ibid., 81–83.

31. Wolin, "Fugitive Democracy," 42–43.

32. Wolin, "Political Theory as a Vocation," 28.

33. Ibid., 37–41 (37).

34. Ibid., 45.

35. Wolin, *Politics and Vision*, 505.

36. Ibid., 515.

37. Ibid., 517.

38. Ibid.

39. Ibid., 514–19.

40. Ibid., 50–51.

41. Wolin, "Fugitive Democracy," 31.

42. Wolin, "People's Two Bodies," 11, 10–11.

43. Wolin, "What Revolutionary Action Means Today," 21, 20–21.

44. Wolin, "People's Two Bodies," 17–19.

45. Ibid., 24.

46. Wolin, "What Revolutionary Action Means Today," 21.

47. Wolin, *Tocqueville between Two Worlds*, 216.

48. Wolin, "Transgression, Equality, and Voice," 66.

49. Ibid., 66, 74.

50. Ibid., 73.

51. Ibid., 66.

52. Ibid., 71.

53. Ibid., 75.

54. Wolin, *Presence of the Past*, 154.

55. Wolin, "Transgression, Equality, and Voice," 75–76.

56. Wolin, "A Look Back at the Ideas That Led to the Events," quoted in Xenos, "Momentary Democracy," 34.

57. Wolin, "Fugitive Democracy," 31, 39.

58. Wolin, *Presence of the Past*, 149.

59. Wolin, "Norm and Form," 43.

60. Wolin, "Fugitive Democracy," 39.

61. Wolin, "Norm and Form," 43.

62. Wolin, "What Revolutionary Action Means Today," 27.

63. Ibid., 27–28.

64. Wolin, *Presence of the Past*, 81; Wolin, "What Revolutionary Action Means Today," 28.

65. Wolin, "What Revolutionary Action Means Today," 28. For "inverted totalitarianism," see Wolin, *Politics and Vision*, 591.

66. Wolin, "Fugitive Democracy," 42.

67. Holmes, "Both Sides Now."

68. Other scholars interpret the Declaration as primarily a liberal document, an articulation of natural rights, not of radically democratic principles. See Zuckert, *Natural Rights Republic*, for example.

69. Wolin, "People's Two Bodies," 11.

70. Wolin, *Tocqueville between Two Worlds*, 269.
71. See Wolin, "Political Theory: From Vocation to Invocation."
72. Wolin, "Fugitive Democracy," 43.
73. Wolin, "What Revolutionary Action Means Today," 27.

# 6—Benjamin Barber and Quixotic Democracy

1. Barber, *Strong Democracy*, 21.
2. Ibid., 32.
3. Ibid., 41.
4. Ibid., 38, 40.
5. Ibid., 21, 106.
6. Ibid., 106.
7. Ibid., 108.
8. Barber, *Superman and Common Men*, 48.
9. Barber, *Strong Democracy*, 118.
10. See, for example, Barber, *A Place for Us*, 19; Barber, *Strong Democracy*, 17; Barber, *An Aristocracy of Everyone*, 155.
11. Barber, *Strong Democracy*, 189–90.
12. Raetia was the subject of Barber's dissertation, which he eventually turned into a book entitled *The Death of Communal Liberty*. I will discuss this book more fully later in the chapter.
13. Barber, *Strong Democracy*, 286–87.
14. Ibid., 247.
15. See the twentieth-anniversary edition of *Strong Democracy*; also see the technology-related essays in Barber's *A Passion for Democracy*.
16. Barber, *A Place for All of Us*, 64–65.
17. Ibid., 40.
18. Ibid., 69.
19. Ibid., 76–79, 101–5.
20. Barber even admits in the introduction of his landmark work of participatory democratic theory, *Strong Democracy*, that he has "been much helped by the tradition of American pragmatism," xii.
21. Barber, *Strong Democracy*, 178.
22. Ibid., 129, 167.
23. Ibid., 166.
24. Barber, *An Aristocracy of Everyone*, 214.
25. Barber, *Strong Democracy*, 166.
26. Ibid., 170.
27. Barber, *Passion for Democracy*, 25.
28. Ibid., 24.
29. Ibid., 26.
30. Ibid.
31. Barber, *Strong Democracy*, 151.
32. Barber stresses the importance of "common work" in the Raetian commune. Citizens did not delegate the implementation of their decisions to experts; they did the work themselves. "For example, the decision to build a new road could not be made in a splendid flurry of democratic spirit and then forgotten, left to some engineer corps to complete. To will the road into being, as it were, entailed building it. Those who willed it built it, and their labor was regarded as an expression of commonality for which no compensation was required." *Death of Communal Liberty*, 176.
33. Ibid., 178.

34. Barber, *Strong Democracy*, 171.

35. Ibid., 160.

36. Barber, *Passion for Democracy*, 61.

37. Barber, *A Place for Us*, 40.

38. Ibid., 90.

39. Barber, *An Aristocracy of Everyone*, 223.

40. Barber, *Strong Democracy*, 152.

41. Ibid., 234.

42. Ibid., 232.

43. Ibid.

44. Ibid., 215.

45. Ibid., 72.

46. Ibid., 75.

47. It is important to note, however, that there are some thinkers in the liberal tradition, including J. S. Mill, T. H. Green, and L. T. Hobhouse, who agree that human nature is not static, that people are capable of moral growth and development. Green and Hobhouse, especially, saw society in organic terms and believed that removing an individual from his social context would destroy his humanity. Embracing a democratic psychology, they maintained that man's relations with others not only helped to define him but could also contribute to his personal growth. Hobhouse comes quite close to advocating participatory democracy when he says: "Democracy is not merely founded on the right or the private interest of the individual. This is only one side of the shield. It is founded equally on the function of the individual as a member of the community. It founds the common good upon the common will, in forming which it bids every grown-up, intelligent person to take a part. No doubt many good things may be achieved for a people without responsive effort on its own part. . . . But democratic theory is that, so obtained, they lack a vitalizing element." Hobhouse, *Liberalism*, 116–17.

48. Barber, *An Aristocracy of Everyone*, 124.

49. Ibid.

50. Ibid.

51. See especially Alan Bloom's famous polemic, *The Closing of the American Mind*. Bloom claimed to be a proponent of liberal democracy, but as a follower of Straussianism, he may have represented a particularly elitist form of it. Barber would argue that this elitist tendency pervades liberal thought.

52. Barber, *Strong Democracy*, 152.

53. Ibid., 240.

54. Ibid., 237.

55. Barber, *Death of Communal Liberty*, 236.

56. Ibid., 240, 241.

57. Ibid., 239.

58. See ibid., the last two chapters, for a detailed account of modernity's impact on the Swiss communes.

59. Ibid., 250.

60. Ibid., 239.

61. Barber, *A Passion for Democracy*, 261.

62. Ibid., 263.

63. Ibid., 258, 252, 254.

64. Ibid., 253.

65. Ibid., 238.

66. Ibid., 260.

67. Ibid., 268.

68. Ibid., 270.

69. Ibid., 259.

70. Ibid.

71. See the last chapter of his *A Place for Us*, 124–47.

72. Barber, *Passion for Democracy*, 259.

73. Ibid., 243.

74. Ibid., 237.

# 7—Participatory Democracy

1. Pinker, *Blank Slate*, 294.

2. See ibid., 44–58, 241–82, 294, 306–36, 372–99.

3. Niebuhr, "Intellectual Autobiography," 15.

4. Niebuhr, *Moral Man and Immoral Society*, xi–xii.

5. Lippmann, *Public Opinion*, 55, 119.

6. Ibid., 126.

7. Niebuhr, *Children of Light*, 40–41.

8. Popper, "Philosophy of Science," 157–58.

9. Popper, *Logic of Scientific Discovery*, 27.

10. Popper, "Philosophy of Science," 171.

11. Popper, *Logic of Scientific Discovery*, 268.

12. Ibid., 260n5.

13. Ibid., 267.

14. Ibid.

15. Ibid., 317.

16. Kuhn, *Structure of Scientific Revolutions*, 167.

17. Ibid., 170.

18. For more on this concept, see Irving, *Victims of Groupthink;* Irving, *Groupthink;* Allison, *Essence of Decision*.

19. Surowiecki, *Wisdom of Crowds*, xi–xiii, (xiii).

20. Giles, "Internet Encyclopedias Go Head to Head," *Nature* (December 2005): 900–901; Schiff, "Know It All," *New Yorker*, July 3, 2006.

21. Read, "Can Wikipedia Ever Make the Grade?" *Chronicle of Higher Education*, October 27, 2006, A31.

22. Giles, "Internet Encyclopedias," *Nature* (December 2005): 900–901.

23. See Hafner, "Growing Wikipedia Revises Its 'Anyone Can Edit' Policy," *New York Times*, June 17, 2006. It is worth noting that only a minuscule fraction of Wikipedia's entries ever receive such protection. According to Hafner, 82 entries were fully protected and another 179 were "semi-protected," which means that only people who had been registered users of the site for at least four days could make edits.

24. Schiff, "Know It All," *New Yorker*, July 3, 2006.

25. Ibid. Schiff also reports that 80 percent of Wikipedians are male, which may give the site a gender bias.

26. Ibid. These are Connolley's words.

27. Ibid. Also see Giles, "Internet Encyclopedias Go Head to Head," *Nature* (December 2005): 900–901.

28. See David Broder's *Democracy Derailed: Initiative Campaigns and the Power of Money*.

29. Surowiecki, *Wisdom of Crowds*, xx–xxi, 268–71.

30. Ibid., 271.

31. Incidentally, in an episode from the fourth season of *Curb Your Enthusiasm*, Larry David defines compromise as a solution that no one is really happy with but that everyone can live with. This sounds right to me. In response, Peirce or James

might have said that a compromise is pragmatically true because it is preferable to the alternative—violent conflict.

32. Some scholars and reformists, such as Lani Guinier, have called for instituting proportional representation in our legislature as the only way to make our political system truly representative of all interests. See Guinier's *Tyranny of the Majority: Fundamental Fairness in Representative Democracy*.

33. Cox and Smolinski, 26–36. Covenant Investment Management conducted the study regarding the financial performance of Standard and Poors 500 companies.

34. See the Web site of the Initiative and Referendum Institute at the University of Southern California: <http://www.iandrinstitute.org>.

35. See H. Bloom, *The Western Canon*.

36. See J. Patterson, *America's Struggle against Poverty*, and Moynihan, *Maximum Feasible Misunderstanding*.

## Epilogue

1. See, for example, Schattschneider, *Semisovereign People*.
2. Kaufman, *Radical Liberal*, 51.
3. Ibid., 51–52.
4. See Foner, *Story of American Freedom*, 278.

# Bibliography

Adams, Larry L. *Walter Lippmann*. Boston: Twayne, 1977.

Allen, Gay Wilson. *William James: A Biography*. New York: Viking, 1967.

Allison, Graham T. *The Essence of Decision: Explaining the Cuban Missile Crisis*. Boston: Little, Brown, 1971.

Anderson, Charles W. *A Deeper Freedom: Liberal Democracy as an Everyday Morality*. Madison: University of Wisconsin Press, 2002.

———. *Pragmatic Liberalism*. Chicago: University of Chicago Press, 1990.

Arnowitz, Stanley. "A Mills Revival?" *Logos* 2.3 (Summer 2003). Online at <http://www.logosjournal.com/issue2.3.pdf>.

Balfour, Arthur James. *The Foundations of Belief*. New York: Longmans, Green, 1895.

Barber, Benjamin. *An Aristocracy of Everyone: The Politics of Education and the Future of America*. New York: Ballantine Books, 1992.

———. *The Conquest of Politics: Liberal Philosophy in Democratic Times*. Princeton, N.J.: Princeton University Press, 1988.

———. *The Death of Communal Liberty: A History of Freedom in a Swiss Mountain Canton*. Princeton, N.J.: Princeton University Press, 1974.

———. *Jihad vs. McWorld*. New York: Times Books, 1995.

———. *A Passion for Democracy*. Princeton, N.J.: Princeton University Press, 2000.

———. *A Place for Us: How to Make Society Civil and Democracy Strong*. New York: Hill and Wang, 1998.

———. *Strong Democracy: Participatory Politics for a New Age*. Berkeley and Los Angeles: University of California Press, 1984.

———. *Superman and Common Men: Freedom, Anarchy, and the Revolution*. New York: Praeger, 1971.

Barzun, Jacques. *A Stroll with William James*. New York: Harper and Row, 1983.

Bell, Daniel. *The End of Ideology: On the Exhaustion of Political Ideas in the Fifties*. New York: Free Press, 1962.

Berlin, Isaiah. *Four Essays on Liberty*. London: Oxford University Press, 1969.

Berns, Walter. *In Defense of Liberal Democracy*. Chicago: Regnery Gateway, 1984.

Bernstein, Richard J. *John Dewey*. New York: Washington Square Press, 1966.

———. "One Step Forward, Two Steps Backward: Richard Rorty on Liberal Democracy and Philosophy." *Political Theory* 15.4 (1987): 538–63.

Bird, Alexander. *Thomas Kuhn*. Princeton, N.J.: Princeton University Press, 2000.

Bloom, Alan. *The Closing of the American Mind*. New York: Simon and Schuster, 1987.

Bloom, Harold. *The Western Canon: The Books and School of the Ages*. New York: Riverhead, 1994.

Boller, Paul F., Jr. *American Thought in Transition: The Impact of Evolutionary Naturalism, 1865–1900*. Chicago: Rand McNally, 1969.

Botwinick, Aryeh, and William E. Connolly, eds. *Democracy and Vision: Sheldon Wolin and the Vicissitudes of the Political.* Princeton, N.J.: Princeton University Press, 2001.

Bourne, Randolph Silliman. *The Radical Will: Selected Writings, 1911–1918.* New York: Urizen Books, 1977.

Brent, Joseph. *Charles Sanders Peirce: A Life.* Bloomington: Indiana University Press, 1998.

Broder, David. *Democracy Derailed: Initiative Campaigns and the Power of Money.* New York: Harcourt, 2000.

Burkhardt, Frederick H., ed. *The Works of William James: Essays in Religion and Morality.* Cambridge, Mass.: Harvard University Press, 1982.

Caspary, William R. *Dewey on Democracy.* Ithaca, N.Y.: Cornell University Press, 2000.

Ceaser, James. *Liberal Democracy and Political Science.* Baltimore: Johns Hopkins University Press, 1990.

Cohen, Mitchell, and Dennis Hale, eds. *The New Student Left: An Anthology.* Boston: Beacon Press, 1966.

Commager, Henry Steele. *The American Mind: An Interpretation of American Thought and Character since the 1880s.* New Haven, Conn.: Yale University Press, 1950.

Connolly, William, ed. *The Bias of Pluralism.* New York: Atherton, 1969.

Cotkin, George. *William James, Public Philosopher.* Baltimore: Johns Hopkins University Press, 1990.

Deneen, Patrick. *Democratic Faith.* Princeton, N.J.: Princeton University Press, 2005.

Dewey, John. *The Early Works, 1882–1898.* Vols. 1–5. Carbondale: Southern Illinois University Press, 1967–1972.

———. *The Later Works, 1925–1953.* Vols. 1–17. Edited by Jo Ann Boydston. Carbondale: Southern Illinois University Press, 1981–1991.

———. *The Middle Works, 1899-1924.* Vols. 1–15. Edited by Jo Ann Boydston. Carbondale: Southern Illinois University Press, 1976–1983.

Dickstein, Morris, ed. *The Revival of Pragmatism: New Essays on Social Thought, Law, and Culture.* Durham, N.C.: Duke University Press, 1998.

Diggins, John Patrick. *The Promise of Pragmatism: Modernism and the Crisis of Knowledge and Authority.* Chicago: University of Chicago Press, 1994.

Dostoevsky, Fyodor. *The Brothers Karamazov.* Translated by Richard Pevear and Larissa Volokhonsky. San Francisco: North Point Press, 1990.

Eastman, Max. *Great Companions: Critical Memoirs of Some Famous Friends.* New York: Farrar, Straus, and Cudahy, 1959.

Eisenhower, Dwight D. "Farewell Address to the Nation." 1961. Available online <http://www.americanrhetoric.com/speeches/dwightdeisenhowerfarewell.htm>. Last retrieved May 2007.

Eldridge, John. *C. Wright Mills.* New York: Tavistock, 1983.

Elliott, W. Y. P. *The Pragmatic Revolt in Politics.* New York: Macmillan, 1928.

Festenstein, Matthew. *Pragmatism and Political Theory: From Dewey to Rorty.* Chicago: University of Chicago Press, 1997.

Fish, Stanley. "Postmodern Warfare: The Ignorance of Our Warrior Intellectuals." *Harper's* (July 2002): 33–40.

———. *The Trouble with Principle.* Cambridge, Mass.: Harvard University Press, 1999.

Foner, Eric. *The Story of American Freedom.* New York: W. W. Norton, 1998.

Fuller, Steve. *Kuhn vs. Popper.* Cambridge: Icon Books, 2003.

Gale, Richard M. *The Philosophy of William James: An Introduction.* Cambridge: Cambridge University Press, 2005.

Gerth, Hans, and C. Wright Mills. *Character and Social Structure: The Psychology of Social Institutions.* New York: Harcourt, Brace, 1964.

Giles, Jim. "Internet Encyclopedias Go Head to Head." *Nature* 438.15 (December 2005): 900–901.

Goudge, Thomas A. *The Thought of C. S. Peirce*. Toronto: University of Toronto Press, 1950.

Guinier, Lani. *The Tyranny of the Majority: Fundamental Fairness in Representative Democracy*. New York: Free Press, 1994.

Gutting, Gary. *Pragmatic Liberalism and the Critique of Modernity*. Cambridge: Cambridge University Press, 1999.

Hafner, Katie. "Growing Wikipedia Revises Its 'Anyone Can Edit' Policy." *New York Times,* June 17, 2006.

Hamilton, Alexander, James Madison, and John Jay. *The Federalist Papers*. New York: Bantam Books, 1982.

Hayden, Tom. "Manifesto Notes: Problems of Democracy." SDS Microfilm, series 1, no. 6, reel 1.

———. "Memo to SDS Executive Committee, Others." SDS Microfilm, series 1, no. 6, reel 1.

———. "Politics, the Intellectual, and SDS." SDS Microfilm, series 1, no. 6, reel 1.

———. *Radical Nomad: C. Wright Mills and His Times*. Boulder, Colo.: Paradigm, 2006.

———. *Reunion: A Memoir*. New York: Random House, 1988.

———. "Student Social Action." SDS Microfilm, series 1, no. 6, reel 1.

Hayden, Tom, and Dick Flacks. "The *Port Huron Statement* at 40." *The Nation,* August 5, 2002, 18–21.

Hayek, F. A. *The Constitution of Liberty*. London: Routledge and Kegan Paul, 1960.

———. *The Road to Serfdom*. London: Routledge and Kegan Paul, 1976.

Held, David. *Models of Democracy*. Cambridge: Polity Press, 1987.

Hobhouse, L. T. *Liberalism*. London: Oxford University Press, 1964.

Hofstadter, Richard. *The Age of Reform*. New York: Vintage Books, 1955.

Holmes, Stephen. "Both Sides Now." *New Republic,* March 4, 2002, 31–38.

Hook, Sidney. *John Dewey: An Intellectual Portrait*. Westport, Conn.: Greenwood Press, 1971.

———. *Out of Step: An Unquiet Life in the Twentieth Century*. New York: Harper and Row, 1987.

Hoopes, James. *Community Denied: The Wrong Turn of Pragmatic Liberalism*. Ithaca, N.Y.: Cornell University Press, 1998.

Horowitz, Irving Louis. *C. Wright Mills: An American Utopia*. New York: Free Press, 1983.

Hutchins, Robert. "Education for Freedom." *Christian Century,* November 15, 1944.

Irving, Janis. *Groupthink: Psychological Studies of Policy Decisions and Fiascos*. 2nd ed. Boston: Houghton Mifflin, 1982.

———. *Victims of Groupthink*. Boston: Houghton Mifflin, 1972.

James, William. *Essays in Pragmatism*. New York: Hafner Press, 1948.

———. *Letters of William James*. Edited by Henry James. Boston: Atlantic Monthly Press, 1920.

———. *Writings 1878–1899*. New York: Library of America, 1992.

———. *Writings 1902–1910*. New York: Library of America, 1987.

Kant, Immanuel. *Critique of Pure Reason*. Translated by Norman Kemp Smith. London: Macmillan, 1956.

Kaufman, Arnold S. "The Affluent Underdog." *The Nation,* November 5, 1960, 349–50.

———. "Human Nature and Participatory Democracy." 1960. Reprinted in Connolly, *Bias of Pluralism,* 178–99.

———. *The Radical Liberal*. New York: Simon and Schuster, 1970.

———. "Teach-Ins: New Force for the Times." In Menashe and Radosh, *Teach-Ins, USA*.

———. "Two Cheers for American Education." *Socialist Commentary* (November 1959): 21–23.

Kautz, Steven. *Liberalism and Community*. Ithaca, N.Y.: Cornell University Press, 1995.

Kloppenberg, James. *Uncertain Victory: Social Democracy and Progressivism in European and American Thought*. New York: Oxford University Press, 1986.

———. *The Virtues of Liberalism*. New York: Oxford University Press, 1998.

Knight, Jack, and James Johnson. "The Political Consequences of Pragmatism." *Political Theory* 24.1 (1996): 68–96.

Knight, Thomas S. *Charles Peirce.* New York: Washington Square Press, 1965.

Kuhn, Thomas S. "The Function of Dogma in Scientific Research." In *Scientific Change: Historical Studies in the Intellectual, Social, and Technical Conditions for Scientific Discovery and Technical Invention, from Antiquity to the Present,* ed. A. C. Crombie. 342–69. New York: Basic Books, 1963.

———. *The Structure of Scientific Revolutions.* Chicago: University of Chicago Press, 1962.

Lasch, Christopher. *The True and Only Heaven.* New York: Norton, 1991.

Lasswell, Harold. *Propaganda Technique in the World War.* New York: P. Smith, 1938.

Lewis, John (with Michael D'Orso). *Walking with the Wind.* New York: Simon and Schuster, 1998.

Lippmann, Walter. "An Open Mind: William James." *Everybody's Magazine* 23.6 (December 1910): 800–801.

———. *The Phantom Public: A Sequel to Public Opinion.* New York: Macmillan, 1927.

———. *Public Opinion.* New York: Macmillan, 1965.

Locke, John. *Two Treatises of Government.* Cambridge: Cambridge University Press, 1988.

MacIntyre, Alasdair. *After Virtue.* Notre Dame, Ind.: Notre Dame University Press, 1983.

Macpherson, C. B. *The Political Theory of Possessive Individualism: From Hobbes to Locke.* London: Oxford University Press, 1962.

Martin, Jay. *The Education of John Dewey.* New York: Columbia University Press, 2002.

Mattson, Kevin. *Intellectuals in Action.* University Park: Pennsylvania State University Press, 2002.

McWilliams, Wilson Carey. *The Idea of Fraternity in America.* Berkeley and Los Angeles: University of California Press, 1973.

Menand, Louis. *The Metaphysical Club: A Story of Ideas in America.* New York: Farrar, Straus, and Giroux, 2001.

Menand, Louis, ed. *Pragmatism: A Reader.* New York: Vintage Books, 1997.

Menashe, Lewis, and Ronald Radosh. *Teach-Ins, USA: Reports, Opinions, Documents.* New York: Praeger, 1967.

Miller, James. *Democracy Is in the Streets.* Cambridge, Mass.: Harvard University Press, 1994.

Mills, C. Wright. *The Causes of World War Three.* New York: Simon and Schuster, 1958.

———. *C. Wright Mills: Letters and Autobiographical Writings.* Edited by Kathryn Mills (with Pamela Mills). Berkeley and Los Angeles: University of California Press, 2000.

———. *The New Men of Power: America's Labor Leaders.* New York: Harcourt, Brace, 1948.

———. *Power, Politics, and People: The Collected Essays of C. Wright Mills.* Edited by Irving Louis Horowitz. New York: Oxford University Press, 1963.

———. *The Power Elite.* London: Oxford University Press, 1956.

———. *The Sociological Imagination.* London: Oxford University Press, 1959.

———. *Sociology and Pragmatism: The Higher Learning in America.* New York: Paine-Whitman, 1964.

———. *White Collar: The American Middle Classes.* London: Oxford University Press, 1951.

Misak, Cheryl, ed. *The Cambridge Companion to Peirce.* New York: Cambridge University Press, 2004.

Moore, Edward C. *American Pragmatism: Peirce, James, and Dewey.* New York: Columbia University Press, 1961.

———. *William James.* Great American Thinkers Series. New York: Washington Square Press, 1966.

Moynihan, Daniel Patrick. *Maximum Feasible Misunderstanding: Community Action in the War on Poverty.* New York: Free Press, 1969.

Mumford, Lewis. *A Golden Day: A Study in American Experience and Culture.* New York: Boni and Liveright, 1926.

Myers, Gerald E. *William James: His Life and Thought.* New Haven, Conn.: Yale University Press, 1986.

Niebuhr, Reinhold. *The Children of Light and the Children of Darkness.* New York: C. Scribner's Sons, 1944.

———. "Intellectual Autobiography." In *Reinhold Niebuhr: His Religious, Social, and Political Thought,* ed. Charles W. Kegley and Robert W. Bretall. 3–23. New York: MacMillan Company, 1956.

———. *Moral Man and Immoral Society.* New York: C. Scribner's Sons, 1932.

Nietzsche, Friedrich. *The Gay Science.* Translated by Walter Kaufmann. New York: Vintage, 1974.

———. *On the Genealogy of Morals and Ecce Homo.* Edited by Walter Kaufmann. New York: Vintage Books, 1989.

———. *Twilight of the Idols / The Anti-Christ.* Translated by R. J. Hollingdale. London: Penguin Books, 1990.

Pateman, Carole. *Participation and Democratic Theory.* Cambridge: Cambridge University Press, 1970.

———. *The Problem of Political Obligation: A Critique of Liberal Theory.* Berkeley and Los Angeles: University of California Press, 1985.

Patterson, James T. *America's Struggle against Poverty, 1900–1980.* 4th ed. Cambridge, Mass.: Harvard University Press, 2000.

Patterson, Thomas E. *The Vanishing Voter: Public Involvement in an Age of Uncertainty.* New York: Alfred A. Knopf, 2002.

Peirce, Charles Sanders. *Collected Papers.* Vols. 1–6. Cambridge, Mass.: Harvard University Press, 1960.

———. *Collected Papers.* Vols. 7–8. Cambridge, Mass.: Harvard University Press, 1931.

———. *The Essential Peirce.* Vol. 1. Edited by Nathan Houser and Christian Kloesel. Bloomington: Indiana University Press, 1992.

Perry, Ralph Barton. *The Thought and Character of William James.* Vols. 1, 2. Boston: Little, Brown, 1935.

Pinker, Steven. *The Blank Slate: The Modern Denial of Human Nature.* New York: Viking Press, 2002.

Popper, Karl. *The Logic of Scientific Discovery.* New York: Basic Books, 1959.

———. "The Philosophy of Science: A Personal Report." In *British Philosophy in the Mid-Century: A Cambridge Symposium,* ed. C. A. Mace. 155–91. London: George Allen and Unwin, 1957.

*Port Huron Statement* (1962). Available online at <http://coursesa.matrix.msu.edu/~hst306/documents/huron.html>. Last retrieved January 2006.

Posner, Richard A. *Law, Pragmatism, and Democracy.* Cambridge, Mass.: Harvard University Press, 2003.

Press, Howard. *C. Wright Mills.* Boston: G. K. Hall, 1978.

Putnam, Hilary. *Pragmatism: An Open Question.* Cambridge, Mass.: Blackwell, 1995.

———. *Renewing Philosophy.* Cambridge, Mass.: Harvard University Press, 1992.

———. *Words and Life.* Cambridge, Mass.: Harvard University Press, 1994.

Putnam, Robert. *Bowling Alone.* New York: Simon and Schuster, 2000.

Putnam, Ruth Anna, ed. *The Cambridge Companion to William James.* Cambridge: Cambridge University Press, 1997.

Ratner, Joseph, ed. *Intelligence in the Modern World: John Dewey's Philosophy.* New York: Modern Library, 1939.

Rawls, John. *Political Liberalism.* New York: Columbia University Press, 1993.

————. *A Theory of Justice*. Cambridge, Mass.: Harvard University Press, 1973.

Read, Brock. "Can Wikipedia Ever Make the Grade?" *The Chronicle of Higher Education*, October 27, 2006, A31.

"Rebels with a Cause." Film. Directed by Helen Garvy. Shire Films, 2000.

Riccio, Barry D. *Walter Lippmann: Odyssey of a Liberal*. New Brunswick, N.J.: Transaction, 1994.

Rockefeller, Steven C. *John Dewey: Religious Faith and Democratic Humanism*. New York: Columbia University Press, 1991.

Rorty, Richard. *Achieving Our Country*. Cambridge, Mass.: Harvard University Press, 1998.

————. *Consequences of Pragmatism: Essays, 1972–1980*. Minneapolis: University of Minnesota Press, 1982.

————. *Contingency, Irony, and Solidarity*. Cambridge: Cambridge University Press, 1989.

————. *Philosophy and Social Hope*. London: Penguin Books, 1999.

————. *Philosophy and the Mirror of Nature*. Princeton, N.J.: Princeton University Press, 1979.

Rousseau, Jean-Jacques. *The Basic Political Writings*. Indianapolis: Hackett, 1987.

Russell, Bertrand. *Philosophical Essays*. New York: Simon and Schuster, 1966.

Ryan, Alan. *John Dewey and the High Tide of American Liberalism*. New York: W. W. Norton, 1995.

Sabine, George H. "The Pragmatic Approach to Politics." *American Political Science Review* 24.4 (1930): 865–85.

————. "The Two Democratic Traditions." *Philosophical Review* 61.4 (1952): 451–74.

Sale, Kirkpatrick. *SDS*. New York: Random House, 1973.

Sandel, Michael J. *Democracy's Discontent: America in Search of a Public Philosophy*. Cambridge, Mass.: Harvard University Press, 1996.

————. *Liberalism and Its Critics*. New York: New York University Press, 1984.

Schattschneider, E. E. *The Semisovereign People*. Hinsdale, Ill.: Dryden, 1975.

Scheffler, Israel. *Four Pragmatists: A Critical Introduction to Peirce, James, Mead, and Dewey*. London: Routledge and Kegan Paul, 1986.

Schiff, Stacy. "Know It All." *New Yorker* 82.23 (July 31, 2006): 36–43.

Schilpp, Paul Arthur, ed. *The Philosophy of John Dewey*. Chicago: Northwestern University Press, 1939.

Schirmer, Daniel. "William James and the New Age." *Science and Society* 33 (Fall–Winter 1969): 434–45.

Schumpeter, Joseph. *Capitalism, Socialism, and Democracy*. New York: Harper and Row, 1950.

Scott, Frederick J. Down, ed. *William James: Selected Unpublished Correspondence, 1885–1910*. Columbus: Ohio State University Press, 1986.

Sharrock, Wes, and Rupert Read. *Kuhn: Philosopher of Scientific Revolution*. Malden, Mass.: Blackwell, 2002.

Shusterman, Richard. "Pragmatism and Liberalism between Dewey and Rorty." *Political Theory* 22.3 (1994): 391–413.

Simon, Linda. *Genuine Reality: A Life of William James*. New York: Harcourt, Brace, 1998.

Stettner, Edward A. *Shaping Modern Liberalism: Herbert Croly and Progressive Thought*. Lawrence: University Press of Kansas, 1993.

Surowiecki, James. *The Wisdom of Crowds*. New York: Anchor Books, 2005.

Tilman, Rick. *C. Wright Mills: A Native Radical and His American Intellectual Roots*. University Park: Pennsylvania State University Press, 1984.

Tocqueville, Alexis de. *Democracy in America*. New York: HarperPerennial, 1988.

Truman, David B. *The Governmental Process*. New York: Alfred A. Knopf, 1951.

West, Cornell. *The American Evasion of Philosophy: A Genealogy of Pragmatism.* Madison: University of Wisconsin Press, 1989.

Westbrook, Robert B. *John Dewey and American Democracy.* Ithaca, N.Y.: Cornell University Press, 1991.

———. "Pragmatism and Democracy: Reconstructing the Logic of John Dewey's Faith." In Dickstein, *Revival of Pragmatism.* 128–40.

White, Morton. *Social Thought in America: The Revolt against Formalism.* London: Oxford University Press, 1976.

Wiener, Philip P. *Evolution and the Founders of Pragmatism.* Cambridge, Mass.: Harvard University Press, 1949.

Wilson, Edmund. *Patriotic Gore: Studies in the Literature of the American Civil War.* New York: Oxford University Press, 1962.

Wolin, Sheldon. "Fugitive Democracy." In *Democracy and Difference: Contesting the Boundaries of the Political,* ed. Seyla Benhabib. 31–45. Princeton, N.J.: Princeton University Press, 1996.

———. "Norm and Form: The Constitutionalizing of Democracy." In *Athenian Political Thought and the Reconstruction of American Democracy,* ed. J. Peter Euben et al. 29–58. Ithaca, N.Y.: Cornell University Press, 1994.

———. "On the Theory and Practice of Power." In *After Foucault,* ed. J. Arac. 179–201. New Brunswick, N.J.: Rutgers University Press, 1988.

———. "The People's Two Bodies." *Democracy* 1 (1981): 9–24.

———. "Political Theory as a Vocation." *American Political Science Review* 63 (1969): 1062–82.

———. *Politics and Vision.* Princeton, N.J.: Princeton University Press, 2004.

———. *The Presence of the Past: Essays on the State and the Constitution.* Baltimore: Johns Hopkins University Press, 1989.

———. *Tocqueville between Two Worlds.* Princeton, N.J.: Princeton University Press, 2001.

———. "Transgression, Equality, and Voice." In *Demokratia: A Conversation on Democracies, Ancient and Modern,* ed. Josiah Ober and Charles Hedrick. Princeton, N.J.: Princeton University Press, 1996.

———. "What Revolutionary Action Means Today." *Democracy* 2 (1982): 17–28.

Xenos, Nicholas. "Momentary Democracy." In Botwinick and Connolly, *Democracy and Vision.* 25–38.

Zuckert, Michael. *The Natural Rights Republic.* Notre Dame, Ind.: University of Notre Dame Press, 1996.

# Index

abduction, 34
Adler, Alfred, 234
Adler, Mortimer, 13, 113
affirmative action, 248, 250–51
American Association of University Professors, 83
American Civil Liberties Union, 83
AmeriCorps, 70
Anti-Federalists, 22
Anti-Imperialist League, 47
Aristotle, 22, 179
Athenian democracy, 179–83, 189–92, 220, 226

Bain, Alexander, 26, 27; *Emotions and the Will*, 26
Balfour, Arthur, 50–51, 54; *Foundations of Belief*, 50
Barber, Benjamin, 10, 21, 23, 24, 198–227, 228, 229–30, 254; on communications technology and media, 222–25; *The Death of Communal Liberty*, 206, 212, 220–21, 226; on free will (democratic metaphysics), 208, 220–26; on human nature (democratic psychology), 208, 215–20, 226; on liberalism, 198–220; *A Place for Us*, 207; on Republic of Raetia, 206, 212, 220–21, 226; on strong democracy, 204–26; *Strong Democracy*, 198–99; on truth (democratic epistemology), 208–15, 226
Bell, Daniel, 134, 135, 158
Bentham, Jeremy, 65, 87, 93
Berkeley, University of California at, 11, 45, 169, 176, 191
Berlin, Isaiah, 20
Black Panthers, 169

*Blank Slate, The*, 230–31
Bloom, Harold, 218, 249
Booth, Paul, 127
Bourne, Randolph, 13, 112
*Brothers Karamazov, The*, 151

Camus, Albert, 167
capitalism, 103–4, 118–19, 131–34, 148, 159, 175, 184, 222
Castro, Fidel, 157, 167
*Causes of World War III, The*, 157
Chautauqua, New York, 75–77
Chesterton, G. K., 12
civic republicanism. *See* republicanism
civil rights movement, 3, 6, 8, 161, 166–69, 247, 254, 256
civil society, 20, 144, 207, 225–26, 256
Civil War, 77, 194, 213
Civilian Conservation Corp, 70
classical liberalism, 87, 89, 90–96, 107, 133, 210
Clifford, William Kingdon, 52
Cold War, 3, 130, 137, 240
Cole, G. D. H., 103, 144
Columbia University, 6, 84, 121
Commager, Henry Steele, 83
communism, 5, 84, 94, 103, 104, 112, 130, 134, 135, 163
communitarianism, 22, 80, 173, 204
community action programs (CAPs), 250
Connolley, William, 244
Constitution, U.S., 194, 213
corporations, 7, 92–94, 104, 123, 129, 132–40, 142, 144, 165, 173, 175–76, 188, 202, 207–8, 214, 221, 222–23, 247, 248
Cotkin, George, 51, 75
Cox, Taylor, 248

*Critique of Pure Reason,* 26
Cuba, 157

Dahl, Robert, 10
Darwin, Charles, 11, 40, 71; *The Origin of Species,* 71
Darwinism, 16, 40, 53, 71, 72, 124
*Death of Communal Liberty, The,* 206, 212, 220–21, 226
Declaration of Independence, 194
deduction, 14, 34, 58, 108–9, 201, 209, 237
deliberative democracy, 21, 157, 229, 254
*Democracy in America,* 7
democratic epistemology, 18, 23–38, 46, 47, 55–67, 107–16, 125, 145–48, 163, 177–87, 195, 208–15, 226, 229–30, 234–46, 249, 251; definition of, 18, 24. *See also* truth
democratic metaphysics, 19, 23–25, 29, 42, 45–54, 71–79, 81, 107, 123–26, 127, 128, 145, 149–60, 164–65, 177, 191–95, 208–9, 220–26, 228–30, 251; definition of, 19, 24. *See also* free will
democratic psychology, 18, 23–25, 40–42, 46, 47, 67–71, 107, 116–23, 125, 148–50, 163–64, 177, 187–91, 192, 195, 208, 215–20, 226, 230–34; definition of, 18, 24. *See also* human nature
democratic realists, 19–20, 99, 119
Descartes, René, 183–84
determinism, 24, 47–55, 71, 131–32, 153
Dewey, John, 6, 8–9, 14, 16–17, 19, 20, 23–24, 26, 46, 58, 81, 82–126, 128, 138–39, 144–47, 149, 158–60, 165, 168, 184–85, 208, 211, 229, 231–33, 252; on education, 84, 85, 87, 91, 120–22; on free will (democratic metaphysics), 107, 123–25; *Freedom and Culture,* 116; on habit, 86, 102, 105, 111, 117–21, 124–25; on human nature (democratic psychology), 107, 116–23, 125; on liberalism, 84, 85, 87–95, 107, 126; *The Public and Its Problems,* 9, 16, 96, 98, 138; on truth (democratic epistemology), 107–16, 125; University of Chicago Laboratory School and, 84, 120
Diggins, John, 11
Dostoyevsky, Fyodor, 12; *The Brothers Karamazov,* 151
Dubois, W. E. B., 46

Eastman, Max, 121
*Economic and Philosophical Manuscripts,* 104
Economic Opportunity Act, 250
Economic Research and Action Project (ERAP), 168
education, 7, 18, 67–68, 70, 77, 80, 84, 85, 87, 91, 120–22, 137, 144, 145, 159, 160, 185–90, 203, 205, 215–19, 223, 230–31, 233, 250
Einstein, Albert, 234
Eisenhower, Dwight, 130
*Emotions and the Will,* 26
empiricism, 46, 59, 124
epistemology, 13, 14, 18, 23, 24, 25–38, 46, 47, 55–67, 83, 107–16, 125, 145–48, 163, 177–87, 195, 208–15, 226, 229–30, 234–46, 247–49, 251
Equal Employment Opportunity Commission (EEOC), 248
*Essais de critique générale,* 51

fallibilism, 14, 32–33, 36, 38, 40
Federal Election Campaign Act, 247
Final Solution, 13, 231
Flacks, Dick, 10
Foucault, Michel, 178
foundationalism, 23
*Foundations of Belief,* 50
Frank, Waldo, 113
Free Speech Movement, 176, 191
free will, 9, 10, 15, 18. *See also* democratic metaphysics
*Freedom and Culture,* 116
Freedom of Information Act, 247, 251
Freedom Riders, 6
Freedom Schools, 161
Freud, Sigmund, 117, 234
fugitive democracy, 22, 241

Galton, Francis, 241–42
Glass Ceiling Commission, 248
Gosnell, Harold, 116
Graubuenden, Switzerland, 206, 212, 220–21, 226
Great Community, 98–99, 101, 104–5, 231
Green, T. H., 87
Gutmann, Amy, 10

habit, 15, 18–19, 25, 27, 31–32, 40–43, 46, 55–56, 67–71, 73–75, 86, 102, 105, 111, 117–21, 124–25, 139, 165, 184, 187–89, 195, 203, 223, 232–33, 235–36

Halavais, Alexander, 242
Harrington, James, 22
Harris, W. T., 120
Hartz, Louis, 204, 208
Hayden, Tom, 6, 7, 10, 161–68, 252; on
free will (democratic metaphysics),
164–65; on human nature (democratic
psychology), 163–64; *Port Huron State-
ment* and, 6–8, 10, 162–69, 252; "Stu-
dent Social Action," 162–63; on truth
(democratic epistemology), 163
Head Start, 250
Herbart, Johann, 120
Holmes, Oliver Wendell, 11, 247
Holmes, Stephen, 193
Hook, Sidney, 117, 233
Horowitz, Irving, 128
human nature. *See* democratic psychology
Hume, David, 27, 61, 235–36
Hutchins, Robert, 13, 112–13

idealist liberalism, 87
individualism, 23, 38, 41, 44, 46, 79, 87,
88, 89, 90, 94, 95, 98, 120, 189, 199,
221, 223
induction, 14, 34–35, 63, 65, 108, 183,
210, 230, 234–38

James, William, 9, 11–12, 14–16, 23, 26,
42, 45–81, 82, 83, 86, 87, 107, 108,
115, 117, 124–25, 128–29, 186, 208,
211, 232, 235, 236; "Dilemma of Determinism," 52; on emotion, 56–57,
74; on free will (democratic metaphysics), 46–53, 71–79; on habit, 46,
55–56, 67–71, 74–75, 124–25; on human nature (democratic psychology),
46, 47, 67–71; *The Meaning of Truth,*
60; metaphysical crisis of, 47–54, 71;
"The Moral Equivalent of War," 69;
"The Moral Philosopher and the
Moral Life," 65; "On a Certain Blindness In Human Beings," 66; "Philosophical Conceptions and Practical
Results," 55; *Pragmatism,* 53, 112, 146,
159; *The Principles of Psychology,* 52,
56, 61, 73, 75; on the problem of evil,
48–54, 76; *Psychology: Brief Course,* 74;
Robert Gould Shaw monument oration, 77–79; "Social Value of the College-Bred," 80; "Talks to Teachers" lecture series, 75; on truth (democratic
epistemology), 46, 47, 55–67, 107;
"What Is an Emotion?," 56; "What
Makes a Life Significant," 75; *The Will
to Believe,* 52, 63
James-Lange Theory of Emotion, 56–57, 74
Jeffrey, Sharon, 5
Job Corps, 250

Kant, Immanuel, 26, 27; *Critique of Pure
Reason,* 26
Kaufman, Arnold, 6, 7–9, 253–54; *The
Radical Liberal,* 8, 253
Kinsey Report, 148
Kloppenberg, James, 17, 114
Kuhn, Thomas, 239–41

Lange, Carl G., 56; James-Lange Theory
of Emotion, 56
Lasswell, Harold, 116, 117
Legal Aid, 250
Lenin, V. I., 6
liberalism, 4, 6, 7, 10, 19–21, 46, 79, 84,
85, 87–96, 101–2, 107, 116, 118–19,
125, 126, 130, 132–42, 150–51,
158–60, 163, 173–75, 179–80, 196,
198–220; classical liberalism, 87, 89,
90–96, 107, 133, 210; idealist liberalism, 87; utilitarian liberalism, 87, 93
Lippmann, Walter, 17, 46, 119, 232–33;
*The Phantom Public,* 232; *Public Opinion,* 232
Lipset, Seymour Martin, 158
*Listen, Yankee!,* 157
Locke, Alain, 46
Locke, John, 61, 87, 89, 199

Machiavelli, Niccolo, 22
MacIntyre, Alisdair, 22
Macpherson, C. B., 10
Madison, James, 174, 199, 212, 232
*Managing Diversity and Glass Ceiling Ini-
tiatives as National Economic Impera-
tives,* 248
Mansbridge, Jane, 10
Marx(ism), 5, 6, 47, 48, 50–51, 104, 128,
130–32, 135; *Economic and Philosophi-
cal Manuscripts,* 104
materialism, 46, 47, 48, 50–51, 56, 131,
189, 216
Max, Steve, 5, 6, 121, 128
McCarthyism, 148
McDew, Charles, 161
Mead, George Herbert, 149
*Meaning of Truth, The,* 60

mechanism, 40
megastate, 21–22, 229
Menand, Louis, 11
Mengele, Josef, 13
Merriam, Charles, 116, 119
Metaphysical Club, 11, 26
*Metaphysical Club, The*, 11
Mill, John Stuart, 87, 150, 175
Millikan, Robert, 238
Mills, C. Wright, 6–7, 8–9, 23, 126–70;
   *The Causes of World War III*, 157; on
   free will (democratic metaphysics),
   145, 149–60; on human nature (democratic psychology), 148–50; on labor,
   141–42; "Letter to the New Left," 6,
   157, 162; on liberalism, 130, 132–42,
   150–51; *Listen, Yankee!*, 157; on Marx-
   ism, 130–32, 135; "Methodological
   Consequences of the Sociology of
   Knowledge," 145; *The New Men of
   Power*, 141; on the permanent war
   economy, 129, 136–37, 141, 144, 151;
   on pluralism, 132, 139, 159; on the
   power elite, 7, 129–30, 135–41, 148,
   151–55, 158, 160–67; *The Power Elite*,
   7, 127, 130; *Sociology and Pragmatism*,
   146; on truth (democratic epistemology), 145–48; *White Collar*, 141
Moore, Edward C., 37
*Moral Man and Immoral Society*, 116–17
Moses, Bob, 161
multiculturalism, 249
Mumford, Lewis, 13, 113

Napoleon, 212, 220
National Association for the Advance-
   ment of Colored People (NAACP), 83
Nazis, 13, 14, 112, 117, 134, 176, 222
negative freedom, 21, 88
New Deal, 7, 70, 84, 134
New Democratic Coalition (NDC), 8
New England town meetings, 10, 180,
   189, 191, 220
New Left, 6–10, 21, 24, 26, 126, 127, 130,
   144, 157, 161–70, 229, 247, 250, 251,
   252
*New Men of Power, The*, 141
*New Republic, The*, 83, 112
New School, the 83
Newton, Isaac, 27, 32
Niebuhr, Reinhold, 116–17, 164, 231–32,
   233–34; *Moral Man and Immoral Soci-
   ety*, 116–17

Nietzsche, Friedrich, 11, 12, 174, 182
nominalism, 27–28, 37, 41, 60, 146

Ockham, 27
Office of Economic Opportunity (OEO),
   250
Old Left, 6, 130–31
*Origin of Species, The*, 71
Outlawry of War movement, 84

participatory democracy, 4–10, 16–24,
   25–26, 44–47, 80–87, 101–7, 115–16,
   125–26, 127–28, 144–45, 156, 159–60,
   161, 163, 166–69, 170–74, 176–80,
   185, 189–90, 193–94, 198, 204–8, 212,
   219–21, 225–30, 234, 238–41, 243,
   245, 247, 250–55
Pateman, Carol, 10
Peace Corps, 70
Peirce, Charles, 9, 11, 14–16, 23, 25–47,
   51, 55–56, 58, 60, 63–65, 67, 72, 81,
   82, 83, 86, 87, 108, 115, 124, 125,
   146, 208, 235, 236, 237; on free will
   (democratic metaphysics), 25, 42–44;
   on habit, 25, 31–32, 40–43; "How to
   Make Our Ideas Clear," 26–29; on human nature (democratic psychology),
   25, 40–42; on truth (democratic epistemology), 25–38; on tychism, 39–40
*Phantom Public, The*, 232
Philippines, 47
Pinker, Steven, 230–31
*Place for Us, A*, 207
Plato, 85, 191, 218; The Republic, 85, 212
pluralism, 20, 53, 54, 124, 132, 139, 159,
   199, 203
*Politics and Vision*, 184
Popper, Karl, 234–39, 241
*Port Huron Statement*, 3–6, 8, 10, 16, 128,
   162–64, 167, 169, 251
positive freedom, 20, 125
positivism, 58–59, 86, 111, 145–47
Potter, Paul, 161
power elite, 7, 129–30, 135–41, 148,
   151–55, 158, 160–67
*Power Elite, The*, 7, 127, 130
pragmatism, 8–18, 22–126, 128, 130,
   145, 149, 158–60, 162–70, 177, 186,
   195, 198, 208, 214, 218, 228, 230,
   234–41, 251–52, 255
*Pragmatism*, 53, 112, 146, 159
*Principles of Psychology, The*, 52, 56, 61,
   73, 75

*Psychology: Brief Course,* 74
*Public and Its Problems, The,* 9, 16, 96, 98, 138
*Public Opinion,* 232
Pullman strike, 84
Putnam, Hilary, 113–14

radical democracy, 7, 21–22, 172, 176, 195, 254
*Radical Liberal, The,* 8, 253
Raetia, Republic of, 206, 212, 220, 226
realism, 27, 41, 63, 148, 199–200, 202
relativism, 12, 43, 46, 57, 59, 63, 218, 249
Renouvier, Charles, 51
*Republic, The,* 85, 212
republicanism, 5, 22–23, 130, 174
Roosevelt, Franklin D., 84
Roosevelt, Theodore, 211–12
Ross, Bob, 5, 127
Rousseau, Jean Jacques, 5, 22, 89, 190, 202, 204, 215–16
Royce, Josiah, 49
Russell, Bertrand, 13, 16, 108
Rwanda, 222

Sandel, Michael, 22
Sanger, Larry, 244
Schiller, F. C. S., 42
scientific method, 12–15, 17, 18, 26, 36–38, 58, 64–65, 82–83, 85–86, 102–3, 107–16, 119, 125, 159, 184–86, 240
Scotus, Duns, 27
Shaw, Robert Gould, 77–79
Smith, Adam, 87
Smolinski, Carol, 248
socialism, 47, 80, 84, 103–4, 115, 144
*Sociology and Pragmatism,* 146
Soviet Union, 132, 243, 253
Spanish-American War, 47
Spencer, Herbert, 50, 71
Stalin, Joseph, 5
statistics, 14, 18, 28, 34–37, 40, 186–87, 234, 237
Stein, Gertrude, 46
Strauss, Leo, 13, 178
*Strong Democracy,* 198–99
*Structure of Scientific Revolutions,* 239–41
Student Non-Violent Coordinating Committee (SNCC), 6, 161, 168–69
Students for a Democratic Society (SDS), 3–9, 17, 127, 161–69, 252, 253

Surowiecki, James, 241–42, 244–46, 249, 250
Switzerland, Swiss democracy, 206, 212, 220–21, 226

Thomas, Norman, 84
Tocqueville, Alexis de, 7, 180, 189, 193; *Democracy in America,* 7
*Tocqueville between Two Worlds,* 180, 193
truth. *See* democratic epistemology
tychism, 39–40

University of California at Berkeley, 11, 45, 169, 176, 191
University of Chicago, 84, 112, 128
University of Michigan, 5, 7, 8, 162
utilitarian liberalism, 87, 93
utilitarianism, 65, 87, 93, 235

Veblen, Thorstein, 128, 141
Versailles Treaty, 84
Vietnam War, 8, 169, 253

Wales, Jimmy, 243
Walzer, Michael, 22
War on Poverty, 250
Weathermen, 169
Weber, Max, 128, 133
*White Collar,* 141
Whitman, Walt, 66
Wikipedia, 242–44
*Will to Believe, The,* 52, 63
*Wisdom of Crowds, The,* 241–42, 244–46, 249, 250
Wolin, Sheldon, 10, 21–22, 23, 24, 169–98, 207–9, 221, 226–30, 241, 254; on Athenian democracy, 179–83, 189–92, 220, 226; on Dewey, 184–85; on free will (democratic metaphysics), 177, 191–95; on human nature (democratic psychology), 177, 187–92, 195; on liberalism, 173–75, 179–80, 196; on the megastate, 21–22, 229; *Politics and Vision,* 184; *Tocqueville between Two Worlds,* 180, 193; on truth (democratic epistemology), 177–87, 195
World War I, 84, 85, 112
World War II, 84, 112, 130, 134, 135, 176
Wright, Chauncey, 11